Digital Banking Revolution and Financial Innovation

Digital Banking Revolution and Financial Innovation

Edited by
Elian Harvey

WILLFORD PRESS
www.willfordpress.com

Published by Willford Press,
118-35 Queens Blvd., Suite 400,
Forest Hills, NY 11375, USA

ISBN: 978-1-64728-526-5

Cataloging-in-Publication Data

Digital banking revolution and financial innovation / edited by Elian Harvey.
    p. cm.
Includes bibliographical references and index.
ISBN 978-1-64728-526-5
1. Internet banking. 2. Banks and banking--Technological innovations. 3. Finance--Technological innovations.
4. Financial services industry--Information technology. 5. Financial institutions--Computer networks.
I. Harvey, Elian.
HG1709 .D54 2023
332.102 85--dc23

For information on all Willford Press publications
visit our website at www.willfordpress.com

Contents

Preface

I am honored to present to you this unique book which encompasses the most up-to-date data in the field. I was extremely pleased to get this opportunity of editing the work of experts from across the globe. I have also written papers in this field and researched the various aspects revolving around the progress of the discipline. I have tried to unify my knowledge along with that of stalwarts from every corner of the world, to produce a text which not only benefits the readers but also facilitates the growth of the field.

Digital banking refers to a type of banking conducted through digital platforms, which eliminates the need of any paperwork such as demand drafts, cheques, or pay-in slips. It entails the digitization of maximum number of traditional banking operations, products, and procedures in order to serve consumers through online channels. The development of new products, services, financial instruments, markets, and institutions is referred to as financial innovation. Lately, varieties of financial innovations have taken place in terms of financial instruments, technology, and payment systems. Financial innovations encompass the technological advancements, which are helping banks broaden their services and satisfy the new expectations of their customers. This book presents researches and studies performed by experts across the globe on digital banking revolution and financial innovation. It will also provide interesting topics for research, which interested readers can take up. Those in search of information to further their knowledge will be greatly assisted by this book.

Finally, I would like to thank all the contributing authors for their valuable time and contributions. This book would not have been possible without their efforts. I would also like to thank my friends and family for their constant support.

Editor

m-Banking Quality and Bank Reputation

Mirjana Pejić Bach [1],*[ID], **Berislava Starešinić** [2], **Mislav Ante Omazić** [1][ID], **Ana Aleksić** [1][ID] and **Sanja Seljan** [3]

[1] Faculty of Economics and Business, University of Zagreb, 10000 Zagreb, Croatia; momazic@net.efzg.hr (M.A.O.); aaleksic@efzg.hr (A.A.)

[2] Privredna banka Zagreb, 10000 Zagreb, Croatia; berislava.staresinic@pbz.hr

[3] Department of Information and Communication Sciences, Faculty of Humanities and Social Sciences, University of Zagreb, Ivana Lučića 3, 10000 Zagreb, Croatia; sanja.seljan@ffzg.hr

* Correspondence: mpejic@efzg.hr

Abstract: m-Banking is developed to support the clients in using various banking services, by using their mobile phones, thus allowing them to overcome the barriers in terms of time and location. Clients are increasingly using m-banking, so for some of them, this is the most used way of communication with the bank and doing banking transactions. Therefore, high-quality m-banking services significantly impact trust towards the bank, and it can influence bank reputation. Given the influence of m-banking, as well as the importance of its perceived quality, the paper aims to investigate the elements of m-banking quality, and to analyze the relation between m-banking quality and bank reputation. We investigate several dimensions of m-banking (safety, simplicity, and variety of m-banking services), and their impact on perceived m-banking quality. Besides, we examine the effect of perceived m-banking quality to bank reputation. For the analysis of these relationships, we use structural equation modeling, based on the survey results on a sample of clients of major banks in Croatia. Results of empirical research indicate that safety, simplicity, and a variety of m-banking services have a significant impact on the perceived m-banking quality, which, in turn, has a positive impact on the bank's reputation.

Keywords: m-banking; service quality; bank reputation; ICT in banks

---

1. Introduction

Increased intensity of competition and globalization in the banking sector, together with technological advancements, has changed banks' approach to clients. To increase the level of client retention, banks are trying to find new sources of competitive advantage, unique capabilities, products, services, or distribution channels that will make them recognizable and distinct on the market.

A growing body of research emphasizes reputation as a specific organizational resource that can have a strategic value for organizations [1,2]. As such, reputation also became critical and particularly important for banks [3,4]. Bank transactions are based on trust, they are the so-called credence goods [5], intangible, which makes their assessment before the transaction very difficult [6,7]. Consequently, the decision to do business with a particular bank is strongly influenced by bank reputation. For banks, as service organizations, one of their major strategic goals, therefore, is to exploit, sustain, and defend their reputation [5].

Technological innovations have brought about fundamental changes in the concept of reputation since the reputation cannot be maintained without consistent and timely application of new technology [8]. For banks, intense demand for increasingly sophisticated products and services is driving them to move from their traditional forms and operations, shifting their focus towards making information technology an integral part of their operations and services [9,10]. Consequently, it offers a diverse portfolio of competitive products and services through technology-driven distribution channels, such as m-banking, which allows them to compete on a global level [11].

Most of the banks have included m-banking as part of their strategic directive [9]. Compared to traditional or internet banking, m-banking offers benefits such as freedom from time and place, thus supporting the efficiency of banking transactions [12].

However, m-banking, as the new distribution channel for banking operations, present a challenge for reputation management. Development of m-banking remains an important tool for building the reputation of banks, retention of existing, and attraction of new clients [13]. Therefore, the impact of m-banking to bank reputation is an important issue. Moreover, it is necessary to analyze which elements contribute to the quality of m-banking service, and consequently, impact bank reputation.

However, very little or no research effort has been done to investigate elements of m-banking quality [14]. There are numerous studies regarding the determinants of computer and internet-based banking, e.g., [15–17]. However, little similar research has been done regarding m-banking. So far, research has focused on determinants of m-banking adoption and usage, e.g., [18–20] or influence of m-banking on client loyalty [21] and satisfaction [22]. Therefore, the purpose of this paper is to analyze the relation between m-banking quality and bank reputation, as well as to investigate elements of m-banking quality. We analyze safety, simplicity, and variability, as specific dimensions of m-banking service quality, as well as the impact of perceived m-banking quality to the bank reputation. For that purpose, we have conducted survey research on a sample of clients from the largest Croatian banks. Although focused on a local financial market, it is necessary to emphasize that results of the research from Croatia can be significant for larger financial markets, as trends regarding m-banking in Croatia follow the trends in European countries [23]. Given the identified global trends, it can be seen that there is a significant potential for growth in the importance of mobile transactions and that further development and understanding of this channel of communication with the bank will be an important element in gaining a competitive advantage in the financial market of Croatia but also wider. The collected data were analyzed using structural equation modeling. The conclusions are used as the basis for the various theoretical and practical implications.

The paper is organized as follows. After the introduction, the literature review is presented, focusing on the bank reputation and quality of m-banking. The research model is elaborated in the third part of the paper, focusing on the development of the research hypothesis. The methodology of the research is presented in the fourth part of the paper, starting with the outline of the research instrument and data collection, and followed by a detailed description of the data analysis. The result section starts with the validity and reliability analysis, then focusing on the assessment of the model fit and hypothesis testing. The final section presents the conclusion of the paper in light of its theoretical and practical contributions.

2. Literature Review

2.1. Bank Reputation

In the banking sector, financial operations are mainly based on trust [24], and services provided by banks can only be evaluated with use and over time, and pre-purchase evaluation of service quality is necessarily vague and incomplete [25]. As this nature of banking services makes them difficult to access, clients rely more on reputation, considering it a strategic signal that reflects the overall quality of business actions [26] and provides clients with the information about future behavior and expectations. Banks' reputation can be defined as a perception of clients that the bank is credible, reliable, responsible, and worthy of their trust [27].

Researchers, as well as practitioners, recognize that reputation is particularly relevant for banks, having an especially important strategic role that helps banks protect their product portfolio, retain and attract clients, differentiate on the market, but also provide systemic value [3,25,26,28].

In general, a good reputation leads to higher financial performance and strategic advantage, reduces operating costs, stimulates loyalty and word of mouth, translates into permanent relationships, and attracts or retains qualified employees [5,26,29,30]. Research among banks indicates a positive relationship between reputation and banks' financial/accounting performance [3,28] and a negative relation to leverage and riskiness profiles [3]. Moreover, reputation also has a significant influence on clients purchasing and repurchasing decisions [25], as well as on bank clients' loyalty and their willingness to make comments or positive recommendations [6].

According to Fombrun [31], reputation can be seen as a result of one's economic value (reputation capital), image (representation), and quality. Neef [32] lists four basic categories leading to reputation—corporate governance, environmental protection, employee rights, and product safety. Grgić [33] emphasizes that reputation encompasses a larger set of criteria, including financial indicators, quality of products and services, employee relations, role within the community, environmental protection, and business ethics. The most common antecedents proposed in the literature on corporate reputation is the quality of products/services [34], although previous research, e.g., [26] shows the importance of reliability and financial strength over product quality in times of crisis. Besides, recent research also recognized corporate social responsibility as an important predictor of bank reputation, e.g., [3].

In bank settings, previous research has, in general, recognized that the quality of products and services can be seen as one of the key antecedents of bank reputation, e.g., [25,30,35,36]. Without high-quality products and services, it is not possible to build a long-term sustainable reputation [37]. Due to the technological advances in banking, the characteristics of technology-driven banking solutions, such as internet banking and m-banking, has become one of the main drivers of the banks' reputation [13].

2.2. Quality of m-Banking

Jun and Palacios [14] emphasize that the development of electronic communication and channels have brought drastic changes to the bank sector's service environment, introducing multi-channel that encompass offline and online communication. Consequently, traditional banking is transforming into the direction of dislocated communications and direct transactions. At the same time, physical interaction between bank employees and clients becomes less important [38].

M-banking has become one of the key forms of virtual banking [39] and is considered as a "new radical innovation in the excellence of service delivery to banks" [40] (p. 2). By integrating mobile communication technology and banking financial services, m-banking has become an increasingly flexible service [41], providing time optimization, independence, convenience, prompt response to clients, decrease in operating costs and efficiency for banking transactions [9,12,42–44].

Still, it is important to note that the introduction of m-banking technology is not without risk. Laukkanen [12] notes that technological innovations, which require fast learning from the clients and are not sufficiently supported by the relevant information, could discourage clients in its adoption. Ha et al. [19] emphasize that client adoption of new technologies, such as m-banking, should consider the estimated cost, risk, benefits, and compliance. Besides, one of the critical elements determining the success of m-banking service is the perceived provider's m-banking service quality [14]. The quality of the m-banking service can be defined as the perception of the bank's clients that the mobile banking system is capable of providing a service that will highly meet their needs and expectations [45].

Numerous researchers provide and investigate the main drivers of the bank's service quality. Two groups of research on the bank's quality are observed, depending on the delivery channels: Traditional (face-to-face) and technology-based channels.

Traditional banking channels have been extensively researched. One of the first studies was conducted by Mersha and Adlakha [46], who provided basic characteristics of good quality related to retail banking. Most of these researchers have been focused on the usage of SERVQUAL as the assessment tool for the overall service and product quality in banks. For example, Culiber and Rojšek [47] stress the importance of assurance, empathy, reliability, responsiveness, access, and tangibles. Arasli et al. [11] emphasize the assurance, while Choudhury [48] emphasize reliability, as the main dimension influencing service quality. Therefore, various researchers using SERVQUAL came to different conclusions concerning the most important service dimensions, depending on the context, i.e., the cultural environment of the banking system itself [49].

Recently, researchers, e.g., [14] have realized that dimension related to traditional offline banking services cannot be applied to the modern banking environment and conducted a substantial effort to develop such a framework for internet-banking. In that sense, most of the studies related to service quality of technology-based services are about online (internet-based) service quality, e.g., [16,17]. There were, however, several attempts to identify key determinants of m-banking service performance and quality. Nisha [50] identifies reliability, privacy, information quality, responsiveness, and empathy as important elements that affect clients' perceptions of the performance of m-banking services. Asfour and Haddad [22] stress reliability, flexibility, privacy, accessibility, ease of navigation, efficiency, safety, as important dimensions, where privacy and accessibility were found to be the most influential comparing to the rest of the m-banking dimensions. Malviya [51] asserts dimensions of assurance, safety, efficiency, convenience, reliability, responsiveness, and satisfaction while Jun and Palacios [14] provide the most comprehensive list of 17 dimensions of m-banking service quality grouped into two categories, namely m-banking application quality and m-banking client service quality. Furthermore, their study revealed m-banking service quality dimensions of accuracy, mobile convenience, ease of use, diverse m-banking services, and features, and continuous improvement, to have strong impacts on client satisfaction.

Research suggests safety and risk issues related to m-banking have been recognized as one of the major concerns of all the clients [40,43]. Moreover, ease of use, simplicity, and different features and products offered have a positive influence on perceived value [43,52].

The security of the mobile banking service is crucial for users, and the perception of risk and safety becomes an important feature affecting quality [52]. Techniques that threaten the security of m-banking today have historically been focused on personal computers. Clients want to know their application is safe, stable, and that all its functionalities are done accurately and on time. Concerns about safety can be seen as one of the most often barriers to the adoption of modern technologically driven bank solutions, e.g., [42,53–56].

Simplicity and ease of use are important as they ensure that the time and effort required to manage finances are kept to a minimum. Namely, simplicity primarily implies the perceived complexity of navigation [57] and potential user's / client's perception of how much effort the selected application will require [58]. It represents an individual response to a technological solution and an important prerequisite for the adoption of innovative technological solutions and perception of its quality [23].

The development of technology and various innovations have led to the creation of an affirmative climate for the placement of m-banking, providing customers with greater availability, convenience, and control of their finances and different financial products [59]. Once the appropriate infrastructure is in place, m- banking has the potential to increase the involvement of social segments of the financial market that have so far been excluded. With the advent of m- banking, the availability of credit and the possibility of investing are growing. In addition to the availability of financial services, an important feature of the adoption of m-banking and perception of its quality is the availability of support systems and personalized communication.

Based on the described research, m-banking services need to provide safety and reflect trustworthiness, as well as to be simple to us and, provide diverse services accurately with high speed. All of these commonly found dimensions are reflecting the unique nature of m-banking, such as ubiquity and mobility [14]. Consequently, these elements can be considered as crucial and important in providing high-quality m-banking service and will be further evaluated.

3. Research Model and Hypothesis Development

M-banking presents an emerging strategic orientation of banks, and its role in bank reputation needs to be further examined [13]. Moreover, since the previous research indicated that there is no consensus of what constitutes the m-banking quality, by this research, we aim to provide a deeper understanding of specific dimensions of m-banking quality, and its impact on the bank reputation. Aiming to integrate the various approaches to m-banking quality and the most common features of m-banking quality that are emphasized as the most important ones in the current literature [22,40,43,50–52], we define the following dimensions of m-banking quality: Safety, simplicity, and variability. As previous literature suggests, banks need to consider how to use mobile banking services easily, to be safe, and provide a variety of services accurately and with high speed [60]. Furthermore, we propose to test the impact of perceived m-banking quality on the bank reputation. The research model is presented in Figure 1, while the support for different hypotheses is provided in the next sections.

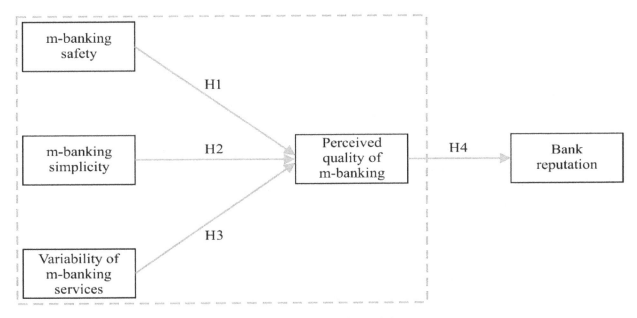

Figure 1. Research model.

3.1. m-Banking Safety

Previous empirical results indicate that client satisfaction increases when they perceive the bank transactions as safe [11], indicating that the safety of bank service is connected with clients' trust, and, finally, a bank reputation [53]. The safety of m-banking is defined as the ability to prevent unauthorized access to information and resources in user accounts, while at the same time allowing customer that the application is stable and that all functionalities of the application are done accurately and on time [23,25]. Concerns about perceived risk and safety seem to be one of the major barriers when it comes to m-banking adoption, e.g., [42,54–56]. Higher risk perception and fear of losses can make people avoid m-banking adoption [44] and question its quality. Safety has been proved as one of the most important determinants for m-banking adoption among generation Y [61]. Clients can easily turn to other bank channels to execute payment and banking services if they have concerns related to m-banking safety and payment technology [41]. As some previous research indicates, safety can be considered an important dimension of m-banking service quality, e.g., [22,51]. To test the effects of safety on m-banking service quality, we propose our first hypothesis:

Hypothesis 1 (H1). *The safety of m-banking service has a positive effect on the perceived quality of m-banking service.*

3.2. m-Banking Simplicity

Simplicity could be defined as the perceived ease of use and complexity of navigation through the application [57]. Previous research, e.g., [60] suggests that banks need to consider how to design their m-banking service to be simple and easy to use. It has been found that simplicity has a positive influence on the perceived value of m-banking services [43], as well as on its actual usage, e.g., [42,43]. When clients perceive that m-banking is easy to learn, with a friendly interface and real-time help, they will have a higher sense of self-efficacy, leading to higher creation of positive image and satisfaction with m-banking [62]. Clients can consider m-banking services less appealing as opposed to traditional services because m-banking services seek more mental effort, are time-consuming, or creating frustration [41]. To test the effects of perceived simplicity of m-banking service, we propose the following hypothesis:

Hypothesis 2 (H2). *The simplicity of m-banking service has a positive effect on the perceived quality of m-banking service.*

3.3. Variability of m-Banking serVices

For m-banking, a wide array of services available to clients through m-banking services become increasingly important. M-banking, in its simplest form, can provide the provision of support for simple banking transactions (e.g., bill payments) but also more complex services, such as arranging savings and investments and contracting additional services, such as insurance contracts. Variability of services over m-banking includes, thus, the availability of different financial services, with the highest level of variability of m-banking services present in those systems that enable the provision of personalized services, as well as personalized marketing messages [23]. Previous research shows that broader variety and features can be seen as significant antecedents of quality, e.g., [25] and that content and quality of available service is important for mobile service quality [52]. In line with previous findings, we propose the following hypothesis:

Hypothesis 3 (H3). *A variety of m-banking services has a positive effect on the perceived quality of m-banking services.*

3.4. Perceived Quality of m-Banking Services and Bank Reputation

Although reputation is a multidimensional construct that differs according to different stakeholders [24], the quality of products and services has been recognized as one of the key antecedents of bank reputation, e.g., [25,30,35,36]. Ennew and Sekhon [37] argue that reputation is developing when services are accompanied by knowledge, expertise, consistency, and shared values, and without the high quality of products and services, it is not possible to build a viable long-term reputation. Through the quality of products and services, organizations show their credibility and get the trust of their stakeholders [5], increase client satisfaction, which leads to a high level of client commitment and loyalty [63]. Ruiz et al. [26] stress that the connection between the perceived quality of services and reputation is important as clients, to assess the perceived risk, rely on a bank reputation when objective and measurable attributes are not present. Bontis et al. [64], Grgić [33], and Wang et al. [25] in their research on the banking sector show that service quality leads to superior bank reputation. In the case of m-banking, m-banking service quality is expected to be a significant factor of bank reputation [51], and to test this relation, we propose the following hypothesis

Hypothesis 4 (H4). *Perceived quality of m-banking service has a positive effect on bank reputation.*

4. Methodology

4.1. Research Instrument and Data Collection

To test our research model and hypothesis, survey research was conducted to collect the responses from bank clients that use m-banking services of major banks in Croatia. The research instrument consists of four parts. The first part of the instrument measured m-banking service characteristics, and it consisted of 18 statements related to safety, simplicity, and variability of services of m-banking. The second part is comprised of five statements measuring the perceived quality of m-banking, while the third part consisted of six statements measuring bank reputation. The aforementioned statements were adapted from previously developed work by Wang et al. [25] and Ponzi et al. [27], which measured these dimensions in the context of internet banking. As both m-banking and internet banking services are technology-based channels, the measures were adjusted to reflect the m-banking instead of internet banking services. The last part of the instrument was related to respondents' data, including the frequency of m-banking usage. All multi-item measures used were based on five-point Likert scales from 1 (strongly disagree) to 5 (strongly agree) and are shown in more detail in Table 1.

Table 1. Research instrument description.

Construct		Code	Item
m-banking characteristics	Safety of m-banking	S1	Upgrade of m-banking application is safe
		S2	m-banking application is stable
		S3	Loading of a new version of the application is executed accurately and on time
		S4	All functionalities of the application are done accurately and on time
		S5	Usage of m-banking application is safe
	Simplicity of m-banking	M1	Download and loading of m-banking application is simple
		M2	Activation of m-banking application is simple
		M3	Search within the m-banking application is simple
		M4	Carry out of payments in the m-banking application is simple
		M5	Contacting bank staff through the m-banking application is simple
	Variability of services over m-banking	V1	The application allows contracting deposit products
		V2	The application allows contracting and/or filling out credit application requirements
		V3	The application allows the purchase of shares in funds
		V4	The application allows contracting insurance policies
		V5	The application allows you to sign up for a card
		V6	The application allows personalized communication
Perceived quality of m-banking		Q1	Overall client service through m-banking is excellent
		Q2	M-banking service of my main bank is of extreme quality
		Q3	M-banking application of my main bank completely satisfies my expectations and needs
		Q4	The average result regarding overall confidence, safety, and simplicity of using m-banking service of my main bank is adequate
		Q5	In general, I am satisfied with the quality of m-banking service of my main bank
Bank reputation		R1	I have a good feeling regarding my bank
		R2	I trust my bank
		R3	I respect my bank
		R4	My bank has a tradition
		R5	My bank has the strength of an international organization
		R6	My bank appreciates me as a client
		R7	Bank has overall a good reputation

Source: Authors' work based on Wang et al. [25] and Ponzi et al. [27].

Bank's volume of assets was a criterion used for the selection of financial institutions, as used in previous studies, e.g., [26]. The selection of respondents was deliberate, corresponding to age and gender of the population structure of the Republic of Croatia available from the last census. The questionnaire was sent to selected respondents via electronic mail on a sample of 500 clients of five major Croatian banks. In total, among 25 banks in Croatia, these banks control up to 70% of assets on the market and are responsible for about 75% of all bank loans. As of their size and importance, they were also the first to provide modern technology-based channels for offering their products and service, and thus their clients were chosen to participate in this study. Each of the respondents received an e-mail invitation to participate in the study, with a brief explanation of the study research goal and objectives. Respondents' anonymity was fully secured. During data collection, it was checked whether the data followed the planned quota design of the sample. After the data collection, the preparation and verification of the data collected by the survey were done by tests aimed at examining atypical values in the data and examining assumptions about the normal distribution of manifest variables.

In total, 154 responses were received. The sample consisted of 53% women, and with 79.8% of respondents with a university or higher level of education degree. Among respondents, 26.6% of them use m-banking several times a week, 20.1% of respondents use m-banking every day, while 13.6% of them use it less than once a month. The distribution of m-banking usage is presented in Table 2.

Table 2. Frequency of m-banking usage.

	Frequency	%
Every day	31	20.1
Several times a week	41	26.6
Once a week	20	12.9
Several times a month	38	24.7
Once a month	3	1.9
Less than once a month	21	13.6
Total	154	100

4.2. Statistical Analysis

Several statistical methods and analyses were done to ensure research validity and reliability, as well as to test our hypotheses.

Primarily, research instrument validity was checked. As the questionnaire items were adapted from the existing literature, and a pilot study was done, a content validity has been ensured. By using explanatory factor analysis to uncover the underlying structure of a relatively large set of variables, which were used under the a priori assumption that any indicator may be associated with any factor [65], convergent validity was done. By using confirmatory factor analysis, we tested for discriminate validity, to determine the degree to which measures of different latent variables are unique enough to be easily differentiated from other constructs [66].

Secondly, using Cronbach's alpha coefficients allowed for reliability analysis that was done to ensure the internal consistency of the items used for calculating scales [67].

Thirdly, to test for possible data validity problems indicated by negative or low correlations [68], our research data were analyzed using descriptive and non-parametric correlation statistics.

Fourthly, using the fit indices Chi-square index, Non-normed-fit index (NNFI), Comparative-fit index (CFI), and Root-mean-square-error (RMSEA) proposed by Hooper et al. [69], structural equations model (SEM) fit was tested.

Finally, SEM was used for testing our hypotheses with the special attention on the signs and statistical significance of the parameters and the amount of variance of endogenous constructs accounted for by independent constructs.

5. Results

5.1. Validity and Reliability Analysis

As the first step in data analysis, validity analysis was done to check the validity of the research instrument used. More specifically, we checked for content validity, convergent validity, and discriminant validity. Content validity was attained by using items from the existing literature, but also through preliminary research that was done on a sample of several randomly selected users of m-banking to test if questionnaire items are clear and if an appropriate level of understanding and interpretation of questionnaire items can be expected.

By using the statistical package SPSS v.23, the explanatory factor analysis was done to investigate the convergent validity. Iterated principal axis factor was combined with varimax rotation extracted five factors, as presented in Table 3.

Table 3. Rotated factor matrix for five factors.

Dimension	Item	Factor				
		1	**2**	**3**	**4**	**5**
Safety of m-banking	S1	0.815				
	S2	0.772				
	S3	0.747				
	S4	0.699				
	S5	0.702				
Simplicity of m-banking	M1		0.727			
	M2		0.709			
	M3		0.864			
	M4		0.873			
	M5		0.859			
Variability of services over m-banking	V1			0.770		
	V2			0.892		
	V3			0.713		
	V4			0.886		
	V5			0.883		
	V6			0.739		
Perceived quality of m-banking	Q1				0.644	
	Q2				0.647	
	Q3				0.746	
	Q4				0.689	
	Q5				0.748	
Bank reputation	R1					0.837
	R2					0.851
	R3					0.841
	R4					0.687
	R5					0.736
	R6					0.827
	R7					0.843

Costello and Osborne [66] suggested applying a loading cut-off value in the magnitude from 0.40 to 0.60. According to the defined criteria, all of the measurement factors were to be retained. Our factor analysis confirmed the existence of five factors.

By applying a confirmatory factor analysis, discriminant validity was assessed. Factor loadings, together with t-values, are presented in Table 4. According to Costello and Osborne [66], all λ's should be higher than the cut-off value of 0.50, and all of the t-values should exceed 1.96. Our data indicated a statistical significance of the observed loading paths.

Table 4 also presents data regarding Cronbach's alpha coefficients that were calculated for the reliability analysis. As internal consistency coefficients of 0.70 or higher are considered to indicate adequate reliability [67], and as all Cronbach's alpha coefficients of items analyzed were above the cut-off value, we can conclude item scales used show internally consistency.

Table 4. Standardized loading estimates and *t*-values, Cronbach's alpha.

Varibale	Item	Standardized Factor Loading	*t*-Values	*p*-Value	R2	Cronbach's Alpha
Safety of m-banking	S1	0.889	37.113	0.000	0.791	
	S2	0.919	41.477	0.000	0.845	
	S3	0.769	13.314	0.000	0.592	0.927
	S4	0.790	16.068	0.000	0.624	
	S5	0.869	25.475	0.000	0.755	
Simplicity of m-banking	M1	0.791	13.579	0.000	0.625	
	M2	0.750	13.048	0.000	0.563	
	M3	0.888	22.398	0.000	0.788	0.932
	M4	0.905	38.320	0.000	0.820	
	M5	0.936	53.281	0.000	0.876	
Variability of services over m-banking	V1	0.694	9.822	0.000	0.482	
	V2	0.912	32.366	0.000	0.831	
	V3	0.630	8.118	0.000	0.397	0.887
	V4	0.901	27.473	0.000	0.811	
	V5	0.876	18.999	0.000	0.768	
	V6	0.736	11.665	0.000	0.541	
Perceived quality of m-banking	Q1	0.891	35.602	0.000	0.793	
	Q2	0.889	27.831	0.000	0.790	
	Q3	0.933	69.254	0.000	0.870	0.965
	Q4	0.935	43.711	0.000	0.874	
	Q5	0.952	73.597	0.000	0.906	
Bank reputation	R1	0.875	21.966	0.000	0.766	
	R2	0.913	19.664	0.000	0.834	
	R3	0.895	30.084	0.000	0.801	0.938
	R4	0.705	10.209	0.000	0.497	
	R5	0.721	10.837	0.000	0.520	
	R6	0.827	19.585	0.000	0.685	

5.2. Correlation Analysis

A non-parametric correlation analysis was done to assess the nature of the connection among analyzed variables. Spearman's correlation coefficients have revealed several very low (near-zero) correlations between some of the examined items (see Tables 5 and 6). However, most coefficients showed that there was a medium to low correlation between items related to the dimension of m-banking service quality, perceived quality, and reputation.

The results, although moderately, emphasize the connection between examined items, which indicates a positive connection between different dimensions, quality, and reputation.

Table 5. Descriptive statistics and correlation coefficients for the dimensions Safety of m-banking, Simplicity of m-banking, and Variability of services over m-banking.

Variable	Mean	Std. Dev.	S1	S2	S3	S4	S6	M1	M2	M3	M4	M5	V1	V2	V3	V4	V5	V6
S1	5.15	1.57	1	0.848 **	0.671 **	0.629 **	0.800 **	0.538 **	0.470 **	0.433 **	0.476 **	0.538 **	0.212 **	0.132	0.258 **	0.163 *	0.146	0.348 **
S2	5.27	1.54		1	0.703 **	0.720 **	0.767 **	0.590 **	0.529 **	0.505 **	0.562 **	0.593 **	0.178 *	0.164 *	0.203 *	0.158 *	0.104	0.276 **
S3	5.21	1.57			1	0.707 **	0.636 **	0.481 **	0.412 **	0.428 **	0.426 **	0.517 **	0.141	0.073	0.212 **	0.118	0.071	0.225 **
S4	5.56	1.43				1	0.712 **	0.552 **	0.422 **	0.497 **	0.456 **	0.510 **	0.106	0.148	0.175 *	0.110	0.070	0.184 *
S6	5.32	1.58					1	0.596 **	0.540 **	0.535 **	0.528 **	0.631 **	0.219 **	0.203 *	0.313 **	0.204 *	0.196 *	0.363 **
M1	5.79	1.48						1	0.688 **	0.737 **	0.688 **	0.721 **	0.208 **	0.162 *	0.183 *	0.166 *	0.085	0.225 **
M2	5.47	1.57							1	0.704 **	0.635 **	0.689 **	0.265 **	0.217 **	0.211 **	0.212 **	0.158	0.322 **
M3	5.68	1.51								1	0.803 **	0.818 **	0.220 **	0.232 **	0.182 *	0.240 **	0.211 **	0.264 **
M4	5.73	1.44									1	0.865 **	0.221 **	0.211 **	0.204 *	0.199 *	0.172 *	0.290 **
M5	5.81	1.45										1	0.223 **	0.211 **	0.275 **	0.217 **	0.169 *	0.304 **
V1	3.88	2.00											1	0.667 **	0.657 **	0.589 **	0.563 **	0.246 **
V2	3.43	1.90												1	0.535 **	0.823 **	0.790 **	0.445 **
V3	4.10	2.05													1	0.547 **	0.577 **	0.387 **
V4	3.38	2.00														1	0.806 **	0.457 **
V5	3.55	2.01															1	0.405 **
V6	3.90	1.92																1

Note: ** statistically significant at 1%; * 5%.

Table 6. Descriptive statistics and correlation coefficients for the dimensions Perceived quality of m-banking and Bank reputation.

Variable	Mean	Std. Dev.	Q1	Q2	Q3	Q4	Q5	R1	R2	R3	R4	R5	R6	R7
Q1	5.30	1.43	1	0.849 **	0.820 **	0.802 **	0.846 **	0.517 **	0.529 **	0.474 **	0.485 **	0.456 **	0.434 **	0.482 **
Q2	5.39	1.47		1	0.837 **	0.824 **	0.821 **	0.587 **	0.613 **	0.528 **	0.557 **	0.514 **	0.494 **	0.542 **
Q3	5.34	1.55			1	0.876 **	0.902 **	0.458 **	0.516 **	0.398 **	0.443 **	0.491 **	0.368 **	0.458 **
Q4	5.40	1.41				1	0.892 **	0.562 **	0.603 **	0.469 **	0.492 **	0.523 **	0.434 **	0.506 **
Q5	5.37	1.55					1	0.485 **	0.509 **	0.402 **	0.458 **	0.488 **	0.382 **	0.462 **
R1	5.00	1.67						1	0.818 **	0.768 **	0.642 **	0.640 **	0.708 **	0.713 **
R2	4.94	1.78							1	0.865 **	0.646 **	0.611 **	0.728 **	0.704 **
R3	4.82	1.74								1	0.603 **	0.585 **	0.747 **	0.740 **
R4	5.29	1.53									1	0.557 **	0.536 **	0.586 **
R5	5.03	1.71										1	0.610 **	0.719 **
R6	4.82	1.81											1	0.797 **
R7	5.23	1.59												1

Note: ** statistically significant at 1%.

5.3. Assessment of Model Fit

Developing a structural equations model according to the proposed conceptual model was done by using the SAS module. It produced a chi-square of 658.034 with 343 degrees of freedom. Table 7 presents the indices used for assessing the overall model validity. Besides chi-square, other indices were additionally used to assess the overall model fit.

Table 7. Fit indices for the hypothesized model.

Fitness Indicator	Model Estimated	Explanations
Chi-square (χ^2)	658.034	χ^2 is not significant
Degrees of freedom (df)	343	
p-value	0.000	
χ^2/df	1.918	Very good, close to 2
NNFI	0.897	Good fit, >0.8
CFI	0.907	Satisfactory fit, >0.9
RMSEA	0.077	Acceptable fit, <0.08
90% confidence interval of RMSEA	(0.068–0.086)	Upper limit <0.10, a good result

The values of the Non-Normed-fit index (NNFI), as well as the Comparative-fit index (CFI), were near the proposed value of 0.90, which indicated a good fit. Root-mean-square-error (RMSEA) indicated results 0.077 which is acceptable e.g., [61]. In other words, we may conclude that our hypothesized model fulfilled the aforementioned requests.

5.4. Hypothesis Testing

As the overall model exhibited a good fit, we were able to further examine the model to assess if proposed theoretical relationships can be applied in a specific research context. The structural equation model was used for statistical testing of the hypothesis, the statistical significance of the parameters (measured by t-value), and the amount of variance of endogenous constructs accounted for by independent constructs (measured by the squared multiple correlation coefficient—R^2).

In Figure 2, the results of the path analysis are presented. As can be seen, the path coefficient for all the hypothesis was supported and with statistical significance present at the 1% level. Detailed results are presented in Table 8.

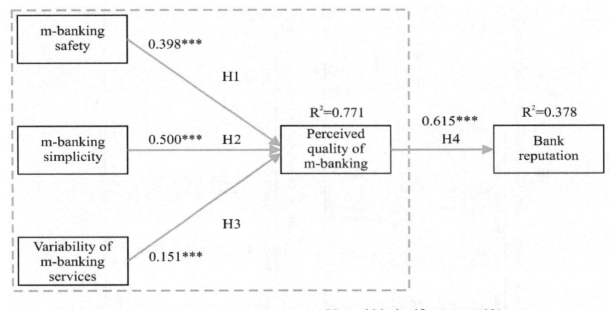

Note: *** significant > at 1%

Figure 2. Path Diagram with path coefficients estimates and their significance levels.

Table 8. Direct effects of path coefficients.

Hypothesis	Path Coeffcient	Std. Error	Z-Value	p-Value	R-Squared
safety → perceived quality	0.398	0.123	3.235	0.001 ***	
simplicity → perceived quality	0.500	0.120	4.172	0.000 ***	0.771
variability → perceived quality	0.151	0.044	3.455	0.001 ***	
perceived quality → reputation	0.615	0.078	7.934	0.000 ***	0.378

Note: *** statistically significant at 1%.

6. Discussion

Given the influence of m-banking, as well as possible effects of m-banking service quality, the paper aimed to analyze the relation between m-banking quality and bank reputation and to investigate elements of m-banking quality. With the emphasis on the application of relevant aspects of theory and practice and perception of m-baking clients, the goal of the paper was to conceptualize the components of the quality of m-banking services, an aspect of research somehow neglected in the examination of m-banking [14]. Besides, the goal was to provide a better insight into their relationship with the reputation of banks. Applying the structural equation modeling method allowed us to investigate the direct and indirect determinants of banks' reputation.

Corporate reputation is an important intangible asset of a company that can be linked to the most important financial indicators and long-term sustainable competitive advantage of the company. Determining a bank's competitive position is no longer solely the result of traditional measures such as financial indicators (ROA, ROE, EBITDA) and/or market share, but also qualitative measures that can be linked to intangible assets as bank's reputation. In that sense, exploring elements leading to bank reputation can be seen as an important step in this new market positioning.

Confirming one of the most common assumptions on the impact of product quality on bank reputation [34] and in line with previous similar research e.g., [25,26,33,64], our study has validated that the perceived quality of m-banking service has a positive effect on bank reputation. To differentiate on the market, banks have to take into account not only the development of modern technology-based services but also ensure their quality.

In line with previous research, e.g., [43,52], safety, ease of use, and variability of services offered have a positive influence on perceived quality, thus stressing the importance of these aspects in designing and providing the service of m-banking. These elements can be considered important not only to retain an existing client but also to attract new ones [42].

Not only that, as literature reveals, but risk and safety are also major contributing factors for the slow uptake of mobile banking [43], as our research has shown, safety affects the perceived quality. Due to their reputation, banks make great efforts to maintain the security of their systems and invest in the development of security systems of the latest technology. User education, automation, and the legal framework can reduce the likelihood of abuse, but they cannot eliminate it. Thus, safety and low perception of risk need to be accompanied by m-banking service.

Due to the particular nature of m-banking, which requires a certain level of knowledge and skill, simplicity seen as the ease of use and navigation through the system also plays a crucial role in determining m-banking quality. In line with previous research, e.g., [60], ease of using financial management services has been proven as crucial in the process of defining and designing quality of m-banking service. By maximizing interactivity and achieving ease of navigation, time and effort for financial management are kept to a minimum, thus, leading to a higher perception of quality. In this process, customer support can serve as support and have an educational element for customers.

If bank customers do not benefit from using m-banking services, consequently, they will leave this service, and banks will significantly decrease resources used to support it [42]. Thus, it is viable for banks to offer a variability of products in their m-banking service. In line with previous research, a broader variety and features, as well as the content of available service, can be seen as significant antecedents of m-banking quality, e.g., [25,52].

7. Conclusions and Implications

With an emphasis on the application of relevant aspects of theory and practice, the components of the quality of m-banking services have been conceptualized, which enabled a better insight into their connection with the reputation of banks. Through the understanding of key measures and indicators of the quality of m-banking services, the cause-and-effect relations are pointed out, which enables the creation of active practices of connection with the reputation of banks by encouraging the development of the use of information and communication technologies. In this way, a set of activities can be designed that best suits the local conditions in which banks operate and making it possible to create a competitive advantage for banks. Through this research, this paper has oriented towards understanding the importance of m-banking service quality and its connection to reputation. Moreover, as of scarcity in the existing research, the paper also explored antecedents of m-banking quality. In this paper, the aim was to contribute to the current literature by identifying those aspects of m-banking that are most likely to drive the growth of banks' reputation. We analyzed the responses of 154 users of m-banking services of five major banks in Croatia. Results show that all analyzed elements of m-banking quality, namely: Safety, simplicity, and variability of m-banking services have a positive effect on the perceived quality of m-banking service, thus confirming our first three hypotheses. In addition, it was hypothesized that the quality of m-banking service will be correlated with bank reputation, which this research has confirmed. Results reveal that the perceived quality of m-banking service has a positive effect on bank reputation, confirming our fourth hypothesis.

M-banking services, as one of the disruptive technologies that change the way of communication and business operations, are becoming increasingly widespread service, enabling us to have instant insight into the financial situation. Clients, on the other hand, are more informed about banks through different communication channels, they are more demanding and ask to have secure and instant bank service and banks are starting to exploit new digital opportunities moving to more agile technologies [70].

High-quality m-banking services (characterized by safety, simplicity, and variety) build trust towards the bank and, therefore, directly influence the bank's reputation, one of the bank's major strategic goals.

The implementation of information and communication technology through m-banking services demonstrates a movement from the traditional way of doing business towards the integration of information technology as an integral part of the bank's services. Consequently, banks offer their services through various channels and promote themselves on the global market. Still, as of specifics of bank services, the reputation of banks plays one of the crucial roles in clients' purchasing decisions, and it is an important element of bank differentiation strategies in various markets.

The results of the research can provide the basis for making recommendations concerning the use of information and communication technologies in the field of mobile communications, as an incentive for the growth of banks' reputation. Upon designing an m-banking services, organizations should emphasize and develop a service that is safe, easy to use but also offers a diverse set of possibilities. Understanding the key measures and quality indicators of m-banking services highlights the cause-and-effect relationships that enable the creation of active marketing and organizational practices that can lead to client satisfaction. This can allow designing activities that are best suited for the local conditions in which banks operate and enables them to create their specific competitive advantage.

Given that reputation is a perception or a public image of a bank, it is not under the direct control and is, therefore, difficult to manipulate [71]. Banks, therefore, seek to defend and sustain their reputation, aiming to provide novel service with an adequate level of quality. The risk of reputation, or the likelihood of occurrence of circumstances causing loss of trust, is of great importance for each bank. Therefore, it must be supervised and managed [72–74].

There are certain limitations of the study that need to be emphasized. First, the research sample is relatively small and from a single-country study, capturing only customers of major banks in Croatia. Thus, the sample could be more extensive to get more generalized results. Similar studies in the future should be conducted on a larger and international sample of m-banking users.

Second, a cross-sectional design was used in our study. Although this kind of research design is ideal for conducting descriptive analyses, we used it to test a causal model of the influence of m-banking quality on banks' reputation. Consequently, our research had to deal with the internal validity problem in establishing a cause-and-effect relationship without a time dimension. To resolve the issue of internal validity, future research activities should include a cohort analysis as a series of repeated cross-sectional studies. Such a design could be used to describe the aggregate change in m-banking quality and the bank's reputation over time. Besides, a longitudinal research design would enable us to test the causality determined in this study. It could also be effectively conducted by applying a multiple case study approach.

Future research should encompass a wider number of respondents and try to incorporate more objective measures to assess the quality of m-banking service, as well as reputation. Moreover, additional elements that can affect the perceived quality of m-banking need to be incorporated. Overall bank reputation can be dependent on the quality of different products and services bank offers, so a deeper understanding of bank reputation needs to take a wider aspect, analyzing bank portfolio and reputation from the employee, client, supplier, and general pubic point of view.

Author Contributions: Conceptualization, M.A.O. and B.S.; methodology, M.P.B. and B.S.; validation, A.A., M.A.O. and S.S.; formal analysis, B.S.; data curation, B.S.; writing—original draft preparation, B.S., A.A. and S.S.; writing—review and editing, M.P.B.; visualization, M.P.B.; supervision, M.A.O. All authors have read and agreed to the published version of the manuscript.

References

1. Barney, J.B.; Clark, D.N. *Resource-Based Theory—Creating and Sustaining Competitive Advantage*; Oxford University Press Inc.: New York, NY, USA, 2007.
2. Dierickx, I.; Cool, K. Asset stock accumulation and sustainability of competitive advantage. *Manag. Sci.* **1989**, *35*, 1504–1513. [CrossRef]
3. Dell'Atti, S.; Trotta, A.; Iannuzzi, A.P.; Demaria, F. Corporate social responsibility engagement as a determinant of bank reputation: An empirical analysis. *Corp. Soc. Responsib. Environ. Manag.* **2017**, *24*, 589–605. [CrossRef]
4. Ruiz, B.; García, J. Modelling customer-based bank reputation: The moderating role of uncertainty avoidance. *Int. J. Bank Mark.* **2019**, *37*, 340–361. [CrossRef]
5. Fombrun, C. *Reputation: Realizing Value from the Corporate Image*; Harvard Business School Press: Boston, MA, USA, 1996.
6. Ruiz, B.; Esteban, A.; Gutiérrez, S. Determinants of reputation of leading Spanish financial institutions among their customers in a context of economic crisis. *BRQ Bus. Res. Q.* **2014**, *17*, 259–278. [CrossRef]
7. Sanchez, J.L.F.; Luna, L. The creation of value through corporate reputation. *J. Bus. Ethics* **2007**, *76*, 335–346. [CrossRef]
8. Barrios, S.; Burgelman, J.C. Europe needs more Lisbon to make the ICT investments effective. *Inter Econ.* **2008**, *43*, 124–134. [CrossRef]
9. Afshan, S.; Sharif, A. Acceptance of mobile banking framework in Pakistan. *Telemat. Inform.* **2016**, *33*, 370–387. [CrossRef]
10. Reis, J.R.G.; Ferreira, F.A.F.; Monteiro Barata, J.M. Technological innovation in banking services: An exploratory analysis to perceptions of the front office employee. *Prob. Perspect. Manag.* **2013**, *11*, 34–49.
11. Arasli, H.; Katircioglu, S.T.; Mehtap-Smadi, S. A comparison of service quality in the banking industry: Some evidence from Turkish- and Greek-speaking areas in Cyprus. *Int. J. Bank Mark.* **2005**, *23*, 508–526. [CrossRef]
12. Laukkanen, T. Mobile banking. *Int. J. Bank Mark.* **2017**, *35*, 1042–1043. [CrossRef]
13. Calisir, F.; Gumussoy, C.A. Internet banking versus other banking channels: Young consumers' view. *Int. J. Inf. Manag.* **2008**, *28*, 215–221. [CrossRef]
14. Jun, M.; Palacios, S. Examining the key dimensions of mobile banking service quality: An exploratory study. *Int. J. Bank Mark.* **2016**, *34*, 307–326. [CrossRef]

15. Ganguli, S.; Roy, S.K. Generic technology-based service quality dimensions in banking: Impact on customer satisfaction and loyalty. *Int. J. Bank Mark.* **2011**, *29*, 168–189. [CrossRef]

16. Jayawardhena, C. Measurement of service quality in internet banking: The development of an instrument. *J. Mark. Manag.* **2004**, *20*, 185–207. [CrossRef]

17. Rod, M.; Ashill, N.J.; Shao, J.; Carruthers, J. An examination of the relationship between service quality dimensions, overall internet banking service quality and customer satisfaction: A New Zealand study. *Mark. Intell. Plan* **2009**, *27*, 103–126. [CrossRef]

18. Akturan, U.; Tezcan, N. Mobile banking adoption of the youth market: Perceptions and intentions. *Mark. Intell. Plan* **2012**, *30*, 444–459. [CrossRef]

19. Ha, K.H.; Canedoli, A.; Baur, A.W.; Bick, M. Mobile banking—Insights on its increasing relevance and most common drivers of adoption. *Electron. Mark.* **2012**, *22*, 217–227. [CrossRef]

20. Zhou, T. Understanding users' initial trust in mobile banking: An elaboration likelihood perspective. *Comput. Hum. Behav.* **2012**, *28*, 1518–1525. [CrossRef]

21. Sagib, G.K.; Zapan, B. Bangladeshi mobile banking service quality and customer satisfaction and loyalty. *Manag. Market.* **2014**, *9*, 331–346.

22. Asfour, H.K.; Haddad, S.I. The impact of mobile banking on enhancing customers' e-satisfaction: An empirical study on commercial banks in Jordan. *Int. Bus. Res.* **2014**, *7*, 145–169. [CrossRef]

23. Staresinic, B. Povezanost Kvalitete Mobilnog Bankarstva i Reputacije Banaka. Ph.D. Thesis, Faculty of Economics and Business, University of Zagreb, Zagreb, Croatia, 2019.

24. Trotta, A.; Cavallaro, G. Measuring corporate reputation: A framework for Italian banks. *Int. J. Econ. Financ. Stud.* **2012**, *4*, 21–30.

25. Wang, Y.; Lo, H.P.; Hui, Y.V. The antecedents of service quality and product quality and their influences on bank reputation: Evidence from the banking industry in China. *Manag. Serv. Qual.* **2003**, *13*, 72–83. [CrossRef]

26. Ruiz, B.; García, J.A.; Revilla, A.J. Antecedents and consequences of bank reputation: A comparison of the United Kingdom and Spain. *Int. Mark. Rev.* **2016**, *33*, 781–805. [CrossRef]

27. Ponzi, L.J.; Fombrun, C.J.; Gardberg, N.A. RepTrak™ Pulse: Conceptualizing and validating a short-form measure of corporate reputation. *Corp. Reput. Rev.* **2011**, *14*, 15–35. [CrossRef]

28. Roberts, P.W.; Dowling, G.R. Corporate reputation and sustained superior financial performance. *Strateg. Manag. J.* **2002**, *23*, 1077–1093. [CrossRef]

29. Flatt, S.J.; Kowalczyk, S.J. Corporate reputation as a mediating variable between corporate culture and financial performance. In Proceedings of the 2006 Reputation Institute Conference, New York, NY, USA, 25–28 May 2006.

30. Krzakiewicz, K.; Cyfert, S. Organizational reputation risk management as a component of the dynamic capabilities management process. *Manag. Sci.* **2015**, *19*, 6–18. [CrossRef]

31. Fombrun, C.J. Corporate reputations as economic asset. In *The Blackwell Handbook of Strategic Management*; Hitt, M., Freeman, E.R., Harisson, S.J., Eds.; Blackwell Publishers: Oxford, UK, 2001; pp. 289–312.

32. Neef, D. *Managing Corporate Reputation and Risk*; Routledge: New York, NY, USA, 2012.

33. Grgić, D. Indeks reputacije poduzeća: Empirijsko istraživanje u bankovnom sektoru. *Market Rev. Mark. Theory Pract.* **2012**, *24*, 23–45.

34. Barnett, M.L.; Jermier, J.M.; Lafferty, B.A. Corporate reputation: The definitional landscape. *Corp. Reput. Rev.* **2006**, *9*, 26–38. [CrossRef]

35. Rindova, V.P.; Williamson, I.O.; Petkova, A.P.; Sever, J.M. Being good or being known: An empirical examination of the dimensions, antecedents, and consequences of organizational reputation. *Acad. Manag. J.* **2005**, *48*, 1033–1049. [CrossRef]

36. Vitezić, N. Corporate reputation and social responsibility: An analysis of large companies in Croatia. *Int. Bus. Econ. Res. J.* **2011**, *10*, 85–96. [CrossRef]

37. Ennew, C.; Sekhon, H.S. *Trust and Trustworthiness in Retail Financial Services*; Routledge: London, UK, 2014.

38. Bitner, M.J.; Brown, S.W.; Meuter, M.L. Technology infusion in service encounters. *J. Acad. Mark. Sci.* **2000**, *28*, 138–149. [CrossRef]

39. Lin, H.F. An empirical investigation of mobile banking adoption: The effect of innovation attributes and knowledge-based trust. *Int. J. Inf. Manag.* **2011**, *31*, 252–260. [CrossRef]

40. Dash, M.; Bhusan, P.B.; Samal, S. Determinants of customers' adoption of mobile banking: An empirical study by integrating diffusion of innovation with attitude. *J. Internet Bank. Commer.* **2014**, *19*, 1–21.

41. Chen, C.S. Perceived risk, usage frequency of mobile banking services. *Manag. Serv. Qual.* **2013**, *23*, 410–436. [CrossRef]

42. Gakere, G.M. An Investigation on the Effects of Mobile Banking Services on Service Quality among United States International University Students. Master's Thesis, Chandaria School of Business, United States International University-Africa, Nairobi, Kenya, 2016.

43. Govender, I.; Sihlali, W. A study of mobile banking adoption among university students using an extended TAM. *Mediterr. J. Soc. Sci.* **2014**, *5*, 451–459. [CrossRef]

44. Malaquias, R.F.; Hwang, Y. An empirical study on trust in mobile banking: A developing country perspective. *Comput. Hum. Behav.* **2016**, *54*, 453–461. [CrossRef]

45. Ennew, C.T.; Waite, N. *Financial Services Marketing: An International Guide to Principles and Practice*; ButterworthHeinemann Elsevier: Oxford, UK, 2007.

46. Mersha, T.; Adlakha, V. Attributes of service quality: The consumers' perspective. *Int. J. Serv. Ind. Manag.* **1992**, *3*, 34–45. [CrossRef]

47. Culiberg, B.; Rojšek, I. Identifying service quality dimensions as antecedents to customer satisfaction in retail banking. *Econ. Bus. Rev.* **2010**, *12*, 151–166.

48. Choudhury, K. Service quality and customers' purchase intentions: An empirical study of the Indian banking sector. *Int. J. Bank Mark.* **2013**, *31*, 529–543. [CrossRef]

49. Sangeetha, J.; Mahalingam, S. Service quality models in banking: A review. *Int. J. Islam. Middle East. Financ. Manag.* **2011**, *4*, 83–103. [CrossRef]

50. Nisha, N. Exploring the dimensions of mobile banking service quality: Implications for the banking sector. *Int. J. Bus. Anal.* **2016**, *3*, 60–76. [CrossRef]

51. Malviya, S. Exploring mobile banking service quality dimensions for public and private sector banks in Indore district of Madhya Pradesh. *Int. J. Adv. Res. Comput. Sci. Manag. Stud.* **2015**, *3*, 243–252.

52. Ozer, A.; Argan, M.T.; Argan, M. The effect of mobile service quality dimensions on customer satisfaction. *Procedia Soc. Behav. Sci.* **2013**, *99*, 428–438. [CrossRef]

53. Hamzah, Z.L.; Lee, S.P.; Moghavvemi, S. Elucidating perceived overall service quality in retail banking. *Int. J. Bank Mark.* **2017**, *35*, 781–804. [CrossRef]

54. Alalwan, A.A.; Dwivedi, Y.K.; Rana, N.P.P.; Williams, M.D. Consumer adoption of mobile banking in Jordan: Examining the role of usefulness, ease of use, perceived risk and self-efficacy. *J. Enterp. Inf. Manag.* **2016**, *29*, 118–139. [CrossRef]

55. Munoz-Leiva, F.; Climent-Climent, S.; Liébana-Cabanillas, F. Determinants of intention to use the mobile banking apps: An extension of the classic TAM model. *Span. J. Market. ESIC* **2017**, *21*, 25–38. [CrossRef]

56. Wessels, L.; Drennan, J. An Investigation of Consumer Acceptance of M-Banking in Australia. In Proceedings of the Australian and New Zealand Marketing Academy Conference 2009: Sustainable Management and Marketing, Melbourne, Victoria, 30 November–2 December 2009; Luxton, S.S., Ed.; Promaco Conventions Pty Ltd.: Bateman, Australia, 2009; pp. 1–7.

57. Peevers, G.; Douglas, G.; Jack, M.A. A usability comparison of three alternative message formats for an SMS banking service. *Int. J. Hum. Comput. Stud.* **2008**, *66*, 113–123. [CrossRef]

58. Davis, F.D.; Bagozzi, R.P.; Warshaw, P.R. User acceptance of computer technology: A comparison of two theoretical models. *Manag. Sci.* **1989**, *35*, 982–1003. [CrossRef]

59. Hayashi, F. Mobile payments: What's in it for consumers? *Econ. Rev. Fed. Reserve Bank Kans. City* **2012**, *97*, 35–66.

60. Gu, J.C.; Lee, S.C.; Suh, Y.H. Determinants of behavioral intention to mobile banking. *Expert Syst. Appl.* **2009**, *36*, 11605–11616. [CrossRef]

61. Boonsiritomachai, W.; Pitchayadejanant, K. Determinants affecting mobile banking adoption by generation Y based on the unified theory of acceptance and use of technology model modified by the technology acceptance model concept. *Kasetsart J. Soc. Sci.* **2017**, *40*, 349–358. [CrossRef]

62. Huili, Y.; Shanzhi, L.; Yinghui, Y. A study of user adoption factors of mobile banking services based on the trust and distrust perspective. *Int. Bus. Manag.* **2013**, *6*, 9–14.

63. Shanka, M.S. Bank service quality, customer satisfaction and loyalty in Ethiopian banking sector. *J. Bus. Admin. Manag. Sci. Res.* **2012**, *1*, 1–9.

64. Bontis, N.D.; Booker, L.D.; Serenko, A. The mediating effect of organizational reputation on customer loyalty and service recommendation in the banking industry. *Manag. Decis.* **2007**, *45*, 1426–1445. [CrossRef]
65. Hair, J.F.; Black, W.C.; Babin, B.J.; Anderson, R.E.; Tathan, R.L. *Multivariate Data Analysis*; Prentice Hall: Upper Saddle River, NY, USA, 2006.
66. Costello, A.B.; Osborne, J. Best practices in exploratory factor analysis: Four recommendations for getting the most from your analysis. *Pract. Assess. Res. Eval.* **2005**, *10*, 1–9.
67. Feldt, L.S.; Kim, S. A comparison of tests for equality of two or more independent alpha coefficients. *J. Educ. Meas.* **2008**, *45*, 179–193.
68. De Vaus, D. *Research Design in Social Research*; Sage Publications: London, UK, 2001.
69. Hooper, D.; Coughlan, J.; Mullen, M.R. Structural equation modelling: Guidelines for determining model fit. *Elecron. J. Bus. Res. Methods* **2008**, *6*, 53–60.
70. Marrara, S.; Pejic-Bach, M.; Seljan, S.; Topalovic, A. FinTech and SMEs—the Italian case. In *FinTech as a Disruptive Technology for Financial Institutions*; Rafay, A., Ed.; IGI-Global: Hershey, PA, USA, 2019; pp. 42–60.
71. Dean, D.H. Consumer perception of corporate donations effects of company reputation for social responsibility and type of donation. *J. Advert.* **2003**, *32*, 91–102. [CrossRef]
72. Carter, R.B.; Dark, F.H. An empirical examination of investment banking reputation measures. *Financ. Rev.* **1992**, *27*, 355–374. [CrossRef]
73. Casalo, L.V.; Flavián, C.; Guinalíu, M. The role of security, privacy, usability and reputation in the development of online banking. *Online Inf. Rev.* **2007**, *31*, 583–603. [CrossRef]
74. Dowling, G.R.; Gardberg, N.A. Keeping score: The challenges of measuring corporate reputation. In *The Oxford Handbook of Corporate Reputations*; Pollock, T.G., Barnett, M.L., Eds.; Oxford University Press: Oxford, UK, 2012; pp. 34–68.

2

Towards Sustainability in E-Banking Website Assessment Methods

Witold Chmielarz and Marek Zborowski *⬛

Faculty of Management, University of Warsaw, Krakowskie Przedmieście 26/28, 00-927 Warsaw, Poland;
witek@wz.uw.edu.pl
* Correspondence: mzborowski@wz.uw.edu.pl

Abstract: Nowadays, banking services have evolved from offline financial services to online platforms available in the form of websites and mobile applications. While multiple methods exist for evaluation of generic-purpose websites, the appraisal of banking services requires a more sophisticated approach. Multiple factors need to be taken into consideration, revolving not only around technical and usability aspects of the sites, but also considering the economic and anti-crisis factors. Moreover, due to the fact that one of the groups of people interested in banking services assessment are potential clients, which might or might not be technically and theoretically literate, a sustainable approach to banking services evaluation is needed. The main contribution of this paper is a sustainable approach balancing the evaluation accuracy with usage simplicity and computational complexity of evaluation methods. Also, a reference model for banking services evaluation is provided. In practical terms, a set of all significant commercial banking services in Poland is assessed. Last, but not least, a preliminary study of practical applicability of various evaluation methods amongst computer-literate banking clients is performed.

Keywords: internet banking; website evaluations; multi-criteria evaluation methods

---

1. Introduction

One of the most important problems associated with bank management at present is how to maintain the existing clients and how to acquire new ones. It is particularly difficult in the case of individual clients, whose choices are determined not only by measurable economic or technical factors but also non-measurable aspects, for example, trends, unwillingness to make changes and cultural or psychological determinants. These choices are influenced also by factors that are independent of clients, such as economic policy of a given country. Moreover, from the banks' perspective, such choices are frequently associated with the possibility of their further operations and functioning in an increasingly competitive market. It is important to note that the bank is perceived by individual clients mainly through the perspective of contact or the efficiency with which tasks are carried out or the client's financial problems are solved. This points to the importance of information technology in providing clients with the highest quality services such as HCI (human computer interaction).

Presently, the common manifestations of these services are mainly the two most popular e-banking tools: i-banking and m-banking. The first one refers to the use of website browsers, and the second one to the use of mobile applications of particular banks. The significance of the problem is indicated by the fact that in the European countries like Norway, Finland, etc., which are most developed in terms of e-banking, the penetration rate at the end of 2018 amounted to over 90%, in Europe the level reached 54%, and in Poland, it was estimated at the level of 44% [1]. In the case of Poland, this means that at the end of the third quarter of 2019, over 18 million clients actively used i-banking and more than 10 million used m-banking services [2].

In the banking sector, the basic categories of users include individual and institutional clients, as well as the representatives of the website/application owners (bank employees). A banking software analyst/designer is a separate category in this case. Each of them has different skills, knowledge, diverse education or training, and different requirements resulting from intuition or awareness of using computer systems. The category of individual e-banking clients is the most diversified, so there is a need for "optimization", both in terms of the methods of communication and the scope of functionality of banking systems. One should also pay attention to the need of finding a common language for such diverse categories of users.

Websites and applications should be tailored to the sector of the services they represent. In particular, one should take into account the fact that banking systems contain a number of characteristics/criteria related to typically financial assessment, which on the one hand, affects their designing process, and on the other, their assessment by the user. In the literature, however, there are universal, unified guidelines for creating websites and internet applications [3,4], but in practice, there is a need to use specific, individual assessment criteria, tailored both to the users' requirements or anticipated needs and the requirements and conditionings of the economic sector.

The considerations to date show that the assessment and selection of the banking system requires an individual client to make decisions based on many complex, diverse factors (criteria) specific to the system. The above situation meets the conditions that locate it among the solutions associated with solving multi-criteria problems: There are many criteria, often contradictory or poorly structured, which are subjectively perceived by individual users. Contrary to single-criteria optimization methods, multi-criteria methods do not present the optimal value for one indicator, but rather a specific "compromise" Pareto-optimal value [5–7]. However, the basic research problem is the question of selecting the best MCDA method for the decision-maker to the problem under consideration. As far as methodology is concerned, this issue is increasingly present in the literature on the subject [8–10].

Although there is a considerable number of methods for evaluating general-purpose websites, such as eQual [11], Web Portal Site Quality [12], SiteQual [13], or SERVQUAL [14], banking platforms are more sophisticated systems, which require a more comprehensive evaluation approach. Not only does the list of evaluation criteria need to be expanded, but also the selection of MCDA aggregation method is crucial, as selection of an improper method can result in completely different final rankings [15]. Nonetheless, the analytical capabilities of individual clients should also be taken into consideration when selecting the evaluation method. This, in turn, constitutes the research gap, which this paper tries to address.

The authors' main contribution in this paper is aiming towards a sustainable approach to banking service assessment, taking into account three pillars: Evaluation methods' computational complexity, usage simplicity, as well as the methods' accuracy. Moreover, a reference bank services assessment model comprised of 18 criteria divided into three groups is provided. In practical terms, a comprehensive multi-method assessment of all significant banks in Poland is performed. Last, but not least, an additional contribution is provided in the form of a survey study of practical applicability of the proposed evaluation methods. Statistical familiarity and preference of users regarding various evaluation methods was studied.

After this introduction, in Section 2, a literature review justifying the research problem is presented. In Section 3, the proposed methodological framework is explained. The empirical research follows in Section 4. Conclusions and possible future works are indicated in Section 5.

2. Literature Review

Since the emergence of information technology systems, one of the key issues was how to assess and select the best IT systems to be used in the organization. In the 1990s, the problem gained recognition due to the widespread use of IT systems and the implementation of expensive integrated, IT systems. In this context, the biggest problem from the managers' point of view was how to achieve a return on their investment, i.e., the reimbursement of increasingly higher costs of IT solutions, and how to achieve the functionality resulting from the implementation of information system [16]. The reasons indicated above partially explain why the researchers and business practitioners have strived to look for the best method of achieving economic efficiency with regard to the use of IT systems and focused on their broadly understood utility [17]. It was not a trivial task, however after years of searching, most researchers came to the conclusion that there is no one universal measure of effectiveness or one widely applicable measure of utility/usefulness [18–20]. Searching for universal indicators based on the amount of time allocated to developing software did not bring the expected results [21] even though there were many attempts to include these factors into the standards of IT systems' evaluation, at least in terms of the assessment of software itself, not its application. It is currently believed that the method of solving this problem should rather be adapted to the decision-making situation [22]. It is important to note that the situation regarding the assessment of online tools is not very different in this respect.

The assumptions of most e-banking evaluation methods are largely based on e-commerce website assessment models [23–25]. These are methods traditionally derived from simple methods applied since the 1990s, based on sets of criteria specified for a given industry and their assessment according to the adopted scale. It is important to indicate that technical and functional factors predominate among the criteria groups [26]. It is difficult to talk about objectivity in this case, since many of these sets contain highly subjective factors, such as readability of the text, the attractiveness of color schemes, photos or videos, high quality of presentation, ease of navigating the site, etc.). Frequently, achieving the desired results can be carried out with the use of several tailored sample assessment criteria (such as the Web Assessment Index method, which focuses on four categories: speed, availability, screen navigation and content analysis [27]). Practitioners often choose methods that are as simple as possible from the point of view of providing input information for establishing indicators or the ease of interpretation, which is needed to make a decision concerning the adoption of a new IT system or changes to an existing solution. The literature on such assessment of electronic banking systems is very extensive and shows that the banking websites are analyzed from the point of:

- Usability (site map, address directory) [27,28],
- Functionality (search mechanisms, navigation, the relevance of content) [29,30],
- Visualization (color scheme, background, graphics, lettering) [31,32],
- Reliability and availability [33],
- Quality (as a combination of previous variants) [34].

This multitude of factors considered prior to selection of a bank creates an interesting research problem of multi-criteria evaluation of banking websites. Whilst the problem of generic websites' evaluation was widely studied and resulted in evaluation methods such as eQual [11], Web Portal Site Quality [12], SiteQual [13], SERVQUAL [14], or PEQUAL [35,36], the study of multi-criteria evaluation of banking services is still in its preliminary stage, which constitutes the research gap addressed in this paper.

3. Methodology

3.1. MCDA Foundations of the Bank Websites' Evaluation

There are numerous approaches for multi-factor decision making that can be divided into five categories. The first one, simple methods such as scoring methods [37,38], are often used in large-scale research; being easy to apply and not requiring explanations to users, they provide easy and transparent in interpretation. These methods are based on an unambiguous scoring scale applied to assess various qualitative features. They allow for establishing a single value for all the criteria features. A variation of the scoring method is the scoring method with preferences related to individual criteria or their groups. The usability of these methods depends on the proper selection of criteria features, in line with the user's expectations. Their subjectivity is mitigated by averaging mass results.

The second category, pairwise comparison, is a group of methods based on the AHP/ANP method (AHP, ANP, Modified AHP, Fuzzy AHP, Fuzzy ANP, e.g., [39]), allowing not only to assess the absolute value of a given feature and the total assessment index, but also the strength of the relationship of a given criterion feature to other characteristics. Such methods need prior instructions given to users, and it is troublesome to use in surveys, due to the large number of inversely scaled answers given by the user to complete the procedure. This method is affected by the rank reversal phenomenon. The ambiguity of the comparisons of different types of features, which the AHP method was accused of, has been partially mitigated by the assumptions of the ANP method [40,41].

The third group, parametric methods, are the methods in which respondents are encouraged to assign values to specific additional parameters. Evaluators avoid such methods because the determination of these indicators is often vague and ambiguous for them. This group of methods include, for example, PROMETHEE II [42], where the main problem connected with using such a method is a necessity—similarly to the AHP method—to educate the respondents before the assessment is to take place [43–45].

The fourth category, i.e., two or multi-criteria methods, is represented by the methods where in the first stage, the criteria and evaluation scale (or preferences) are established, and data are collected without the scoring analysis, and in the second stage, the researchers apply other multi-criteria methods [9,46]. The researchers differentiated nearly 300 of such methods, based on various theoretical assumptions, taking into account the assumed user preferences, distance from the assumed optimal levels, etc. While the first stage is relatively easy for the user, the second stage is sometimes difficult to adapt and apply due to the problems associated with the interpretation of the findings.

The last category comprises the combinations of aforementioned methods. These are hybrids, such as AHP + TOPSIS, Fuzzy AHP + TOPSIS, etc. The combination of methods aims at eliminating possible deficiencies of the well-known methods or bringing them closer to the standards related to findings interpretation [47].

In general, the consideration of multi-criteria assessment methods from the users' perspective is based on their opinions or their attitudes to: (1) The accuracy of the selection of criteria (attributes) in relation to the issue under consideration, even when these attributes are contradictory; (2) the ease and intuitiveness of using the assessment scale or the scale of the proposed preferences (when some criteria are more important for the user than others) applied to collect data; and the (3) ease and versatility of interpreting the evaluation results and the possibility of recommending taking specific decisions. The final selection of the evaluation method can differ depending on the nature of the decision maker (DM). While DMs in large corporations are accustomed to business analytics mechanisms and are less interested in the method of obtaining results, more in their interpretation and recommendations, the DMs from SMEs might prefer simpler and easier methods that can easily be used on less-educated individuals, not accustomed to making strategic-decisions to large extent.

In this paper, the sustainability concept is used to compare several evaluation methods and look for ones that balance the complexity of the method and amount of work required to arrive at a result, while obtaining the result that would be satisfactory enough for the user.

3.2. Criteria for Bank Websites' Evaluation

All methods presented in Section 3.1, regardless of the category to which they belong, require a set of criteria. Whilst there are numerous works proposing evaluation criteria for generic websites evaluation, online banks' evaluation has not been studied thoroughly yet. In this paper, a set of criteria for evaluating online banks is proposed. The proposed criteria are divided into 3 groups: Economic, technological, and anti-crisis.

- The economic criteria include:

  - A1   Annual nominal interest rate on personal accounts,
  - A2   Account maintenance PLN/month,

- A3 Fee for a transfer to own bank,
- A4 Fee for transfer to another bank,
- A5 Payment order,
- A6 Fee for issuing a debit card,
- A7 Monthly fee for a card PLN/month,
- A8 Interest rate on savings account,
- A9 Interest rate on deposits PLN 10,000,
- A10 Interest rate on loans PLN 10,000.

- The technological criteria include:

  - A11 Additional services,
  - A12 Account access channels,
  - A13 Security,
  - A14 Visualization,
  - A15 Navigation,
  - A16 Readability and user-friendliness,
  - A17 The scope of functionality.

Last, but not least, the anti-crisis group consists a single criterion A18 representing anti-crisis measures.

3.3. Sustainability in e-Banking Website Assessment

In this paper, the sustainability in e-banking website assessment is explored. In order to study how the methods' accuracy, usage simplicity, and computational complexity balance each other, the authors have adopted the following procedure:

- Definitions of a set of attributes (criteria) for assessing the functionality of electronic banking websites,
- Verification of the clarity and correctness of the set of questions for a particular, randomly selected client, using a randomly selected group of users,
- Adopting an unambiguous scale for evaluating attributes during the data collection process,
- Conducting a survey to obtain data and their initial verification,
- Analysis of the results for simple scoring methods (without preferences and with imposed, sample preferences),
- Adopting selected evaluation methods and performing calculations on the data provided by the research sample,
- Comparison of the obtained findings and discussion of their compliance,
- Conclusions resulting from the comparison of the applied methods.

3.4. Bank Websites' Evaluation Results Aggregation Scheme

In this paper, a comparative study between four groups of possible approaches is performed:

- A simple scoring method and a simple scoring method with preferences [48],
- Authors' own conversion method [49],
- Parametric methods Promethee II [50] and PROSA [18],
- TOPSIS Method [35].

The methodological foundations of each of the compared approaches are presented below.

3.4.1. Simple Scoring Method

In the case of a simple scoring method, the researchers measure either the sum of the average scores obtained in the study or the average distance from the maximum value (according to the adopted scale) for a given attribute. It refers to the value of the criterion and the distance is the same when we measure it from the first to the second criterion, and vice versa. However, the relationship between the individual criteria is not specified. Assigning the preference scale, adding up to 100%, particular criteria (or the group of criteria) can be seen as such a measure. The linear scale of preferences in its normalized form determines, in turn, the share of individual criteria in the final score. The scoring methods are considered to be subjective, although their subjectivity seems to decrease as the number of people surveyed increases and the preference scale is used. These methods are widely used, and their findings are easy to interpret. Other types of methods, which are based on measuring the relationship between individual attributes, are generally regarded as more objective. However, on the other hand, e.g., the AHP method [51], the Promethee II, Electre I and III, TOPSIS, and other methods are more complicated to apply and they are not very transparent in terms of interpretation of the findings. They often rely on the calculation of relative distances to another attribute (assessment criterion) or the adopted significance ranges. Users, both those evaluating banking services and later decision-makers, are reluctant to use them in the cases where the work efforts needed to identify input data as well as those related to subsequent interpretation are greater than those required in the case of a scoring method. The authors' research related to the use of such website evaluation methods as Promethee II, AHP etc. [50,52] suggests that in the case of the above-mentioned methods, respondents perceive that the process of completing the questionnaire as very difficult. As a result, it often leads to ill-considered and accidental assessment, and frequently depends on the order in which particular criteria appear.

3.4.2. Authors' Own Conversion Method

In order to minimize the problems encountered in simple scoring methods, the authors have developed their own method of evaluating websites—the conversion method. It does not require respondents to estimate any additional parameters, while calculations use the same data as in the scoring method. It is based on average distances from a possible maximum value. A detailed description of this method, together with the algorithm of its solution, can be found in [49]. Its main advantages are: The ease of collecting data for the evaluation, minimal amount of data necessary to obtain, the ease of application for non-experts in a given field, and the fact that there are no additional indicators that might be difficult to understand, such as in the case of ELECTRE method—the veta threshold, which may not be transparent for the respondent [53]—and the result of calculations in the form of the range of evaluations of the examined objects are easy to interpret. This method is still subject to verification; however, it constitutes an additional reference point for the results obtained with the use of other methods.

The method consists of determining the relation of each criterion to other criteria, based on averaged distances from the maximum potential value established on the basis of previous scoring evaluation. Data received from the scoring evaluation are the starting point for a conversion method. Then, we adopt the following assumptions: After constructing the experts' table of evaluations of particular criteria for each website, we need to perform the conversion with the established preference vector of the superior level criteria. Next, the authors perform the transformation of the combined scoring table into the preference vector (first converter).

The next steps are:

- Constructing a matrix of distances from the maximum value for each criterion in every website, establishing the maximum value (Equation (1)):

$$P_{i.max} = Max\{f_i(a_j), \ldots, f_n(a_m)\} \text{ for } i = 1, \ldots, n \text{ and } j = 1, \ldots, m \qquad (1)$$

- Establishing the matrix of the distances from the maximum value (Equation (2))

$$\delta\,(f_i(a_j)) = P_{i,max} - f_i(a_j) \text{ for } i = 1, \ldots, n \text{ and } j = 1, \ldots, m \qquad (2)$$

- Calculating the average distance from the maximum value for each criterion (Equation (3)),

$$F_{i,j} = \sum\nolimits_{(m,j=1)} \delta(f_i(a_j))/m \qquad (3)$$

- As a result of the above operation, constructing a matrix of differences in the distance from the maximum value and the average distance according to criteria,
- For each bank website: Constructing conversion matrices—modules of relative distances of particular criteria to remaining criteria (the distance from the same criterion is 0), the obtained distances below the diagonal are the converse of the values over the diagonal,
- Averaging criteria conversion matrices—creating one matrix of average modules of values for all criteria (Equation (4)):

$$A_{i,j} = \sum\nolimits_{(n,m,i=1,j=1)} (\alpha_{i,j} - \alpha_{i+2,j})/n \qquad (4)$$

- Transforming the conversion matrix of criteria into a superior preference matrix (calculating squared matrix, adding up rows, standardization of the obtained preference vector; repeated squaring, adding up rows, standardization of preference vector—repeating this iteration until there are minimum differences in subsequent preference vectors).

As a result of the above operations we establish a criteria conversion matrix Ta_{mx1}. Subsequently, the authors performed a transformation of the scores presented by experts on the level of a matrix specifying expert websites' evaluations for particular criteria (second converter).

The results have been obtained in an analogical way:

- Constructing a matrix of distances from the maximum value for each criterion and each website:
- establishing the maximum value (Equation (5)):

$$P_{i.max} = Max\{f_i(a_j), \ldots, f_n(a_m)\} \text{ for } i = 1, \ldots, n \text{ and } j = 1, \ldots, m \qquad (5)$$

- Establishing the matrix of distances from the maximum value (Equation (6)):

$$\delta\,(f_i(a_j)) = P_{i,max} - f_i(a_j) \text{ for } i = 1, \ldots, n \text{ and } j = 1, \ldots, m \qquad (6)$$

- Calculating the average distance from the maximum value for each website (Equation (7)),

$$F_i = \sum\nolimits_{(m,j=1)} \delta(f_i(a_j))/m \qquad (7)$$

- Constructing a matrix of the differences of deviations from the maximum value and the average distance of the features from the maximum,
- For each criterion: Constructing a matrix of transformations (conversions) of the differences of the average distance from the maximum value between the websites, analogically as presented above values below the diagonal are the converse of the values over the diagonal,
- Constructing a module matrix of transformations of the differences of average distance from the maximum value between the websites, for each criterion (Equation (8)),

$$A_{i,j} = \sum\nolimits_{(n,m,i=1,j=1)} (\alpha_{i,j} - \alpha_{i+2,j})/n \qquad (8)$$

- For each module matrix of the transformation of the differences of the average distance from the maximum value between the websites, squaring it, adding up rows, standardization of the obtained ranking vector and repeating this operation until the obtained differences between two ranking vectors for each criterion will be minimal.

As a result of the above-presented operations we obtain a conversion matrix of websites' evaluations Equation (9)):

$$Tf_{mx1} \tag{9}$$

- Using the obtained vectors to construct a combined ranking matrix—returning to the matrix where in,
- In its side-heading, there are criteria; in the heading, names of bank websites by appropriate transfer of the obtained preference vectors for each criterion, multiplying the matrix obtained in such a way by the previously calculated preference vector Equation (10)),

$$T' = Tf*Ta \tag{10}$$

- Analyzing final results and drawing conclusions (note: the lowest distances in this case are the most favorable, comparability adjustments to other methods can be obtained by subtracting these values from 1 and their repeated standardization).

3.4.3. Promethee II

The Promethee II method has a limited effect of linear compensation of criteria, and in contrast to other methods referred to as "European school" (e.g., the Electre methods), the result of its application is the full final ranking of alternatives with their quantification. The Promethee II method allows for obtaining a complete ranking of the resulting alternatives [54]. After determining the compliance factors for each pair of variants, dominance flows are determined for each of the variants:

- Output dominance flow describing how much the variant i a exceeds the other variants Equation (11)):

$$\Phi^+(a_i) = \sum_{(n,j=1)} \pi(a_i,b_j) \tag{11}$$

- Input dominance flow, indicating how much variant i a is dominated by other variants Equation (12)):

$$\Phi^-(a_i) = \sum_{(n,j=1)} \pi(b_j,a_i) \tag{12}$$

In turn, the decision-maker may create a total ranking of variants. In the Promethee II method, in order to create a complete order of variants, one should calculate the net dominance flow described by Equation (13):

$$\Phi(a_i) = \Phi^+(a_i) - \Phi^-(a_i) \tag{13}$$

In the Promethee II method, relations in a broad sense are defined as follows:

- Preference relation (threshold)—strict preference—variant a_i exceeds variant (Equation (14)):

$$b_j \ (a_i \ L \ b_j) \text{ when } \Phi(a_i) > \Phi(b_j) \tag{14}$$

- Indifference relation (threshold)—equivalence—variant a_i is equivalent to variant (Equation (15)):

$$b_j \ (a_i \ I \ b_j) \text{ when } \Phi(a_i) = \Phi(b_j) \tag{15}$$

3.4.4. PROSA

The PROSA method originated from the aforementioned Promethee II method. The basic assumptions for the PROSA methodology and the results of the procedure are set out as follows.

After determining the value $\Phi_{net}(a)$ and $\Phi_j(a)$ for $j = 1 \ldots n$, the decision-maker can determine the balance/compensation of criteria for particular decision-making alternatives:

- $\Phi_j(a) << \Phi_{net}(a)$ means that for the alternative a, the performance of criterion j is compensated by other criteria (alternative a is not balanced in terms of criterion j),
- $\Phi_j(a) >> \Phi_{net}(a)$ means that for the alternative a, the performance of criterion j is compensated by other criteria (alternative a is not balanced in terms of criterion j),
- $\Phi_j(a) \sim \Phi_{net}(a)$ means that for the alternative a is balanced in terms of criterion j.

The operators $>>$ and $<<$ mean the relations "much greater than" and "much less than". These relations express the subjective view of the decision-maker about whether the value on the right of the operator is much greater/much less than the value on the right of the operator, and thus whether the alternative a is balanced in terms of the criterion j or not.

In the next step, the value of the mean absolute deviation in a weighted form is determined taking into consideration the balance factor (compensation), according to the Equation (16):

$$WMAD(a) = \sum_{(n,j=1)} |\Phi_{net}(a) - \Phi_j(a)| w_j s_j \tag{16}$$

where s_j is the compensation factor for criterion j. It is easy to note that WMAD(a) is a specific type of weighted average distance of the solution $\Phi_{net}(a)$ from the solutions $\Phi_j(a)$ obtained for individual criteria.

The final assessment of the alternatives, i.e., PSV_{net} (PROSA Sustainable Value Netto), is calculated based on the Equation (17):

$$PSV_{net}(a) = \Phi_{net}(a) - WMAD(a) \tag{17}$$

This evaluation allows for compiling a complete ranking of objects.

3.4.5. TOPSIS

The TOPSIS method is made of six stages. Initially, the decision maker (DM) describes the decision problem (DP) with n criteria and m alternatives. A decision matrix $D[x_{ij}]$ is then constructed, with rows representing the decision attributes of the alternatives, and columns representing the criteria Equation (18):

$$D[x_{ij}] = (x_{11}, \ldots, x_{mn}) \tag{18}$$

Subsequently, the decision matrix undergoes normalization in the second step, with the following Equations (19) and (20):

$$r_{ij} = (x_{ij} - min_i(x_{ij}))/(max_i(x_{ij}) - min_i(x_{ij})) \tag{19}$$

$$r_{ij} = (max_i(x_{ij}) - x_{ij})/(max_i(x_{ij}) - min_i(x_{ij})) \tag{20}$$

for the benefit and cost criteria, respectively.

In the following step, the weights are imposed on the normalized decision matrix, thus resulting in a weighted normalized decision matrix, where each element is computed with the Equation (21):

$$v_{ij} = w_j * r_{ij} \tag{21}$$

In the fourth step, the positive (PIS) and negative (NIS) ideal solutions are obtained (V^+_j and V^-_j) (Equations (22) and (23)).

$$V^+_j = \{v^+_1, v^+_2, \ldots, v^+_n\} \tag{22}$$

$$V^-_j = \{v^-_1, v^-_2, \ldots, v^-_n\} \tag{23}$$

The best alternative should be as close as possible to PIS and as far as possible from NIS. Therefore, the Euclidean distances between each alternative and PIS and NIS are computed in the fifth step(Equations (24) and (25)):

$$D^+_i = (\sum_{(n,j=1)}(v_{ij} - v^+_j)^2)^{1/2} \tag{24}$$

$$D^-_i = (\sum_{(n,j=1)}(v_{ij} - v^-_j)^2)^{1/2} \tag{25}$$

Finally, in the last step of the algorithm, a relative closeness to the ideal solution is obtained (Equation (26)):

$$CC_i = D^-_i/(D^-_i + D^+_i) \tag{26}$$

The obtained closeness coefficient CC_i is the score value produced by the TOPSIS method and is used to construct the ranking of alternatives.

4. Empirical Research

4.1. Research Sample and Its Initial Preparation

The set of attributes used in the research is partly based on the set adopted in 2006, consulted at that time with Polish experts in the field of electronic banking. In 2008, this set was expanded to include factors that may indicate anti-crisis activities, and in 2017 after extending this set to approximately 70 attributes, the correctness and comprehensibility of all criteria and their significance for respondents was verified on a group of over 240 people. This allowed reducing the set of attributes to the current form used since 2018. In 2019, the preferences were re-evaluated limited to the previous set of attributes and the authors selected 18 attributes with the significance of above 60%, on a scale of 1–100% (Table 1).

The respondents did not report any problems in the case of a scoring method; however, the data for the study were collected in the first two weeks of April 2019. Over 940 people were asked to fill in the data needed to evaluate electronic banking services. The authors adopted a simplified, standardized Likert scale [55] to carry out the evaluation of the various criteria distinguished by bank clients.
The scale was as follows:

- complete fulfilment of the evaluation criterion (attribute),
- 0.75—almost complete fulfilment of the criteria,
- 0.50—partial fulfilment of the criteria,
- 0.25—minimum fulfilment of the criteria,
- failure to fulfil the criteria conditions.

In the study, the authors have indicated an additional condition for the respondents related to the provision of data. They should have the experience of using at least three online banking websites and evaluate three of the banks which are best known to them. This condition resulted from the requirement to receive answers from experienced respondents dealing with various electronic banking services. More than half of the respondents expressed their willingness (51%) to assess only one bank, and 19%—two banks. Two hundred and seventy-six individuals (less than 30% of the entire sample) assessed the websites of three banks. This represents a total of 828 ratings of electronic bank websites obtained as part of the study.

After the next verification and taking into account the recent comments of respondents, in their study, the authors considered 18 attributes (criteria), divided into the following three groups: Economic, technical, and anti-crisis criteria. A detailed list of attributes is provided in Table 1.

Table 1. The averaged value of significance and preference indicators for particular attributes.

No.	Criterion	Significance for the Respondent TOPSIS	Preference for the Respondent Scoring	Strict Preference for Promethee II Method	Indifference for Promethee II Method
	Economic	78.07%	55.60%	0.5019	0.5633
A1	Annual nominal interest rate on personal accounts	74.32%	5.29%	0.4822	0.5658
A2	Account maintenance PLN/month	89.03%	6.34%	0.5359	0.6066
A3	Fee for a transfer to own bank	88.51%	6.30%	0.5497	0.6188
A4	Fee for transfer to another bank	90.24%	6.43%	0.5572	0.6241
A5	Payment order	67.19%	4.78%	0.4549	0.5082
A6	Fee for issuing a debit card	69.58%	4.96%	0.4735	0.5360
A7	Monthly fee for a card PLN/month	88.27%	6.29%	0.5584	0.6281
A8	Interest rate on savings account	78.36%	5.58%	0.4580	0.5036
A9	Interest rate on deposits PLN 10,000	69.29%	4.93%	0.4403	0.4921
A10	Interest rate on loans PLN 10,000	65.92%	4.69%	0.5088	0.5497
	Technological	78.33%	39.05%	0.5177	0.5729
A11	Additional service	66.22%	4.72%	0.4705	0.5379
A12	Account access channels	82.64%	5.89%	0.5132	0.5811
A13	Security	92.72%	6.60%	0.5777	0.6373
A14	Visualisation	69.39%	4.94%	0.4954	0.5336
A15	Navigation	75.00%	5.34%	0.5071	0.5596
A16	Readability and user-friendliness	83.47%	5.94%	0.5373	0.5880
A17	The scope of functionality	78.89%	5.62%	0.5227	0.5725
	Anti-crisis	75.14%	5.35%	0.0535	0.0535
A18	Anti-crisis measures	75.14%	5.35%	0.5028	0.0050
	Average of group indicators	77.18%	33.33%	35.77%	39.66%

Apart from the significance assessment, the respondents defined their preferences regarding the share of individual attributes in the quality evaluation of the banking service. As far as individual attributes were concerned, it turned out that they do not deviate in any significant way from the average of 5.56%. However, the scores were fundamentally different in the case when the attributes were divided into groups. The highest average significance for respondents was recorded in the case of technological attributes, and the scores were slightly lower for economic factors. It is important to point out that the highest preferences that were indicated in the study, which should be taken into consideration when using a scoring method, concerned economic attributes—they amounted to nearly 56%, in the case of technological aspects they constituted only 39%, and for anti-crisis measures the result was estimated at just over 5% (Table 1). Economic attributes, which are a manifestation of the bank's current policy, in the eyes of the respondents are often decisive factors in terms of assessing the quality of the service and the latter translates into the bank's ability to retain existing customers or acquire new ones.

In addition, the respondents completed two further preference and indifference parameters needed for the PROMETHEE II method. The indifference index meant, in this case, the indication of the value (for each of the attributes) for which the difference in the evaluation of a particular attribute in relation to another is not important, which generally applies to the immediate environment of a given attribute (scale 1–100%). The beginning of the scale means a low difference and the end means a large difference. The preference index was defined as the value for which this difference is significant, and it is described using the same scale in the study as the level of indifference (Table 1).

Also, in a pilot study, a population of 32 individuals (12% of the selected group) presented their subjective assessments of the website evaluation methods, which they were familiar with taking into consideration the following features: Advanced knowledge/expertise needed to apply a particular method, the convenience/ease of collecting basic data, the need to estimate additional parameters, the ease of performing calculations for the analyses, the need to use specialized calculation software, methodological correctness, ease of making extensive analyses for decision making as well as the reliability of results.

The respondents did not report any problems in the case of a scoring method; however, there was some difficulty related to the assessment of the indifference and preference indicators for the Promethee II method. Despite this, the respondents still chose the Promethee II and not the AHP method that requires filling in more tables indicating relationships between particular attributes, which they perceived as uncertain or doubtful.

The respondents assessed 22 banking websites of the following banks: Alior Bank (Alior Bank SA), Bank BPS Grupa BPS (Bank Polskiej Spółdzielczości SA), Bank Millennium (Bank Millennium SA), Bank Pekao (Bank Polska Kasa Opieki SA), Bank Pocztowy (Bank Pocztowy SA), BGŻ BNP Paribas (Bank BGŻ BNP Paribas SA), BGŻ Optima (Bank BGŻ BNP Paribas SA), BOŚ Bank (Bank Ochrony Środowiska SA), Citi Handlowy (Citi Handlowy, Bank Handlowy w Warszawie SA), Credit Agricole (Credit Agricole Bank Polska SA), Eurobank (Euro Bank SA), Get In Bank (Getin Noble Bank SA), Idea Bank (Idea Bank SA), ING, ING Bank Śląski (ING Bank Śląski SA), INTELIGO, PKO Bank Polski (Bank Polski SA), iPKO, PKO Bank Polski (Bank Polski SA), mBank (mBank SA), Nest Bank (Nest Bank SA), Raiffeisen POLBANK (Bank BGŻ BNP Paribas SA), SGB Spółdzielcza Grupa Bankowa (Spółdzielcza Grupa Bankowa SA), T-Mobile Usługi Bankowe (Alior Bank SA), and Toyota Bank Polska SA (Toyota Bank Polska SA). The group of the most popular banks in this population included: MBank—one of the oldest and largest internet banks—services of the largest Polish banks: iPKO banks (Bank PKO BP SA) and Bank Pekao (Bank Polska Kasa Opieki SA), as well as the most modern banks such as Alior Bank (Alior Bank SA) and Bank Millennium (Bank Millennium SA).

The study was a case of purposeful sampling. The respondents included students of the last years of specialization studies at the University of Warsaw. The survey was distributed after the completion of a series of lectures on e-business website ratings. The fact that the sample consisted of individuals aged 18–25, selected from randomly chosen groups, could affect the results of the survey (96% of the population in Poland are potential online banking customers, 48% are active users of online banking, and 25% are active users of mobile banking); the surveyed age group accounts for over 60% of users) [56]. The sample was made up of 75% of women and 25% of men. Over 95% of the surveyed population declared having secondary education, Bachelor's degree or engineering studies were indicated by over 2% of the sample, and over 2% pointed out that they have higher education. The majority (65%) described themselves as working students and 35% as students. Most people (24%) stated that they come from cities with over 500,000 residents, the second largest group (21%) indicated that they come from cities below 50,000, and 17% of residents were born in the countryside.

4.2. Comparison of the Results of the Scoring Method without Preferences and the Scoring Method with Preferences

In order to carry out the analysis based on the scoring method the authors used the output tables exported from the survey system. In the survey, each client evaluated the banks' offers for selected e-banking services as well as the fees related to the use of bank accounts, which can be managed via the Internet. Subsequently, on the basis of the completed questionnaires, the researchers created a summary table of average ratings of criteria with the scores that were generated by users. This way, they could analyze and discuss the obtained results (Table 2). The individual rows contain the attributes of the evaluated website and the columns include the names of banks, which are listed in alphabetical order.

Table 2. Average scoring evaluations for equivalent attribute ratings.

A-attributes/C-banks	C1	C2	C3	C4	C5	C6	C7	C8	C9	C10	C11	C12
A1	0.62	0.58	0.62	0.61	0.66	0.57	0.68	0.62	0.66	0.69	0.44	0.65
A2	0.75	0.65	0.83	0.80	0.71	0.74	0.62	0.65	0.73	0.78	0.76	0.86
A3	0.87	0.61	0.89	0.88	0.78	0.86	0.75	0.68	0.85	0.89	0.89	0.96
A4	0.81	0.66	0.85	0.81	0.73	0.75	0.67	0.75	0.80	0.83	0.81	0.89
A5	0.76	0.55	0.79	0.79	0.72	0.73	0.64	0.68	0.81	0.77	0.70	0.81
A6	0.78	0.65	0.81	0.80	0.72	0.75	0.67	0.66	0.74	0.78	0.87	0.88
A7	0.73	0.62	0.83	0.79	0.71	0.74	0.59	0.66	0.74	0.78	0.74	0.90
A8	0.65	0.61	0.64	0.62	0.57	0.55	0.71	0.62	0.58	0.62	0.53	0.70
A9	0.62	0.57	0.62	0.62	0.58	0.52	0.67	0.63	0.60	0.58	0.58	0.66
A10	0.58	0.58	0.60	0.59	0.59	0.57	0.69	0.59	0.60	0.52	0.52	0.54
Economic	7.19	6.07	7.48	7.31	6.76	6.79	6.68	6.54	7.12	7.24	6.83	7.84
A11	0.70	0.64	0.74	0.74	0.47	0.67	0.61	0.61	0.72	0.74	0.57	0.76
A12	0.82	0.60	0.85	0.84	0.36	0.81	0.48	0.69	0.80	0.75	0.76	0.83
A13	0.80	0.74	0.82	0.82	0.60	0.75	0.64	0.68	0.83	0.74	0.73	0.82
A14	0.74	0.61	0.80	0.76	0.43	0.70	0.72	0.64	0.75	0.67	0.74	0.78
A15	0.72	0.57	0.76	0.73	0.49	0.69	0.64	0.64	0.73	0.69	0.71	0.79
A16	0.76	0.60	0.80	0.77	0.57	0.74	0.80	0.72	0.73	0.69	0.80	0.83
A17	0.76	0.58	0.81	0.78	0.49	0.71	0.57	0.69	0.71	0.67	0.72	0.79
Technological	5.29	4.33	5.57	5.44	3.41	5.07	4.45	4.67	5.27	4.95	5.04	5.59
A18	0.68	0.58	0.71	0.66	0.57	0.62	0.36	0.63	0.66	0.59	0.63	0.62
Anti-crisis	0.68	0.58	0.71	0.66	0.57	0.62	0.36	0.63	0.66	0.59	0.63	0.62
Total	13.16	10.98	13.76	13.42	10.74	12.48	11.49	11.84	13.05	12.78	12.50	14.05
%% max. score	73.11%	61.01%	76.47%	74.55%	59.68%	69.35%	63.83%	65.80%	72.51%	71.01%	69.42%	78.07%

A-attributes/C-banks	C13	C14	C15	C16	C17	C18	C19	C20	C21	C22	Suma	%% max. score
A1	0.60	0.67	0.69	0.63	0.63	0.57	0.55	0.45	0.65	0.82	13.66	62.08%
A2	0.76	0.81	0.94	0.84	0.84	0.83	0.74	0.76	0.78	0.78	16.95	77.04%
A3	0.86	0.91	1.00	0.93	0.91	0.90	0.80	0.77	0.83	0.98	18.80	85.44%
A4	0.73	0.86	0.99	0.85	0.87	0.85	0.77	0.59	0.82	0.99	17.67	80.31%
A5	0.65	0.81	0.89	0.80	0.78	0.73	0.72	0.80	0.78	0.81	16.54	75.18%
A6	0.69	0.80	0.83	0.79	0.79	0.83	0.73	0.88	0.73	0.75	16.92	76.91%
A7	0.79	0.78	0.92	0.79	0.82	0.83	0.67	0.72	0.77	0.92	16.83	76.52%
A8	0.53	0.67	0.63	0.58	0.64	0.57	0.57	0.52	0.77	0.75	13.61	61.86%
A9	0.54	0.63	0.59	0.58	0.61	0.56	0.55	0.55	0.75	0.85	13.44	61.09%
A10	0.49	0.61	0.58	0.57	0.59	0.45	0.61	0.57	0.72	0.65	12.79	58.13%
Economic	6.63	7.56	8.05	7.34	7.49	7.11	6.70	6.59	7.60	8.29		
A11	0.59	0.76	0.72	0.70	0.79	0.57	0.64	0.51	0.77	0.73	14.75	67.04%
A12	0.75	0.83	0.78	0.87	0.90	0.69	0.72	0.68	0.65	0.54	15.99	72.70%
A13	0.81	0.81	0.86	0.85	0.82	0.73	0.75	0.82	0.74	0.97	17.12	77.84%
A14	0.69	0.83	0.80	0.80	0.87	0.72	0.66	0.61	0.74	0.76	15.80	71.83%
A15	0.57	0.78	0.86	0.80	0.81	0.72	0.66	0.69	0.73	0.72	15.49	70.42%
A16	0.72	0.80	0.91	0.83	0.84	0.75	0.74	0.73	0.80	0.71	16.63	75.57%
A17	0.73	0.79	0.82	0.82	0.84	0.75	0.69	0.60	0.73	0.65	15.71	71.43%
Technological	4.85	5.58	5.74	5.69	5.88	4.93	4.87	4.64	5.15	5.08		
A18	0.61	0.70	0.74	0.69	0.70	0.53	0.70	0.66	0.75	0.75	14.16	64.36%
Anti-crisis	0.61	0.70	0.74	0.69	0.70	0.53	0.70	0.66	0.75	0.75		
Suma	12.08	13.85	14.53	13.72	14.07	12.57	12.28	11.88	13.49	14.12		
%% max. score	67.14%	76.93%	80.72%	76.24%	78.17%	69.85%	68.23%	66.02%	74.96%	78.43%		

%% maximum score—the share of a particular bank's website in the maximum favorable score expressed in the percentages or a share of a given attribute in the maximum score of each criterion. total—sum of points according to a standardized five-point Likert scale (0–1).

The analysis of the data collected and processed using the scoring method without preferences (equivalent attribute weights) indicates that the first place in the ranking was taken by the Inteligo PKO BP SA website, which meets over 80% of customer requirements. This coincides with the calculations made for the respondents' preferences. Toyota Bank's website ranks close to the previous position, i.e., it takes the second place in the ranking of points, and the third position in the ranking according to customer preferences due to good economic indicators. MBank is also rated highly. In the assessment influenced by customer preferences, Getin Noble Bank was also able to reach a high position, due to favorable conditions related to the credits and deposits offered by the bank. In this case, the worst results were indicated for Bank Pocztowy and Bank BPS Grupa BPS (Bank Polskiej Spółdzielczości SA). Considering the significance of the implementation of individual attributes, the most important aspects included fees for transfers to the user's own bank and to another bank, account maintenance, and the last positions taken by interest rates on savings accounts, deposits, and loans. It follows that bank customers perceive Internet-access accounts as a tool for implementing a current policy, rather than conducting a strategy of managing financial resources. However, the distribution of significance of individual attributes indicates the high importance of financial criteria in the evaluation of e-banking websites. In the case of e-commerce websites, technological factors are more prevalent [57].

Based on the table presented above, four variants were considered in the study. One of the methods limiting the specific subjectivity of the group of experts or users in the case of a scoring method is the application of unit preferences to individual criteria or groups of criteria. The study categorized all attributes (criteria) into three groups: Economic, technical, and anti-crisis criteria. The fourth group of criteria was adopted as a result of customer preferences indicated in the stages preceding the analyses. For each group, the authors adopted one variant with a group of dominant criteria:

- Economic (70% for economic criteria, 15% for the remaining ones),
- Technological (70% for technological criteria, 15% for the remaining ones),
- Anti-crisis (70% for anti-crisis criteria, 15% for the remaining ones).

The fourth variant calculated in the study were the average preferences presented by the respondents (56% economic criteria, 39%—technological, 5%—anti-crisis criteria, see Table 1. Column 4). Based on the calculations, the authors were able to establish an unambiguous ranking of places occupied by individual banks in the order of numerical values, assigned according to specific criteria. A comparison for these variants is provided in Table 3.

Imposing an absolute advantage (70%) on the group of economic attributes resulted in significant shifts both in relation to the variant related to customer preferences as well as to the ranking without preferences. That is why BGŻ BNP Paribas achieves the first position in the economic and anti-crisis variant (Bank BGŻ BNP Paribas SA). In the ranking, BGŻ BNP Paribas is followed by Bank Pocztowy, which attracts its customers with relatively good economic conditions, though is perceived by clients as less attractive than Inteligo or Toyota Bank. The best anti-crisis measures are provided by BGŻ BNP Paribas (Bank BGŻ BNP Paribas SA) and BGŻ Optima (Bank BGŻ BNP Paribas SA) as well as by Idea Bank (Idea Bank SA). IPKO, PKO Bank Polski (Bank Polski SA) and Bank Millennium (Bank Millennium SA) received the lowest scores in this area. A significant advantage of technical attributes caused a shift in the first positions: The most modern e-banking websites of Idea Bank (Idea Bank SA) and Nest Bank (Nest Bank SA) moved them to the top of the ranking. ING, ING Bank Śląski (ING Bank Śląski SA) obtained the lowest scores in this respect. The large discrepancy between the results of the version of the ranking related to the client (respondent's) preferences and the economic variant seems strange. In both cases, economic criteria of assessment have a significant advantage over other types of attributes. An experiment showed specific sensitivity to the assignment of extreme preferences to the distinguished groups of attributes, compared with studies carried out a year before [58]. In the authors' opinion, this points to the fact that in the spring of 2019, the relations between different banks and their clients appeared uncertain and rapidly changing. At that time, we could observe a specific disturbance in a temporarily established financial balance between banks and, what follows, changes in the clients' perception of e-banking websites.

Table 3. Ranking of the quality of banks' websites for the respondent, economic, technological, and anti-crisis variants (effects of sensitivity to changes in selected preference scales).

Symbol	Bank/Weights with a Predominance of Factors	Technological	Anti-crisis	Economic	Respondent	No Preference
C1	Alior Bank (Alior Bank SA)	11	12	4	22	10
C2	Bank BPS Grupa BPS, (Bank Polskiej Spółdzielczości SA)	10	18	11	21	21
C3	Bank Millennium (Bank Millennium SA)	12	21	8	5	6
C4	Bank Pekao (Bank Polska Kasa Opieki SA)	20	11	7	6	9
C5	Bank Pocztowy (Bank Pocztowy SA)	8	8	2	18	22
C6	BGŻ BNP Paribas (Bank BGŻ BNP Paribas SA)	4 *	1	1	13	15
C7	BGŻ Optima (Bank BGŻ BNP Paribas SA)	19	2	20	12	20
C8	BOŚ Bank (Bank Ochrony Środowiska SA)	15	13	17	20	19
C9	Citi Handlowy (Citi Handlowy, Bank Handlowy w Warszawie SA)	13	14	19	11	11
C10	Credit Agricole (Credit Agricole Bank Polska SA)	5	6	9	9	12
C11	Eurobank (Euro Bank SA)	17	4	12	17	14
C12	Get In Bank (Getin Noble Bank SA)	7	15	16	2	4
C13	Idea Bank (Idea Bank SA)	1	3	6	16	17
C14	ING, ING Bank Śląski (ING Bank Śląski SA)	22	9	3	15	5
C15	INTELIGO, PKO Bank Polski (Bank Polski SA)	21	10	10	1	1
C16	iPKO, PKO Bank Polski (Bank Polski SA)	6	22	13	10	7
C17	mBank (mBank SA)	9	5	15	4	3
C18	Nest Bank (Nest Bank SA)	2	7	21	8	13
C19	Raiffeisen POLBANK (Bank BGŻ BNP Paribas SA)	3	17	18	14	16
C20	SGB Spółdzielcza Grupa Bankowa (Spółdzielcza Grupa Bankowa SA)	16	16	5	19	18
C21	T-Mobile Usługi Bankowe (Alior Bank SA)	14	19	22	7	8
C22	Toyota Bank Polska SA (Toyota Bank Polska SA)	18	20	14	3	2

* each number in the table represents a place in the ranking.

4.3. Comparison of the Results of the Scoring Methods with the Conversion, Promethee II, PROSA and TOPSIS Methods

Among the scoring methods with preferences, the scoring method with the respondent's preferences pointed to the largest discrepancies in terms of its comparison with other variants. Similar discrepancies were observed in the result of the ranking established with the application of the conversion method. Similar to previous studies, the conversion method contributed to the "flattening" of the results, reducing the maximum spread of significance obtained as a result of using other methods. Nevertheless, the discrepancies in the results of the ranking obtained by this method compared to the rankings established with other methods were the largest. Thus, the top places in the ranking were occupied by the banks that in April 2019 completed the process modernizing their websites. They included: mBank (mBank SA), Raiffeisen POLBANK (Bank BGŻ BNP Paribas SA), and ING, ING Bank Śląski (ING Bank Śląski SA). Unfortunately, this resulted in a specific shift in the ranking: The banks that held much higher positions in the rankings obtained by other methods moved to further positions. The most stable position was recorded by mBank (mBank SA), where the difference between different assessments amounted to four places and INTELIGO PKO Polish Bank (Bank SA Polish) where the difference between the evaluations was limited to five positions.

Due to the advantages of Promethee II method, e.g., the relative (in reference to the scoring method) evaluation objectivity and the fact that a significant number of criteria or services does not cause a considerable increase in the number of questions included in the form, it seemed that the results obtained with the application of this method would be more objective than in the case of the scoring methods. However, they do not differ greatly from the ranking obtained with the use of other methods. Perhaps the reasons are certain disadvantages associated with this method, such as specific additional measures that respondents had to enter (such as weights and significance, parameters of indifference and strict preference), which may be difficult to understand for the respondents and the fact that when obtaining results one needs to use dedicated software. Thus, it is possible that indicators of indifference and strict preferences were determined without a deep understanding of their meaning, despite earlier instructions provided to the participants of the study. The average results presented in Table 1 show that they are very similar. The second important issue is the different preference weights used in the calculations—both when using the scoring, conversion, Promethee II, and the PROSA method, preference weights were used in relation to the attributes distinguished by the respondents (clients). In addition, calculations were made for the scoring method and Promethee II method without using a preference scale (all attributes were equivalent). This resulted in additional implications for the rankings of bank websites (Table 4).

Banks in Table 4 have been ordered according to the sum of places obtained in individual rankings. The smaller the sum obtained, the smaller the discrepancy between the results obtained with the application of the distinguished methods. The most stable position in this ranking belongs to INTELIGO, PKO Bank Polski (Bank Polski SA): in six out of eight rankings this bank held the first position in the scoring method (without preferences), Promethee II (without preferences), PROSA and TOPSIS (without and with preferences) method. The situation of mBank (mBank SA) is largely similar, the bank occupies the second position in the conversion method, in the Promethee II method without preferences, PROSA and TOPSIS with preferences method, and it takes the third place in the calculations made in the case of the scoring method without preferences and TOPSIS without preferences. The next two positions are very close to each other, ING, ING Bank Śląski (ING Bank Śląski SA) and Toyota Bank Polska SA (Toyota Bank Polska SA); however, the sum of their obtained positions is at least twice as high as in the case of the first two places. The last places are occupied by Bank BPS Grupa BPS, (Bank Polskiej Spółdzielczości SA) and Bank Pocztowy (Bank Pocztowy SA) (the sum of positions is over 8 times higher than in the case of the first positions).

The results in Table 5 were additionally used to calculate the differences between all the pairs of methods used and the so-called city block distance, which is the sum of the absolute values of the differences between the results obtained (in this case, places in the ranking).

Table 4. Comparison of internet banking website rankings according to individual methods.

No	Bank/Place in the Ranking According to a Method	Scoring Method without Preference	Scoring Method with Weights	Conversion Method	Promethee II without Preferences	Promethee with Weights	PROSA	TOPSIS without Preference	TOPSIS with Weights	Total
C1	INTELIGO, PKO Bank Polski (Bank Polski SA)	1	5	6	1	1	1	1	1	17
C2	mBank (mBank SA)	3	6	2	2	5	2	3	2	25
C4	ING, ING Bank Śląski (ING Bank Śląski SA)	5	22	3	4	3	4	4	4	49
C3	Toyota Bank Polska SA (Toyota Bank Polska SA)	2	13	9	7	2	7	5	5	50
C5	Get In Bank (Getin Noble Bank SA)	4	21	11	3	4	3	2	3	51
C6	iPKO, PKO Bank Polski (Bank Polski SA)	7	18	7	6	6	6	7	7	64
C8	Bank Millennium (Bank Millennium SA)	6	11	20	5	7	5	6	6	66
C7	T-Mobile Usługi Bankowe (Alior Bank SA)	8	12	5	9	9	9	9	8	69
C10	Bank Pekao (Bank Polska Kasa Opieki SA)	9	9	18	8	8	8	8	9	77
C9	Citi Handlowy (Citi Handlowy, Bank Handlowy w Warszawie SA)	11	2	13	11	11	11	11	11	81
C11	Credit Agricole (Credit Agricole Bank Polska SA)	12	1	17	12	12	12	12	12	90
C12	Raiffeisen POLBANK (Bank BGŻ BNP Paribas SA)	16	4	1	16	16	16	16	16	101
C14	Alior Bank (Alior Bank SA)	10	20	22	10	10	10	10	10	102
C13	Nest Bank (Nest Bank SA)	13	15	8	13	18	13	13	14	107
C15	BGŻ BNP Paribas (Bank BGŻ BNP Paribas SA)	15	10	15	15	13	15	14	13	110
C17	Eurobank (Euro Bank SA)	14	16	12	14	17	14	15	15	117
C16	Idea Bank (Idea Bank SA)	17	8	10	19	14	17	17	17	119

Table 4. *Cont.*

No	Bank/Place in the Ranking According to a Method	Scoring Method without Preference	Scoring Method with Weights	Conversion Method	Promethee II without Preferences	Promethee with Weights	PROSA	TOPSIS without Preference	TOPSIS with Weights	Total
C18	SGB Spółdzielcza Grupa Bankowa (Spółdzielcza Grupa Bankowa SA)	18	17	4	18	20	18	19	19	133
C19	BGŻ Optima (Bank BGŻ BNP Paribas SA)	20	3	14	17	21	20	20	20	135
C20	BOŚ Bank (Bank Ochrony Środowiska SA)	19	14	16	20	15	19	18	18	139
C21	Bank Pocztowy (Bank Pocztowy SA)	22	7	19	21	22	21	22	22	156
C22	Bank BPS Grupa BPS, (Bank Polskiej Spółdzielczości SA)	21	19	21	22	19	22	21	21	166

Table 5. Comparison of internet banking assessment pair methods distance.

Comparison Methods Pairs	City-Block Distance (Sum of Absolute Values)	Fisher-Snedeckor Test $\alpha > p = 2.084$	Significance
Scoring without and preferences	172	0.7131	Y
Scoring without preferences and conversion method	122	0.0047	Y
Scoring without preferences and Promethee II with preferences	20	0.1825	Y
Scoring without preferences and Promethee II without preferences	30	0.1933	Y
Scoring without preferences and PROSA	14	0.0170	Y
Scoring without preferences and TOPSIS without preferences	12	0.0174	Y
Scoring without preferences and TOPSIS with preferences	12	2.0160	Y
Scoring with preferences and conversion method	164	0.0066	Y
Scoring with preferences and Promethee II without preferences	172	0.2560	Y
Scoring with preferences and Promethee II with preferences	164	0.2711	Y

Table 5. *Cont.*

Comparison Methods Pairs	City-Block Distance (Sum of Absolute Values)	Fisher-Snedeckor Test $\alpha > p = 2.084$	Significance
Scoring with preferences and PROSA	172	0.0239	Y
Scoring with preferences and TOPSIS without preferences	170	0.0245	Y
Scoring with preferences and TOPSIS with preferences	168	28273	N
Conversion method and Promethee II with preferences	118	38,7582	N
Conversion method and Promethee II without preferences	134	41,0507	N
Conversion method and PROSA	120	36160	N
Conversion method and TOPSIS without preferences	124	37035	N
Conversion method and TOPSIS with preferences	122	428,1083	N
Promethee II without and with preferences	42	10591	Y
Promethee II without preferences and PROSA	6	0.0933	Y
Promethee II without preferences and TOPSIS with preferences	18	0.0956	Y
Promethee II without preferences and TOPSIS without preferences	20	11,0456	N
Promethee II with preferences and PROSA	36	0.0881	Y
Promethee II with preferences and TOPSIS without preferences	28	0.0902	Y
Promethee II with preferences and TOPSIS with preferences	28	10,4288	N
PROSA and TOPSIS without preferences	12	10242	Y
PROSA and TOPSIS with preferences	14	118,3914	N
TOPSIS without and with preferences	6	115,5951	N

In addition, two hypotheses have been formulated: H0 hypothesis assumed there is difference between each pair of analyzed methods, and H1 hypothesis assumed the existence of such differences, with a potential probability at the level of 0.95. In order to substantiate the hypotheses, the authors calculated the significance level α for the probability distribution of the inverse (right-sided) function of Fisher–Snedecor. It can be applied in the Fisher–Snedecor test to compare the degree of variability of two result sets for the same populations and compare it with the p value determined on the basis of test statistics. If $p \leq \alpha$, we reject H0 and take H1, if $p \geq \alpha$, we reject H1 and take H0.

The lowest city-block distance value in this case means the best method match from the point of view of the results achieved. Almost identical results, in terms of ranking, were obtained with the use of the Promethee II method without preferences and the PROSA method, if we calculated the absolute differences between the places obtained in the ranking (6 in total). The same result was calculated for combination TOPSIS without preferences and TOPSIS with preferences. Small differences also occurred in the results obtained by the scoring method without preferences and TOPSIS with and without preferences or PROSA as well as the scoring method without preferences and Promethee II without preferences. The biggest differences appeared in three cases: Scoring method according to the average weights and PROSA; the scoring method without preference and Promethee II without preferences; or the scoring method with preferences versus TOPSIS without preferences.

However, if we consider the calculated Fisher–Snedecor test indicators, they served as a no confirmation of the above conclusions. The H_0 hypothesis for individual criteria was confirmed only in 36% of cases, in one case of comparison Promethee II without preferences and PROSA methods despite the city block indicator result. However, the differentiation—compared to the findings from other methods—of results obtained thanks to the conversion method and scoring with preferences was confirmed. The results of the calculations are presented in Table 5, too.

4.4. Comparison of the Results of the Scoring Method without Preferences and the Scoring Method with Preferences

A pilot study has been carried out to assess the characteristics of individual evaluation methods from the client's point of view. The results of this study are of preliminary nature, but they confirm the observations made to date. The respondents in the survey, who were clients of different banks, most frequently assigned positive scores to the simplest methods, which they were familiar with and whose results they were able to check in person. Sophisticated, scientific research methods based on complex and complicated methodologies, requiring expert knowledge and specialized (often paid or costly) software for making calculations were not particularly appreciated during mass testing (even in the case of experienced users). It is widely believed that these tend to be methods for field experts or that they are not particularly useful. The detailed results for the pilot sample are shown in Table 6.

Table 6. Comparison of the possibilities of the application of methods in clients' evaluation (assessment dominant).

Features of the Method Which Are Significant for the Client	Scoring Method without Preferences	Scoring Method with Preferences	Conversion Method	Promethee II without Preferences	Promethee with Preferences	PROSA	TOPSIS without Preferences	TOPSIS with Preferences
No requirement of advanced knowledge to apply the method	1	1	1	0.75	0.75	0.5	1	0.75
The convenience of collecting basic data	1	1	1	1	1	1	1	0.75
No need to estimate additional parameters	1	0.75	1	0.75	0.5	0.5	0.75	0.75
Easy calculation for analysis	1	1	0,5	0,5	0.5	0.5	0.75	0.75
No need to use specialized calculation software	1	1	0,5	0.5	0.5	0.5	0.75	0.75
Methodical correctness	0,5	0,5	1	1	1	1	1	1
The ease of making extensive analyzes	1	1	0.75	0.5	0.5	0.5	0.75	0.75
Reliability of results	0,75	0,75	1	0.75	1	1	1	1
Total	7.25	7.00	6.75	5.75	5.75	5.50	7.00	6.50
%% of the share in maximum possible score	90.63%	93.75%	84.38%	71.88%	71.88%	68.75%	87.50%	81.25%

5. Conclusions

Banking services have evolved from offline financial services to highly available i-banking and m-banking platforms. Such online exposition of these services increases such services' penetration in the population, which in turn justifies the researchers' and clients' interest in assessment and competitive comparison of such services. Whilst there are numerous methods to evaluate general-purpose websites, banking services evaluation requires a more sophisticated approach, with extended set of criteria, as economic, technological, and anti-crisis aspects of each platform need to be considered. However, the accuracy of the evaluation method is not the only aspect that needs to be taken into account—the methods' usage simplicity as well as computational complexity are also very important factors.

The main contribution of this paper was its proposed sustainable methodological approach to banking services' evaluation, balancing the accuracy, computational complexity, and usage simplicity factors. Moreover, a reference model for banking services assessment was provided. In practical terms, all significant banks in Poland were appraised. As the results of the conducted analyses suggest, respondents (clients) of online banking mainly chose websites that, on the one hand, offered the lowest possible costs associated with having an account, and on the other, those that give the greatest potential technological benefits such as good functionality, navigation, modern communication media, etc.

Last, but not least, additional contribution is also provided. An attempt was made to evaluate the practical applicability of the proposed methods. The statistical preference and familiarity of technical-literate users regarding various evaluation methods was studied. Surprisingly, the surveyed group was more prone to using less accurate, yet simple methods than more accurate, yet computationally and theoretically complex ones.

First of all, the group of respondents was intentionally limited to the most experienced clients with the experience of using at least three banking services. Another limitation of the sample indicated in the study was the age of the surveyed respondents: The sample included individuals aged 18–25 years. This was a deliberate assumption because according to research and statistics, this group includes the most active users who are most aware of the possibilities offered by the Internet. On the other hand, the conclusions drawn on the basis of their opinions are difficult to generalize because of the lack of opinions of other age groups. Therefore, the surveyed group of respondents could be expanded in future research.

For the purposes of managing e-banking services of individual banks, an in-depth analysis concerning the differences in the assessment of individual attributes of banking services would also be necessary, which may be the next stage of the present research procedure. Future studies should also expand the group of the analyzed evaluation methods to include other popular MCDA methodologies.

Author Contributions: Conceptualization, W.C., M.Z.; methodology, W.C., M.Z.; Literature Review, W.C., M.Z.; Results, W.C., M.Z.; Conclusion and Abstract, W.C., M.Z.; writing—review and editing, W.C., M.Z. All authors have read and agreed to the published version of the manuscript.

References

1. Online Banking Penetration in Selected European Markets in 2019. Available online: https://www.statista.com/statistics/222286/online-banking-penetration-in-leading-european-countries/ (accessed on 1 August 2020).
2. Barbrich, P. NetB@nk, Bankowość Internetowa i Mobilna, Płatności Bezgotówkowe, 3 Kwartał 2019. Związek Banków Polskich, Warszawa. Available online: https://www.zbp.pl/getmedia/053cb32a-a816-4825-8c45-982ee6fe817a/Raport-Netbank_Q3-2019_fin2 (accessed on 20 June 2020).
3. Nielsen, J.; Budiu, R. *Mobile Usability*; New Riders Press: Indianapolis, IN, USA, 2012.
4. Nielsen, J. *Designing Web Usability: The Practice of Simplicity*; New Riders Publishing: Indianapolis, IN, USA, 1999.
5. Roy, B. *Multicriteria Methodology for Decision Aiding*; Springer: New York, NY, USA, 1996.

6. Keenney, R.I.; Raiffa, H. *Decision Analysis with Multiple Conflicting Objectives*; Wiley & Sons: New York, NY, USA, 1976.
7. Nijkamp, P.; van Delft, A. *Multi-Criteria Analysis and Regional Decision-Making*; Springer: New York, NY, USA, 1977.
8. Wątróbski, J. Outline of Multicriteria Decision-making in Green Logistics. *Transp. Res. Procedia* **2016**, *16*, 537–552. [CrossRef]
9. Wątróbski, J.; Jankowski, J. Guideline for MCDA Method Selection in Production Management Area. In *New Frontiers in Information and Production Systems Modelling and Analysis: Incentive Mechanisms, Competence Management, Knowledge-based Production*; Różewski, P., Novikov, D., Bakhtadze, N., Zaikin, O., Eds.; Springer International Publishing: Cham, Switzerland, 2016; pp. 119–138.
10. Wątróbski, J.; Jankowski, J.; Piotrowski, Z. The Selection of Multicriteria Method Based on Unstructured Decision Problem Description. In *Computational Collective Intelligence. Technologies and Applications*; Springer: Cham, Switzerland, 2014; pp. 454–465. [CrossRef]
11. Barnes, S.J.; Vidgen, R. Measuring web site quality improvements: A case study of the forum on strategic management knowledge exchange. *Ind. Manag. Data Syst.* **2003**, *103*, 297–309. [CrossRef]
12. Shih, H.-P. Extended technology acceptance model of Internet utilization behavior. *Inf. Manag.* **2004**, *41*, 719–729. [CrossRef]
13. Webb, H.W.; Webb, L.A. SiteQual: An integrated measure of Web site quality. *J. Enterp. Inf. Manag.* **2004**, *17*, 430–440. [CrossRef]
14. Buttle, F. SERVQUAL: Review, critique, research agenda. *Eur. J. Mark.* **1996**, *30*, 8–32. [CrossRef]
15. Wątróbski, J.; Jankowski, J.; Ziemba, P.; Karczmarczyk, A.; Zioło, M. Generalised framework for multi-criteria method selection. *Omega* **2018**. [CrossRef]
16. Myers, B.; Kappelman, L.; Prybutok, V.R. A Comprehensive Model for Assessing the Quality and Productivity of the Information Systems Function. *Inf. Resour. Manag. J.* **1997**, *10*, 6–25. [CrossRef]
17. Boudreau, M.-C.; Gefen, D.; Straub, D.W. Validation in Information Systems Research: A State-of-the-Art Assessment. *MIS Q.* **2001**, *25*, 1–16. [CrossRef]
18. Melone, N.P. A Theoretical Assessment of the User-Satisfaction Construct in Information Systems Research. *Manag. Sci.* **1990**, *36*, 76–91. [CrossRef]
19. Dudycz, H.; Dyczkowski, M. *Efektywność Przedsięwzięć Informatycznych Podstawy Metodyczne Pomiaru*; Przykłady Zastosowań; Uniwersytet Ekonomiczny we Wrocławiu: Wroclaw, Poland, 2007.
20. Lech, P. *Metodyka Ekonomicznej Oceny Przedsięwzięć Informatycznych Wspomagających Zarządzanie Organizacją, Lech Przemysław, Wydawnictwo Uniwersytetu Gdańskiego: Ekonomiczna Księgarnia Internetowa EKI.*; Wydawnictwo Uniwersytetu Gdańskiego: Gdańsk, Poland, 2007.
21. Czarnacka-Chrobot, B. *Wymiarowanie Funkcjonalne Przedsięwzięć Rozwoju Systemów Oprogramowania Wspomagających Zarządzanie*; Szkoła Główna Handlowa w Warszawie: Warszaw, Poland, 2009.
22. Wątróbski, J. An Ontology Supporting Multiple-Criteria Decision Analysis Method Selection. In *Intelligent Decision Technologies 2016: Proceedings of the 8th KES International Conference on Intelligent Decision Technologies (KES-IDT 2016)*; Springer: Cham, Switzerland, 2016; pp. 89–99.
23. Whiteley, D. *E-commerce: Strategy, Technologies and Applications*; McGraw-Hill: London, UK, 2000.
24. Evans, J.R.; King, V.E. Business-to-Business Marketing and the World Wide Web: Planning, Managing, and Assessing Web Sites. *Ind. Mark. Manag.* **1999**, *28*, 343–358. [CrossRef]
25. Selz, D.; Schubert, P. Web Assessment—A Model for the Evaluation And the Assessment of Successful Electronic Commerce Applications. *Electron. Mark.* **1997**, *7*. [CrossRef]
26. Chmielarz, W. Methodological Aspects of the Evaluation of Individual E-Banking Services for Selected Banks In Poland. In *Infonomics for Distributed Business and Decision-Making Environments. Creating Information System Ecology*; Pańkowska, M., Ed.; IGI Global, Business Science Reference, Hershey-New York: New York, NY, USA, 2010; Chapter 11; pp. 201–216.
27. Miranda, F.J.; Cortés, R.; Barriuso, C. Quantitative evaluation of e-banking web sites: An empirical study of Spanish banks. *Electron. J. Inf. Syst. Eval.* **2006**, *9*, 73–82.
28. Diniz, E.; Porto, R.M.; Adachi, T. Internet Banking in Brazil: Evaluation of Functionality, Reliability and Usability. *Electron. J. Inf. Syst. Eval.* **2005**, *8*, 41–50.
29. Guru, B.; Shanmugam, B.; Alam, N.; Perera, J. An Evaluation of Internet Banking Sites in Islamic Countries. *J. Internet Bank. Commer.* **2003**, *8*, 1–11.

30. Saraswat, A.; Katta, A. Quantitative Evaluation of E-Banking Websites: A Study of Indian Banks. *Icfai Univ. J. Inf. Technol.* **2008**, *3*, 32–49.

31. Mateos, M.B.; Chamorro, A.; Gonzalez, F.J.M.; Lopez, O.R.G. A New Web Assessment Index: Spanish Universities Analysis. *Internet Res. Electron. Appl. Policy* **2001**, *11*, 226–234. [CrossRef]

32. Chiemeke, S.C.; Evwiekpaefe, A.E.; Chete, F.O. The Adoption of Internet Banking in Nigeria: An Empirical Investigation. Available online: http://www.icommercecentral.com/open-access/the-adoption-of-internet-banking-in-nigeria-an-empirical-investigation-1-9.php?aid=38546 (accessed on 10 July 2020).

33. Hadhémi, A. An evaluation of internet banking and online brokerage in Tunisia. In Proceedings of the 1st International Conference on E-Business and E-learning (EBEL), Amman, Jordan, 23–24 May 2005; pp. 147–158.

34. Migdadi, Y.K. Quantitative Evaluation of the Internet Banking Service Encounter's Quality: Comparative Study between Jordan and the UK Retail Banks. *J. Internet Bank. Commer.* **2008**, *13*, 2–7.

35. Wątróbski, J.; Jankowski, J.; Karczmarczyk, A.; Ziemba, P. *Integration of Eye-Tracking Based Studies into e-Commerce Websites Evaluation Process with eQual and TOPSIS Methods*; Springer: Berlin/Heidelberg, Germany, 2017; pp. 56–80. [CrossRef]

36. Wątróbski, J.; Ziemba, P.; Jankowski, J.; Wolski, W. PEQUAL-E-commerce websites quality evaluation methodology. In Proceedings of the 2016 Federated Conference on Computer Science and Information Systems (FedCSIS), Gdansk, Poland, 11–14 September 2016; pp. 1317–1327.

37. Hasan, L.; Abuelrub, E. Assessing the quality of web sites. *Appl. Comput. Inform.* **2011**, *9*, 11–29. [CrossRef]

38. Jin-Young, K.; Linda, C. An analysis of smart tourism system satisfaction scores: The roleof priced versus average quality. *Comput. Hum. Behav.* **2015**, *50*, 610–617.

39. Saaty, T.L. Fundamentals of the Analytic network process. In Proceedings of the 5th International Conference on th Analytic Hierarchy Process, Kobe, Japan, 12–14 August 1999; pp. 20–33.

40. Shaaban, M.; Scheffran, J.; Böhner, J.; Elsobki, M.S. Sustainability Assessment of Electricity Generation Technologies in Egypt Using Multi-Criteria Decision Analysis. *Energies* **2018**, *11*, 5. [CrossRef]

41. Toklu, M.C.; Taşkın, H. A Dynamic Performance Evaluation Model for SMEs Based on Fuzzy DEMATEL and Fuzzy ANP. *Int. J. Oper. Res. Inf. Syst. (IJORIS)* **2019**, *10*, 16–30. [CrossRef]

42. Dadashpour, I. Identifying and ranking of alternative fuels by using AHP and PROMETHEE II methods to find best fuel for bus rapid transit system. *Int. J. Bus. Anal.* **2018**, *5*. [CrossRef]

43. Piwowarski, M.; Ziemba, P. Metoda PROMETHEE II w wielokryterialnej ocenie produktów. *Pol. Stow. Zarządzania Wiedzą* **2009**, *18*, 135–144.

44. Vivas, R.; Sant'anna, Â.; Esquerre, K.; Freires, F. Measuring Sustainability Performance with Multi Criteria Model: A Case Study. *Sustainability* **2019**, *11*, 21. [CrossRef]

45. Priyadarshinee, P. Examining Critical Success Factors of Cloud Computing Adoption: Integrating AHP-Structural Mediation Model. *Int. J. Decis. Support Syst. Technol. (IJDSST)* **2020**, *12*, 80–96. [CrossRef]

46. Tupenaite, L. Sustainability Assessment of the New Residential Projects in the Baltic States: A Multiple Criteria Approach. *Sustainability* **2018**, *10*, 5. [CrossRef]

47. Mardani, A. Application of decision making and fuzzy sets theory to evaluate the healthcare and medical problems: A review of three decades of research with recent developments. *Expert Syst. Appl.* **2019**, *137*, 202–231. [CrossRef]

48. Chmielarz, W.; Zborowski, M. Comparative Analysis of Electronic Banking Websites in Poland in 2014 and 2015. In *Information Technology for Management*; Springer: Cham, Switzerland, 2016; pp. 147–161. [CrossRef]

49. Chmielarz, W.; Zborowski, M. Conversion Method in Comparative Analysis of e-Banking Services in Poland. *Lect. Notes Bus. Inf. Process.* **2013**, *158*, 227–240.

50. Zborowski, M. Universites with an Economic Profile Websites Modelling. Ph.D. Thesis, Faculty of Management at the University of Warsaw, Warsaw, Poland, 2013.

51. Saaty, T. How to Make a decision. The Analytic Hierarchy Process. *Eur. J. Oper. Res.* **1990**, *48*, 9–26. [CrossRef]

52. Chmielarz, W.; Szumski, O.; Zborowski, M. *Kompleksowe Metody Ewaluacji Jakości Serwisów Internetowych*; Wydawnictwo Naukowe WZ UW: Warszawa, Poland, 2011.

53. Buchanan, J.; Sheppard, P.; Vanderpooten, D. Project Ranking Using Electre III. Available online: http://goldenchance.ir/wp-content/uploads/2016/10/580b046cb2a191.717560451477117036.pdf (accessed on 10 July 2020).

54. Trzaskalik, T. *Wielokryterialne Wspomaganie Decyzji*; Polskie Wydawnictwo Ekonomiczne: Warsaw, Poland, 2014.

55. Likert, R. *A Technique for the Measurement of Attitudes*; Archives of Psychology: New York, NY, USA, 1932.

56. Barbrich, P. NetB@nk, Bankowość Internetowa i Mobilna, Płatności Bezgotówkowe, 2 Kwartał 2019. Związek Banków Polskich, Warszawa. Available online: https://www.zbp.pl/getmedia/02918dd2-bf12-4cf7-a70a-09c1a297471c/Report-Netbank_Q2-2019 (accessed on 10 June 2020).

57. Chmielarz, W.; Zborowski, M. Ocena e-bankowości i e-płatności w Polsce—Perspektywa klienta. In *Roczniki Kolegium Analiz Ekonomicznych/Szkoła Główna Handlowa, nr 49 Społeczno-Ekonomiczne Aspekty Rozwoju Gospodarki Cyfrowej: Koncepcje Zarządzania i Bezpieczeństwa*; Szkoła Główna Handlowa: Warsaw, Poland, 2018; pp. 441–453.

58. Chmielarz, W.; Zborowski, M.; Atasever, M. *On Aspects of Internet and Mobile Marketing from Customer Perspective*; Springer: Cham, Switzerland, 2020; pp. 27–41.

3

Sustainable Financial Products in the Latin America Banking Industry: Current Status and Insights

Juan Camilo Mejia-Escobar [1,2], **Juan David González-Ruiz** [3,*] **and Eduardo Duque-Grisales** [4]

[1] Departamento de Ingeniería de la Organización, Facultad de Minas, Universidad Nacional de Colombia, Avenida 80 No. 65-223 Medellín, Colombia; jcmejiae@unal.edu.co
[2] Facultad de Producción y Diseño, Institución Universitaria Pascual Bravo, Calle 73 No. 73A-226 Medellín, Colombia
[3] Departamento de Economía, Facultad de Ciencias Humanas y Económicas, Universidad Nacional de Colombia, Cra. 65 #59a-110 Medellín, Colombia
[4] Facultad de Ingeniería, Institución Universitaria Pascual Bravo, Calle 73 No. 73A-226 Medellín, Colombia; e.duque@pascualbravo.edu.co
[*] Correspondence: jdgonza3@unal.edu.co

Abstract: The purpose of this study is to analyse the extant literature on sustainable financial products (SFP) with a comprehensive understanding of the status quo and research trends as well as characterise the existing SFP in the Latin America banking industry. In this way, research papers derived from Scopus as well as institutional reports such as main documents, sustainability reports, and product portfolios publicly available on webpages from public, private, and development banks are used to create a database of SFP where their main characteristics are included and classified. Based on the research trends identified, the results show the development of financial products focused on environmental, social, and government (ESG) matters, mainly from the credit side, of more sustainable financial markets and products under fintech ecosystems. The results show that because of regulatory and government support through mechanisms such as green protocols and social and environmental responsibility policies, private financial institutions of Brazil, Colombia, and Argentina have led the development of both social and green financial products. These study's findings may be used for several policymakers to broaden the opportunities available in sustainable financing and thus, provide a roadmap that researchers and practicing professionals can use to improve their understanding of SFP. Finally, the study presents the potential for further research in the field, both with a qualitative and a quantitative approach.

Keywords: sustainable finance; sustainable financial products; sustainable banking; SDGs; sustainable development; Latin America; ESG.

1. Introduction

Climate change is one of the greatest—if not the greatest—threats to humanity. In order to avoid reaching critical levels, such as the one represented by an increase of 2° Celsius above the levels before the pre-industrial era, sustainability would play a pivotal role [1]. Recent research suggests that, if this limit is exceeded, it could lead to continuous warming of the earth no matter what actions were taken by humans to reduce CO_2 emissions [2]. On the other hand, global pressures determined by imbalances at the social and economic level, with vast inequalities between countries, accelerated population growth with limited access to primary resources, and more than 1 billion people considered multidimensionally poor demonstrate that commitment on the part of all actors is required, especially governments and private agents [3,4]. In this scenario, it is crucial to mobilise huge financial resources to achieve the relevant changes. Therefore, there is a substantial opportunity for the banking industry in developing financial products that favour the expansion of sustainable finance and thus, align their activities with a sustainable and green economy [5].

The concept of sustainability has ceased to be a matter merely focused on compliance with regulations or a move towards corporate reputation improvement with activities of merely a philanthropic type [6,7]. At present, it is also considered as an integral part of the business and generator of financial value [8,9]; in particular, green practices impact on both a company's future market value and its profitability [10].

Concepts such as Corporate Social Responsibility (CSR) or Environmental Management are part of the new sustainability perspective as a type of management oriented towards all stakeholders [11–14]. Moreover, a desirable paradigm to implement is Environmental, Social and Government Policy (ESG) throughout the business cycle as a strategy to take advantage of and unleash all the capacities that investors can contribute to reaching the Sustainable Development Goals (SDGs), whose central axis is sustainability [15]. ESG is considered as a strategic factor, which contributes to competitiveness by doing differentiation [16].

In the last decades, for the banking industry, both responsibility and climate concerns have been considered as the main drivers for developing new business models, mainly focused on sustainable banking [17–20]. Given its pivotal role as the leading financial intermediary and cornerstone in the granting of credits for the development of projects, business growth and the weighting of risks embedded therein, the effects that the incorporation of ESG criteria could have on the design of its products and financial services are extensive in the banking industry [21–24].

Since the banking industry is vital for economic growth, this has a considerable indirect impact on the environment and society. Thus, sustainable banks could help provide the estimated US $5 to the US $7 trillion per year needed for reaching the SDGs by 2030 [25]. In this sense, the responsible banking industry can be thought of as the appropriation of the industry of the broadest concept of sustainable finance, a term for which there is no single definition and coexists with others such as green finance or social finance and points to new sustainable business models [23,26,27]. However, despite the importance of banks in promoting a transition towards a more sustainable form of growth, the activities related to banks have received little to no attention from sustainable finance scholars [28].

According to [29], sustainable finance refers to financial products or services that integrate ESG criteria in business or investment decisions. This is how multiple initiatives focused on building sustainable banks have been promoted at different levels such as the Sustainable Banking Network (SBN), the International Developed Financial Club and Global Alliance for Banking on Values, and very recently the Principles for Responsible Banking [30] in an attempt to move sustainable banking into the mainstream [31]. For its part, green finance varies on its definition from institution to institution but despite these differences can be well declared as defined by [32] as "financing of investments that provide environmental benefits". Regarding social finance though, there is no consensus in the industry about its scope [33], as stated in [34] "it may be understood as a broad area wherein various forms of capital are structured in ways that consider and value both financial performance and social value creation". In the end, both are defined based on the orientation of their funds (environmental versus social) and by the fact that they both are covered under the umbrella of sustainable finance.

Despite being a relatively new trend, several studies have been conducted to aim at examining how the incorporation of ESG criteria can be carried out in the banking industry. Among them, analyses conducted by [35–38] have contributed to understanding how customer sustainability and financed activities can have an impact on financial performance, thus being a promoter of change towards a more responsible economy. However, the evidence shows some unawareness of the implications of an accurate administration focused on sustainability and impact on stakeholders [39]. Some studies argue that it is a trend that is due to solutions using market logic rather than ethics of the firm and shifts towards a private responsibility for the provision of welfare services and poverty treatment [33]. Studies conducted by [40] and [41] suggest measuring the performance and degree of sustainability of the banks through ratings that evaluate their commitments together with environmental and social indirect impacts generated by credit recipients. They also suggest the existence of two types of banks, and consequently, two different business models: Those of a reactive nature that only adopt certain sustainable banking practices due to regulatory pressures and others that truly recognise the importance of rethinking the business and pretend to be ahead of standards and regulations [40,42,43].

Banks, meanwhile, by developing sustainable financial products (SFP) not only gain first-hand expertise but can also obtain benefits for their corporate image and reputation [44,45], as well as customer loyalty improvements [43,46]. Not to mention that seeing the implementation of more sustainable practices as a resounding alleviation to facing financial crises is something which diverse financial institutions agree upon [23,47]. Regarding profitability, previous research focused on Latin America (Latam) has shown that the performance of those SFP portfolios, particularly green ones, has a significantly better loan performance as well as high growth rates of about 50% year-on-year [48].

Moreover, these products demonstrate a real commitment to international voluntary initiatives to which they have joined and capitalise on an opportunity of a small business niche, but with significant growth. It is worth clarifying, however, that transparency and the real reach of banks that embark on such purposes can be questioned in several cases, as highlighted in [49–51]. Therefore, the inclusion of SFP strengthens overall sustainability performance, as explained by [23] and [52]. Despite this, very few studies have deepened in this specific field, and for the few inquiries that have been made, most have been carried out in European or North American countries, justifying a greater focus on emerging regions.

Thus, from researchers and practicing professionals' perspectives, little attention has been given to research on the SFP available in the market, which have ESG criteria, and what are the features and advantages that they offer to potential users of these products. For capital users, it is essential to know these types of products because obtaining financing through sustainable financial instruments offers companies and project developers a tangible benefit in terms of lower interest rates, which positively impacts on the cost of capital [53–55]. Also, benefits in the granting of loans such as longer terms, longer grace periods, and special guarantees provide valuable conditions to borrowers to comply with debt servicing [56]. The operative part of the projects that look for this type of financing is also favoured since they usually receive technical assistance and even have indirect operating cost reductions such as insurance premiums due to less exposure to ESG risks.

Furthermore, the value of SFP diversity relative to other financing products also lies in allowing green financing to be made available to the real economy and to actors (for example, individuals and SMEs) that do not have sufficiently large financing needs and/or the necessary experience to directly access the green bond market or be of interest to investment funds with climatic/sustainable criteria.

Studies conducted by the North American Task Force of the Finance Initiative of the United Nations Environment Programme [57] and [5] have aimed at mapping and providing a description of green financial products and identifying actors pushing the Italian financial sector to become increasingly greener, respectively. In the same way, studies conducted by [58,59] have deepened the analysis and applications of SFP. However, to the best of the authors' knowledge, no elements in the current literature analyse research on SFP or the mapping of this type of products, especially in Latin America. Latam serves as an interesting and rather unique context for testing old theories and for generating new insights about SFP, and specifically for identifying the effect that these products have on the regional banking industry. It is important to emphasise that in the context of emerging economies, the social, cultural, and managerial practices are significantly and systematically different from developed economies, which could condition the development of effective SFPs.

To help bridge the identified knowledge gap, this study aims at analysing the extant literature on SFP with a comprehensive understanding of the status quo and research trends in this topic. Additionally, this study characterises the existing SFP in the Latam banking industry. This paper contributes to the literature in two ways. First, in order to have a better understanding of SFP, an in-depth review that allows for analysing the research areas, trending topics, and evolution in this arena is carried out. Secondly, the characterisation of the SFP allows having a road map of the offering of this type of products in the Latam bank industry. Thus, to achieve a greater understanding of the motivations of the banks in the incorporation of ESG criteria in their business model, the results obtained are compared with previous analyses on the archetypes adopted by them [22]. This study will help practitioners, consumers, and bank managers to expand their knowledge of the opportunities available in sustainable financing and build on the experience and advances of other banks. The results could be equally useful for policymakers and regulators in the design of public sustainability policies. Besides, the study presents the potential for further research in the field, both with a qualitative and a quantitative approach.

The paper is organised as follows: After this introduction, which provides a context on the main elements of the study, the methodology section is presented. Next, the literature review on sustainable banking and sustainable finance is provided, followed by the results and discussion. Finally, the last section summarises the conclusions and significance of this study, followed by further research topic recommendations.

2. Methodology

This study carried out a comprehensive, systematic, and holistic literature review covering all research papers published in leading journals in the fields related to sustainability, environmental studies, economics, finance, and management as well as categorising the leading development of SFP. In this way, research papers derived from the bibliographic database Scopus as well as main institutional documents such as annual reports, sustainability reports, and product portfolio summaries publicly available on webpages from public, private, and national development banks are used in order to create a database of SFP where its main characteristics are included and classified.

To have an in-depth understanding of SFP, a scientometric review that allows analysing the research areas, trending topics, and evolution in this arena is carried out. According to [60], Scopus is among the databases with the highest academic research reputation. For having concise results from the database, combinations based on these keywords are used: sustainable banking, sustainable finance, green financing, green loans, and SFP. Concerning scientometric analysis, [61] argue that this technique allows characterising specific scientific knowledge by identifying structural patterns and research trends by means of an illustrative map. To do this, VosViewer software is used. Given that this tool is substantially useful in mapping knowledge areas through illustrations with graphical maps, several studies such as [62–64] have used it. Figure 1 shows the general methodology of this research and is detailed below.

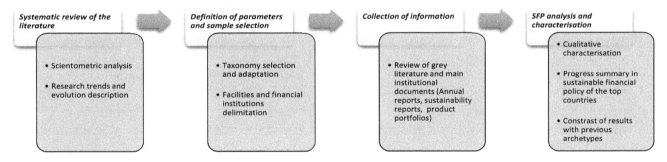

Figure 1. Overall methodology implemented.

For the searching, identifying, and conduction of this study, a broadly accepted set of sustainability-related guidelines were selected seeking despite lacking unified terms and concepts, the adoption of widespread categories and definitions related to SFP. Specifically, what can be understood as a green or social financial product, and some of the more meaningful taxonomies that cover SFP were sought. For this, the Green Loan Principles (GLP) [65] and the Social Bond Principles (SBP) [66] were chosen as referents for SFP, the former for those is more intended to bring mainly environmental benefits, and the latter for more socially-oriented products. These are both international voluntary forms of guidance that are the result of collaborative work between some of the main market actors, and which seek to foster the market development and guarantee the integrity of the products offered.

Although the GLP and SBP refer to different instruments and impacts (green versus social), both establish the same core components necessary to certify a green loan or social bond: the use of proceeds, the process for project evaluation and selection, management of proceeds, and reporting. For the analysis, SFP is considered to be any financial product existing in the market, whose only destination is the financing or refinancing, whether total or partial, of projects that bring environmental, social, or mixed benefits and that fall within the non-exhaustive categories of eligibility stated in the GLP or SBP.

It must be stressed that the last category in the green-oriented products sphere shown in Table 1—Multiple—does not belong to the original categories included in the GLP; however, it was added to better account for those products that encompass activities or projects related to two or more categories simultaneously, a possibility that the GLP also mentions.

Table 1. Taxonomies for Sustainable Financial Products (SFP).

Categories for Social-Oriented Products	Categories for Green-Oriented Products
Affordable basic infrastructure	Renewable energy
Access to essential services	Energy efficiency
Affordable housing	Climate change adaptation
Employment generation including through the potential effect of (SME) financing and microfinance	Pollution prevention and control
Food security	Environmentally sustainable management of living natural resources and land use
Socioeconomic advancement and empowerment	Terrestrial and aquatic biodiversity conservation
	Clean transportation
	Sustainable water and wastewater management
	Eco-efficient and/or circular economy adapted products, production technologies and processes
	Green buildings
	Multiple

The consideration of these taxonomies reflects the approach of sustainable finance adopted, which is not merely restricted to green categories as tends to be believed [67], and is in line with the recommendations of the G20 Sustainable Finance Study Group [25]. Additionally, this separation of products allows a more comprehensive analysis by having higher specificity regarding the use of funds.

On the other hand, the financial institutions considered were local financial institutions (LFI), which include private commercial banks and microfinance banking institutions, and public financial institutions (PFI) that comprise national development banks, state-owned commercial banks, special guarantee funds, or government trusts. The selection of institutions was made by including the banks that met the aforementioned characteristics and that belonged to one of the banking associations listed as active members of the Latin American Federation of Banks (FELABAN). FELABAN is an institution that groups banking associations from all over the continent and gathers more from 600 banks and financial institutions. The chosen associations by country and the number of financial institutions (FI) analysed are shown in Table 2.

Additionally, the SFP considered were limited to saving, credit, and grants-related products. This excluded insurance and investment products, mostly given that the institutions analysed were mainly commercial banks and because governments make the vast majority of clean economy investments, as well as corporations, private equity, and venture capital firms [68], which are outside of the scope of this study. This decision was made because the analysis of these kinds of products has been much more significant in the literature.

Besides, it should be noted that only products that explicitly indicated the sustainable purposes and/or categories of the facilities were considered. Therefore, several were either discarded or not considered given inaccuracies, or precarious disclosure in the media examined, which attends to the recommendations of the GLP and is consistent with the Climate Bonds Initiative (CBI) methodology for tracking of green bonds [69].

Table 2. Selected national banking associations. Source: Author's own research.

Country	Member Association	FI Examined
Argentina	Asociación de bancos de la Argentina	62
Bolivia	Asociación de Bancos Privados de Bolivia	15
Brazil	Federacao Brasileira de Bancos (FEBRABAN)	79
Chile	Asociación de Bancos e Instituciones Financieras de Chile A.G.	20
Colombia	Asociación Bancaria y de Entidades Financieras de Colombia (ASOBANCARIA)	32
Costa Rica	Asociación Bancaria Costarricense	14
Ecuador	Asociación de Bancos Privados del Ecuador	28
El Salvador	Asociación Bancaria Salvadoreña (ABANSA)	13
Honduras	Asociación Hondureña de Instituciones Bancarias (AHIBA)	16
Mexico	Asociación de Bancos de México	54
Guatemala	Asociación Bancaria de Guatemala	18
Nicaragua	Asociación de Bancos Privados de Nicaragua	7
Panama	Asociación Bancaria de Panamá	44
Paraguay	Asociación de Bancos de Paraguay	15
Peru	Asociación de Bancos del Perú	20
Uruguay	Banco de la República Oriental del Uruguay	11

With this in mind, together with the characterisation and analysis of the main SFP offered in the Latin American market, a catalogue of the main policies and regulations that have favoured the leadership and development of sustainable finances in the best-ranked countries is presented. Likewise, some progress indicators related to SFP provided by the SBN are evaluated. Its inclusion responds to its unique character as a global community that groups financial sector regulatory agencies and banking associations directed at emerging economies, and that in general seeks to provide a knowledge platform for the acceleration and commitment of these economies with the best international practices of sustainable finance [70]. Also, it is a major global player; SBN's 38 member countries are valued at $43 trillion in total, which is around 85 per cent of emerging market banking assets, 11 of which are Latin American [70].

Finally, the results obtained in terms of categories are contrasted with the most relevant developments in terms of archetypes for the advancement of business models for sustainability in the banking industry exposed in [22].

Literature Review

Although the existing literature lack a common definition for it, SFP can be understood as the practical instrument of sustainable finance. Based on the previous definition of sustainable finance [29], SFP could be specified as financial instruments whose issues and whose deployment points to the allocation of funds to causes related to sustainability improvements, an approach that we consider most significant and will be adopted throughout the study. The above can take place both with totally new products and by adapting non-sustainable financial products, namely traditional ones.

In the most significant contributions to SFP, concepts such as sustainable development, corporate social responsibility, and impact investing have the most attention, while only recent and very few research studies have managed to identify an explicit and comprehensive approach to SFP [58,59,71–73].

Figure 2 presents the most relevant keywords obtained after refining the search with the words previously mentioned in the methodology. It allows observing a variety of terms among which, at least directly, it is not possible to observe SFP, responsible financial products, new financial instruments, or anything else that could be a synonym for SFP. All these terms appear in the universe of results; however, they are notably small, suggesting they are of relatively little relevance, highly novel, and poorly related to the rest of the resulting words. Such an outlook in the academy is consistent with [71] in exposing the incipient development of responsible financial products, especially in emerging market and developing countries, and which has only recently begun to emerge. In this context, three well-defined research development trends can be identified in the scientific literature.

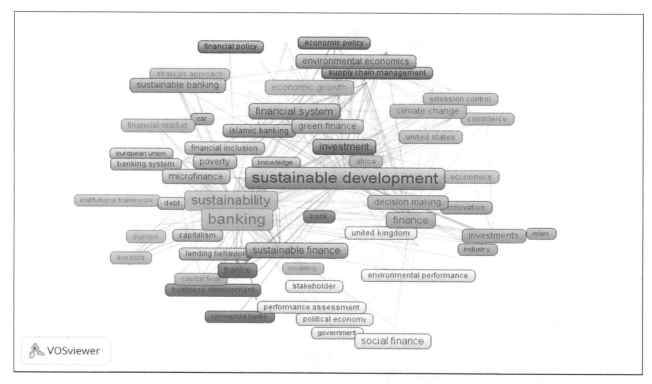

Figure 2. Most important keywords in the Sustainable Financial Products (SFP) research. Source: Author's own research.

A first research development trend focuses on a set of topics that cover risk management, sustainable banking practices, processes, environmental risks, and sustainability measurement as well as the business performance and sustainability relationship. Within this trend, the contributions conducted by [35,74] stand out as referents in the field for rethinking the credit risk management process framed in terms of sustainability. In [74] the benefits for both parties of considering the sustainability profile in the granting of credit were analysed.

In this regard, the bank for its part reduces reputational, regulatory, and credit risks arising from an imprecise risk rating and borrowers can enhance their perceived solvency thanks to lower exposure to ESG risk with the improvement in the negotiating power that is highlighted by [35].

Likewise, there is evidence of the benefits of integrating ESG ratings on traditional credit risk ratings from obtaining improvements in the accuracy of default predictions of a loan, as shown by this author with a significant sample of credit assessments, which is extremely useful for loans to small to middle-sized enterprises (SME) whose qualification is a challenge. Furthermore, these results are complemented by [75] who through regression analysis of several different Chinese banks focused on the effects of China's green credit policy on their bank's credit risk, discovering that banks with a higher proportion of green loans are associated with a lower non-performance loans ratio. This trend is characterised by the connection between financial and sustainability performance. For example, [76] contributes to refuting the incompatibility paradigm between financial performance and sustainability efforts by identifying a two-way causality relationship between these two variables for Chinese banks. Meanwhile, the bidirectional nature of the relationship between financial results and sustainability performance of the organisation is also defended by [77], pointing this time to French banks using a regression panel model and a sample of 68 banks for this purpose.

Within this research trend, assess sustainability risk is common among authors. [41] suggests a sustainability credit score system based on stages as a practical way to strengthen usual credit rating models in light of the sustainability considerations normally ignored in the banking industry. The authors of [78] for their part propose a framework to quantify, analyse, compare, and glimpse water risks by making investment decisions. The question about the actions taken to involve biodiversity in the bank's operations and the motivators for this purpose are addressed by [17]. The relations between a bank's CSR policies and the countries' peculiarities in developing countries have been conducted [12]; however, there is a scarcity of studies on these topics in Latam.

A second research development trend is about sustainable banking's evolution, which includes incorporated practices and the barriers, obstacles, and pitfalls faced as well as schemes and propositions of solutions. In this trend, studies on analysis at the institutional, sector, and macro regulatory level are common. Thus, the importance of banking industry in the mobilisation of resources towards sustainable finance is generally recognised; however, as is highlighted by [48,56,79], the practical understanding of how to develop sustainable finance in their product portfolio is vague. In line with the above, [80] focuses on the approaches that seek to embody sustainable solutions in the bank's operation, arguing their usefulness to the extent that banks can impact the business models and strategic decisions of their clients given their potential to determine whether projects can obtain the requested capital or not based on sustainability considerations, which can be measured by ESG when considering the viability of a loan.

Although disparities regarding concepts of what can be classified as sustainable finance, diverse types of barriers for the development of financial innovations have been identified, as stated by [19]. These authors also examine the concept of financial eco-innovation and recompile several existing barriers to its expansion and the suggested instruments to undertake them. On the other hand, [81] analyses difficulties due to information gaps on social and environmental impacts and risks that transcend the purely monetary perspective as well as the widespread predilection for short-term returns and investments with relative security, asserting that the combination of both constitutes a crucial barrier that negatively affects financing for sustainable activities. The above is supported by [56], who focuses on fostering of green lending and acknowledges the incompatibility between the terms granted by traditional bank loans and the typical time horizon of benefits in sustainable projects.

Likewise, concerns relative to high costs associated with the development of departments dedicated to sustainable loans within banks, non-existent mechanisms for managing the risks of such loans, and the insufficient capacity for evaluation and segmentation once they are granted are addressed by [56] and [82]. To help sustainable lending get to gain traction among banks, [83] suggest considering certain minimum times being required before noticing an improvement in the return on assets, and differences on their magnitudes according to the degree of development of the financial market in question.

In this regard, [21] aims at considering monetary policies dedicated to easing lending conditions for the low-carbon firm, since nationally developed market schemes such as carbon pricing through carbon markets are insufficient to meet the imperative need for credit that sustainable activities entail, and also do not address the high capital costs associated with investments in clean technologies depicted in [84].

Hence, the insufficient disclosure and offers in the bank industry of SFP make it possible to identify a knowledge gap, particularly in having a better understanding of the existing SFP [16,22,85–87].

Finally, the third research development trend discusses new financing instruments, namely sustainable ones, the redevelopment of traditional products, and microfinance schemes. This trend is characterised by the fact that it contains research with a greater focus on SFP, or at least more directly related than the rest. For instance, [71] exposes the incipient development of responsible financial products, especially in emerging market and developing countries, which have only recently begun to develop. This study also highlights the role of SMEs as clear potential users of this type of products, particularly in the environmental area with feasible investments in renewable energy, resource efficiency, and pollution abatement, among others.

On the other hand, [73] conducted a study to identify investors' preferences regarding ESG criteria, their real-life investment needs, and the most relevant SFP in the Spanish market, with special focus on Socially Responsible Investing (SRI) funds, bonds, SR loans, and SR current accounts and savings. This study concludes there is a need to adapt the SRI products to those of the public investor's preferences, and, at the same time, to promote knowledge of the characteristics of these products, for instance, their risks and returns, to eliminate supply and demand's mismatch.

In this regard, [72] addresses the supply-demand discrepancy of SFP in Germany. Based on this, it is necessary to diversify, customise, and make known to current banking customers the existing SFP. This study also argues that new SFP can allow the growth of sustainable finance in risk-averse countries such as Germany, where the stock market stands as the principal sustainable investment alternative. Within this development trend, a study conducted by [58] delves into the understanding of the state-of-the-art in green leasing in theory and practice from a stakeholder perspective. In this way, [59] suggest a finance framework that serves the financing of environmentally friendly practices in EU agriculture through SFP. On this issue, a securitisation system that allows various sources of financing for farmers, for the most part obtained through public subsidies and improving efficiency in the placement of public resources, is outlined. On the other hand, in [75,88], micro and social finance schemes are discussed. In the former, the case of a Canadian community credit institution dedicated to social finance and that is on the path to realising a 100% social finance portfolio is studied. In the latter, successes, errors, and recommendations are detailed based on a microfinance program in rural areas of Bangladesh [67].

Within these research development trends, the importance of SFP to support the expansion of the banking sector can be clearly observed. However, there is a scarcity of studies that allow having a better understanding of SFP since, although the research that addresses the concerns of massifying sustainable banking has abounded, it has focused mostly on the first two trends described and some other complementary issues, but has hardly delved into the third one. This scene is at least surprising and represents a conjunctural opportunity, since [22] proposes the SFP as one of the new archetypes to be adopted with the greatest potential to materialise sustainable finances towards bank users. In this sense, this gap can be noticed, especially in the Latam context. Therefore, it is necessary to analyse the evolution and characteristics of this type of products in the banking industry.

3. Results and Discussion

3.1. Results by Countries

In summary, 448 banks from 16 countries were analysed, with 267 of them with at least one SFP and thus obtaining a record of 1.709 SFP. The results show the number of SFP by countries, as shown in Figure 3. The top three (i.e., best-ranked) countries by offered SFP were Brazil, Colombia, and Argentina. Below are some of the main regulatory milestones that have contributed to their role as leaders in the region and the comparison with some indicators developed by the SBN to assess the performance and coverage of member countries with established national sustainable finance policies. After the selection of these indicators, the relevance of their scope was deemed to judge the progress in SFP. These countries are followed by Mexico and Ecuador that also show significant progress in sustainable finance, and that together account for 61.56% of all identified SFP.

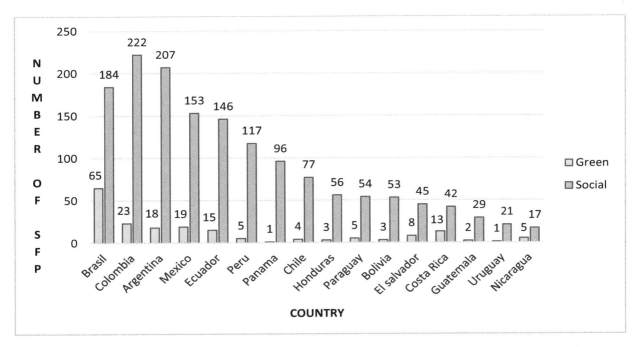

Figure 3. Sustainable financial products in Latin America. Source: Author's own research.

3.1.1. Brazil

Brazil is the most developed country in the region, working on the subject for more than a decade. In 2008, it established the green protocol and since 2013 it has been annually measuring financial resources for the green economy. In 2014, it established the framework for the creation and implementation of a social and environmental responsibility policy, and in 2016 it generated the guidelines for the issuance of green bonds. More recently, Brazil made progress in monitoring the environmental benefits of its banks' portfolios, while also beginning the creation of a methodology for calculating exposure to climate risks oriented to the national regulatory bodies. The country also has a great variety of national and regional state banks that are mainly active in the supply of SFP. For example, Banco Nacional de Desenvolvimento Econômico e Social is one of the largest banks with a vast number of products, which mark the development and supply of SFP nationwide and that place it above the rest of the relevant countries.

Another peculiar characteristic of Brazil is the special attention given to agricultural activity reflected in multiple products and services oriented to this sector by both PFI and LFI, although to a lesser extent for the latter. This scenario is logically clearly related to its role as a notable producer and exporter of many agricultural products, but it requires some restructuring and consolidation regarding PFI. That is, despite the positive nature of the existence of many programs to support sustainable agriculture, this favours a complex environment of financing that paradoxically hinders the understanding of available opportunities and ultimately hinders the proposed SFP disbursement objectives, as echoed in [69]. Finally, up to 2019, Brazil led investments in the fintech ecosystem, which necessarily drive the existence of a more significant number of SFP of a social nature oriented to financial inclusion and digitalisation of financial services.

The SBN framework contemplates two indicators to measure the progress in the sub pillar "Products and services", within the pillar "Climate and green finance" [70]. They are the indicators 4 and 5: "Defining sustainable assets and financial products" and "Green finance product guidelines", respectively. According to these indicators, Brazil has a 35% gap in that Climate and green finance area, thus being above the regional and global average. This stands out from the framework that provides valuable definitions for green sectors and green bonds, which are in accordance with existing standards such as the Green Bond Principles or Climates Bond Standards. However, according to [89], for further improvement, there is a planned extension of guidelines for green financial assets that are different from green bonds; they also further detail the definitions and examples of social and sustainable assets.

3.1.2. Colombia

Colombia traces its first and most significant advance in the promotion of sustainable finance to the Green Protocol issued by Asobancaria in 2012, the same regulatory entity that issued general guidelines for the implementation of environmental and social risk analysis in 2016. This was then supported in 2017 by a roadmap of actions to launch a green bond market in Colombia. Recently, in 2018, the leading financial regulator (Superintendencia Financiera—SF-) has been striving to establish clear definitions of sustainable finance, and the scope of the Green Protocol has been extended to include other associations in the sector such as insurers and microfinance entities. Besides, Colombia is working on its national emission reduction objective aligned with the Sustainable Colombian Initiative framework (covering 2015-2030) as well as the National Decree on Climate Change. The above, together with its flourishing and diversified thematic bond market (that is, green, social, and sustainable bonds) led by financial institutions issuers augurs well for the expansion of other types of products and services within the spectrum of sustainable banking [69].

Concerning digital finance, Colombia ranks as the third largest fintech ecosystem in Latam behind Brazil and Mexico, favouring and urging on opportunities for innovation and financial inclusion from traditional banks, but there is still much to be done [90]. On the other hand, various support mechanisms used by the central government can only be granted to companies that meet the criteria established by the Mipyme Law in 2000 such as preferred credit lines for working capital, acquisition of productive assets and investment, guarantees to facilitate access to credits through the National Guarantee Fund, and diverse programs to support growth and innovation.

According to the SBN framework [91], within the pillar "climate and green finance", Colombia has a 60% gap in the sub pillar "products and services". However, it is above the regional and global average in the two indicators used. In this sense, national regulations define green assets, set targets to develop a green bond sector, and recommend the development of SFP to banks, yet, Colombia needs to develop a greater clarity through more specific taxonomies and more explicit definitions of social and sustainable assets. This is a task that is underway and according to the most updated information from SF, is about to be completed very soon.

3.1.3. Argentina

In terms of sustainable banking, Argentina has been behind other countries in the region, including smaller or less developed financial markets. However, it has made several notable efforts beyond the stock market level. These actions include the development of environmental and social impact financing guidelines as well as the launching of a sustainable finance investor awareness campaign by the National Securities Commission, the first Argentinan sustainability index promoted by Bolsas y Mercados Argentinos (BYMA) in cooperation with the Inter-American Development Bank, and the agreement between the Buenos Aires Stock Exchange and the Mexican Stock Exchange to work together on the development of environmental markets. Additionally, in June 2019, the Sustainable Finance Protocol of Argentina was launched, which will be the guide to bringing sustainability to the financial sector. Also, one of the strategic axes of this crucial protocol will be to create financial products and services to support the financing of projects with a positive environmental and social impact, so the outlook is positive.

Argentina, despite being a member of the SBN, does not have a national sustainable finance policy and was not subject to specific evaluation and therefore, there are no indicators related to SFP. This apparent contradiction suggests that despite the lack of a national policy that serves as a frame of reference, the concept does exist in the national banking market. At the same time, it has an important number of products that can be classified as SFP and in some cases products that are unintentionally related in some way to sustainability. This country also reveals great future potential once the recent sustainable finance protocol or similar initiatives are consolidated and implemented, as this would provide integrity to the SFP and promote collective learning among the actors involved. Nonetheless, it should be highlighted that greater political involvement with these initiatives and sectoral efforts is desirable.

3.2. Results by Kind of Institution

Regarding the kind of institutions analysed, only 18.08% were PFI, which in turn translates into approximately 38.27% of the total SFP compared to 61.73% of the LFI, as illustrated in Figure 4a,b. Although this does not represent a majority, it is an important number considering the low participation in the universe of registered financial institutions.

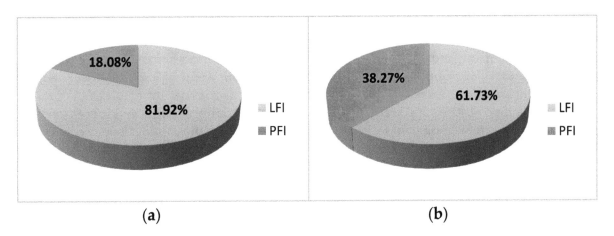

(a)   (b)

Figure 4. (a) Financial institutions examined; (b) Financial institutions offering SFP. Source: Author's own research.

Table 3 shows the first ten banks according to the number of SFP, with a predominance of banks in Colombia and Brazil, in addition to Argentina, Ecuador, and Chile. Although for this ranking the ratio of LFI versus PFI is the same, what is observed is that almost all of them are banks of considerable size and relative importance within the countries where they are located and that somehow gives indications of what has already been suggested about the bidirectional relationship between financial capacity and materialisation of strategies related to sustainability in its business model. In this sense, the average number of SFP per bank is approximately 6, which, however, is affected by the presence of large institutions with enough SFP in their portfolio. It is noteworthy that despite the financial institutions that have 1–4 SFP representing 50%, that is, approximately 132 institutions, only 19 of them are PFI. Then, the best description of the variable number of SFP per institution is that of a distribution skewed to the right with a median of 5 and the most frequent value of SFP equal to 2.

Table 3. Leading banks by the number of SFP. Source: Author's own research.

Country	Financial Institution	Kind of Institution	No. of SFP Identified
Brazil	Banco Nacional de Desenvolvimento Econômico e Social	PFI	48
Argentina	Banco de la Pampa	PFI	30
Colombia	Davivienda	LFI	29
Brazil	Banco do Nordeste do Brasil	PFI	29
Chile	Banco del Estado de Chile	PFI	27
Brazil	Banco Bradesco	LFI	24
Colombia	Bancolombia	LFI	23
Ecuador	Banco Pichincha	LFI	22
Colombia	Banco Agrario de Colombia	PFI	21
Colombia	Banco de Bogotá	LFI	21

3.3. Results by Products

All the products that are both social and green identified are part of the universe of sustainable finance and are some of the ways selected by financial institutions to adhere to this trend, that is to say, archetypes, but more precisely they are framed in the ways described by [22]. Analysing in depth the rationality on the part of financial institutions towards the offer of SFP is not the central focus of this study, but it is closely related. Thus, in addition to the aforementioned benefits derived from this, [22] has advanced a rigorous inspection of the motivations that drive them. That is why to shed light on this point, such archetypes were contrasted with the results, specifically four of them, which are: "Substitute with digital processes", "Inclusive value creation", "Resilience in loan granting", and "Sustainable financial products".

The main resulting categories for both social and green SFP indicate which are the archetypes of greater adoption in Latam and preliminarily suggest their pertinency in the region. Socially, the categories of SME financing and microfinance, access to essential services, socioeconomic development, empowerment, and even affordable housing account for the archetypes 'Substitute with digital processes' and 'Inclusive value creation'. There are associations that do not result in the reality of the region with emerging countries and multiple inequities and social problems, and that is evidenced for example in the low figures of financial inclusion. No less obvious is the predominance of informality in business and SMEs in regional economies, and so, by addressing these imbalances with SFP, financial institutions, as highlighted in [22], serve the most disadvantaged and generate opportunities in new markets. The other social categories also respond to a lesser extent to these archetypes.

As Figure 5 shows, products with a social focus are closely related to the unbanked population. These aim at creating opportunities for financial inclusion through microfinance, digital banking, and low-cost initiatives as well as financing of nascent enterprises to improve socio-economic conditions of disadvantaged communities. These products promote the development of SMEs as well as access to essential services.

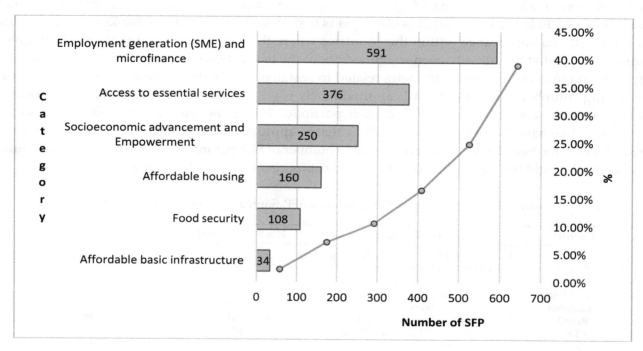

Figure 5. Results obtained for social-oriented SFP. Source: Author's own research.

It should also be noted that some of these institutions achieve their mission of sustainability using only one of those archetypes, such as a substitute with digital processes. In this sense, the results support what is stated by [22] regarding the persistence of institutions that prefer archetypes of high visibility and relatively easy and fast implementation over others, with more significant strategic and operational implications for their accomplishments. Once again, short-termism is present.

In products whose main sustainability benefit is environmental, in turn, the SFP, regardless of the category are framed in the archetype 'Sustainable financial products' and 'Resilience in loan granting'. As for green products, the generation of alternative energy, energy efficiency, and sustainable use of the land and its resources, or simply general environmental investments are the main focus of financial institutions as Figure 6 shows. In this sense, the results by categories are also consistent with previous analysis of green products and services in Latam [48,92].

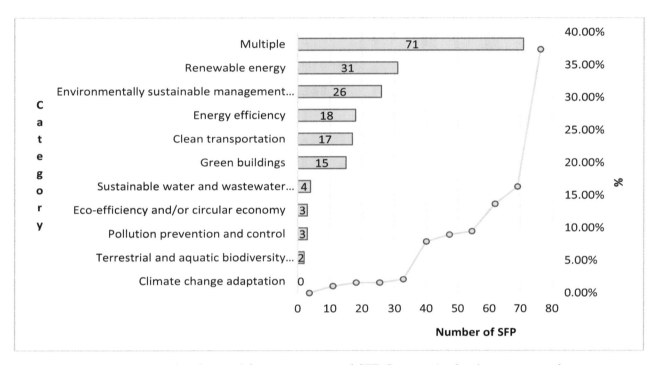

Figure 6. Results obtained for green-oriented SFP. Source: Author's own research.

On the other hand, the fact that the category 'Multiple' is by far the largest group of products identified with 38% of the total reflects that several financial institutions through their aim to include SFP develop general ecological products (regardless of the type of facility) that help potential clients to accomplish any activity that generates environmental benefits. The above is quite logical and may be explained by widely recognised barriers such as a lack of knowledge within the bank in terms of sustainability [22,48,56,92], and thus, these types of products are the easiest to structure and practical to use to venture into the SFP.

Lastly, the importance of PFI in the promotion of SFP in Latam should be highlighted, not only for their role in encouraging LFI for the development of their own SFP, but also in a less commented aspect, that of their role in the adjustment and development of SFP according to the environmental and social needs, and economic vocation of the areas where they are located. Evidence of this may be that countries that have diverse state banks in their different regions were clear leaders in some key categories such as the case of Brazil in "Renewable energy" and "Environmentally sustainable management of living natural resources and land use", and to some extent Argentina in "Employment generation through SME financing and microfinance". SFP were characterised according to the category, type of facility, and features of the products identified in the financial institutions of Latam and are shown in Table 4.

Table 4. Characterisation of SFP.

Category	Type of Facility	Instrument for Delivering Sustainability
		Social-oriented SFP
Affordable basic infrastructure	Credit/Grants	Refundable and non-refundable loans to meet the credit needs of municipal, regional, and national governments that carry out public investment projects in the energy, transportation, construction, sanitation, communication, and social equipment sectors. Up to 100% of the projects are financed and for the most part the financing is provided by PFI
	Credit	Long-term loans with differentiated repayment schemes for infrastructure and public services projects developed as public-private partnerships
		Personal loans for the installation of natural gas or domestic sanitation networks in houses. These products have fixed interest rates and do not require any guarantee.
	Savings	Savings accounts with returns and without opening, maintenance, or minimum balance requirements charges, and/or that offer exemption or lower commissions on transactions
Access to essential services		100% digital savings accounts, with a special interest rate, debit card, and free transfers
		Savings/currents accounts or integral portfolios specifically designed for SME that meet their basic banking needs and have minimum documentation requirements. Some do not charge for maintenance and include debit cards as well as both cheques and protection for free
		Accounts or savings plans programmed for use in specific personal projects, with automatic debit and where the holder defines the term. They provide interest rates higher than those of traditional savings accounts and allow the choice of deposit frequency
	Credit	Preferential rate credits to afford one's own and family medical procedures and treatments
		Free destination online loans, without guarantee requirement and a lower rate than conventional credit.
		Credit cards with an easy approval (without verification of income or financial references), benefits in the interest rate, discounts in stores and/or an annuity free
		Specific credit cards that donate a percentage of purchases to support a foundation or non-profit organisation dedicated to solutions related to health or education
		Loans to entities, companies, or financial intermediaries for the development of the inclusion and offer of financial services in specific sectors with a deficit of access to credit
Affordable housing	Savings	Savings accounts that offer tax benefits to natural persons who seek to save in the medium or long term to acquire housing. There is no charge for maintenance fees or minimum opening amounts
		Savings accounts to verify or complete the income needed to access government subsidies for social and/or priority interest housing
	Credit	Mortgage loans for the purchase of social interest housing, land for construction, expansion, improvement, or legalisation of housing (either traditional or productive housing) for low-income families
		Mortgage loans intended for legalisation, purchase, repair, construction, and expansion of productive housing (houses and businesses in the same space)
		Social lease programs offered by PFI structured as a long-term loan, with a low initial fee and a low monthly fee that offer a 0% purchase option at the end of the lease term
		Loans to developers, builders, and housing production agencies for social housing development projects (public and private) with interest rates and more convenient structures.
	Grants	Funds granted by PFI to families for free, to strengthen or improve housing at the structural level

Table 4. *Cont.*

Category	Type of Facility	Instrument for Delivering Sustainability
Employment generation (SME financing and microfinance)	Credit	Loans and credit lines to SME in the formal/informal sector to finance indifferent or exclusively working capital, equipment projects, purchase of fixed assets, and investments to increase productivity. Normally, they leave to the borrower' the choice of payment method and the grace period according to the cash flow.
		Credit cards aimed especially at entrepreneurs and SMEs for expenses on supplies and fixed assets. Usually with benefits in associated stores and some are exempt from an annuity
		Microcredits mostly oriented to established SMEs but also for those who want to start their own business or professionals who want to grow their line of work. They offer fast disbursement, convenient repayment schemes according to the ability to pay, and generous grace periods
Food Security	Credit	Loans, credit lines, and microcredits for agricultural and livestock working capital and investment. Many of these include technical assistance
		Credit cards to finance exclusively the purchase of supplies, machinery, and services necessary to fully cover the agricultural or livestock production cycle or related industries through flexible payment plans in line with the natural cycles of the productive project. They feature special discounts at certain distributors and stores, as well as a preferential interest rate. Some are free of monthly maintenance fees
	Savings/Credit	Debit cards and fiduciary guarantee loans for the payment of food pensions legally ordered
		Special plans for products and services aimed at small and medium enterprises linked to rural businesses or family/subsistence farmers.
	Savings	Current and savings accounts free of commissions or charges for opening, use, or maintenance intended for artisans, vulnerable populations such as victims of armed conflict, or marginalised rural areas.
		Savings accounts designed for immigrants and their remittances, as well as for the receipt of subsidies and state aid from government social programs. They are exempt from fee collection, minimum balance, or annuity and with direct credit.
Socioeconomic advancement and Empowerment		Collective savings accounts with which people can save collectively achieve goals with friends or family, and communal credits through the formation of a group with a certain minimum of participants who must be active micro-entrepreneurs. There may be individualised fees.
	Savings/Credit	Current accounts, savings accounts, and/or loans for investment, social development projects or patrimonial recovery for cooperatives, civil society organisations or associations of the popular and solidarity economy, with a personalised payment frequency according to the cash flow and productive cycle.
		Current savings accounts, or unsecured loans directly to the account for retirees and pensioners with special interest rates and without account maintenance fees. The opening and usage of some of these are digital.
		Bank accounts and financing of activities that are framed in the productive sectors, strategic adaptation of infrastructure, or the purchase of goods and services for people with disabilities.
		Loans and credit cards for personal expenses, household equipment, or for development of economic activities led by women and associations or organisations in situations of violence, with benefits in shops and associated businesses, with no spouse signature requirement and the possibility of training and emergency assistance.
	Credit	Accessible educational loans and credit lines for technical, technological, pre-graduate, or postgraduate programs accessible under conditions according to the type of program such as a preferential fixed rate, flexible payment plan, ease of early cancellation, and grace period for the entire period of studies.
		Special financing provided by PFI for municipalities and government entities for the construction or improvement of public space, community equipment, green areas and/or co-ownership land in neighbourhoods with problems of urban deterioration, segregation, and social vulnerability; this also includes the implementation of social development programs and culture support
		Financing for acquisition of assets and investments for the development of small-scale rural tourism, or adventure and other forms of non-traditional tourism
	Credit/Grants	Non-refundable subsidies and loans for educational institutions and/or applied research, technological development, innovation, and knowledge transfer projects to promote social and territorial development processes

Table 4. *Cont.*

Category	Type of Facility	Instrument for Delivering Sustainability
		Green-oriented SFP
Renewable energy	Credit	Development loans for the expansion/modernisation of the national energy frontier through the financing of projects for the generation and transmission of non-conventional renewable energies
		Loans for the acquisition of solar panels for family use, as well as other household items related to the use of renewable energies that allow the transformation of expenses into energy savings in the family environment under the distributed clean generation scheme, as well as a preferential rate loan for SMEs and corporations with productive projects related to renewable energy.
Energy efficiency	Credit	Loans with preferential conditions for people to invest in high-energy efficiency home appliances or environmental impact reduction technologies for the home, usually in shops designated by the bank.
		Credits for technical advice, investment projects, replacement of machinery and purchase of new energy-efficient equipment that cause lower consumption of electricity, cost reduction, and improvements in the competitiveness of SME and companies. Characterised by payment terms according to needs and the flow of the project to be financed and is subject to a verification/guarantee scheme for potential energy savings.
Pollution prevention and control	Credit	Development loans for institutional level activities of improvement and recovery of contaminated or degraded soils and areas as well as projects to strengthen the business capacity of reduction and mitigation of socio-environmental risks.
Environmentally sustainable management of living natural resources and land use	Credit	Loans with extended rate and grace period bonus, and non-refundable subsidies to prevent, monitor, and combat deforestation, in addition to promoting the conservation of protected areas and the sustainable use of forests with responsible exploitation and certification practices.
		Loans for investments in low carbon agriculture programs and agro-ecologic productive systems with sustainable practices such as waste management, pasture reform, irrigated agriculture, biotechnology, and eco-efficiency technologies from small to large scale.
Terrestrial and aquatic biodiversity conservation	Credit	Credit lines for investments in the recovery and conservation of ecosystems and biodiversity provided by PFI.
		Collaboration credit cards, which donate a certain percentage of funds from purchases made to funds/NGOs dedicated to promoting wildlife conservation and biodiversity.
Clean transportation	Credit	Loans for the acquisition of bicycles, motorcycles, and automobiles (mostly private but also commercial) hybrids, electric, or lower emissions vehicles. They offer a lower interest rate than the credits for traditional vehicles and finance up to 100% of the commercial value with a quick disbursement by being able to exempt the vehicle from an initial fee or co-debtor. Car conversion to vehicular natural gas is also supported.
Sustainable water and wastewater management	Credit	Exclusive credit lines to finance projects for the efficient and sustainable use of water for public drainage works and resource reuse in condominiums and houses.
Eco-efficiency and/or circular economy	Credit	Loans provided by PFI for investments in process and product efficiency through the application of a preventive or clean production approach and use of supplies from renewable sources or of less environmental impact as rawmaterial
Green buildings	Credit	Loans for builders and real estate developers for projects (housing or commerce) with sustainable architecture or access to eco-efficiency certifications
Multiple	Credit/Grants	Mortgage loans, green leases, and state subsidies to access housing units and projects built under sustainability criteria or with environmental certifications, and with a lower financial cost than other similar alternatives.
	Savings	Green low-cost savings accounts, debit, and credit cards which raise funds for the placement of environmental credits or where the customer can support sustainability issues by contributing with its use to the maintenance and development of non-profit environmental organisations
	Credit	Loans, microcredits, and ecological credit lines to finance projects that explicitly focus on two or more green categories mentioned above, or which through their generality enable a vast range of destinations for general sustainability or environmental protection and improvement projects with differentiated interest rates, assistance, and schemes of amortisation.

Source: Author's own research.

3.4. Segments

Individuals, SME, corporations, and government entities were considered as segments for SFP. These products can be directed to one or several segments at the same time. Thus, the records obtained are those observed in Figure 7. These show the relationship between projects and the categories associated with significant investment and projects with corporate segments and government entities. In this sense, credit products for infrastructure projects, public programs, and mega-investments in categories such as affordable basic infrastructure, energy renewable, affordable housing, green buildings, and access to essential services (other than financial) are most commonly offered to this segment. As for the segment of individuals, they are significant recipients of products of various modalities, especially in the social field within the categories of access to essential services, microfinance, affordable housing, and socioeconomic development and empowerment. In the environmental field, they have less prominence and the products they can access are focused on the acquisition of energy-efficient products, green buildings, renewable energy for domestic applications, or personal clean transportation solutions. Although SFP are offered to people in general, population groups with some vulnerability or degree of exclusion (e.g., ethnic minorities, disabled persons, or immigrants) are offered these SFPs more frequently by financial institutions.

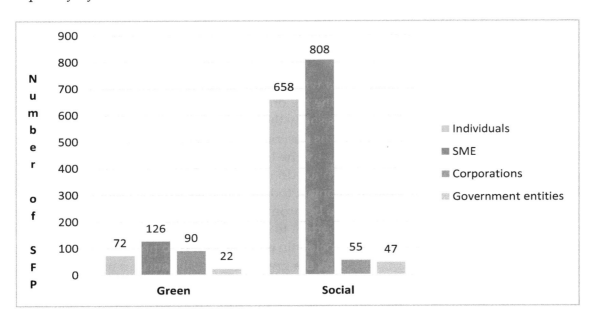

Figure 7. Target segments for SFP. Source: Author's own research.

Finally, the SME segment is the most versatile and attended, leading both the social and green ambits. The main categories are access to essential services (financial), food security, and employment generation through SME financing and microfinance. It is remarkable how attractive SMEs are to deploy SFP not only because the sector is a market of great size and potential, but also because of its recognition as high potential actors due to its mainly familiar nature, dynamism, and significant involvement with the communities that can help to achieve several of the social objectives framed in the different sustainability taxonomies and SDGs.

3.5. Sustainability and Corporate Social Responsibility Reporting

Along with the revision of the SFP, the existence and publication of sustainability reports or reports on socio-environmental policies on the websites of financial institutions was verified. Figure 8 shows that only 29.53% of the banks analysed report their efforts in terms of sustainability, which is eminently a really small part. It should be clarified that the fact that an institution has not been accounted for does not mean that it does not have SFP. It may have these products, but it has not developed adequate communication or does so insufficiently in the media examined. Besides, there is evidence of the confusion of sustainability strategies with solidarity and philanthropic activities in financial institutions that they recurrently advertise in so-called sustainability sections on web pages or annual reports but in many cases, this is nothing more than a compendium of donation activities, allied foundations, or occasional campaigns of volunteer activities within the institution. This alone does not meet the requirements of sustainable banking at all and instead provides a window-dressing practice for stakeholders, and therefore was not considered.

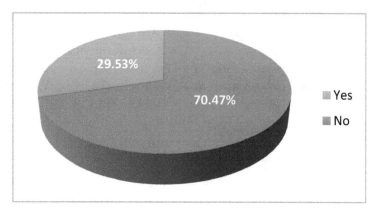

Figure 8. Financial institutions that communicate their sustainability management. Source: Author's own research.

Moreover, this may be one of the reasons why the levels of reporting observed are much lower than previous measurements in this regard in the region [92], in which the consideration of what is and what is not a report of sustainability efforts was solely the perception of financial institutions' managers.

The results are consistent with the previous descriptions of the precarious communication to the interest groups and particularly to the clients by the banks. What is beyond the report is evidence that even institutions with SFP in their portfolios do not promote them with the fortitude that one would expect in the most essential points of contact today, which are virtual channels [21]. The idea is not only to develop SFP, but they should also be promoted and even more privileged in marketing strategies. As echoed in [22,48], it is just as important to publicise the benefits and impact of sustainable banking with financial institutions and civil society in general, as it is to promote the demand for SFP. The faster and more integrated these efforts are, the greater will be the success in the consolidation of sustainable banking.

The SBN framework contemplates one indicator to measure the progress in the sub pillar "Climate and green investment reporting", within the pillar "Climate and green finance" [70]. It is the indicator: "Tracking and disclosure of climate & green finance". According to this, Brazil has a 60% coverage in that area, positioning itself well ahead of the regional and global average. Meanwhile, Colombia has not yet made any progress in this area, and the essential needs should be to compel reporting on climate / green financing flows and stimulate financial institutions to publicly report on green financing activities. This aspect is vital to address for the sake of standardising information that enables effective monitoring. Then, Colombia is called upon to work with its neighbor countries and build on its recognised experience.

4. Conclusions and Further Research

This paper analysed the extant literature on SFP with a comprehensive understanding of the status quo and research trends and, characterised the existing SFP in the Latam banking industry. In this way, this paper contributes to the body of knowledge and practice by being the first to characterise and analyse the SFP in the Latam banking industry. The results of the study show that Brazil, Colombia, and Argentina are the main countries involved in the development of SFP. Because of regulatory and government support such as through Green Protocols and social and environmental responsibility policies, these countries have led both social and green financial product development.

The development of financial products focused on ESG, particularly from the credit side, is highlighted in the first research trend. It is important to highlight that Brazil has one of the most developed financial markets in the region and it has allowed the development and supply of SFP nationwide. Besides, it has a fintech ecosystem which has allowed it to have a greater financial inclusion and digitalisation of financial services, as well as agricultural activity reflected in multiple products and services oriented to this sector, developed by both PFI and LFI.

On the other hand, Colombia began its evolution towards sustainable finance with the Green Protocol issued by Asobancaria in 2012. Even though Colombia has had relevant advances in fintech, much still to be done to have greater financial inclusion as Brazil and Mexico have, though its ecosystem is highly promissory.

This result was in line with the SBN framework; the authors of [91] found that Colombia had a 60% gap in products and services. This suggests that both the public and private sector should develop strategies for boosting the development of SFP based on fintech. This would include greater clarity through more specific taxonomies and more explicit definitions of social and sustainable assets. Although Argentina has a small and less developed financial market, it has made several efforts towards developing SFP. At this point, campaigns in alliance with BYMA, the Inter-American Development Bank, and the Mexican Stock Exchange, as well as its very recently launched national sustainable finance policy have played a pivotal role and therefore, the outlook is positive.

Thus, barriers, obstacles, and pitfalls are being overcome aimed at developing a more sustainable financial system, which is line with the second research trend. Other relevant countries are Mexico and Ecuador, these five countries together account for 61.56% of all SFP identified in this study, which is certainly significant.

Concerning the rest of the Latin American countries, it is highly recommended that they deepen cooperative relationships with these five leaders, especially those that are in the basic stages of development respecting SFP. As it has already been demonstrated with countries in Latam and other regions, success is based on sharing experiences and building from the mistakes of others, which will undoubtedly help with the further development of SFP.

About the kind of institutions, the results show the tremendous importance of PFI, which obtained significant results with almost a 40% participation. The role of a promoter and at the same time as a persuader towards the LFI is confirmed, but it is also important to emphasise the work of PFI in matching regional needs with the potential SFP that address them.

The results also indicate a prominent relationship between SFP and the creation of opportunities for financial inclusion for the unbanked and vulnerable population, as well as with SME financing initiatives. These two factors were the main categories in the social-oriented SFP. On the other hand, in the green-oriented SFP, the main categories were occupied by products with multiple environmental destinations, renewable energies, and activities on sustainable management of natural resources and land use, sectors with huge investment opportunities in the region.

When evaluating the target audience of the different SFP, it can be seen that SME are the most flexible segment. These have the highest amount of SFP, both in the green and social spheres.

Regarding the kind of facilities granted, individuals are recipients of savings products such as checking accounts, savings, debit cards, and credit loans mainly to encourage their insertion into the formal financial system and healthy financial habits. Multiple ecological loans, which are another widespread practice, are the most practical and efficient option for financial institutions (regardless of type) to include in green products in the portfolios, which was raised in the second research trend.

At the same time, low levels of bank sustainability reporting expose the imperative need to improve the dissemination of efforts in this regard. Furthermore, in terms of promotion it is required that in addition to informing the details of traditional products, the banks report whether they have SFP, and if so, what are the mechanisms for evaluation and monitoring adopted.

Despite the contributions of the present study, limitations should be acknowledged. The most significant limitation of this study is the scarce information on SFP that financial institutions publish on websites. Also, there is a lack of homogeneity in the presentation of information as well as a low proportion of institutions that quantify and monitor the flows and performance of SFP if offered. Therefore, it is possible that additional elements not identified may be essential for establishing new features on SFP. This issue should be addressed in further research. Finally, this research is providing a roadmap to SFP in the Latam banking industry so researchers and practicing professionals can improve their understanding of the SFP and thus, they may use these study's findings to broaden the central aspects of this kind of financial products, as the third research trend indicated.

Based on the research trends and results, to go beyond this study, research on topics related to SFP will facilitate improve financial practices for the economic development based on ESG issues. From a practical and research perspective, further research may develop a framework in which each financial institution registers its SFP. It would allow us to determinate the real SFP offers. Likewise, the development of both new metrics for measuring financial leverage from ESG perspective as well as interest rates indexed by ESG issues is required. These issues could complement the sustainability credit score system proposed by [41,74,80]. Additional lines of further research may include:

- Comparing interest rates for similar SFP but in different countries.

- Developing a credit risk framework to measure how much money a sustainable project could borrow.

- Measuring if SFP could boost the generation of economic value added (EVA).

- Analysing the relation between green bonds and SFP in financial institutions.

- Appraising the participation of monetary flows destined to reach green and social loans in the financial markets at a regional level.

- Assessing the applicability of the archetypes established in [21] now for the banking industry in emerging economies.

- In order to have more understanding of the associations and factors determining the offering / not offering of SFP in Latam countries, an analysis by means of numeric analysis, statistic tests, or even econometric models when suitable.

Finally, since only 60% of the banks considered had at least one SFP, and because the average number of SFP among financial institutions is just two, the developing nature of this topic is corroborated. As a result, the topics above represent only a part of the great potential in the SFP research field with both a qualitative and quantitative focus. Thus, greater engagement of public/private agents and awareness-raising for potential users about existing opportunities are the preconditions for triggering a virtuous cycle.

Author Contributions: J.C.M.-E. wrote, reviewed, and analysed literature and data, J.D.G.-R. designed the research framework, conceptualised, wrote, reviewed and developed the manuscript, E.D.-G. analysed literature, and reviewed the paper. All authors have read and agreed to the published version of the manuscript.

Acknowledgments: The authors thank the editor and two anonymous reviewers for their useful comments that allowed us to improve the quality and comprehension of the paper.

References

1.   United Nations. United Nations Framework Convention on Climate Change. In *Adoption of the Paris Agreement*; United Nations: New York, NY, USA, 2015; p. 32.
2.   Steffen, W.; Rockström, J.; Richardson, K.; Lenton, T.M.; Folke, C.; Liverman, D.; Summerhayes, C.P.; Barnosky, A.D.; Cornell, S.E.; Crucifix, M.; et al. Trajectories of the Earth System in the Anthropocene. *Proc. Natl. Acad. Sci. USA* **2018**, *115*, 8252–8259. [CrossRef] [PubMed]
3.   Bassi, S.; Jennifer, E.; Lucas, T.; Leonardo, M.; Volkery, A. *Briefing Green Economy—What Do We Mean by Green Economy?* United Nations Environment Programme: Nairobi, Kenya, 2012.

4. United Nations Development Programme and Oxford Poverty and Human Development Initiative. *Global Multidimensional Poverty Index 2019 Illuminating Inequalities*; United Nations: New York, NY, USA, 2019.
5. Falcone, P.M.; Morone, P.; Sica, E. Greening of the financial system and fuelling a sustainability transition: A discursive approach to assess landscape pressures on the Italian financial system. *Technol. Forecast. Soc. Chang.* **2018**, *127*, 23–37. [CrossRef]
6. Pinillos, A.A.; Fernández, J.L. De la RSC a la sostenibilidad corporativa: Una evolución necesaria para la creación de valor. *Harvard Deusto Bus. Rev.* **2011**, *207*, 4–21.
7. Masud, M.; Hossain, M.; Kim, J. Is Green Regulation Effective or a Failure: Comparative Analysis between Bangladesh Bank (BB) Green Guidelines and Global Reporting Initiative Guidelines. *Sustainability* **2018**, *10*, 1267. [CrossRef]
8. Zhang, D.; Zhang, Z.; Managi, S. A bibliometric analysis on green finance: Current status, development, and future directions. *Financ. Res. Lett.* **2019**, *29*, 425–430. [CrossRef]
9. González-Ruiz, J.D.; Arboleda, A.; Botero, S.; Rojo, J. Investment valuation model for sustainable infrastructure systems: Mezzanine debt for water projects. *Eng. Constr. Archit. Manag.* **2019**, *26*, 850–884. [CrossRef]
10. Miroshnychenko, I.; Barontini, R.; Testa, F. Green practices and financial performance: A global outlook. *J. Clean. Prod.* **2017**, *147*, 340–351. [CrossRef]
11. Kaufer, J. Social responsibility as a core business model in banking: A case study in the financial sector. *J. Sustain. Financ. Invest.* **2014**, *4*, 76–89. [CrossRef]
12. Hu, V.I.; Scholtens, B. Corporate social responsibility policies of commercial banks in developing countries. *Sustain. Dev.* **2014**, *22*, 276–288. [CrossRef]
13. Sarfraz, M.; Qun, W.; Hui, L.; Abdullah, M.I. Environmental Risk Management Strategies and the Moderating Role of Corporate Social Responsibility in Project Financing Decisions. *Sustainability* **2018**, *8*, 2771. [CrossRef]
14. Miralles-Quirós, M.M.; Miralles-Quirós, J.L.; Redondo Hernández, J. ESG Performance and Shareholder Value Creation in the Banking Industry: International Differences. *Sustainability* **2019**, *11*, 1404. [CrossRef]
15. United Nations. Transforming Our World: The 2030 Agenda For Sustainable Development United Nations. United Nations: New York, NY, USA, 2015.
16. Pomering, A.; Dolnicar, S. Assessing the prerequisite of successful CSR implementation: Are consumers aware of CSR initiatives? *J. Bus. Ethics* **2009**, *85* (Suppl. 2), 285–301. [CrossRef]
17. Mulder, I.; Koellner, T. Hardwiring green: How banks account for biodiversity risks and opportunities. *J. Financ. Invest.* **2011**, *1*, 103–120.
18. Conley, M.; Williams, C.A. Global Banks as Global Sustainability Regulators? The Equator Principles. *Law Policy* **2011**, *33*, 542–575. [CrossRef]
19. González-Ruiz, J.D.; Botero-Botero, S.; Duque-Grisales, E. Financial Eco-Innovation as a Mechanism for Fostering the Development of Sustainable Infrastructure Systems. *Sustainability* **2018**, *10*, 4463. [CrossRef]
20. Stern, N. *The Economics of Climate Change: The Stern Review*; Cambridge University Press: Cambridge, UK, 2007.
21. Campiglio, E. Beyond carbon pricing: The role of banking and monetary policy in financing the transition to a low-carbon economy. *Ecol. Econ.* **2016**, *121*, 220–230. [CrossRef]
22. Yip, W.H.; Bocken, N.M.P. Sustainable business model archetypes for the banking industry. *J. Clean. Prod* **2018**, *174*, 150–169. [CrossRef]
23. Jeucken, H.A.; Bouma, J.J. The changing environment of banks. *Greener Manag. Int.* **1999**, *27*, 20–35. [CrossRef]
24. Alexander, K. *Stability and Sustainability in Banking Reform: Are Environmental Risks Missing in Basel III?* Cambridge and Geneva: Geneva, Switzerland, 2014.
25. United Nations. *Environment Programme, Sustainable Finance Progress Report*; United Nations: Geneve, Switzerland, 2019.
26. Jeucken, M. *Sustainable Finance and Banking: The Financial Sector and the Future of the Planet*, 1st ed.; Routledge: London, UK, 2001.
27. Jeucken, M. *Sustainability in Finance: Banking on the Planet*; Eburon Academic Publishers: Delft, The Netherlands, 2004.
28. Urban, M.A.; Wójcik, D. Dirty Banking: Probing the Gap in Sustainable Finance. *Sustainability* **2019**, *11*, 1745. [CrossRef]

29. Clarke, T.; Boersma, M. *Sustainable Finance? A Critical Analysis of the Regulation, Policies, Strategies, Implementation and Reporting on Sustainability in International Finance*; United Nations Environment Programme: Sydney, Australia, 2016.

30. United Nations. Environment Programme Finance Initiative, Principles for Responsible Banking: Key Steps to be Implemented by Signatories. United Nations: Washington, DC, USA, 2020.

31. Korslund, D.; Spengler, L. *Financial Capital and Impact Metrics of Values Based Banking*; Global Alliance for Banking on Values: Zeist, The Netherlands, 2012.

32. Bergedieck, L.; Maheshwari, A.; Avendano, F. *Green Finance A Bottom-Up Approach to Track Existing Flows*; International Finance Corporation: Washington, DC, USA, 2017.

33. Rosenman, E. The geographies of social finance: Poverty regulation through the 'invisible heart' of markets. *Prog. Hum. Geogr.* **2019**, *43*, 141–162. [CrossRef]

34. Emerson, J.; Freundlich, T.; Fruchterman, J.; Berlin, L.; Stevenson, K. *Nothing Gained: Addressing the Critical Gaps in Risk-Taking Capital for Social Enterprise*; Oxford University: Oxford, UK, 2007.

35. Weber, O.; Scholz, R.W.; Michalik, G. Incorporating sustainability criteria into credit risk management. *Bus. Strateg. Environ.* **2010**, *19*, 39–50. [CrossRef]

36. Fijałkowska, J.; Zyznarska-Dworczak, B.; Garsztka, P. Corporate social-environmental performance versus financial performance of banks in Central and Eastern European Countries. *Sustainability* **2018**, *10*, 772. [CrossRef]

37. Nizam, E.; Ng, A.; Dewandaru, G.; Nagayev, R.; Nkoba, M.A. The impact of social and environmental sustainability on financial performance: A global analysis of the banking sector. *J. Multinatl. Financ. Manag.* **2019**, *49*, 35–53. [CrossRef]

38. Jan, A.; Marimuthu, M.; Hassan, R. Sustainable business practices and firm's financial performance in islamic banking: Under the moderating role of islamic corporate governance. *Sustainability* **2019**, *11*, 6606. [CrossRef]

39. Paulet, E.; Parnaudeau, M.; Relano, F. Banking with Ethics: Strategic Moves and Structural Changes of the Banking Industry in the Aftermath of the Subprime Mortgage Crisis. *J. Bus. Ethics* **2015**, *131*, 199–207. [CrossRef]

40. Raut, R.; Cheikhrouhou, N.; Kharat, M.B. Sustainability in The Banking Industry: A Strategic Multi-Criterion Analysis. *Bus. Strateg. Environ.* **2017**, *26*, 550–568. [CrossRef]

41. Zeidan, R.; Boechat, C.; Fleury, A. Developing a Sustainability Credit Score System. *J. Bus. Ethics* **2015**, *127*, 283–296. [CrossRef]

42. Shum, K.; Yam, S.L. Ethics and Law: Guiding the Invisible Hand to Correct Corporate Social Responsibility Externalities. *J. Bus. Ethics* **2011**, *98*, 549–571. [CrossRef]

43. Igbudu, N.; Garanti, Z.; Popoola, T. Enhancing bank loyalty through sustainable banking practices: The mediating effect of corporate image. *Sustainability* **2018**, *10*, 4050. [CrossRef]

44. Dell'Atti, S.; Trotta, A.; Iannuzzi, A.P.; Demaria, F. Corporate Social Responsibility Engagement as a Determinant of Bank Reputation: An Empirical Analysis. *Corp. Soc. Responsib. Environ. Manag.* **2017**, *24*, 589–605. [CrossRef]

45. Ibe-Enwo, G.; Igbudu, N.; Garanti, Z.; Popoola, T. Assessing the Relevance of Green Banking Practice on Bank Loyalty: The Mediating Effect of Green Image and Bank Trust. *Sustainability* **2019**, *11*, 4651. [CrossRef]

46. Ferreira, F.A.; Jalali, M.S.; Meidutė-Kavaliauskienė, I.; Viana, B.A. A metacognitive decision making based-framework for bank customer loyalty measurement and management. *Technol. Econ. Dev. Econ.* **2015**, *21*, 280–300. [CrossRef]

47. Bossle, M.B.; de Barcellos, M.D.; Vieira, L.M.; Sauvée, L. The drivers for adoption of eco-innovation. *J. Clean. Prod.* **2016**, *113*, 861–872. [CrossRef]

48. International Finance Corporation. *FELABAN, and EcoBusiness Fund, Green Finance Latin America 2017 Report: What is the Latin American Banking Sector Doing to Mitigate Climate Change?* International Finance Corporation: Washington, DC, USA, 2017.

49. Dingwerth, K.; Eichinger, M. Tamed transparency: How information disclosure under the global reporting initiative fails to empower. *Glob. Environ. Polit.* **2010**, *10*, 74–96. [CrossRef]

50. Rasche, A. A Necessary Supplement: What the United Nations global compact is and is not. *Bus. Soc.* **2009**, *48*, 511–537. [CrossRef]

51. Windolph, S.E. Assessing Corporate Sustainability Through Ratings: Challenges and Their Causes. *J. Environ. Sustain.* **2011**, *1*, 1–22. [CrossRef]

52. Scholtens, B. Corporate social responsibility in the international banking industry. *J. Bus. Ethics* **2009**, *86*, 159–175. [CrossRef]
53. Figge, F.; Hahn, T. The cost of sustainability capital and the creation of sustainable value by companies. *J. Indust. Ecol.* **2005**, *9*, 47–58. [CrossRef]
54. Ng, C.; Rezaee, Z. Business sustainability performance and cost of equity capital. *J. Corp. Financ.* **2015**, *34*, 128–149. [CrossRef]
55. Ruiz, J.G.; Arboleda, C.A.; Botero, S. A Proposal for Green Financing as a Mechanism to Increase Private Participation in Sustainable Water Infrastructure Systems: The Colombian Case. *Procedia Eng.* **2016**, *145*, 180–187. [CrossRef]
56. Shishlov, I.; Bajohr, T.; Deheza, M.; Cochran, I. *Using Credit Lines to Foster Green Lending: Opportunities and Challenges*; Institute for Climate Economics: Paris, France, 2017.
57. United Nations. *Environment Programme Finance Initiative, Green Financial Products and Services Current Trends and Future Opportunities in North America*; United Nations: Toronto, ON, Canada, 2007.
58. Collins, D. Green leases and green leasing in theory and in practice: A state of the art review. *Facilities* **2019**, *37*, 813–824. [CrossRef]
59. Migliorelli, M.; Dessertine, P. Time for new financing instruments? A market-oriented framework to finance environmentally friendly practices in EU agriculture. *J. Sustain. Financ. Invest.* **2018**, *8*, 1–25. [CrossRef]
60. Waltman, L. A review of the literature on citation impact indicators. *J. Informetr.* **2016**, *10*, 365–391. [CrossRef]
61. Olawumi, T.O.; Chan, D.W.M. A scientometric review of global research on sustainability and sustainable development. *J. Clean. Prod.* **2018**, *183*, 231–250. [CrossRef]
62. Dominko, M.; Verbič, M. The Economics of Subjective Well-Being: A Bibliometric Analysis. *J. Happiness Stud.* **2019**, *20*, 1973–1994. [CrossRef]
63. Ertz, M.; Leblanc-Proulx, S. Sustainability in the collaborative economy: A bibliometric analysis reveals emerging interest. *J. Clean. Prod.* **2018**, *196*, 1073–1085. [CrossRef]
64. Nájera-Sánchez, J. A Systematic Review of Sustainable Banking through a Co-Word Analysis. *Sustainability* **2019**, *12*, 278. [CrossRef]
65. Loan Market Association. *Green Loan Principles, Supporting Environmentally Sustainable Economic Activity*; Loan Market Association: London, UK, 2018.
66. International Capital Market Association. *Social Bond Principles, Voluntary Process Guidelines for Issuing Social Bonds*; International Capital Market Association: París, France, 2018.
67. Forstater, M.; Zhang, N. *Definitions and Concepts: Background Note*; United Nations Environmental Programme: Geneva, The Netherlands, 2016.
68. European Political Strategy Centre. Financing Sustainability: Triggering Investments for the Clean Economy. *EPSC Strateg. Notes* **2017**, *25*, 18.
69. Almeida, M.; Filkova, M. *América Latina y el Caribe Estado Del Mercado De Las Finanzas Verdes*; Climate Bonds Initiative: London, UK, 2019.
70. Sustainable Banking Network. *Global Progress Report of the Sustainable Banking Network: Innovations in Policy and Industry Actions in Emerging Markets*; Sustainable Banking Network: Washington, DC, USA, 2019.
71. Lindlein, P. Mainstreaming environmental finance into financial markets—Relevance, potential and obstacles. In *Greening the Financial Sector: How to Mainstream Environmental Finance in Developing Countries*; Springer: Heidelberg/Berlin, Germany, 2012; pp. 1–30.
72. Heinemann, K.; Zwergel, B.; Gold, S.; Seuring, S.; Klein, C. Exploring the supply-demand-discrepancy of sustainable financial products in Germany from a financial advisor's point of view. *Sustainability* **2018**, *10*, 944. [CrossRef]
73. Escrig-Olmedo, E.; Muñoz-Torres, M.J.; Fernández-Izquierdo, M.Á. Fernández-Izquierdo, Sustainable development and the financial system: Society's perceptions about socially responsible investing. *Bus. Strateg. Environ.* **2013**, *22*, 410–428. [CrossRef]
74. Weber, O.; Fenchel, M.; Scholz, R.W. Empirical analysis of the integration of environmental risks into the credit risk management process of European banks. *Bus. Strateg. Environ.* **2008**, *17*, 149–159. [CrossRef]
75. Geobey, S.; Weber, O. Lessons in operationalising social finance: The case of Vancouver City Savings Credit Union. *J. Sustain. Financ. Invest.* **2013**, *3*, 124–137. [CrossRef]
76. Weber, I. Corporate sustainability and financial performance of Chinese banks. *Sustain. Account. Manag. Policy J.* **2017**, *8*, 358–385. [CrossRef]

77. Laguir, I.; Marais, M.; El Baz, J.; Stekelorum, R. Reversing the business rationale for environmental commitment in banking: Does financial performance lead to higher environmental performance? *Manag. Decis.* **2018**, *56*, 358–375. [CrossRef]

78. Nikolaou, I.E.; Kourouklaris, G.; Tsalis, T.A. A framework to assist the financial community in incorporating water risks into their investment decisions. *J. Sustain. Financ. Invest.* **2014**, *4*, 93–109. [CrossRef]

79. Zimmermann, S. Same same but different: How and why banks approach sustainability. *Sustainability* **2019**, *11*, 2267. [CrossRef]

80. Bowman, M. The Role of the Banking Industry in Facilitating Climate Change Mitigation and the Transition to a Low-Carbon Global Economy. *Environ. Plan. Law J.* **2010**, *27*, 448–468.

81. Clark, R.; Reed, J.; Sunderland, T. Bridging funding gaps for climate and sustainable development: Pitfalls, progress and potential of private finance. *Land Use Policy* **2018**, *71*, 335–346. [CrossRef]

82. Polzin, F. Mobilising private finance for low-carbon innovation—A systematic review of barriers and solutions. *Renew. Sustain. Energy Rev.* **2017**, *77*, 525–535. [CrossRef]

83. Jo, H.; Kim, H.; Park, K. Corporate Environmental Responsibility and Firm Performance in the Financial Services Sector. *J. Bus. Ethics* **2015**, *131*, 257–284. [CrossRef]

84. Steckel, C.; Jakob, M. The role of financing cost and de-risking strategies for clean energy investment. *Int. Econ.* **2018**, *155*, 19–28. [CrossRef]

85. Amin, A.L.; Dimsdale, T.; Jaramillo, M. Greening the Financial Sector—From Demonstration to Scale in Green Finance. In *Designing Smart Green Finance Incentive Schemes: The Role of the Public Sector and Development Banks*; E3G Working Paper; Third Generation Environmentalism: London, UK, 2014; p. 32.

86. Carolina Rezende de Carvalho Ferreira, M.; Amorim Sobreiro, V.; Kimura, H.; Luiz de Moraes Barboza, F. A systematic review of literature about finance and sustainability. *J. Sustain. Financ. Invest.* **2016**, *6*, 112–147. [CrossRef]

87. Sobhani, F.A.; Amran, A.; Zainuddin, Y. Sustainability disclosure in annual reports and websites: A study of the banking industry in Bangladesh. *J. Clean. Prod.* **2012**, *23*, 75–85. [CrossRef]

88. Rahman, A. Micro-Credit initiatives for equitable and sustainable development: Who pays? *World Dev.* **1999**, *27*, 67–82. [CrossRef]

89. Sustainable Banking Network. *A Sustainable Banking Network (SBN) Brazil Flagship Report Addendum to SBN Global Progress Report*; Sustainable Banking Network: Washington, DC, USA, 2019.

90. Inter-American Development Bank. *Informe Fintech en América Latina 2018: Crecimiento y Consolidación*; Inter-American Development Bank: Washington, DC, USA, 2018.

91. Sustainable Banking Network. *A Sustainable Banking Network (SBN) Colombia Flagship Report Addendum to SBN Global Progress Report*; Sustainable Banking Network: Washington, DC, USA, 2019.

92. United Nations. *Environment Programme Finance Initiative, Integración de la Sostenibilidad en las Instituciones Financieras Latinoamericanas: Énfasis en los Aspectos Medio Ambientales*; United Nations: Ginebra, Switzerland, 2012.

4

European Financial Services SMEs: Language in their Sustainability Reporting

Esther Ortiz-Martínez * and Salvador Marín-Hernández

Department of Accounting and Finance, University of Murcia, 3100 Murcia, Spain; salvlau@um.es
* Correspondence: esther@um.es.

Abstract: In this study we concentrate on the segment of small companies in the financial sector in Europe. Services in this sector are developing rapidly and are not necessarily provided only by traditional banks and financial companies. Many nonfinancial companies provide financial services, and this may open the sector to additional risk. In this context, the aspects of both financial and nonfinancial reporting are important and need to be taken into consideration as a whole to provide a complex picture of a particular institution. The goal of this paper is to analyze sustainability reporting according to the Global Reporting Initiative (GRI) by European financial services small and medium-sized enterprises (SMEs). First, we conducted a descriptive analysis of the features of nonfinancial information and its assurance, studying a sample of all European SMEs reporting according to the GRI from 2016 to 2018. Then, we chose only financial services SMEs to apply lexical analysis to their narrative reporting based on a corpus of 102,056 words. We conclude that nonfinancial information does not have the same importance as traditional financial information, and this sustainability reporting only complies with the minimum requirements. Thus, there is still a long way to go in this field.

Keywords: European financial services; SMEs; nonfinancial information; sustainable reporting; disclosure; lexical analysis; nonfinancial reporting

1. Introduction

Initially, disclosure of nonfinancial information was voluntarily assumed by companies, mainly large global ones. The European Commission decided that the heterogeneity in this field was an inconvenience for transparency and comparability, so it required the compulsory issuance of nonfinancial information by big European groups [1]. Although the transposition of this directive can vary and includes certain flexibility in order to be adopted by each Member State, no state has extended the obligation of issuing this sustainable information to small and medium-sized enterprises (SMEs) [2]. Bearing in mind that most of the companies in Europe are SMEs, it is important to study the nonfinancial information that they provide because disclosure of nonfinancial information is a way to improve companies' transparency and communication of social and ethical practices. The first contribution of this paper is to show which European SMEs are disclosing sustainability reports according to the Global Reporting Initiative (GRI) voluntarily, which will add important knowledge to this field of research traditionally based on large companies.

SMEs are the backbone of the European economy and are traditionally dependent on bank loans for their external financing. The last financial crisis and now the situation generated by COVID-19 have increased both the need for financial resources and the difficulties in accessing it. The European Commission highlights these difficulties and promotes the provision of suitable alternatives to bank loans, so it enacted a specific regulation "to make SMEs more visible to investors and markets more attractive and accessible for SMEs. Regulatory changes will keep the right balance between prudential regulation and financing of SMEs, and between investor protection and tailored measures for SMEs" [3]. This sector is also in the spotlight of transparency after the recent crisis and has an additional obligation with society to try to balance the unequal distribution of information [4]. We focused our study on European financial services SMEs that provide sustainability reports according to GRI standards. The development of this sector is linked to economic growth [5], and the effect of the recent crisis on bank credit has increased the importance of other types of financial resources, such as trade credit [6]. Thus, the recent evolution of the financial sector has turned to SMEs to provide these services because their traditional problems in obtaining financial resources can be more easily solved by other SMEs [7]. Although at first sight the small size can seem to be a limitation to operating in the financial sector, it can be an important advantage because specializing as another SME or in retail services in order to provide a more similar service is seen as a positive way to attract SMEs to this sector [7]. Banks and, by extension, financial services companies are expected to approach climate risks and other risks related to sustainability in the same way that they approach any other financial risks [8].

The development of regulations in Europe to require sustainability reporting by financial services companies and obtain financial resources is under discussion, and recently a roadmap of regulation on taxonomy-related disclosures was launched by undertaking the reporting of nonfinancial information included in the European Commission's Action Plan on financing sustainable growth [9]. European financial sector companies have their own regulatory and supervisory bodies that do not depend on their size in terms of national and international financial compliance, although groups of European listed companies are directly regulated by European Union–International Financial Reporting Standards (EU-IFRS). IFRS also include requirements on disclosure as a response to the need for high-quality standards in order to be endorsed in Europe. In this line, in 2018 the European Securities and Markets Authority (ESMA) expanded its supervisory activities to nonfinancial information on environmental, social, and governance (ESG) matters assessing compliance with IFRS, and in 2019 it continued to focus on this disclosure. When speaking specifically about regulation of nonfinancial disclosure, large financial services companies are mainly considered entities of public interest in each Member State, which means that they are compulsorily required to disclose nonfinancial reporting according to Directive 2014/95/EU, although the specific requirements depend on its transposition by each Member State [1]. Hence, financial services SMEs that publish sustainability information do it voluntarily because they are not within the scope of the directive, and this field is not regulated.

Background information on the field of sustainability reporting of financial services SMEs is scarce and far from sufficient to develop requirements about it now when the European Commission is working on a review of nonfinancial reporting. Studying nonfinancial information is also difficult due to its mainly qualitative and narrative nature, which makes the information heterogeneous. Although most companies are using GRI standards, this does not suppose comparable homogeneous information. Hence, it is necessary to look for another type of methodology, such as lexical analysis, which means studying the words used in the narratives of sustainability reports by European financial sector SMEs, and this is the main objective of this study.

There are three main streams of theoretical framework on which this paper is based. The first refers to disclosure of nonfinancial information and global trends in this subject, such as the general use of GRI standards. Background information about the disclosure of nonfinancial information is mainly based on large companies, which are accustomed to listing because they try to inform their stakeholders and cope with the requirements established by the capital markets [10–12]. All global trends in this field have been adopted by large companies, which are globally shaping the features of disclosure with their voluntary reporting [13]. The generally accepted standards of nonfinancial information are GRI standards because "the GRI guidelines seem to fulfil the need for standards when reporting, identifying and implementing sustainable practices in the companies, since the GRI framework has become, de facto, the standard in sustainability reporting around the world" [14]. Reporting according to GRI standards means there is some kind of homogeneous disclosure as well as use of the GRI database [15–22].

Another important global trend in nonfinancial information is to verify it externally, or to gain assurance, which is linked to disclosure of these issues [23]. All of these practices have been extensively studied at the level of big companies, but background information on SMEs is scarce. Some studies have tried to obtain differences in disclosure between big companies and SMEs [24]. SMEs have fewer resources to report nonfinancial information [10], which does not mean that they do not behave in a sustainable way or do not have a sustainable culture. Studies have also argued that SMEs adopt better corporate social responsibility (CSR) practices, although they do not issue information about it [25]. Until recently, all sustainable reporting was issued voluntarily, but for a few years the European Union has made some kind of nonfinancial information on large companies compulsory [1], and some SMEs issue this information due to the influence of large companies [26] or because they want to gain a competitive advantage [12].

Currently, important work is being done to advise SMEs on how to voluntarily issue nonfinancial information. This is being done by regulators (such as the European Commission), the regulators' advisors (the European Financial Reporting Advisory Group (EFRAG) advises the European Commission, focusing on disclosure requirements), and professional organizations (the International Federation of Accountants (IFAC) and active organizations representing European SMEs such as the European Federation of Accountants and Auditors for SMEs (EFAA for SMEs) and SMEunited). However, the literature on sustainability reporting by SMEs is scarce and mainly based on a single research method, surveys, which means there is a need for further studies that combine other methods to add additional conclusions about this subject [27]. In this line, we point out the situation of voluntary sustainability reporting according to the GRI by European SMEs, which provides another point of view in a field of research traditionally based on large companies.

Second, there is background information focused on disclosure of financial services companies due to their important role in the economy. This sector has traditionally been a determinant of social issues of companies [28–30] because the information being issued depends on the kind of activity of the firm. Financial services companies are vital agents in the economy, so they are a benchmark for greater transparency [31–33]. They are also under special supervision and regulation in each country, with specific requirements on top of those applied for nonfinancial entities [34], and there can be an effect of the type of market economy on banks' disclosure (coordinated or liberal market economy) [35]. This vital activity and the effects of the recent crisis have increased research on the relationship between social responsibility and profitability in financial services companies and companies operating in other sectors [36–43]. Nowadays, there is also "ethical banking" in comparison to "conventional banking" because it is supposed to be more responsible and issue more information, both financial and nonfinancial, in response to stakeholders [44,45]. Notwithstanding ethical banking, traditional banking is supposed to take care of different aspects of its social responsibility such as consumer satisfaction [46] and the opinions of providers of financial resources [47]. The European Commission is promoting alternative financial plans for SMEs, trying to make it easier for SMEs to access markets [3], while not forgetting investor protection, which also includes sustainable reporting to respond to the increasing pressure to provide nonfinancial information [48].

The third theoretical framework is related to the methodology that we used in this paper: lexical analysis. The area of study, disclosure of nonfinancial information, is complex because it mainly consists of heterogeneous qualitative and narrative information. It is true that most companies are using GRI standards, but this does not mean there is comparable information, as there are different levels of adherence, and the formats of presenting the information can be quite diverse and flexible. Hence, analyzing disclosure implies many problems, which the majority of studies have tried to solve using content analysis or disclosure indices to measure this information (one recent study using indices is [49]), or to check if there is any relationship between disclosure and other features, although there are proven disadvantages when using this methodology [50]. Lexical analysis has been used in research having to do with semantics and language in a variety of fields, such as in [51,52], which strictly refer to language skills, as well as in analyzing qualitative narrative information in the field of economics, such as [53], which examined statements by the chairman and CEO in BP plc's Annual Report 2010 [54], which used lexicometric analysis to study a corpus comprising speeches of European Central Bank presidents; [55], which analyzed the results of open-ended interviews in the field of management; and [56], which used lexical analysis to try to extract the sentiments of a group of people to predict the movement of the stock market. Studies using lexical analysis of nonfinancial reporting are scarce, and none has analyzed disclosure by European financial sector SMEs. Mainly they have focused on big firms, such as [57], which conducted lexical analysis of annual reports of Shell plc.; [58], which reviewed previous research on sustainable banks for three periods depending on the financial crisis and used a descriptive bibliometric analysis and a co-word analysis to study the topics in the literature; [59], which applied lexical analysis to environmental disclosure of listed companies; [60], which asserted that the discourse included in the social reports of BP and IKEA was constructed to present the face that the companies wanted to show; and [61], which created two corpora from seven corporate governance reports of listed companies.

In this paper we use lexical analysis to study disclosure of nonfinancial information because it is mainly narrative, and this is a good way to obtain conclusions from the text provided and the words used to compose the narrative. The analysis is based on reporting by European financial sector SMEs, and the background on this field is scarce. Sustainability reporting in the financial sector is mainly inadequate and focused on financial aspects rather than on material issues, as highlighted by the UN when studying sustainability reporting in the financial sector [62]. Only a few of these initiatives of sustainability reporting provide a picture of all sustainability factors of financial companies [62]. In addition, the overwhelming majority of SMEs perceive sustainability reporting as a burden, and it appears that SMEs either do not have the capacity to comply or are reluctant to invest the necessary resources [63], so taking all this together, we propose the following research questions:

Research Question 1. *Are European financial sector SMEs preparing their sustainability reports only in accordance with minimum nonfinancial disclosure requirements?*

Research Question 2. *Are European financial sector SMEs still more influenced by financial terms in their nonfinancial reporting?*

The paper is organized as follows: first we describe the methodology, in the next section we discuss the results, and in the final section we wrap up the paper and describe the limitations and future research.

2. Materials and Methods

As the first goal of this paper is to point out the situation of sustainability reporting according to GRI voluntarily disclosed by European SMEs, we obtained the sample from the GRI database. Bearing in mind that GRI nonfinancial reporting standards are the most widely used all over the world and that SMEs in Europe are not compelled to issue this information, this database is a suitable resource to get these data. The search tool of the GRI database allows searches for nonfinancial reports according to firm size, and specifically reports issued by SMEs. We made our search on 11 November 2019 with the following criteria: firm size—SMEs; region—Europe; report type—GRI-Standards. Although previous versions of the GRI standards are included in the report type, these are the latest ones, published by GRI on 1 July 2018, replacing the GRI 4 version (https://www2.globalreporting.org/standards/g4/Pages/default.aspx). In total, 116 organizations and 157 reports were found. This means that there are firms (or other types of organizations) that issued more than one report because these standards refer to 2016, 2017, 2018, and even 2019. As shown in Table 1, there are many sectors in which SMEs that issue nonfinancial information operate.

Table 1. Nonfinancial information issued by European small and medium-sized enterprises (SMEs) according to Global Reporting Initiative (GRI).

		Frequency	%			Frequency	%
Sector	Real estate	16	10.2	**Country**	Sweden	26	16.6
	Tourism/leisure	3	1.9		Slovenia	1	0.6
	Energy utilities	3	1.9		Belgium	3	1.9
	Food and beverage products	4	2.5		Andorra	1	0.6
	Media	3	1.9		Poland	2	1.3
	Healthcare services	7	4.5		Greece	5	3.2
	Nonprofit services	15	9.6		Austria	5	3.2
	Commercial services	10	6.4		Portugal	3	1.9
	Telecommunications	1	0.6		Russian	1	0.6
	Textiles and apparel	6	3.8		Denmark	2	1.3
	Forest and paper products	2	1.3		United Kingdom	1	0.6
	Agriculture	4	2.5		Netherlands	8	5.1
	Conglomerates	1	0.6		Norway	1	0.6
	Mining	2	1.3		Spain	38	24.2
	Waste management	8	5.1		Iceland	3	1.9
	Aviation	1	0.6		Germany	18	11.5
	Universities	1	0.6		Switzerland	8	5.1
	Construction	7	4.5		France	4	2.5
	Energy	7	4.5		Italy	20	12.7
	Metal products	3	1.9		Finland	7	4.5
	Healthcare products	6	3.8		Total	157	100
	Household and personal products	4	2.5	**Grouped Sector**	Real estate	16	10.2
	Logistics	3	1.9		Agriculture and mining	6	3.8
	Public agencies	2	1.3		Industry	34	21.6
	Consumer durables	1	0.6		Services	38	24.2
	Water utilities	1	0.6		Public agencies and services	6	3.8
	Construction materials	1	0.6		Nonprofit services	15	9.6
	Automotive	3	1.9		Financial services	9	5.7
	Financial services	9	5.7		Construction and construction materials	8	5.1
	Railroads	1	0.6		Energy	7	4.5
	Retailers	1	0.6		Other	18	11.5
	Chemicals	3	1.9		Total	157	100
	Other	18	11.5		–	–	–
	Total	157	100		–	–	–

Second, if we focus on the financial services sector, due to the specific features that we highlighted previously, we see that there are only nine reports to analyze. Hence, there are nine sustainability reports by European financial sector SMEs according to GRI, which supposes an important number of reports according to sector based on the breakdown in Table 1, and a percentage of reports (5.7%) important in comparing nearly all sectors, with the exception of real estate, nonprofit services, commercial services, and others. It was necessary to group the sectors in order to get higher percentages of sustainability reports (grouped sector breakdown in Table 1).

Analyzing the language of these reports to see if they can be investigated more deeply, we find (Table 2) that only four out of nine reports are written in English, and the others are in the mother tongue. Although there is no English financial services SME in the sample, the majority of SMEs use English to prepare this information. It does not seem logical to prepare nonfinancial information according to GRI using the mother tongue in response to the market and stakeholders, but we must bear in mind that we focus on SMEs, and their goals in disclosing this information may not be so global.

Table 2. Nonfinancial information issued by European financial services SMEs according to GRI.

		Frequency	%			Frequency	%
Country	Sweden	1	11.1	**Year**	2016	1	11.1
	Iceland	1	11.1		2017	4	44.4
	Germany	2	22.2		2018	4	44.4
	Italy	3	33.3		Total	9	100
	Finland	1	11.1	**Format of Report**	Pdf	9	100
	Belgium	1	11.1		Html	0	0
	Total	9	100	**Adherence Level**	In accordance core	7	77.7
Language of Report	Swedish	1	11.1		In accordance comprehensive	1	11.1
	English	4	66.6		GRI referenced	1	11.1
	German	1	11.1		Total	9	100
	Italian	3	11.1	**Integrated Report**	Yes	3	33.3
	Total	9	100		No	6	66.6
					Total	9	100

Hence, only four European financial services SMEs issued nonfinancial information according to GRI standards and, fulfilling the methodological requirements, reported in English. We used all the data obtained from the GRI database during this period, so the sample is the whole population of European financial services SMEs that complied with GRI standards from 2016 to 2018 and wrote their reports in English. From the point of view of the lexical analysis methodology, the studied sample has the appropriate size, measured by the size of the corpus (number of words or tokens) compared to previous valid studies [57,64,65].

We used SPSS to analyze the features of the nonfinancial information and its assurance, showing the frequencies in absolute values and percentages. All features were taken from the GRI database. After describing the features of the nonfinancial information issued by European financial services SMEs in English, we studied the narrative discourse of these reports, as this is the best way to analyze qualitative heterogeneous information. Hence, it was necessary to look for another type of methodology, such as lexical analysis, which involves studying the words used in the narrative. The reports are in PDF format in the GRI database, and to do a lexical analysis it is necessary to convert them into TXT files. We used free PDF-to-text software (https://pdftotext.com/es/) to get four TXT files correspondingly organized according to firm. These files made up the corpus for analyzing nonfinancial disclosure. To analyze the narrative reporting, we used another statistical methodology that allowed us to compare the disclosure to obtain the main characteristics of a corpus and find word patterns. The chosen tool was WordSmith Tools 7 software (version 7, Oxford University Press, Oxford, UK), published by Lexical Analysis Software and Oxford University Press since 1996. We used different utilities that this lexical analysis software offers, which are explained in the Results section.

3. Results

3.1. Features of Nonfinancial Information and Its Assurance of European Financial Services SMEs

First, 5.7% of all European SMEs that voluntarily disclosed nonfinancial information according to GRI (9 out of 157) operated in the financial services sector (Table 1). The most important sector in this sample was real estate companies (10.2%; Table 1), and financial services occupies an important position of nonfinancial information according to sector. The nine financial services companies that issued nonfinancial information came from different EU countries (Table 2). There are two effects to bear in mind. First, sometimes SMEs that need credit have to report on some sustainability aspects to align with banks' sustainability requirements. Second, these SMEs provide financial services, which means they have to report on their own sustainability [63]. As previously pointed out, only four of the nine used the English language to report their nonfinancial information, and five used their mother tongue, although it is supposed that these reports are published for global stakeholders (Table 2).

To get an idea of the importance of this type of SME in Europe, we can highlight that two of the four are asset managers, one in Germany and one in Finland. According to the European Fund and Asset Management Association [65], in 2017 there were 380 asset management companies in Germany (one of the leading European countries with this type of company) and 26 in Finland. Hence, bearing in mind that these numbers are not detailed by company size, we can say that these two SMEs are a good sample to study. The other two European financial services SMEs are a bank in Iceland, a state-owned bank created from an old bank during the last crisis (a national bank, thus its small size), and a provider of financial market infrastructure services in Belgium. The bank's main services are based on consumer, corporate, and private banking; mortgage loans, private equity, wealth management, and credit cards. The German asset manager offers one global investment platform focused on multi-asset alternative credit, real asset debt, and sustainable investments through a digital environment for retail investors. The Belgian provider of financial market infrastructure services acts as an international central securities depository (ICSD) and as the central securities depository (CSD) for some other securities. Retail investors can also have direct accounts in their local CSD. The Finnish asset manager offers asset management solutions and financial advice globally to private investors, institutions, professional athletes, and artists. Finally, the analyzed companies offer a valuable picture of the narrative discourse included in sustainability reports, taking into account particular niches in the financial industry. At the same time, these reports are comparable because all the companies are SMEs operating in the financial services sector, bearing in mind that the sector is one of the most important determinant variables influencing nonfinancial reporting [66–68].

As regards the adherence level, most of the nine European financial services SMEs (80%) adjust their information to the core level of GRI, which is referred to as the "in accordance" core, and prefer not to prepare integrated reports (Table 2). Thus, it seems as if these companies try to issue nonfinancial information following the minimum established standards as highlighted by the UN when it studies sustainability reporting in the financial sector and says that it is not offering information about all sustainability factors of financial companies [69], even more if we are speaking about SMEs.

Bearing in mind the assurance of this information (Table 3), two-thirds of these financial services companies verified the disclosure externally. The predominant level of assurance is limited/moderate, and the assurance scope is a specified section as defined by GRI. The assurance providers in the analyzed reports were mainly accountants (55.5%); one-third of verifications were done by one of the Big Four companies, KPMG (33.3%), and one-third were done following the ISAE 3000 assurance standard. However, the financial services companies did not issue information about this assurance after they verified their nonfinancial information (at least four of them, or 44.4%, did not have this information available; Table 3).

Table 3. Features of nonfinancial assurance of European financial services SMEs.

		Frequency	%			Frequency	%
External Assurance	Yes	6	66.6	**Type of Assurance Provider**	Accountant	5	55.5
	No	3	33.3		Not available	4	44.41
	Total	9	100		Total	9	100
Level of Assurance	Not available	4	44.4	**Assurance Scope**	Not available	5	55.5
	Limited/moderate	5	55.5		Specified sections	4	44.4
	Total	9	100		Total	9	100
Assurance Standard	Not available	4	44.4	**Assurance Provider**	Not available	4	44.4
	ISAE 3000	3	33.3		KPMG	3	33.3
	AA1000AS	1	11.1		Deloitte	2	22.2
	National	1	11.1		Total	9	100
	Total	9	100				

3.2. Lexical Analysis of Sustainability Reporting of European Financial Services SMEs

First, we used the WordList application to obtain the principal characteristics of the text analyzed. The main features are shown in Table 4. Although the companies are in different countries and the reports are from different years, these data are comparable because all are SMEs and operate in the financial services sector. Finally, we analyzed 102,056 words, which are called tokens, and all together are defined as a corpus. The size of the corpus, and thus of the sample, is appropriate to apply lexical analysis (the number of analyzed words or tokens is always bigger than the corpus analyzed in previous valid studies [57,64,65]).

Table 4. Principal characteristics of analyzed sustainability reports.

Corpus/SME	Country	Year	Words (Tokens)	Types * (Distinct Words)	Type–Token Ratio (TTR)	Standardized ** TTR	Sentences
Corpus	–	–	102,056	7927	7.77%	40.63%	3800
SME1	Iceland	2018	38,753	4214	10.87%	38.01%	1423
SME2	Germany	2018	29,795	3659	12.28%	42.46%	1150
SME3	Belgium	2017	23,728	3570	15.05%	42.37%	725
SME4	Finland	2016	9780	1870	19.12%	41.37%	502

* Types: different words that are not repeated in the text. ** Standardized TTR: TTR that does not depend on different text lengths.

It can be seen that the four companies are in different European countries. There are no big differences between words in the reports of the last three years, except that in 2016 the reports were much briefer than in the following years. This may be due to the early application of GRI standards or to the fact that companies show greater effort "from year to year in giving more information in order to comply with the transparency principle, or at least to give this appearance" [57]. The same can be checked in the different words used in the reports, which are called "types" in this software, and in the type–token ratio (TTR), calculated as different words over total words, which increases when the number of total words decreases (Table 4). However, when the TTR is calculated without considering the extension of the whole text, standardized TTR, the largest number of different words, without repetition, is found in the latter reports, with the exception of the report of the Icelandic financial services company, which seems to repeat words more frequently although the report is the most extensive (more words and more sentences; Table 4). Perhaps more words are used to say the same thing, and the opposite was the case in the 2016 report; fewer words were used to say the important things, which were not repeated. Although, as mentioned, there is value in a reporting narrative, that does not mean it is an extensive report because a sustainability report is not for storytelling [70]. Previous studies on the relationship between disclosure length and greater readability, transparency, or complexity were inconclusive [71] and were not focused on financial services SMEs.

The next tool used in the lexical analysis was the word list (results are shown in Table 5). This counts the frequency of words used in the corpus, i.e., how often each word appears in the whole text, and their percentage of use in the text. The position is the ranking of the most frequently used words. We included in Table 5 the most significant frequent words for this analysis (the first position is included as an example). Only the word "risk" appeared in more than 1% of the cases in the corpus (1.04%), in position 8, followed by "bank" in position 12 and "management" in position 20. To classify these most frequent words, we created three groups: words that are basically related to financial meaning such as "risk", "bank", "management", "financial", "capital", "investment", "business", and "funds"; other words that have to do with the core sense of nonfinancial information, such as "employees", "sustainability", "board", "environmental", "committee", "governance", "pillar", and "GRI"; a group with words related to information and requirements, such as "information", "compliance", "reporting", "disclosures", and "requirement". This classification was based on the assignment of a certain term to a concept, which can be done in specialized languages, as in this case, when analyzing sustainability reporting; for example, the word "meager" is identified as a specialized term in the realm of finance, since it is very commonly used in expressions such as "meager economic recovery" and "meager 10%" [71]. Although the word "pillar" is included in the financial group, it could also be included in the second group related to nonfinancial aspects, which we called sustainable most frequent words. This is due to the Basel II and III requirements, which ask for reporting on financial and nonfinancial items of these kinds of companies, so it contains both dimensions of the concept, financial and nonfinancial. Although these three groups of most frequent words were made following the assignment of terms to concepts in specialized languages [72], sometimes some words refer to more concepts and the assignment is not so simple.

The following results were obtained from the analysis of the most frequent words, shown in Tables 6–8. The number of occurrences of the search word (hits), occurrences of each word per 1000 words, and their dispersion are calculated. To establish comparisons, it is better to use hits per 1000 words as a homogeneous measurement. As can be seen, "financial" words are used the most: the occurrences per 1000 words were clearly the highest for these kinds of words. The most used was "risk" (10.16 times per 1000 words), followed by "bank", "management", and then a sustainable word, "sustainability" (3.75 times per 1000 words; Table 7) followed by other financial words: "financial", "capital", "investment", "business" (2.40 times per 1000 words), and then "employees", previously included in the group of sustainable words (2.29 times per 1000 words) and "GRI" (2.13 times per 1000 words). This means that what counts the most in sustainable reports is the financial information over the nonfinancial information, or at least the typical financial aspects of the business are highlighted more with the use of the language. These companies do not seem to include sustainable words in their vocabulary and, hence, in their culture. Although the four companies are in different countries and operate in different niches of financial services, the results are similar when classifying the most used words.

Analyzing the information on the use of these frequent words considering the four reports separately, we can see that some of the words appear to be used more because they are used very often in some reports, which increases the global frequency in the corpus. This is the case of the words "risk", "bank", and "capital" (20.15, 18.23, 6.80 per 1000 words; Table 6), which occur frequently in the report of the financial services company in Iceland. The word "sustainability" appears as the second most frequent in this group due to its use in the Finnish company's 2016 report, although it is only used in three of the four reports (8.10 per 1000 words; Table 7). Something similar happens with the word "employees", whose use increases due to the Finnish company's report (5.36 per 1000 words, Table 7). The case of the word "pillar" deserves some reflection because, although it is a frequent word in the corpus, the detailed analysis of the reports showed that it was only used in two, and essentially only in one because the frequency of use in the other was very low. Thus, "pillar" was exclusively used by the financial services company in Iceland in its 2018 report (Table 7). Another example is the term "GRI", which would be expected to appear in all of the reports, given that all are prepared according to GRI standards, yet it did not appear in one report, which is one of the most recent ones (Table 7).

Table 5. Word analysis of sustainability reports.

Position	Word	Frequency	%
1	The	5001	4.90%
8	Risk	1103	1.08%
12	Bank	899	0.89%
20	Management	566	0.55%
24	Financial	374	0.37%
26	Capital	356	0.35%
41	Investment	276	0.27%
44	Business	261	0.26%
45	Employees	248	0.24%
46	Sustainability	234	0.23%
52	Board	207	0.2%
53	Information	206	0.2%
69	Responsibility	157	0.15%
73	Compliance	153	0.15%
74	Reporting	147	0.14%
75	Disclosures	147	0.14%
76	Requirements	145	0.14%
77	environmental	145	0.14%
79	Committee	143	0.14%
82	Governance	135	0.13%
83	Pillar	134	0.13%
84	GRI	133	0.13%
86	Funds	131	0.13%

Table 6. Statistics of the most important financial words in sustainability reports.

Words	Risk			Bank			Management			Financial		
Corpus/SME	Hits *	Per 1000 **	Dis.	Hits	Per 1000	Dis.	Hits	Per 1000	Dis.	Hits	Per 1000	Dis.
Corpus	1103	10.16	0.831	899	8.28	0.796	566	5.22	0.839	374	3.45	0.811
SME1	931	20.15	0.818	842	18.23	0.777	237	5.13	0.711	170	3.68	0.699
SME2	95	3.25	0.728	28	0.96	0.753	187	6.40	0.797	114	3.90	0.796
SME3	68	2.88	0.497	28	1.19	0.630	103	4.36	0.814	59	2.50	0.652
SME4	9	0.95	0.340	1	0.11	0.000	39	4.10	0.736	31	3.26	0.802

Words	Capital			Investment			Business			Funds		
Corpus/SME	Hits *	Per 1000 **	Dis.	Hits	Per 1000	Dis.	Hits	Per 1000	Dis.	Hits	Per 1000	Dis.
Corpus	356	3.28	0.630	276	2.54	0.852	261	2.40	0.834	131	1.21	0.820
SME1	314	6.80	0.595	41	0.89	0.618	80	1.73	0.729	69	1.49	0.727
SME2	11	0.38	0.665	169	5.78	0.755	96	3.29	0.806	38	1.30	0.607
SME3	16	0.68	0.646	16	0.68	0.410	58	2.46	0.820	10	0.42	0.553
SME4	15	1.58	0.435	50	5.26	0.653	27	2.84	0.669	14	1.47	0.646

* Hits: number of occurrences of the search word. ** Per 1000 words: number of occurrences per 1000 words. Dis., dispersion.

Table 7. Statistics of the most important sustainable frequent words in sustainability reports.

Words	Employees			Sustainability			Board			Environmental		
Corpus/SME	Hits *	Per 1000 **	Dis.	Hits	Per 1000	Dis.	Hits	Per 1000	Dis.	Hits	Per 1000	Dis.
Corpus	248	2.29	0.802	234	3.75	0.732	207	1.91	0.732	145	1.34	0.733
SME1	12	0.26	0.184	–	–	–	99	2.14	0.563	1	0.02	0.000
SME2	92	3.15	0.688	147	5.03	0.722	62	2.12	0.718	64	2.19	0.612
SME3	93	3.94	0.704	10	0.42	0.528	37	1.57	0.498	57	2.41	0.608
SME4	51	5.36	0.551	77	8.10	0.682	9	0.95	0.340	23	2.42	0.489

Digital Banking Revolution and Financial Innovation

Table 7. *Cont.*

Words	Committee			Governance			Pillar			GRI		
Corpus/SME	Hits *	Per 1000 **	Dis.	Hits	Per 1000	Dis.	Hits	Per 1000	Dis.	Hits	Per 1000	Dis.
Corpus	143	1.44	0.648	135	1.24	0.730	134	1.78	0.785	133	2.13	0.810
SME1	103	2.23	0.452	29	0.63	0.630	133	2.88	0.783	-	-	-
SME2	7	0.24	0.270	74	2.53	0.639	1	0.03	0.000	68	2.33	0.767
SME3	33	1.40	0.485	22	0.93	0.665	-	-	-	53	2.25	0.751
SME4	-	-	-	10	1.05	0.419	-	-	-	12	1.26	0.184

* Hits: number of occurrences of the search word. ** Per 1000 words: number of occurrences per 1000 words. Dis., dispersion.

Table 8. Statistics of the most important frequent words related to information and compliance in sustainability reports.

Words	Information			Compliance			Reporting			Disclosures		
Corpus/SME	Hits *	Per 1000 **	Dis.	Hits	Per 1000	Dis.	Hits	Per 1000	Dis.	Hits	Per 1000	Dis.
Corpus	206	1.90	0.813	153	1.41	0.751	147	1.35	0.841	147	1.35	0.806
SME1	84	1.82	0.703	48	1.04	0.572	42	0.91	0.681	118	2.55	0.759
SME2	85	2.91	0.741	66	2.26	0.526	56	1.92	0.829	11	0.38	0.356
SME3	10	0.42	0.419	36	1.52	0.725	28	1.19	0.747	17	0.72	0.651
SME4	27	2.84	0.620	3	0.32	0.299	21	2.21	0.600	1	0.11	0.000

Words	Requirements		
Corpus/SME	Hits *	Per 1000 **	Dis.
Corpus	145	1.34	0.855
SME1	101	2.19	0.815
SME2	34	1.16	0.730
SME3	6	0.25	0.582
SME4	4	0.42	0.465

* Hits: number of occurrences of the search word. ** Per 1000 words: number of occurrences per 1000 words. Dis., dispersion.

Analyzing Table 8, with the statistics of the most important frequent words related to information and compliance in the sustainability reports, there was one report in which they had less importance, as was previously obtained, that of the Belgian company from 2017. The most used words in the other three reports were those generally obtained as the most frequent words; hence, they follow the general pattern. For example, "information" showed higher frequency per 1000 words in the German and Finnish reports (SME2 and SME4: 2.91 and 2.84, respectively; Table 8) and so on with the other words.

The last three tables of this analysis (Tables 9–11) include the results obtained from the concordance tool of the lexical analysis. The last step is to analyze the most frequent words in their context. This means counting the number of times one word is found in the neighborhood of the chosen word. This tool allows us to discover whether or not the most frequent words are related to the disclosure they supposedly refer to. The method of considering the relationships between certain words and the other words that appear a sentence was used in previous studies, such as [73]. All the tables of concordance include the first eight words with the most important relationships (in the tables, they are in positions from 1 to 8, and position 1 is always the most frequent word analyzed). In the case of the word "requirements", its position 8 showed very low frequency, and it was not included in Table 11.

Table 9. Concordance of most important financial frequent words in sustainability reports.

Position	Word	Total *	Word	Total	Word	Total	Word	Total
1.	Bank	936	Risk	1538	Management	610	Financial	394
2.	Risk	254	Bank	254	Risk	252	Services	33
3.	Arion	190	Management	252	Asset	55	Report	33
4.	2018	139	Credit	210	Bank	53	Statements	28
5.	Disclosures	104	2018	160	Approach	51	Risk	26
6.	Pillar	97	Disclosures	147	Capital	48	Institutions	25
7.	Capital	64	Pillar	118	With	38	Bank	25
8.	Management	53	Arion	110	Senior	36	Undertakings	25
Position	Word	Total	Word	Total	Word	Total	Word	Total
1.	Capital	450	Investment	302	Business	279	Funds	149
2.	Bank	64	Responsible	47	Risk	36	Investment	21
3.	Risk	64	Sustainable	22	With	29	Bank	15
4.	Requirements	64	Funds	21	Bank	20	Pension	13
5.	Buffer	51	Platform	21	Travel	17	Sustainable	12
6.	Requirement	50	Fund	18	Units	17	Capital	11
7.	Management	48	Process	18	Management	17	With	10
8.	Adequacy	32	Into	17	That	13	Risk	10

* Total: number of times the word was found in the neighborhood of the search word.

Table 10. Concordance of most important sustainable frequent words in sustainability reports.

Position	Word	Total *	Word	Total	Word	Total	Word	Total
1.	Employees	260	Sustainability	258	Board	241	Environmental	157
2.	Time	19	Report	129	Committee	53	Social	51
3.	With	16	2018	82	Executive	44	Impacts	15
4.	That	15	Information	36	Directors	42	Impact	14
5.	Have	15	Supplementary	32	Management	27	Group	12
6.	Permanent	15	Topics	25	Risk	27	Assessment	12
7.	Total	12	This	22	Bric	19	Footprint	12
8.	Their	12	Clients	21	Policy	17	Economic	11
Position	**Word**	**Total**	**Word**	**Total**	**Word**	**Total**	**Word**	**Total**
1.	Committee	203	Governance	147	Pillar	148	GRI	133
2.	Board	53	Corporate	46	Risk	118	2017	25
3.	Credit	40	Risk	15	Disclosures	105	Index	24
4.	Risk	25	Data	12	2018	97	Responsibility	24
5.	Management	24	Social	11	Bank	97	With	19
6.	Executive	21	Policy	11	Arion	94	Disclosure	18
7.	Level	17	Body	11	Capital	24	Reporting	16
8.	Arion	14	Environmental	11	Requirements	21	Report	14

* Total: number of times the word was found in the neighborhood of the search word.

Table 11. Concordance of most important frequent words related to information and compliance in sustainability reports.

Position	Word	Total *	Word	Total	Word	Total
1.	Information	214	Compliance	165	Reporting	152
2.	Report	48	With	33	Risk	22
3.	Sustainability	36	Risk	27	Financial	22
4.	Security	35	Officer	19	Sustainability	16
5.	Risk	31	Control	18	Report	14
6.	2018	27	Regulatory	14	Bank	13
7.	Supplementary	26	Management	13	Internal	12
8.	Bank	18	2018	13	Period	11
Position	**Word**	**Total**	**Word**	**Total**		
1.	Disclosures	148	Requirements	155		
2.	Risk	148	Capital	64		
3.	Pillar	106	Regulatory	25		
4.	Bank	104	With	21		
5.	2018	98	Bank	21		
6.	Arion	96	Risk	19		
7.	Credit	21	Buffer	15		
8.	Management	18	–	–		

* Total: number of times the word was found in the neighborhood of the search word.

The words that were previously grouped as financial terms in the analysis of the most frequent words are related to the same type of financial words: bank–risk, management–risk, financial–services, capital–bank–risk, business and risk, and funds–investment–bank (all are in position 1, 2, or 3 in Table 9, which means they appear next to each other). The only most frequent financial word included previously that was more frequently related to other sustainable terms was "investment", appearing in the reports with "responsible" and "sustainable" (Table 9).

The most frequent words about sustainable aspects appeared fewer times that the financial ones (Table 10), and the concordance shows the following:

- The word "employees" is not related to other important words.
- The word "sustainability" is linked mainly to "report", due to the requirement to issue sustainable information, and is totally consistent with the results obtained in Table 11.
- The words "committee" and "board", "environmental" and "social", "governance" and "corporate" are found frequently in the same neighborhood, a result that is totally logical.
- The word "pillar" appears in the neighborhood with two other words, "risk" and "disclosures", as is also seen in Table 11 with "disclosures". This result proves that "pillar" is a word that comes from the Basel II and III requirements regarding these aspects.
- Finally, the most important link is found between "GRI", "2017", and "index", as reports include the GRI index to show that they are elaborated according to GRI standards.

The majority of results included in Table 11 go further in the importance of the words "compliance", "requirements", "disclosures", and "risk". According to GRI good practices for SMEs, sustainability reporting has to comply with the following checklist: it describes the sustainable development and draws objective and available information and measures of sustainable development, presents the performance of sustainable conditions and goals and the magnitude of the contribution to (un)sustainability, and describes the relationship between sustainability and long-term organizational strategy, risks, and opportunities [74]. Thus, if we use this lexical analysis to understand whether these financial services SMEs properly developed their sustainability reporting, the obtained results show that although they used some specific words to meet the minimum requirements, the financial dimension of reporting continues to be more important, and the other information is used to increase the length of the report but still does not reflect significant environmental and social impacts. According to previous studies [75], sustainability reporting in financial companies has as the highest priorities those directly related to their business operations.

4. Discussion

Our analysis is based on European SMEs included in the GRI database, hence the population of SMEs that voluntarily use GRI standards, although only between 10 and 15% of sustainability reports in the database from 2017 to 2018 came from SMEs [76]. Then, we focused on European SMEs operating in the financial services sector. Bearing in mind their specific activity, sustainability reports by European financial sector SMEs represent an important percentage of reports in comparison with nearly all other sectors (5.7%).

The results obtained from the lexical analysis lead us to think that the answer to our first research question is yes because there is no significant use of symbolic concepts in the narrative discourse in the reports analyzed; hence, there is minimum compliance with nonfinancial requirements. Opposite results were obtained by the authors of [53] after applying a lexicometric analysis to speeches delivered by European Central Bank presidents, although in this case we analyzed sustainability reporting.

Although initially it may be thought that sustainability reports are specific for each company, the broader corpus analysis suggests they were prepared similarly and used the same template [52], even more if it is pointed out that the four companies are in different countries and, although operating in financial services, are focused on different niches. As the sector is a strongly determinant variable of nonfinancial reporting [66–68], the analyzed reports follow the same pattern. Financial services companies not only operate in the same sector, but they also have their own regulatory and supervisory bodies. In this case the sector is decisive in following the same financial trend in sustainability information, and as found in KPMG´s 2017 survey, financial services companies are in last place in corporate responsibility reporting [77].

These financial services companies are still imbued with traditional financial objectives and information. This means that what counts most in sustainable reports is financial information over nonfinancial, or at least the typical financial aspects of the business in this important sector are highlighted more through the language used. The analysis of the most frequent words in context shows that all financial terms are related to other financial terms. Hence, our second research question is supported. These results are the same as those obtained in previous studies, although in developing countries, based on financial services companies, because it is argued that the most important priorities of these enterprises are those directly related to their business operations [75].

Although a first view of sustainable reporting may show that companies try to exert more effort to increase the extent of their disclosure, the deep lexical analysis of these reports shows that the language used is not so extensive or rich, as some words are repeated many times, which highlights the problem of the lack of content in sustainability information. This shows evidence of the gap that still exists between financial and nonfinancial information and takes us to the same question posed by other researchers: "If it is like this for disclosing firms, what is happening in the case of nondisclosing firms?" [55].

Future research directions depend on an increase in nonfinancial reports, which will make it possible to get a bigger sample, more companies, and a longer period. Currently, the most important limitation is the number of sustainability reports published according to GRI by European financial services SMEs. Another future research project involves using a proper sample of nonfinancial reports to describe and compare financial sector vs. nonfinancial sector SMEs and financial sector SMEs vs. large financial sector companies.

5. Conclusions

These financial services SMEs should particularly focus on the proper elaboration and publication of sustainability reporting. There are many initiatives to increase the importance of this type of company in Europe and to move toward more sustainable finance. There is a challenge for these companies, taking into account all of their stakeholders, to give the proper role to nonfinancial information. It is desirable that SMEs, as well as those that operate in the financial services sector due to their essential role in the economy, start issuing nonfinancial information, especially now, when alternatives to traditional bank financing are being promoted for financing SMEs. These results and conclusions have theoretical and practical implications for the importance of sustainability reporting. It may be a burden, but it can also have multiple advantages, such as being an opportunity to create value in the company, differentiate from other companies, improve operational performance, or enhance market reputation, among others. Our contribution with this work is to point out that these financial services SMEs play an important role, and sustainability reporting has to mean there is another way to do business [78]. This study provides an opportunity to improve sustainability disclosure and standards considering the specific features of financial services SMEs. Regulators must take into account the specific features of this type of company in order to adapt the standards and requirements. Sustainability reports must include all relevant topics that reflect the organization´s economic, environmental, and social impacts or influence the decisions of stakeholders [74]. The main reasons argued for not having proper sustainability reporting by SMEs are the lack of resources, awareness of sustainability´s importance and potential impacts, access to financing, information and skills to elaborate this information, and regulatory requirements [76]. Thus, this is an opportunity for practitioners, academics, and regulators to try to solve these problems from all points of view, theoretical and practical, to make up for this lack of resources according to their different tasks. Now, when the European Commission is working on amending the nonfinancial reporting directive through the mission of the European Financial Reporting Advisory Group (EFRAG) and its Project Task Force on nonfinancial reporting standards, it is time to think about these specific features of SMEs and financial services companies to make the process of sustainability reporting easier.

Author Contributions: Conceptualization, E.O.-M. and S.M.-H.; methodology, E.O.-M. and S.M.-H.; software, E.O.-M.; validation, S.M.; formal analysis, E.O.-M. and S.M.-H.; investigation, E.O.-M. and S.M.-H.; resources, E.O.-M. and S.M.-H.; data curation, E.O.-M. and S.M.-H.; writing—original draft preparation, E.O.-M. and S.M.-H.; writing—review and editing, E.O.; visualization, S.M.-H.; supervision, E.O.-M. and S.M.-H. All authors have read and agreed to the published version of the manuscript.

References

1. Directive 2014/95/EU of the European Parliament and of the Council of 22 October 2014 Amending Directive 2013/34/EU as Regards Disclosure of Non-Financial and Diversity Information by Certain Large Undertakings and Groups. Available online: https://eur-lex.europa.eu/legal-content/EN/TXT/?uri=CELEX%3A32014L0095 (accessed on 20 May 2019).
2. Lang, M.; Martin, R. The Trickle down Effect-IFRS and accounting by SMEs. European Federation of Accountants and Auditors for SMEs 2017. Available online: http://www.efaa.com/cms/upload/efaa_files/pdf/Publications/Articles/EFAA_Trickle_Down_WEB.pdf (accessed on 10 July 2020).
3. European Commission. Communication from the Commission to the Council, to the European Parliament, to the Committee of the Regions and to the European and Social Committee. An Action Plan to Improve Access to Finance for SMEs 2011. SEC (2011) 1527final. COM (2011) 870 Final. Available online: https://eur-lex.europa.eu/LexUriServ/LexUriServ.do?uri=COM:2011:0870:FIN:EN:PDF (accessed on 11 July 2020).
4. Azofra Palenzuela, V.; López Iturriaga, F.J. La Asimetría Informativa En Los Mercados Financieros: ¿el Hallazgo De Un Nexo De Unión? *An. Estud. Económicos Empresariales* **1996**, *11*, 9–34.
5. Asteriou, D.; Spanos, K. The relationship between financial development and economic growth during the recent crisis: Evidence from the EU. *Financ. Res. Lett.* **2019**, *28*, 238–245. [CrossRef]
6. Palacín-Sánchez, M.-J.; Canto-Cuevas, F.-J.; Di-Pietro, F. Trade credit versus bank credit: A simultaneous analysis in European SMEs. *Small Bus. Econ.* **2018**, *53*, 1079–1096. [CrossRef]
7. Glisovic, J.; Martínez, M. Financiamiento de Pequeñas Empresas: ¿Qué papel Desempeñan las Instituciones Microfinancieras? Available online: https://www.cgap.org/sites/default/files/CGAP-Focus-Note-Financing-Small-Enterprises-What-Role-for-Microfinance-Jul-2012-Spanish.pdf (accessed on 25 July 2020).
8. Feridun, M.; Güngör, H. Climate-related prudential risks in the banking sector: A review of the emerging regulatory and supervisory practices. *Sustainability* **2020**, *12*, 5325. [CrossRef]
9. European Commission. Roadmap: Commission Delegated Regulation on Taxonomy-Related Disclosures by Undertakings Reporting Non-Financial Information. 2020. Available online: https://ec.europa.eu/info/law/better-regulation/have-your-say/initiatives/12440-Commission-Delegated-Regulation-on-taxonomy-alignment-of-undertakings-reporting-non-financial-information (accessed on 30 July 2020).
10. Baumann-Pauly, D.; Wickert, C.; Spence, L.J.; Scherer, A.G. Organizing corporate social responsibility in small and large firms: Size matters. *J. Bus. Ethics* **2013**, *115*, 693–705. [CrossRef]
11. Dincer, C.; Dincer, B. An investigation of Turkish small and medium-sized enterprises online CSR communication. *Soc. Responsib. J.* **2010**, *6*, 197–207. [CrossRef]
12. Torugsa, N.A.; O'Donohue, W.; Hecker, R. Capabilities, proactive CSR and financial performance in SMEs: Empirical evidence from an australian manufacturing industry sector. *J. Bus. Ethics* **2011**, *109*, 483–500. [CrossRef]
13. Nin Ho, F.; Wang, H.-M.D.; Ho-Dac, N.; Vitell, S.J. Nature and relationship between corporate social performance and firm size: A cross-national study. *Soc. Responsib. J.* **2019**, *15*, 258–274. [CrossRef]
14. Ortiz, E.; Marin, S. Global Reporting Initiative (GRI) as recognized guidelines for sustainability reporting by Spanish companies on the IBEX 35: Homogeneity in their framework and added value in the relationship with financial entities. *Intang. Cap.* **2014**, *10*, 855–872. [CrossRef]
15. Albers, C.; Günther, T. Disclose or not disclose: Determinants of social reporting for STOXX Europe 600 firms. *Z. Plan. Unternehm.* **2010**, *21*, 323–347. [CrossRef]
16. Berthelot, S.; Coulmont, M.; Serret, V. Do investors value sustainability reports? A Canadian study. *Corp. Soc. Responsib. Environ. Manag.* **2012**, *19*, 355–363. [CrossRef]

17. Cuganesan, S.; Guthrie, J.; Ward, L. Examining CSR disclosure strategies within the Australian food and beverage industry. *Account. Forum* **2010**, *34*, 169–183. [CrossRef]

18. Etzion, D.; Ferraro, F. The role of analogy in the institutionalization of sustainability reporting. *Organ. Sci.* **2010**, *21*, 1092–1107. [CrossRef]

19. Lopatta, K.; Kaspereit, T. The value relevance of corporate sustainability and sustainability reporting in Europe. *SSRN Electron. J.* **2011**. [CrossRef]

20. Levy, D.L.; Brown, H.S.; De Jong, M. The contested politics of corporate governance. *Bus. Soc.* **2009**, *49*, 88–115. [CrossRef]

21. Lynch, B. An examination of environmental reporting by Australian state government departments. *Account. Forum* **2010**, *34*, 32–45. [CrossRef]

22. Schadewitz, H.J.; Niskala, M. Communication via responsibility reporting and its effect on firm value in Finland. *Corp. Soc. Responsib. Environ. Manag.* **2010**, *17*, 96–106. [CrossRef]

23. González Pérez, M.; Ortiz Martínez, E. Información no financiera y su verificación externa: GRI. *Rev. Responsab. Soc. Empresa* **2017**, *27*, 85–106.

24. Dias, A.; Rodrigues, L.L.; Craig, R.; Neves, M.E.D. Corporate social responsibility disclosure in small and medium-sized entities and large companies. *Soc. Responsib. J.* **2019**, *15*, 137–154. [CrossRef]

25. Ram, M.; Edwards, P.; Gilman, M.; Arrowsmith, J. The dynamics of informality: Employment relations in small firms and the effects of regulatory change. *Work Employ. Soc.* **2001**, *15*, 845–861. [CrossRef]

26. Santos, M.J. CSR in SMEs: Strategies, practices, motivations and obstacles. *Soc. Responsib. J.* **2011**, *7*, 490–508. [CrossRef]

27. Bikefe, G.; Zubairu, U.M.; Araga, S.; Maitala, F.; Ediuku, E.; Anyebe, D. Corporate Social Responsibility (CSR) by small and medium enterprises (SMEs): A systematic review. *Small Bus. Int. Rev.* **2020**, *4*, 16–33. [CrossRef]

28. Griffin, J.J.; Mahon, J.F. The corporate social performance and corporate financial performance debate. *Bus. Soc.* **1997**, *36*, 5–31. [CrossRef]

29. Inoue, Y.; Lee, S. Effects of different dimensions of corporate social responsibility on corporate financial performance in tourism-related industries. *Tour. Manag.* **2011**, *32*, 790–804. [CrossRef]

30. Ioannou, I.; Serafeim, G. What drives corporate social performance? International evidence from social, environmental and governance scores. *J. Int. Bus. Stud.* **2012**, *43*, 834–864. [CrossRef]

31. Khan, C.H.-U.-Z. The effect of corporate governance elements on corporate social responsibility (CSR) reporting. Empirical evidence from private commercial banks of Bangladesh. *Int. J. Law Manag.* **2010**, *52*, 82–109. [CrossRef]

32. Jizi, M.; Salama, A.; Dixon, R.; Stratling, R. Corporate governance and corporate social responsibility disclosure: Evidence from the US banking sector. *J. Bus. Ethics* **2013**, *125*, 601–615. [CrossRef]

33. Gambetta, N.; García-Benau, M.A.; Zorio-Grima, A. Corporate social responsibility and bank risk profile: Evidence from Europe. *Serv. Bus.* **2016**, *11*, 517–542. [CrossRef]

34. Marín, S.; Gras, E.; Ortiz, E. Prudential regulation and financial information in Spanish banks: 1995–2015. *Span. J. Financ. Account. Rev. Española Financ. Contab.* **2019**, *48*, 1–23. [CrossRef]

35. Gallego-Alvarez, I.; Pucheta-Martínez, M.C. Environmental strategy in the global banking industry within the varieties of capitalism approach: The moderating role of gender diversity and board members with specific skills. *Bus. Strat. Environ.* **2020**, *29*, 347–360. [CrossRef]

36. Platonova, E.; Asutay, M.; Dixon, R.; Mohammad, S. The impact of corporate social responsibility disclosure on financial performance: Evidence from the GCC Islamic banking sector. *J. Bus. Ethics* **2016**, *151*, 451–471. [CrossRef]

37. Esteban-Sanchez, P.; De La Cuesta-Gonzalez, M.; Paredes-Gazquez, J.D. Corporate social performance and its relation with corporate financial performance: International evidence in the banking industry. *J. Clean. Prod.* **2017**, *162*, 1102–1110. [CrossRef]

38. Wu, M.-W.; Shen, C.-H.; Chen, T.-H. Application of multi-level matching between financial performance and corporate social responsibility in the banking industry. *Rev. Quant. Financ. Account.* **2016**, *49*, 29–63. [CrossRef]

39. Al-Malkawi, H.-A.N.; Pillai, R. Analyzing financial performance by integrating conventional governance mechanisms into the GCC Islamic banking framework. *Manag. Financ.* **2018**, *44*, 604–623. [CrossRef]

40. Fijalkowska, J.; Zyznarska-Dworczak, B.; Garsztka, P. Corporate social-environmental performance versus financial performance of banks in central and Eastern European Countries. *Sustainability* **2018**, *10*, 772. [CrossRef]

41. Laguir, I.; Marais, M.; El Baz, J.; Stekelorum, R. Reversing the business rationale for environmental commitment in banking: Does financial performance lead to higher environmental performance? *Manag. Decis.* **2018**, *56*, 358–375. [CrossRef]

42. Pérez, A.; Salmones, M.D.M.G.D.L.; Liu, M.T. Maximising business returns to corporate social responsibility communication: An empirical test. *Eur. Bus. Rev.* **2019**, *28*, 275–289. [CrossRef]

43. San-Jose, L.; Retolaza, J.L.; Gutierrez-Goiria, J. Are ethical banks different? a comparative analysis using the radical affinity index. *J. Bus. Ethics* **2011**, *100*, 151–173. [CrossRef]

44. Tse, T. Shareholder and stakeholder theory: After the financial crisis. *Qual. Res. Financ. Mark.* **2011**, *3*, 51–63. [CrossRef]

45. Shoenmaker, D.; Werkhoven, D. *What Is the Appropriate Size of the Banking System?* 2012. No. 28. Available online: https://papers.ssrn.com/sol3/papers.cfm?abstract_id=2158606 (accessed on 25 July 2020).

46. McDonald, L.M.; Rundle-Thiele, S. Corporate social responsibility and bank customer satisfaction: A Research Agenda. *Int. J. Bank Mark.* **2008**, *26*, 170–182. [CrossRef]

47. Goss, A.; Roberts, G.S. The impact of corporate social responsibility on the cost of bank loans. *J. Bank. Financ.* **2011**, *35*, 1794–1810. [CrossRef]

48. European Commission. Consultation Document Review of the Non-Financial Reporting Directive 2020. Available online: https://ec.europa.eu/info/publications/finance-consultations-2020-non-financial-reporting-directive_en (accessed on 10 July 2020).

49. Amor-Esteban, V.; Galindo-Villardón, P.; García-Sánchez, I.-M. A multivariate proposal for a National Corporate Social Responsibility Practices Index (NCSRPI) for international settings. *Soc. Indic. Res.* **2018**, *143*, 525–560. [CrossRef]

50. Ortiz, E.; Clavel, J.G. Índices de revelación de información: Una propuesta de mejora de la metodología. Aplicación a la información sobre recursos humanos incluida en los Informes 20F. *Rev. Española Financ. Contab.* **2006**, *35*, 87–113. [CrossRef]

51. Bakhtiar, M.; Weekes, B. Lexico-semantic effects on word naming in Persian: Does age of acquisition have an effect? *Mem. Cogn.* **2014**, *43*, 298–313. [CrossRef] [PubMed]

52. Marchenko, O.O. A method for automatic construction of ontological knowledge bases. I. Development of a semantic-syntactic model of natural language. *Cybern. Syst. Anal.* **2016**, *52*, 20–29. [CrossRef]

53. D'Northwood, G.; Mundy, J. BP plc 2010—A case of linguistic legitimation? *J. Appl. Account. Res.* **2017**, *18*, 480–495. [CrossRef]

54. Morales, A. Uso de la Familia Léxica de Sovereignty en los Discursos de la Presidencia del Banco Central Europeo 2003–2016. Available online: http://hdl.handle.net/10201/53021 (accessed on 20 May 2020).

55. Madeira, A.B.; Lopes, M.; Giampadi, V.; Silveira, J.A.G. Análise proposicional quantitativa aplicada. Á pesquisa em administrasao. Quantitative propositional analysis as applied to business administration research. Análisis proposicional cuantitativo aplicado a la investigación en administración. *RAE* **2011**, *51*, 396–410.

56. Sohangir, S.; Petty, N.; Wang, D. Financial sentiment lexicon analysis. In Proceedings of the 2018 IEEE 12th International Conference on Semantic Computing (ICSC), Laguna Hills, CA, USA, 31 January–2 February 2018; pp. 286–289. [CrossRef]

57. Martinez, E.O.; Crowther, D. Is disclosure the right way to comply with stakeholders? The Shell case. *Bus. Ethics Eur. Rev.* **2007**, *17*, 13–22. [CrossRef]

58. Nájera-Sánchez, J.-J. A systematic review of sustainable banking through a co-word analysis. *Sustainability* **2019**, *12*, 278. [CrossRef]

59. Figueira Marquezau, L.H.; Seibert, R.M.; Bartz, D.; Gomes Barbosa, M.A.; Wickstrom Alves, T. Análise dos Determinantes do disclosure Verde em Relatórios Anuais de Empresas Listadas na BM&FBOVESPA. *Contab. Gest. Gov. Brasilia* **2015**, *18*, 127–150.

60. Fuoli, M. Assessing social responsibility: A quantitative analysis of Appraisal in BP's and IKEA's social reports. *Discourse Commun.* **2012**, *6*, 55–81. [CrossRef]

61. Miller, C.V.; Tripp, E.R.; Rasco, M.A. A Linguistic Analysis and Comparison of Hong Kong and US Corporate Governance Reports 2010. Available online: https://digitalcommons.wpi.edu/iqp-all/651 (accessed on 5 April 2020).

62. UN Environment. Sustainability Reporting in the Financial Sector. A Governmental Approach 2017. Available online: https://wedocs.unep.org/handle/20.500.11822/17375 (accessed on 26 April 2020).

63. GRI. Empowering Small Business. Recommendations for Policy Makers to Enable Corporate Sustainability Reporting for SMEs 2018. Available online: file:///C:/Users/UM/Downloads/empowering_small_business_policy_recommendations%20(1).pdf (accessed on 22 July 2020).

64. Kaity, M.; Balakrishnan, V. An automatic non-English sentiment lexicon builder using unannotated corpus. *J. Supercomput.* **2019**, *75*, 2243–2268. [CrossRef]

65. Kocoń, J.; Miłkowski, P.; Zaśko-Zielińska, M. Multi-level sentiment analysis of PolEmo 2.0: Extended corpus of multi-domain consumer reviews. In Proceedings of the 23rd Conference on Computational Natural Language Learning, Hong Kong, China, 3–4 November 2019; Association for Computational Linguistics: Stroudsburg, PA, USA, 2019; pp. 980–991.

66. Bonsón, E.; Escobar, T. La Difusión Voluntaria de Información Financiera en internet. Un Análisis Comparativo entre Estados Unidos, Europa del Este y la Unión Europea. *Rev. Española Financ. Contab.* **2004**, *33*, 1063–1101. [CrossRef]

67. Xiao, J.Z.; Yang, H.; Chow, C.W. The determinants and characteristics of voluntary internet-based disclosures by listed Chinese companies. *J. Account. Public Policy* **2004**, *23*, 191–225. [CrossRef]

68. Oyelere, P.; Laswad, F.; Fisher, R. Determinants of internet financial reporting by New Zealand Companies. *J. Int. Financ. Manag. Account.* **2003**, *14*, 26–63. [CrossRef]

69. EFAMA. *Asset Management in Europe. An Overview of the Asset Management Industry*, 11th ed.; EFAMA: Brussels, Belgium, 2019; Available online: https://www.efama.org/Publications/Statistics/Asset%20Management%20Report/AssetManagementReport2019.pdf (accessed on 19 June 2020).

70. Sutton, J. Why There Is Not Role for Storytelling in Your Sustainability Report 2017. Available online: https://sustainablebrands.com/read/marketing-and-comms/why-there-is-no-role-for-storytelling-in-your-sustainability-report (accessed on 27 April 2020).

71. Nazari, J.A.; Hrazdil, K.; Mahmoudian, F. Assessing social and environmental performance through narrative complexity in CSR reports. *J. Contemp. Account. Econ.* **2017**, *13*, 166–178. [CrossRef]

72. Moreno-Ortiz, A.; Fernandez-Cruz, J. Identifying polarity in financial texts for sentiment analysis: A corpus-based approach. *Procedia Soc. Behav. Sci.* **2015**, *198*, 330–338. [CrossRef]

73. Ito, R.; Izumi, K.; Sakaji, H.; Suda, S. Lexicon creation for financial sentiment analysis using network embedding. *J. Math. Financ.* **2017**, *7*, 896–907. [CrossRef]

74. GRI IOE. Small Business Big Impact. SME Sustainability Reporting from Vision to Action. Available online: https://www.ioe-emp.org/fileadmin/ioe_documents/publications/Policy%20Areas/sustainability/EN/20171113_Small_business__big_impact_-_publication_ENGLISH_version.pdf (accessed on 30 July 2020).

75. Kumar, K.; Prakash, A. Examination of sustainability reporting practices in Indian banking sector. *Asian J. Sustain. Soc. Responsib.* **2019**, *4*, 2. [CrossRef]

76. Accountancy Europe. SME Risk Management: Sustainability. Factsheet July 2020. Available online: https://www.accountancyeurope.eu/publications/sme-risk-management-sustainability/ (accessed on 30 July 2020).

77. KPMG. The Road Ahead. The KPMG Survey of Corporate Responsibility Reporting 2017. Available online: https://integratedreporting.org/wp-content/uploads/2017/10/kpmg-survey-of-corporate-responsibility-reporting-2017.pdf (accessed on 20 April 2020).

78. Alonso, A.; Marqués, J.M. *Innovación Financiera para una Economía Sostenible*; Documentos Ocasionales; Banco de España: Madrid, Spain, 2019.

5

Construction and Empirical Research on the Dynamic Provisioning Model of China's Banking Sector under the Macro-Prudential Framework

Xiaofeng Hui [1,*] and Aoran Zhang [2,*]

[1]   School of Economics and Management, Harbin Institute of Technology, Harbin 150001, China
[2]   Antai College of Economics and Management, Shanghai Jiao Tong University, Shanghai 200030, China
*   Correspondence: xfhui@hit.edu.cn (X.H.); zhangaoran@sjtu.edu.cn (A.Z.)

Abstract: Since the international financial crisis in 2008, to achieve the political goal of financial stability, academic circles, financial industry, and regulatory authorities worldwide have deeply reflected on the current economic regulatory theories and policy adjustment tools through introducing the macroprudential policy. The dynamic provisioning system is a counter-cyclical policy tool in the macro-prudential adjustment framework widely used in the world. This paper uses the binary Gaussian Copula function to combine the measurement method of the default distance in the contingent claims analysis method with the risk warning idea based on the Probit model and proposes the contingent claims analysis (CCA)–Probit–Copula dynamic provisioning model based on nine forward-looking indicators. Based on China's actual conditions, this model solves present problems faced by the current dynamic provisioning system in China, such as insufficient historical credit data reserves of commercial banks, excessive reliance on subjective judgments, and conflicts with the current accounting system. Moreover, this model can put forward corresponding counter-cyclical provisioning requirements according to the influence degree of macro-cyclical factors to different commercial banks' own default risk, which not only takes into account the security and liquidity of commercial banks, but also ensures their profitability and competitiveness. Based on the empirical test of historical data from listed commercial banks in China, it proves that the dynamic provisioning requirements proposed in this model can effectively adjust the overall credit scale of the banking industry in counter-cyclical ways, thereby achieving the policy goals of counter-cyclical adjustment under the macro-prudential framework and maintaining the security of China's financial system and the sustainable development of the macroeconomy.

Keywords: dynamic provisioning; macroprudential supervision; counter-cyclical adjustment

1. Introduction

For a long time, maintaining the steady growth and sustainable development of the national economy has been the fundamental purpose of macroeconomic policy adjustment and the common pursuit of macroeconomic theory. Since the 1990s, the financial systems of major countries in the world have shown a trend of rapid development and deepening. The development of finance and the improvement of its functions have greatly reduced the financing costs and information costs of the real economy, making finance increasingly the center of the modern economic system. Meanwhile, financial security and stability have also become new key factors that determine the economy's health and sustainable development. Traditional economic adjustment tools have policy objectives that are mainly price stability, economic growth, full employment, and balance of international payments. The key to policy adjustment is to weigh the output target and the price target. However, the introduction of the political goal of financial stability has created a new conflict: when the macroeconomy is in a period of low inflation and high growth, it will promote the accumulation of potential financial systemic risks instead. According to Tinbergen's rule and policy comparative advantage theory, major countries generally choose to introduce macro-prudential policies as a supplement to traditional economic adjustment policy tools, which has the effect of promoting sustainable and stable economic development.

Before the international financial crisis in 2007, the conventional wisdom in dealing with financial risk was "monetary policy plus micro-prudential regulation". Micro-prudential regulation believes that systemic risk can be prevented by ensuring the safety of individual financial institutions. In fact, micro-prudence does not guarantee the overall safety of the financial system, but promotes the failure and collapse of the financial system to some extent. On the contrary, macro-prudential policies are intended to examine the prevention, remedy, and distribution of responsibility for systemic risks among financial institutions from the top to bottom with a more macro and holistic perspective, so as to achieve the goal of maintaining the stability and security of the financial system through external review and internal regulation. The starting point of macro-prudence can be considered from horizontal and vertical dimensions. From a horizontal perspective, macro-prudential policies focus on risk contagion among financial institutions; from a vertical perspective, macro-prudential policies are mainly aimed at the pro-cyclical problems in the financial system. In China, an economic system dominated by indirect financing, commercial bank credit is the main financing method for the real economy. Moreover, maintaining the continuity of commercial bank credit is the key to ensuring the sustained and stable development of China's economy. However, the cyclical financial crisis and the pro-cyclicality of bank credit operations have made economic entities' inevitable liquidity difficulties, which have intensified the cyclical crisis of the macro economy. Therefore, counter-cyclical credit adjustment is an inevitable requirement for maintaining the sustainable and stable development of China's economy. Besides, the dynamic provisioning requirements discussed in this paper can be used as a macroprudential tool for counter-cyclical credit adjustment.

Under the micro-prudential framework, banks only focus on the changes of their own present level of risk but lack an overall and forward-looking vision, so they often have the phenomenon of pro-cyclical credit operation. Borio, 2003 [1] argued that Basel II did not prevent the accumulation of risks in the entire financial system, but enhanced the pro-cyclical nature of the bank credit market and even the overall economy. Capital adequacy ratio, the core regulatory indicator in Basel II, has helped prompt this phenomenon. On the one hand, when the economy goes up, the risk weighting of the corresponding asset goes down as the market price of collateral goes up. Under the fixed capital adequacy ratio standard, the existing capital adequacy ratio level will be surplus, which will inevitably prompt most financial institutions to expand their balance sheets by increasing liabilities to avoid being punished by the stock market for perceived lack of leverage. On the other hand, when the economy goes down, as the market price of collateral falls, the risk weighting of the corresponding asset increases, tightening the existing capital adequacy ratio level. Because financial regulators typically require financial institutions in crisis to maintain the required capital adequacy level, financial institutions whose capital adequacy ratios are close to standard levels will choose to sell assets and offset their liabilities in order to scale back their balances.

As an important policy tool for macro-prudential counter-cyclical regulation, a dynamic provisioning ratio requires financial institutions to increase capital provision in the stage of economic upturn, improve the minimum leverage ratio of financial institutions, prevent excessive statement expansion, and increase the foresight of potential risks. During downturns, the dynamic provisioning ratio will be lowered accordingly, which improves the buffer of commercial banks to deal with losses, prevents the rapid contraction of the balance sheets of large-scale financial institutions, and avoids the amplification and contagion of systemic risks. Therefore, the dynamic provisioning requirement can be used as a capital buffer mechanism to smooth the financial cycle and is a powerful tool to increase the effectiveness of macro-prudential policies, maintain the security of the financial system, and promote the sustainability of macroeconomics. Thus, the purpose of this paper is to propose a dynamic provisioning model suitable for China's national conditions on the basis of analyzing the limitations of the current dynamic provisioning model in China and to prove the effectiveness of the counter-cyclical adjustment of the model through empirical tests.

2. Literature Review

The regulation of capital adequacy ratio has aggravated the pro-cyclical problem among deposit-taking financial institutions. Kashyap et al., 2004 [2] proposed the time-varying capital requirements to this model: the idea is that banks should tolerate higher bankruptcy risks when they are short of capital and tighter credit supply than in booms, which means that banks in distress should be required to meet lower capital adequacy requirements during economic downturns. This thought coincides with the dynamic capital requirement put forward by the Chinese scholar Liu, 2012 [3]. In 2008, Kashyap et al. 2008 [4] proposed to solve the pro-cyclical problem of capital adequacy ratio by issuing contingent convertibles or reverse convertibles. Such financial instruments usually set a threshold value for the issuer's capital or stock market value. When the reference index falls below this threshold value, these bonds will automatically turn into the issuer's stock, thus achieving the purpose of replenishing capital and reducing liabilities. Samuel, Kashyap et al. 2011 [5] proposed an improved solution for PCA, incorporating limits on the amount of capital into the PCA's regulatory indicators so that we can effectively discourage financial institutions from opting to sell assets rather than replenish capital in the event of economic downturns, a surge in risk, or actual losses.

In general, the above methods are all improvements or supplements to the regulatory indicator of capital adequacy ratio. However, if the capital requirements are not "stratified" and the capital adequacy ratio is solely relied on for counter-cyclical adjustment, the expected target is often not achieved. In addition, the existence of moral hazard will further lead to the deviation of policy results and policy objectives.

As a result, Basel III adopts the method of provision dynamic provisioning to carry out counter-cyclical adjustment. Dynamic provisions require financial institutions to increase capital provisions in the stage of economic upturn to improve the foresight of potential risks, and lower the standard of capital provisions in the stage of economic downturn to increase the buffer against losses and prevent the amplification and contagion of risks.

The existing dynamic provisioning model mainly has two forms: the dynamic provisioning model represented by Spain and based on anticipated loan losses, and the dynamic provisioning model represented by Peru and based on a triggering mechanism. In addition, Mexico et al. 2012 [6] transform operational objects from commercial banks to various types of assets in the application of dynamic provisioning systems, but specific modeling ideas continue with the Spanish or Peruvian model.

Academic circles have undertaken a lot of empirical tests on the policy effectiveness of the counter-cyclical adjustment of the dynamic provision system. The research results of Kanagaretnam, et al., 2005 [7] showed that the loan loss provision and provision operation of commercial banks in the uptrend period was more pro-cyclical compared with the downtrend period. Jin et al., 2013 [8] took 1419 banks from different countries and regions as samples. Their study indicated that banks in Asia were more likely to show pro-cyclicality of loan loss provision in the economic downtrend. Balla et al., 2009 [9] substituted the historical data of commercial banks in the United States from 1993 to 2008 into the Spanish dynamic provision model for simulation testing. It was found that, compared with the current US reserve system for loan provision based on occurred or estimable events, the capital provision required in the crisis stage can be extracted at an earlier time, thus smoothing the income of commercial banks and reducing the pro-cyclical nature of commercial bank credit under the framework of dynamic provision. Martha et al., 2014 [10] analyzed the historical credit data of Colombia's commercial banks and pointed out that the counter-cyclical adjustment effect of the dynamic provision system is mainly achieved in two ways: (i) it is effectively suppressed by the excessive credit expansion of commercial banks in the boom, and the credit expansion is mainly due to excessive competition between commercial banks; (ii) the accumulation of provisions during the economic boom can show a buffer during the recession. Jimenez et al., 2017 [11] used the historical data of the commercial banks in Spain to prove that dynamic provision can effectively smooth the credit cycle. The study believes that the realization of this mechanism is because the cost of loan loss provision during the economic boom is much less than the cost of capital replenishment and macro-policy adjustment in times of crisis, but the study also stated that while implementing the Spanish dynamic provision system, it should be alert to the possibility of regulatory arbitrage. In addition, Santiago et al., 2010 [12], through analyzing historical experiences of Spain, Colombia, and Peru, believed that only in the process of implementing the dynamic provisioning system, taking into account the policy rules and discretionary decisions, can the policy goal of counter-cyclical regulation be effectively achieved. Meanwhile, the transparency between financial institutions and financial regulators is also a key factor to determine the effect of counter-cyclical regulation. Santiago et al., 2013 [13] also believed that, from a theoretical perspective, the dynamic reserve system could also be regarded as a mechanism to correct disaster myopia, herd behavior, information asymmetry, and short-term behavior of bank managers. In fact, the introduction of the dynamic provision system woul improve the bank managers' awareness of credit risks, so as to properly record and recognize credit risks in advance and reduce the pro-cyclicality of credit provisions. Huang et al., 2014 [14] and Gao et al., 2017 [15], Chinese scholars, proved that the introduction of a forward-looking dynamic provisioning system in China would effectively restrain the cyclical economic fluctuations and the pro-cyclical credit behavior by constructing a new Keynes DSGE model with an independent banking sector. Zhang et al., 2004 [16] believed that, in the light of the experience of countries that already have dynamic provisioning systems, such as Spain, the implementation of the dynamic provisioning system can help to smooth out the cyclical fluctuations in the provision for loan losses and help to enhance the stability of the banking system. However, in the process of introducing the dynamic provisioning system into China's banking supervision system, it is necessary to combine with China's national conditions.

Li, 2009 [17] believed that when the current international dynamic provisioning model is introduced into China's macro-prudential supervision system, there are three difficulties: (i) Provision for losses not yet incurred violated the principle of the current accounting standards that provision can only be made for losses that have occurred or that have been conclusively demonstrated to be occurring; (ii) the subjective factors in the current dynamic provisioning process in the world will give an opportunity to artificially smooth the profits; (iii) China's data reserve on indicators such as long-term loan loss rate of commercial Banks cannot support the direct application of the current international model in China.

Specifically, the basic requirements of both dynamic provisioning models are statistical analysis of historical data on commercial bank loans in a full cycle, both in Spain and Peru, where the non-performing loan ratio has experienced a full cycle of surges and falls. However, China's non-performing loan rate data began to be counted in 2004 and has not yet shown completely cyclical characteristics, and since 2008, China's banking sector non-performing loan rate has been at a historically low level and maintained a relatively stable state. Therefore, it is difficult to put forward an effective dynamic provisioning model through the statistical analysis of the historical data of non-performing loans. Because of this, the China Banking Regulatory Commission (CBRC), in reference to the existing international dynamic provisioning model, proposed the current dynamic provisioning model in China [18]. The model is

$$GP = L \times NLR \times (PCR + \delta) - SP \tag{1}$$

GP stands for general provisions made in the current period. L represents all loans in the current period. NLR stands for the historical non-performing loan ratio. PCR stands for loan provision coverage in the current period, with a lower limit of 2.5%. δ is the adjustment factor. SP is a special provision for the current period.

Compared with the dynamic provisioning model implemented in Spain, China's current model is not only based on statistics of historical non-performing loan rates, but also affected by adjustment factor δ when making loan provisioning. The main reason is that China's commercial banks have insufficient historical data reserves for the indicator of non-performing loan ratio, so subjective adjustment factor δ is needed to help achieve the policy goal of counter-cyclical adjustment.

This model considers the problem of insufficient statistics of historical data in China. Therefore, when determining the historical non-performing loan ratio and provision coverage in the corresponding period, it adopts the five-year moving window period to take the average value and solidifies after a complete economic cycle. However, the non-performing loan rate of the country's commercial banking industry has been at a historically low level and remained relatively stable since 2008. Therefore, even if the method of moving windows is adopted, it will still be difficult to make the model have forward-looking effects, and it is difficult to truly achieve the policy goal of macro-prudential counter-cyclical supervision. Additionally, as a key parameter to achieve "dynamic" in this model, the adjustment coefficient does not have an exact method to determine its value. Instead, the adjustment, with a certain degree of subjectivity, is based on macroeconomic indicators, the overall risk level of the banking sector, and the financial index deviation of financial institutions. Through empirical analysis, Chen et al., 2015 [19] and Zhang et al., 2016 [20] have found that the provision for loan losses is widely used in China's commercial banking industry to smooth profits. Bushman et al., 2012 [21] argued that forward-looking provisions based on smoothing profits rather than covering future loan losses would significantly increase the risk level taken by banks. In addition, due to the subjective judgmental factors in the model, time lag will occur in the process of adjusting the dynamic provisioning requirements. As a counter-cyclical adjustment tool, the dynamic provision system places more emphasis on time variability and timeliness. The time inconsistency phenomenon may promote economic fluctuations instead. Moreover, the loan provisioning rate based on the current model completely relies on the historical non-performing loan rate, which is contrary to the current accounting system proposing the principle of loan provision based on real or predictable losses.

In order to solve the problem of subjectivity in the dynamic provisioning model, Li et al., 2008 [22] drew on the idea of the credit rating migration matrix adopted by Moody's and applied the Markov chain prediction theory to construct a forward-looking dynamic provisioning model. Moreover, the defects of the original model that could not cover the macroeconomic cyclical fluctuation factors were corrected. The specific method is to measure the credit risk migration matrix during the economic period and recession period, respectively, and introduce the dynamic weighting, which can be adjusted according to macroeconomic changes to construct a weighted migration matrix to indicate dynamic provisioning. However, this method has some limitations: on the one hand, the determination of dynamic weights in this model requires historical data on the change of non-performing loan rate in the complete economic cycle; on the other hand, when this model is used to analyze the changes of credit risks in bank loans, it does not distinguish the macro cyclical factors from the micro individual factors, but all of them are viewed from the cyclical perspective, which weakens the ability of Banks to resist credit risks to some extent. In addition, Xu et al., 2011 [23] estimated the degree of bank loan default loss and the dynamic law of loan default probability through dynamic random modeling of the return on assets of borrowing enterprises, so as to realize the dynamic and forward-looking provision for loan losses. However, there are two limitations to modeling dynamic provisioning rates in this way: first, the bank's counterparties are not only businesses, but also individuals, peers, and government agencies. In addition, some of the borrowing enterprises are not listed, making it difficult to obtain real and accurate asset return data, so the dynamic provisioning requirements proposed by the model will also be biased. Second, dynamic provisioning requirements are a macro-prudential tool; their role is to inhibit the bank's pro-cyclical operation and offset the financial macro-cyclical changes brought about by the risk. However, taking the return on assets of borrowing enterprises as the dynamic provisioning model indicating variables, the results will be influenced by micro-factors such as the enterprise's own characteristics and business behavior, which makes it difficult to meet the requirements of macro-prudential regulation.

Therefore, proposing a dynamic provisioning model that is suitable for China's financial system and can avoid subjectivity to a certain extent is important to enrich China's macro prudential "toolbox" and achieve the goal of counter cyclical regulation.

3. Methods

3.1. Construction of Dynamic Provisioning Model

This paper usds the contingent claims analysis method (CCA) to measure the risk of default by financial institutions due to bankruptcy (hereinafter referred to as default risk). The model was first applied in papers by Gray et al., 2007 [24] and then further extended by Jobst et al., 2010 [25]. The CCA model is a theoretical model based on financial market data and financial institutions' balance sheets to assess the risk of default and can use current data to calculate the probability of default risk. The model can measure the risk of default of individual institutions from a micro level as well as the systemic risk of the whole system at the macro level.

The CCA model, like the B–S–M option pricing formula, assumes the geometric brown movement of asset price A_t subject to μ_A as drift rate and σ_A as volatility. According to mathematical deduction, the following formula can be obtained.

$$A_t = A_0 exp[(\mu_A - \frac{\sigma_A^2}{2})t + \sigma_A \sqrt{t}\cdot\varepsilon] \tag{2}$$

where, $\varepsilon \sim N(0,1)$.

Merton, 1974 [26] argues that a company's stock E can be considered a call option, while the company's total assets A can be considered as the underlying asset of the call option, and the company's liability B can be considered as the execution price. The maturity date of the liability is determined to be T. If the total assets of the company $A_T > B_T$ at the T moment, the total return of the shareholders of the company is $A_T - B_T$; If the total assets of the company $A_T < B_T$ at the T moment, the total return of the shareholders of the company is 0, and the company is in bankruptcy and default.

Additionally, at maturity T, the probability of default due to the bankruptcy of the target financial institution is

$$P(A_T \le B_T) = P(A_0 \exp[(\mu_A - \frac{\sigma_A^2}{2})T + \sigma_A \sqrt{T}\cdot\varepsilon] \le B_T) = P(\varepsilon \le -DD) = \Phi(-DD) \tag{3}$$

$$DD = \frac{ln(\frac{A_0}{B_T}) + (\mu_A - \frac{\sigma_A^2}{2})T}{\sigma_A \sqrt{T}} \tag{4}$$

It can be found that the DD and the probability of default are inversely variable: the larger the DD, the smaller the probability of default, and the smaller the DD, the greater the probability of default by the institution, which is the one-to-one correspondence. Therefore, DD can be used as an indicator of the risk of default by financial institutions.

Further observation shows that in addition to the time constant T, there are three variables affecting the change of DD: the drift rate of asset return μ_A, the volatility of asset return σ_A, and the ratio of the present value of total assets to the maturity date of liabilities A_0/B_T. In addition, A_0/B_T can represent the leverage ratio of the financial institution to some extent. According to Moody's treatment, the B_T value is the sum of the book value of short-term liabilities and 0.5 times the book value of long-term liabilities, so the B_T value has a one-to-one correspondence with the total debt level. Additionally, the ratio of A_0/B_T will be inversely variable to the leverage of the agency at this stage. For convenience, the variable K is used below to represent A_0/B_T. The above three influencing factors were used to obtain the partial derivative of DD.

$$\frac{\partial DD}{\partial \sigma_A} = -\frac{ln(K) + (\mu_A - \frac{\sigma_A^2}{2})T}{\sigma_A^2 \sqrt{T}} - \sqrt{T} < 0 \tag{5}$$

$$\frac{\partial DD}{\partial \mu_A} = \frac{\sqrt{T}}{\sigma_A} > 0 \tag{6}$$

$$\frac{\partial DD}{\partial K} = \frac{1}{K \cdot \sigma_A \sqrt{T}} > 0 \tag{7}$$

DD is in the same direction as the drift rate of return on assets μ_A, and in the opposite direction as the volatility rate of return on assets σ_A of the financial institution. The variable K is inversely correlated with the leverage ratio of the institution and positively correlated with the DD of the institution.

According to the "risk neutral" idea proposed by Cox et al., 1976 [27], when applying the B–S–M option pricing formula, all risky assets do not require risk compensation. When calculating the default distance DD, most of the relevant studies adopted the idea of "risk neutrality" to replace the return drift rate of assets μ_A with risk-free interest rate r.

Risk-free interest rate r is affected to some extent by cyclical changes in the macro economy. This paper uses the average of the seven-day fixing repo rate to represent the average of the risk-free interest rate in a year, which is usually in the same direction as the year-on-year level of nominal GDP, as shown in Figure 1.

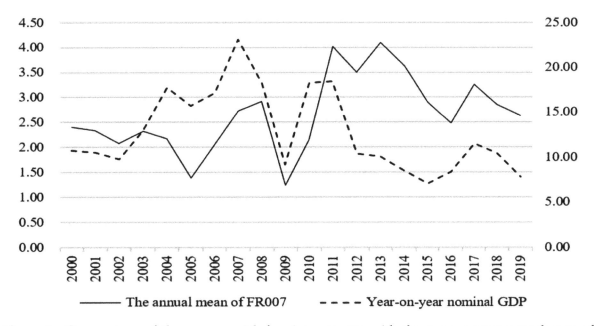

Figure 1. Comparison of the average risk-free interest rate with the year-on-year growth rate of nominal GDP.

This is because the benchmark interest rate level is regulated by monetary policy and is usually equated with the risk-free interest rate, while promoting economic growth and maintaining prices are included in our monetary policy objectives. As one of the common monetary policy rules of central banks, Taylor's Law reflects the influence of these two policy objectives on monetary policy making. It argues that the base rate level is also affected by both the price gap and the output gap, apart from the trend item.

$$r_t = \rho_0 + \beta_{GDP}\left(E_t \Delta GDP_{t+1} - \Delta GDP^*_{t+1}\right) + \beta_\pi\left(E_t \pi_{t+1} - \pi^*_{t+1}\right) \tag{8}$$

ρ_0 represents the trend item. The difference between the expected year-on-year real GDP growth rate and the potential GDP growth rate represents the output gap, and the potential GDP growth rate is obtained from the year-on-year real GDP level processed by the H–P filtering method. The difference between the expected rate of inflation and the target level of monetary policy represents the price gap. The output gap is partly related to the possibility of an expected overheating, and the price gap can be used to measure the level at which expected inflation exceeds policy objectives. When the economy is in an upward cycle, real economic growth rises and is usually accompanied by higher inflation, which is reflected in the increase of output gap and price gap, and leads to the tightening of monetary policy and the rise of benchmark interest rates. Otherwise, it goes down. Therefore, theoretically both β_{GDP} and β_π are positive. In addition, nominal GDP equals the product of the real GDP and GDP deflator, so that the year-on-year growth rate of nominal GDP will also be affected by both real economic growth and inflation level. Therefore, the year-on-year growth level of nominal GDP usually has the same trend as the benchmark interest rate and risk-free interest rate.

According to Sharpe's definition, systemic risk refers to the risk that cannot be eliminated by diversification. Therefore, from a relatively long-term perspective, the volatility of the financial institution's asset return σ_A and the volatility of the market return σ_M show a certain degree of the same trend.

From the above analysis, there is a certain correlation between macro-economic cycle changes and financial cycle changes. During the boom, the return on assets of financial institutions μ_A generally rose, while the level of market volatility σ_M showed a downward trend, which usually promoted the upward trend of the financial cycle. During a recession, the return on assets of financial institutions μ_A generally declines, while the level of market volatility σ_M tends to rise, usually driving down the financial cycle. However, financial cyclical changes and economic changes are not completely synchronized, and systemic risks do not all come from macroeconomic changes. Factors such as international capital flows, asset pricing bubbles, and even shadow banking may trigger systemic risks. At the same time, the excessive correlation of balance sheets between financial institutions and unreasonable internal incentives have amplified this process. As a result, there may also be increased systemic risks and cyclical downwards in finance during boom period. In addition, failures within the financial system may also contribute to and accelerate the surge in systemic risks when the downturn in the economy leads to a systemic increase. Therefore, when discussing the impact factors of default risk of micro-financial institutions from the perspective of "top-down" macro-prudence, we should consider both macroeconomic fluctuations and internal factors of the financial system.

When the financial cycle goes up, the drift rate of asset return μ_A generally rises, and the volatility of asset return σ_A is affected by the level of market volatility σ_M, which also has a downward trend, resulting in an increase in the default distance of financial institutions and a decrease in the risk of default. This reduction in the risk of default is usually reflected in a decrease in the risk weighting of the corresponding assets, resulting in an increase in the level of capital adequacy, at which point most financial institutions usually choose to expand their balance sheets by increasing leverage to maximize the value of the company and shareholders' interests. In the process, financial institutions will create a new combination of leverage and default risk.

$$(K', DD') \in \left\{ (K, DD) \middle| K \leq K \leq K^*, DD \leq DD \leq DD^* \right\} \tag{9}$$

The following relationship exists under the condition of risk-neutral pricing.

$$DD = \frac{ln(K) + (r' - \frac{\sigma_A'^2}{2})T}{\sigma_A' \sqrt{T}} \tag{10}$$

$$DD^* = \frac{ln(K^*) + (r' - \frac{\sigma'^2_A}{2})T}{\sigma'_A \sqrt{T}} \tag{11}$$

K^* and DD^* represent, respectively, the original ratio of A_0/B_T at the time of risk prediction and the correspondingly measured default distance, and $K\prime$, $DD\prime$, $r\prime$, and σ'_A, respectively, represent the A_0/B_T ratio, default distance, risk-free interest rate level, and volatility of asset yield after the upward change in the economy. K represents the A_0/B_T ratio corresponding to the adjustment of the default distance back to the original level when the financial cycle changes upward, which is the lower limit of K'. When the financial cycle changes upward, DD represents the distance to default when the financial cycle changes downward and the corresponding leverage ratio is not adjusted, namely the lower limit of $DD\prime$.

When there is a cyclical downturn in finance, the drift rate of asset return μ_A usually falls generally, while the volatility of asset return σ_A tends to rise, at which time the default distance of financial institutions decreases and the risk of default increases. Usually, the risk weight of corresponding assets rises and the capital adequacy ratio drops. In order to meet the regulatory requirements on capital adequacy ratio and reduce the risk of default, most financial institutions sell risky assets and reduce their leverage ratio. In the process, financial institutions will also create a new combination of leverage and default risk.

$$(K'', DD'') \in \left\{ (K, DD) \middle| K^* \le K \le \overline{K}, DD^* \le DD \le \overline{DD} \right\} \tag{12}$$

Additionally, there is the following relationship:

$$\overline{DD} = \frac{ln(\overline{K}) + (r'' - \frac{\sigma''^2_A}{2})T}{\sigma''_A \sqrt{T}} \tag{13}$$

$$DD^* = \frac{ln(K^*) + (r'' - \frac{\sigma''^2_A}{2})T}{\sigma''_A \sqrt{T}} \tag{14}$$

K^* and DD^* still represent, respectively, the original ratio of A_0/B_T at the time of risk prediction and the correspondingly measured default distance, and K'', DD'', r'', and σ''_A represent the A_0/B_T ratio, default distance, risk-free interest rate level, and volatility of the assets return, respectively, after the downward change in the financial cycle. $\overline{K}$ represents the A_0/B_T ratio corresponding to the adjustment of the default distance back to the original level after the downward change in the economy, which is the upper limit of K''. $\overline{DD}$ represents the distance to default when the financial cycle changes upward and the corresponding leverage ratio is not adjusted, which is the upper limit of DD''.

It should be emphasized that the CCA model cannot accurately calculate the change range of K, or the adjustment range of leverage ratio, but the model can calculate the range that K can float when the economy changes periodically. The boundary of the value of K in the process of financial cyclical changes is exactly the object that needs supervision.

The core of the so-called counter-cyclical adjustment is that when the systemic risk changes, the financial institutions should not only consider the change of their own default risk during the measurement period, but also increase the forward-looking expectation of the cyclical change of systemic risk, and make comprehensive judgment and adjust the leverage accordingly.

The concept of marginal expected shortfall proposed by Acharya et al., 2016 [28] is adopted to measure the expected loss suffered by individual financial institutions when left-tail extreme events occur in the overall financial system.

$$MES^i_\alpha = -\frac{\partial \sum_i y_i E[r_i | R \le -VaR_\alpha]}{\partial y_i} = -E[r_i | R \le -VaR_\alpha] \tag{15}$$

$$R = \sum_i y_i r_i \tag{16}$$

In the formula, MES_α^i represents the expected loss of financial institution i when the left-tail extreme event occurs under the $(1 - \alpha)$ confidence level. R represents the rate of return of the overall financial system. y_i represents the proportion of financial institution i in the overall financial system. r_i represents the rate of return of financial institution i.

The higher the MES_α^i value, the greater the degree of exposure to systemic risk on behalf of financial institutions, and the greater the degree of loss in the event of a systemic crisis. This potential loss increases the risk of default caused by non-individual factors in micro-financial institutions, which is precisely the object of forward-looking dynamic provisioning.

When putting forward dynamic provisioning requirements for micro-financial institutions and weakening pro-cyclical changes of systemic risks, this paper draws on the idea of a crisis early warning mechanism to enable micro-financial institutions to anticipate the cyclical changes of losses suffered by systematic risks, thus reducing the degree of pro-cyclical operations of financial institutions. First, this paper calculates the historical data of quarter MES_α^i of each financial institution and calculates its mean. After that, when the current MES_α^i of the financial institution i is below 3% and, in the next four quarters, the MES_α^i rises above 3%, it is considered that the potential loss of financial institution i due to the influence of systemic risk picks up in the following year, recorded as Event 1. When the MES_α^i of financial institution i is above 5% at the present stage, and the MES_α^i falls below 5% in the next four quarters, it is considered that the possible losses of financial institution i due to the influence of systemic risks fall in the following year, recorded as Event 2. As the main purpose of this operation is to meet the requirement of increasing counter-cyclicality under macro-prudential conditions, the objective of this paper is to measure the probability of a change in the degree of loss of financial institutions by systemic risk. Event 1 is regarded as a representative event of the pick-up of the loss degree, while Event 2 is regarded as a representative event of the decline of the loss degree. The reason for event setting is detailed in Appendix A.

In this paper, the binary Probit model is used to predict the probability of Event 1 and Event 2 appearing, respectively. The idea of the Logit/Probit model was first proposed by Frankel et al., 1996 [29], namely the FR model. In their paper, they analyzed the factors that caused the currency crisis in developing countries. It is most reasonable to choose quarterly as the frequency of data extraction. This is because, if monthly data is used, when predicting the probability of loss change in the next year, it is equivalent to looking forward 12 units of time. The forecasting period is relatively long, reducing the accuracy of the forecast. If the annual data are used for analysis, there will be few historical data, and the regression results will not be representative. This paper selects the Probit model to build an early warning mechanism, because the Probit model and the default distance in the CCA model are based on the standard normal distribution, which reflects a certain degree of "compatibility". This is conducive to introducing the Probit model into the traditional CCA model to modify, and finally put forward, the dynamic provisioning model.

When analyzing the probability of the MES value of financial institutions to pick up, this paper constructs the dummy variable Y_1 and stipulates

$$\begin{aligned} &Y_1 = 1, \ MES_t \leq 3\% \,, \exists MES_j \geq 3\%, t+1 \leq j \leq t+4 \\ &Y_1 = 0, \ \text{else} \end{aligned} \tag{17}$$

MES_t represents the MES_α^i value of the financial institution i in the t period, representing the expected loss level of financial institution i at the $1 - \alpha$ confidence level when a left-tail extreme event occurs in the financial system.

Set the dummy variable $n.e.d_1$ that satisfies the normal distribution, and set a threshold $n.e.d_1^*$. Let A be linearly dependent on the explanatory variable. Assume that when the dummy variable exceeds the threshold, $Y_1 = 1$. Establish regression model

$$n.e.d_1 = \beta_0 + \sum \beta_s \cdot I_s \tag{18}$$

I_s stands for the selected forward-looking indicators.

The probability of $n.e.d_1^* \leq n.e.d_1$ can be calculated by the standard normal cumulative distribution function.

$$P_L^i = P(Y_1 = 1|\Omega) = P\big(n.e.d_1^* \leq n.e.d_1\big) = \Phi\Big(\beta_0 + \sum \beta_s I_s\Big) \tag{19}$$

P_L^i is the probability of Event 1.

Similarly, when analyzing the probability of the MES value of financial institutions to decline, this paper constructs the dummy variable Y_2 and stipulates

$$\begin{aligned}
&Y_2 = 1, \ MES_t \geq 5\% \ \exists MES_j \leq 5\%, t+1 \leq j \leq t+4 \\
&Y_2 = 0, \ \text{else}
\end{aligned} \tag{20}$$

Set the dummy variable $n.e.d_2$ that satisfies the normal distribution, establish the threshold value $n.e.d_2^*$, and establish the regression model.

$$n.e.d_2 = \beta_0' + \sum \beta_s' \cdot I_s \tag{21}$$

When $n.e.d_2^* \leq n.e.d_2$, $Y_2 = 1$. Calculate the probability

$$P_S^i = P(Y_2 = 1|\Omega) = P\big(n.e.d_2^* \leq n.e.d_2\big) = \Phi\Big(\beta_0' + \sum \beta_s' \cdot I_s\Big) \tag{22}$$

P_S^i is the probability of Event 2.

The business activities of financial institutions, especially the credit operations of commercial banks, have pro-cyclical characteristics. The reason is that when financial institutions measure their own bankruptcy risks, they often start from the current economic environment and ignore the cyclical changes in systemic risks that will occur in the future. This reflects the short-sightedness of financial institutions, which leads to the phenomenon of pro-cyclical adjustment of financial institutions' balance sheets. Therefore, the premise of constructing a dynamic provisioning model suitable for China's commercial banking industry is to propose a modified CCA model with a forward-looking mechanism, which can consider the possibility of bankruptcy events in the future when the loss degree caused by systemic risk changes in the future of commercial banks.

$$\Phi(-MDD_s) \equiv P(A_T \leq B_T|Y_s = 1) = \frac{F(-DD, n.e.d_s)}{\Phi(n.e.d_s)} \tag{23}$$

MDD_s are defined as the modified default distance, used to reflect changes in the default risk of financial institutions under the condition of forward-looking future systemic risk changes. $F(\cdot, \cdot)$ represents the joint cumulative distribution function. $s = 1, 2$.

As the theoretical analysis above can determine that the default distance DD and the dummy variable $n.e.d_s$ both meet the standard normal distribution, the binary Gaussian Copula function should be introduced for the calculation of their joint cumulative distribution.

$$\begin{aligned}
F(-DD, n.e.d_s) &= C(U, V) \\
&= \int_{-\infty}^{\Phi^{-1}(U)} \int_{-\infty}^{\Phi^{-1}(V)} \frac{1}{2\pi \sqrt{1-\rho^2}} exp\big(-\frac{\delta^2 - 2\rho\delta\eta + \eta^2}{2(1-\rho^2)}\big) d\delta d\eta
\end{aligned} \tag{24}$$

$$U = \Phi(-DD)$$

$$V = \Phi(n.e.d_s)$$

$\Phi^{-1}(\cdot)$ represents the inverse function of the standard normal cumulative distribution. ρ represents the correlation between random variables.

Considering the future rise and fall of the systemic risk level, the upper and lower limits of the MDD value are determined, respectively. When the DD value is higher than the historical average, MDD takes the lower limit. When the DD value is lower than the historical average, MDD takes the upper limit.

In the modified CCA model, it can be found that in addition to measuring their own default risk based on current indicators, financial institutions also consider the possibility of changes in their own default risk due to cyclical changes in systemic risks in the next year. It has narrowed the room for adjustment of the leverage ratio of commercial banks, thus achieving the goal of increasing forward-looking and counter-cyclical regulation.

The counter-cyclical regulation effect of the modified CCA model on the financial system is realized by extracting dynamic provisions. In the research of applying the CCA model, there are two mainstream ways to determine the value of B_T. One is the treatment method of Moody's, and the other is directly expressed by the level of book total liabilities. However, a large number of existing research conclusions indicate that both calculation results are almost the same. Therefore, this paper adopts Moody's method in calculating the default distance, that is, the sum of the book value of short-term liabilities and 0.5 times the book value of long-term liabilities to represent B_T. Assuming that the proportion of long-term liabilities of financial institution i in total liabilities is v, the relationship between the book value of total liabilities B and B_T is:

$$B_T = B \cdot (1 - 0.5v) \tag{25}$$

Then the K value in the modified CCA model has a one-to-one correspondence with the leverage ratio of financial institutions:

$$L = \frac{K(1 - 0.5v)}{K(1 - 0.5v) - 1} \tag{26}$$

As the K value and the leverage ratio L have a reverse relationship, the limits of the leverage ratio adjustment can be judged in the process of changes in the default risk of financial institutions.

The requirement of the dynamic provisioning ratio (DPR) of financial institutions is the difference between the leverage ratio obtained by the modified CCA model and the original CCA model. This is because loan provision is regarded as an expense in accounting, decreasing "undistributed profit" and included in the "asset impairment provision" account. According to the requirements of Basel III to calculate the leverage ratio of commercial banks using Tier 1 capital, when the actual level of assets and liabilities remains unchanged, the higher the dynamic provisioning ratio is, the lower the calculated leverage ratio will be. On the contrary, the lower the dynamic provisioning ratio, the higher the calculated leverage ratio. Therefore, when the financial cycle goes up, by increasing the provisioning ratio, the leverage ratio of financial institutions can be reduced, and pro-cyclical balance sheet expansion can be suppressed; when the financial cycle goes down, by reducing the provisioning ratio, it can increase the level of leverage of financial institutions and curb pro-cyclical balance sheet reduction behavior. The dynamic provisioning model constructed in this paper is designed to withdraw loss provisions for the overall assets of commercial banks. The advantage of this design is that it can not only make commercial banks subject to the counter-cyclical adjustment of the dynamic provisioning rate during credit operations, to a certain extent, but also prevent the phenomenon of shadow credit arising from commercial banks' evasion of supervision.

$$DPR = L_1 - L_2 = \frac{K_1(1 - 0.5v) - 1}{K_1(1 - 0.5v)} - \frac{K_2(1 - 0.5v) - 1}{K_2(1 - 0.5v)} = \frac{K_2^{-1} - K_1^{-1}}{1 - 0.5v} \tag{27}$$

$$K_1 = \exp[DD^* \cdot \sigma_A \sqrt{T} - (r - \frac{\sigma_A^2}{2})T]$$

$$K_2 = \exp[MDD_s^* \cdot \sigma_A \sqrt{T} - (r - \frac{\sigma_A^2}{2})T]$$

DD^* and MDD_s^*, respectively, represent the default distance and modified default distance of the measure, and L_1 and L_2, respectively, represent the leverage adjustment limits calculated by the CCA model and modified CCA model.

When the default distance is lower than the historical average, the DPR value is positive, which means extracting dynamic provisions and restraining the tendency of excessive leverage of financial institutions, that is, preventing the accumulation of potential risks in the upward stage of the financial cycle. When the default distance is higher than the historical average, the DPR value is negative, which means releasing dynamic provisions, preventing large-scale risk aversion of financial institutions, and maintaining the security of the financial system in the downward phase of the financial cycle. From a horizontal perspective, the extraction of the dynamic provisioning rate is related to the degree to which financial institutions are impacted by systemic risks. From a vertical perspective, the dynamic provisioning rate is related to the level of systemic risk and changes in macroeconomic indicators. The model constructed in this paper is dynamic in both horizontal and vertical dimensions and makes up for the shortcoming of the original dynamic provisioning model, which is still pro-cyclical to some extent.

Compared with the traditional dynamic provision model, the dynamic provisioning model constructed in this paper has achieved the following five improvements:

- The model is based on multi-factor indicators, which is helpful to solve the problem of insufficient data reserves when only the historical credit data of commercial banks are used for dynamic provision adjustment.
- The dynamic provisioning rate calculated in this paper is a supplementary provisioning rate that has a corrective effect on the micro-prudential loan provisioning rate based on a five-tier classification method, so it does not cover up the real risk situation of commercial banks in the current period and resolves the conflict with the current accounting system.
- The model excludes subjective factors, so as to avoid the provision behavior of commercial banks based solely on smoothing profits rather than resisting risks.
- The model has different requirements for dynamic provision of different commercial banks, avoiding a one-size-fits-all regulatory model. While maintaining the safety of commercial banks, it also takes into account competitiveness and profitability.
- The model is designed to set aside provisions for the whole assets of commercial banks. The advantage of this design is that it can not only make the credit operation of commercial banks subject to the counter-cyclical regulation through extracting dynamic provisions, but also prevent the phenomenon of regulatory arbitrage of commercial banks and distortion of resource allocation to a certain extent.

3.2. Selection of Forward-Looking Indicators

According to the theoretical analysis above, it can be seen from formula (4) that when the leverage ratio of commercial banks remains unchanged, the default risk of commercial banks is influenced by external factors through two channels: volatility of assets and interest rate. Based on previous research results (Behn et al., 2013 [30]; Detken et al., 2014 [31]; Shen Yue et al., 2008 [32]; Ma Jun et al., 2019 [33]), combined with the theoretical analysis in Section 3.1, this paper selects macroeconomic and financial credit indicators. This paper foresees the changes in the default risk of commercial banks from nine aspects: output gap, inflation, unemployment, credit, foreign debt, foreign exchange reserves, foreign trade balance, credit, the stock market, and the real estate market, which enhances the risk prediction capabilities of commercial banks and achieves the policy objectives of counter-cyclical adjustment of credit. The specific index setting method is shown in Table 1.

Table 1. Setting method of forward-looking indicators.

Indicator (Quarterly)	Abbreviation	Setting Method
Output gap	OG	The difference between real GDP year-on-year growth rate and potential GDP year-on-year growth rate
Inflation	I	Cumulative year-on-year GDP deflator
Unemployment rate	UR	Urban unemployment year-on-year growth rate
Foreign debt	FD	The ratio of quarterly increase in foreign debt balance to nominal GDP
Foreign exchange reserves	FER	The ratio of quarterly increase in foreign exchange reserves to nominal GDP
Foreign trade balance	FTB	The ratio of quarterly increase in current account balance to nominal GDP
Credit	C	Domestic non-financial sector credit year-on-year growth rate
Stock market	SM	The ratio of quarterly increase in total market value of A-shares to nominal GDP
Real estate market	REM	Cumulative new construction site area year-on-year growth rate

The risk level of commercial banks is periodically affected by the macroeconomic output level. Meanwhile, the change of macroeconomic output level will also cause the monetary policy to adjust accordingly, and the adjustment of monetary policy will weaken or even reverse the impact of the cyclical change of macroeconomic output level on the risk level of commercial banks. Therefore, the effect of GDP change on bank default risk in the above two ways should be discussed separately when establishing forward-looking dynamic provisioning indicators. By formula (13), it can be seen that the effect of macroeconomic output on monetary policy is achieved through the expected output gap. Under the conditions of adaptive expectations, the policy makers' judgment on the expected output gap will be largely affected by the current output gap, so this paper selects the current output gap as an indicator to measure the impact of the total output level on the default risk of commercial banks through the transmission of monetary policy. The value of the output gap is equal to the difference between the actual GDP year-on-year growth rate and the potential GDP year-on-year growth rate. The potential GDP year-on-year growth rate is obtained by H–P filtering the actual GDP year-on-year growth rate.

An unemployment indicator to measure the cyclical changes in economic production was chosen. Due to the existence of a natural unemployment rate, the rise of the unemployment rate indicates that the macro economy tends to be depressed, while the decline of the unemployment rate indicates that the macro economy tends to be overheated. As China has long adopted the registered unemployment rate instead of the survey unemployment rate, the statistical unemployment rate is often difficult to measure the accurate unemployment situation in China. The urban unemployment rate is obtained through the census of urban permanent residents, which is more reliable. Therefore, this paper chooses the index of urban unemployment year-on-year growth rate to represent the unemployment situation in China.

In order to meet the quarterly statistical requirements of the forward-looking indicators of the dynamic provisioning model constructed in this paper, the cumulative year-on-year GDP deflator is selected to represent the level of inflation. The expected inflation target announced by China is based on the CPI, and the statistical calibers of the CPI and the GDP deflator are different. Additionally, the expected inflation target is relatively stable. Therefore, this paper does not calculate the inflation gap, but directly uses the current GDP deflator to measure the impact of inflation level on default risk of commercial banks.

The purpose of choosing the three indicators of foreign debt, foreign exchange reserves, and foreign trade balance is to measure the impact of external economic factors on the default risk of Chinese commercial banks. As the three indicators of foreign debt, foreign exchange reserve, and current account balance are calculated in USD, the quarter-end value of the USD–CNY reference rate is used to calculate the ratio of current increment to nominal GDP.

In order to exclude the influence of seasonal credit changes, this paper chooses the year-on-year growth rate of domestic non-financial sector credit to represent the change of China's credit scale. At the same time, due to the pro-cyclical changes in the prices of collateral and pledges, which promoted the pro-cyclical operation of bank credit, this paper selects two indicators, the total market value of A-shares and cumulative new construction site area year-on-year growth rate, to forecast the default risk of commercial banks, which will strengthen the counter-cyclicality of commercial bank credit. It is worth emphasizing that the year-on-year growth rate of new construction area can better represent the real estate market. During the boom period, due to the active inventory replenishment operations of real estate companies, the year-on-year growth rate of new construction site area increased; during the downturn, because of the active destocking operations of real estate companies, the year-on-year growth rate of new construction site area decreased.

This paper defines the three indicators of C, SM, and REM as credit forward-looking indicators, and other indicators as economic cyclical indicators. The former reflect the correlation between financial sub-markets, while the latter reflect the impact of cyclical changes in macroeconomic indicators on the financial system.

4. Empirical Analysis

4.1. Study Data

This paper selected 14 listed commercial banks in China, all of which have completed the A-share listing before 2008. Through the Wind database, this paper obtained the data related to the total liabilities, total assets, and the proportion of long-term liabilities disclosed in the annual reports of these 14 commercial Banks from 2007 to 2019, and regarded them as the assets and liabilities situation at the beginning of the next year. Additionally, according to formula (25), the corresponding execution price B_T in the CCA model was calculated. In order to correspond with the data disclosed in the annual report, the year-end total market value of common shares of each bank under the CSRC algorithm was obtained through the Wind database, which was used as the total market value at the beginning of next year in turn. In this paper, the seven-day fixed repo rate from 2008 to 2019 was selected as the risk-free interest rate of the corresponding year. This paper assumed that when commercial banks make default risk prediction at the beginning of the year, the beginning level of the seven-day fixed repo rate used in the calculation process represents the risk-free interest rate of the whole year and that the annual volatility of ROA of commercial banks in this year remains the level of the annual volatility in the previous year.

When calculating volatility of ROA, this paper first used the weekly closing price of common shares of each bank in the secondary market to calculate the volatility of logarithmic return and converted it into the corresponding annual volatility. The reason why weekly closing price was chosen to calculate volatility is that after one week of price adjustment, weekly closing price can more reasonably show market information. Therefore, this paper argues that the volatility calculated by weekly closing price can more accurately reflect the risk level of the corresponding stock. The relationship between annual volatility σ_E and weekly volatility σ is

$$\sigma_E = \sqrt{52}\sigma \tag{28}$$

$$\sigma = \sqrt{\frac{1}{n-1}\cdot\sum_{t=1}^{n}(u_t - u)^2} \tag{29}$$

$$u_t = ln\frac{P_t}{P_{t-1}} \tag{30}$$

P_t represents the closing price of the stock in week t. P_{t-1} represents the closing price of the stock in week $t-1$. u_t represents the logarithmic rate of return in week t. u represents the annual average of the logarithmic rate of return. n represents the number of trading weeks in a year. It was supposed that the stock price follows logarithmic normal distribution.

Then, formula (31) and the B–S–M option pricing formula were iteratively calculated to output the volatility of ROA under the condition that the error is less than 0.0001.

$$\sigma_E = \frac{\Phi(d_1)\cdot A_0}{E_0}\cdot\sigma_A \tag{31}$$

σ_E represents the volatility of ROE. σ_A represents the volatility of ROA. A_0 represents total assets of listed commercial banks at the beginning of the year. E_0 represents the total market value of the stocks of listed banks at the beginning of the year.

The B–S–M option pricing formula is,

$$E_0 = A_0\Phi(d_1) - B_T e^{-rT}\Phi(d_2) \tag{32}$$

where r represents the risk-free interest rate. The value of T is 1, which represents unit time. B_T represents the total liabilities of listed banks at the end of the year.

As the above 14 banks all completed the listing before October 2007, this paper used the Wind database to obtain the daily closing price and the total market value of the 14 banks from 9 October 2007 to 31 December 2019. The day-on-day growth rate of Shenwan Bank index was taken as the overall stock return rate of the banking industry, and the tail expected losses of each listed commercial bank from the fourth quarter of 2007 to the fourth quarter of 2019 were calculated, respectively, under the 95% confidence level according to the method shown in formula (15). The forward-looking indicators for the corresponding quarter were obtained. Descriptive statistics are shown in Table 2.

4.2. Regression Results

In this paper, according to the Probit regression model proposed in Section 3.1, the probability of the occurrence of Event 1 and Event 2 was regressed, respectively, and the corresponding parameters were estimated. The heteroscedasticity of random terms is a common phenomenon in the regression of binary discrete models. Therefore, this paper adopted the White correction of robust standard error to heteroscedasticity. In addition, each explanatory variable had a certain theoretical correlation. In order to prevent the existence of multicollinearity, this paper used AIC and SC as the basis and adopted the stepwise regression method. The criterion is to increase the explanatory variable in the model if the AIC value or SC value can be reduced. The regression results are shown in Tables 3 and 4.

4.3. Discussion

Through the regression analysis of Event 1 and Event 2, it can be found that the larger the output gap in the current period, the more generally inhibiting the effect on the default risk of the commercial banking industry. Theoretically, this is because the policy makers' judgment on the expected output gap is a weighted average of the historical number of the indicator under the conditions of adaptive expectations. Additionally, the closer the time is, the greater the weight will be applied to the judgment. Therefore, the expected output gap will largely depend on the current output gap level. When the current output gap is large, monetary policy makers will expect that the future economy will have a tendency to overheat, and therefore will raise the level of risk-free interest rates to drive the overall interest rate level upward. According to formula (4), the increase in interest rates will increase the default distance, that is, the default risk of commercial banks has a downward trend. The increase in interest rates will reduce the duration of commercial banks' credit assets, shorten the period required to recover the principal, and reduce the bank's default risk accordingly.

The cumulative year-on-year GDP deflator is significantly negatively correlated with the occurrence probability of Event 1. It can be understood that when the loss of financial institutions from systemic risks is at a historically low level, the higher the level of inflation, the less likely the loss will rise in the next year. This is because the level of systemic risk is low and credit activities generally tend to expand under the upward phase of the financial cycle. The expansion of credit is one of the manifestations of loose monetary policy. Yi et al., 2002 [34] believe that the expansion of monetary policy will cause the stock market to rise before the inflation level in the short term, and the subsequent monetary policy tightening brought by the inflation would bring back the excessively rising stock market in the early stage. It can be seen that when the level of systemic risk is low, the increase in inflation actually inhibits the overheating of the stock market, thereby inhibiting the blind credit expansion that occurred during the overheating stage of the stock market, maintaining the credit quality of commercial banks, and preventing the risk from rising due to the future fall of the stock market. The cumulative year-on-year GDP deflator is also significantly negatively correlated with the occurrence probability of Event 2. It can be understood that when the loss of financial institutions from systemic risks is at a historically high level, the higher the inflation level, the less likely the loss will fall. This is because the level of systemic risk is high, and credit activities generally shrink during the downward phase of the financial cycle. At this time, the tight monetary policy brought by high inflation further suppressed the price of assets in the market, which prompts financial institutions to further sell assets and increases the systemic risk and the volatility of ROA of micro-financial institutions.

Table 2. Descriptive statistics.

Indicators	Mean (%)	Maximum (%)	Minimum (%)	Median (%)	Standard Deviation (%)
OG	−0.0646	2.6092	−4.4480	−0.1800	1.2016
I	3.5862	9.2100	−0.9800	3.1800	3.0763
UR	1.3456	10.9100	−2.0100	0.5500	2.8118
C	16.1958	33.1500	10.1900	15.1400	5.2204
FD	0.0160	0.2900	−0.0500	0.0100	0.0471
FER	−0.0307	0.0600	−0.1700	−0.0200	0.0498
FTB	0.0309	0.1200	−0.0100	0.0200	0.0280
SM	0.0269	1.0600	−1.3100	0.0100	0.4100
REM	8.0788	34.1000	−17.2744	7.4000	11.0717
$MES_{5\%}(BOB)$	2.8567	7.6825	0.2424	2.6778	1.6909
$MES_{5\%}(ICBC)$	2.3188	6.3178	0.4141	1.8245	1.6017
$MES_{5\%}(HXB)$	3.4414	9.0823	0.6441	3.0618	2.0274
$MES_{5\%}(CCB)$	2.5160	7.5438	−1.1957	2.3547	1.8034
$MES_{5\%}(BCM)$	3.1825	8.8084	0.3155	2.8477	2.0020
$MES_{5\%}(CMBC)$	3.0042	7.5143	0.8844	2.4681	1.7294
$MES_{5\%}(NJCB)$	3.3603	9.8108	0.6306	2.8801	2.0746
$MES_{5\%}(NBBANK)$	3.5824	8.3472	1.1519	3.3139	1.8716
$MES_{5\%}(SPABANK)$	3.6243	7.8368	0.0000	3.1213	2.0302
$MES_{5\%}(SPDB)$	3.4216	8.2442	0.8305	2.7384	1.8345
$MES_{5\%}(CIB)$	3.4579	7.8659	0.7896	3.0855	1.9586
$MES_{5\%}(CMB)$	3.2992	9.4372	0.8803	2.8517	1.7329
$MES_{5\%}(BOC)$	2.1903	6.5244	0.1761	1.7219	1.4162
$MES_{5\%}(CITIC)$	3.4881	7.4035	0.8184	3.2361	1.8095
DD(BOB)	0.9203	1.7598	0.3859	0.7131	0.5080
DD(ICBC)	1.0059	1.6012	0.5011	0.8989	0.4069
DD(HXB)	0.6915	1.5740	0.1645	0.5097	0.4353
DD(CCB)	0.8437	1.3817	0.4464	0.7773	0.2990
DD(BCM)	0.8511	1.5797	0.2693	0.8324	0.4449
DD(CMBC)	0.7901	1.5887	0.2977	0.7179	0.4198
DD(NJCB)	0.7086	1.1121	0.3419	0.7307	0.2345
DD(NBBANK)	0.6362	1.0126	0.3022	0.6199	0.2449
DD(SPABANK)	0.5333	1.2552	0.0627	0.5279	0.3037
DD(SPDB)	0.7035	1.3419	−0.2586	0.6655	0.4588
DD(CIB)	0.6777	1.4472	0.0034	0.5734	0.4535
DD(CMB)	0.6393	1.0232	0.1790	0.6745	0.2182
DD(BOC)	1.0909	1.7820	0.3374	1.1328	0.4348
DD(CITIC)	0.6415	1.1214	0.2089	0.6202	0.2989

Table 3. Regression results on the probability of Event 1.

Banks	c	OG	I	UR	C	FD	FER	FTB	SM	REM
BOB	−1.009	−0.989 ** (0.017)	−0.446 ** (0.018)	—	—	—	—	—	1.545 ** (0.025)	0.053 * (0.063)
ICBC	−0.916	−0.364 * (0.080)	—	—	—	—	—	—	—	0.043 ** (0.039)
HXB	0.055	—	—	−0.281 ** (0.010)	—	—	—	—	0.978 ** (0.042)	—
CCB	2.832	—	−0.370 *** (0.003)	—	−0.169 *** (0.008)	—	−19.971 *** (0.008)	—	—	—
BCM	6.423	−1.652 *** (0.005)	—	−0.326 * (0.063)	−0.450 *** (0.002)	—	—	−21.770 ** (0.038)	—	0.049 * (0.081)
CMBC	1.631	−0.862 ** (0.027)	—	−0.445 ** (0.017)	−0.106 * (0.073)	—	—	—	1.670 ** (0.013)	—
NJCB	0.768	—	−0.206 ** (0.010)	−0.302 ** (0.010)	—	—	—	—	—	—
NBBANK	3.937	−0.794 ** (0.013)	—	—	−0.271 *** (0.004)	—	—	−28.101 *** (0.009)	—	0.063 ** (0.020)
SPABANK	2.187	−0.853 *** (0.002)	—	—	−0.216 *** (0.000)	—	—	—	1.764 ** (0.010)	0.095 *** (0.002)
SPDB	−0.308	—	−0.210 * (0.055)	—	—	—	—	—	—	—
CIB	3.410	−0.811 * (0.068)	—	−0.286 * (0.069)	−0.267 ** (0.020)	—	—	—	—	0.046 * (0.053)
CMB	0.566	—	−0.272 *** (0.003)	−0.336 * (0.052)	—	—	—	—	—	—
BOC	1.871	—	−0.301 *** (0.007)	—	−0.133 ** (0.038)	—	−17.849 ** (0.011)	—	—	—
CITIC	2.673	—	−0.147 * (0.057)	—	−0.183 *** (0.006)	—	—	—	—	0.051 ** (0.018)

***, **, * indicate significance at the 0.01, 0.05, and 0.10 level, respectively.

Table 4. Regression results on the probability of Event 2.

Banks	c	OG	I	UR	C	FD	FER	FTB	SM	REM
BOB	−1.041	0.525 * (0.053)	—	—	—	—	−12.146 * (0.082)	—	—	−0.070 * (0.090)
ICBC	−0.512	—	—	—	−0.10973 ** (0.048)	—	−18.604 ** (0.039)	—	—	—
HXB	−1.363	—	—	—	—	—	—	17.058 ** (0.018)	—	—
CCB	−1.740	—	−0.137 * (0.098)	—	—	—	—	18.986 ** (0.017)	−1.586 ** (0.050)	—
BCM	17.039	—	—	40.511 *** (0.000)	−18.374 *** (0.000)	−139.812 *** (0.000)	−125.262 *** (0.000)	4640.601 *** (0.000)	—	−6.800 *** (0.000)
CMBC	15.192	—	—	—	2.146 ** (0.023)	−1.518 ** (0.014)	−116.758 *** (0.009)	—	—	−0.252 ** (0.015)
NJCB	−0.455	1.212 *** (0.002)	−0.379 ** (0.012)	—	—	−53.973 *** (0.007)	−18.660 * (0.074)	27.735 ** (0.014)	−2.464 ** (0.023)	—
NBBANK	−1.235	—	−0.289 *** (0.005)	—	—	—	—	38.942 *** (0.000)	−2.147 *** (0.001)	—
SPABANK	−1.335	—	—	—	—	—	—	20.222 *** (0.000)	−1.474 ** (0.024)	—
SPDB	−1.756	—	—	—	0.173 ** (0.011)	—	—	18.484 ** (0.015)	—	—
CIB	−1.705	—	—	—	0.173 ** (0.011)	—	—	18.484 ** (0.015)	—	—
CMB	−1.591	—	—	—	48.593 *** (0.000)	−20.831 *** (0.000)	−107.995 *** (0.000)	5558.682 *** (0.000)	—	−6.903 *** (0.000)
BOC	0.255	—	—	—	−0.1296 ** (0.014)	−12.846 ** (0.035)	—	—	—	—
CITIC	1.038	0.451 ** (0.019)	−0.231 * (0.072)	—	−0.125 * (0.072)	—	−15.914 * (0.099)	17.250 ** (0.041)	—	—

***, **, * indicate significance at the 0.01, 0.05, and 0.10 level, respectively.

The year-on-year growth rate of urban unemployment has a significant negative correlation with the probability of Event 1 and a significant positive correlation with the probability of Event 2. This indicates that no matter whether the losses of commercial banks from systemic risks are at a historical high or low level at the present stage, the lower the level of unemployment, the more likely commercial banks will encounter default events triggered by systemic risks in the next year. Conversely, the higher the level of unemployment, the lower the probability that commercial banks will default in the next year. This is because the fluctuation of the unemployment level represents the deviation of the actual unemployment rate from the natural unemployment rate. When the unemployment level is lower, it indicates that the current macro economy has a tendency to overheat, and when the unemployment level is higher, it indicates that the current macro economy is more depressed. As the macro economy is characterized by cyclical changes, commercial banks should put forward higher provision requirements when the level of unemployment is lower, so as to prevent a surge in non-performing loans of commercial banks and an increase in their own default risk due to future economic recessions. In contrast, when the unemployment level is higher, commercial banks should reduce their provision requirements accordingly, so as to adapt to the future economic recovery. It can be seen that the dynamic provisioning model constructed in this article realizes the prospect of cyclical fluctuations in the macro economy due to the inclusion of the unemployment indicator.

Compared with China's current dynamic provisioning model, the model proposed in this paper introduces three forward-looking indicators, the output gap, the cumulative year-on-year GDP deflator, and the year-on-year growth rate of urban unemployment, which make the model more sensitive to fluctuations in macroeconomic cycles while taking into account the credit cycle.

The domestic non-financial sector credit year-on-year growth rate has a significant negative correlation with the occurrence probability of events 1 and 2. When the financial cycle is downward and the level of systemic risk is high, the expansion of credit will restrain the decline of default risk in the banking industry, further promoting the level of systemic risk in the next year. When the financial cycle goes up and the level of systemic risk is low, the expansion of credit scale will restrain the rise of default risk in the banking industry and maintain a low level of systemic risk. This regression result shows that when the fluctuation of systemic risk occurs before the counter-cyclical credit adjustment policy, the policy will promote systemic risk instead. This further illustrates that counter-cyclical policy adjustments should be forward-looking.

The ratio of the quarterly increase in foreign debt to nominal GDP has a significant negative correlation with the probability of Event 2. This shows that when the level of systemic risk is high, the increase in China's foreign debt will lead to a general increase in the default risk of commercial banks in the next year. This phenomenon is not significant when the systemic risk is low. The main reason for this phenomenon is that there is a huge difference between the foreign debt volume and the treasury bonds volume in China. The increase in the level of foreign debt cannot replace the issuance of treasury bonds, nor can it optimize the debt structure of central finance in China. At the same time, the increase in the volume of foreign debt requires a country to have sufficient foreign exchange reserves as a guarantee, which weakens the country's ability to use foreign reserves to maintain exchange rate stability, and exchange rate fluctuations will increase the default risk of sovereign debt. Gorzelak et al.2019 [35] used panel data regression to analyze developed and developing countries from 1970 to 2012 and found that the default risk of sovereign debt has a significant non-linear positive correlation with the default risk of the private sector. Therefore, when the default risk of foreign debt rises, it will trigger a "spiral rise" in the default probability of sovereign debt and the default probability of the private sector, which will eventually cause the systemic risk to increase sharply, the credit quality of commercial banks to generally deteriorate, and banks default risks to generally increase.

There is a significant negative correlation between the ratio of quarterly increase in foreign exchange reserves to nominal GDP and the occurrence probability of Event 1 and Event 2. Foreign exchange reserves have both advantages and disadvantages for a country's macroeconomic development. On the one hand, the increase in foreign exchange reserves is conducive to enhancing the ability of the central bank of China to intervene in the foreign exchange market, meeting the needs of maintaining the stability of exchange rate and blocking the transmission of international economic fluctuations to the country. On the other hand, when a country's foreign exchange reserves are higher than the appropriate scale, it will cause waste of social resources and decline in output. Agarwal 1971 [36], when studying the appropriate scale of foreign exchange reserves of developing countries, proposed that if the foreign exchange held by them that exceeds the appropriate size is used to import production, the underemployment situation in developing countries can be improved, so as to enhance the output level of the country. Therefore, when a country holds excessive foreign exchange reserves, it can be seen as suppressing the country's overall investment returns to a certain extent. As a result, the default risk of China's commercial banks generally rises, and the systemic risk also goes up. Foreign exchange reserves have opposite effects on the default risk of commercial banks from the channels of interest rate and asset volatility, respectively. Through the above results, it can be found that when the level of systemic risk is low, the increase of foreign exchange reserve increment will restrain the increase of default risk of commercial banks in the next year. When the level of systemic risk is high, the increase of foreign exchange reserve increment will keep the default risk of commercial banks at a high level.

The ratio of quarterly increase in current account balance to nominal GDP has a significant negative correlation with the probability of Event 1 and a significant positive correlation with the probability of Event 2, which shows that the foreign trade surplus will bring about a general decline in the default risk of commercial banks in the next year. This is because the increase of current account surplus is conducive to improving China's foreign exchange reserves, reducing the pressure on the central bank to use foreign exchange in adjusting the foreign exchange market and preventing the transmission of external risks to China through the price mechanism.

The ratio of quarterly increase in total market value of A-shares to nominal GDP and cumulative new construction site area year-on-year growth rate has a significant positive correlation with the probability of Event 1 and a significant negative correlation with the probability of Event 2. The reason is that, due to the general rise in stock prices and real estate prices, there is an over-expansion trend in credit that uses listed company stocks as collateral or real estate as collateral, which makes the average credit quality of commercial banks decline. Moreover, the extent of losses caused by systemic risks in commercial banks will generally rise in the next year. Conversely, the general decline in stock prices and real estate prices will inhibit the blind expansion of commercial bank credit and reduce the impact of systemic risks on commercial banks.

The introduction of forward-looking indicators, the ratio of the quarterly increase in foreign debt to nominal GDP, and the ratio of quarterly increase in foreign exchange reserves to nominal GDP allows the dynamic provisioning model to take into account the impact of the external economy on China's economy when making counter-cyclical adjustments. In addition, the introduction of forward-looking indicators, the ratio of quarterly increase in current account balance to nominal GDP, and the ratio of quarterly increase in total market value of A-shares to nominal GDP makes it possible to refer to the driving factors of fluctuations in the credit cycle when calculating the dynamic provision rate and makes the model more forward-looking. The above two aspects reflect the advanced nature of the model proposed in this paper relative to the current model in China.

4.4. Counter-Cyclical Validity Test

The dynamic provisioning model can realize the effectiveness of counter-cyclical adjustment, which means that it has the following two functions. First, the loan provision behavior of commercial banks can be adjusted counter-cyclically, and it forms excess provision for non-performing loans in the upward stage of the cycle, the provision which acts as a buffer for the downward stage of the cycle. Second, it can regulate the credit behaviors of commercial banks in a counter-cyclical manner, restrain the excessive expansion of credit in the upward stage of the cycle, and prevent the rapid contraction of credit in the downward stage of the cycle.

As shown in Table 5, according to formula (24), the correlation coefficients between the default distances of 14 listed commercial banks and their thresholds of Event 1 and Event 2 in the binary Gaussian Copula model are calculated. Then, according to formulas (23) and (27), the dynamic provisioning ratio of the 14 listed commercial banks from 2008 to 2019 is back-tested.

Table 5. The correlation coefficients in the binary Gaussian Copula model.

BANK	EVENT 1	EVENT 2
BOB	0.373	−0.367
ICBC	0.023	−0.064
HXB	−0.522	0.496
CCB	−0.120	0.266
BCM	−0.489	−0.218
CMBC	−0.337	0.113
NJCB	−0.354	−0.044
NBBANK	−0.400	0.316
SPABANK	−0.150	0.224
SPDB	−0.549	0.609
CIB	−0.502	0.474
CMB	−0.527	−0.103
BOC	−0.140	−0.354
CITIC	−0.185	−0.083

It is necessary to emphasize that the dynamic provisioning rate provided in this paper is not the total loan loss provision ratio provided by commercial banks during credit operations. It is a supplementary provisioning rate that is additionally set based on a forward-looking view of cyclical systemic risk and has a corrective effect on the micro-prudential loan provision rate based on a five-tier classification method.

As shown in Figure 2, the dynamic provisioning rate based on the model in this paper has a strong counter-cyclical characteristic. Affected by the U.S. financial crisis, the default distances of 14 listed commercial banks in China from 2009 to 2011 were all at a relatively low level, indicating that China's banking industry was also affected during the global financial crisis. At this stage, the dynamic provisioning requirements in this paper are also at a historically low level, releasing credit creation capabilities and helping to supplement the overall economic liquidity. During the period from 2012 to 2013, because the default risk of commercial banks was generally alleviated, the dynamic provisioning rate also increased accordingly, so that the loss reserve coul be accumulated at a lower cost for the subsequent rise of systemic risks. From 2014 to 2016, the supply-side structural reforms and the policy orientation of preventing financial risks worsened the default risk of the country's commercial banks, and the dynamic provisioning rate measured back declined, which can promote the overall economic stability. Since 2017, the default distance of listed commercial banks has been at a historically high level. In order to limit the blind expansion of bank credit, the dynamic provisioning rate level of the commercial banking industry has risen, achieving the characteristics of counter-cyclical adjustment. In addition, this paper has different requirements for dynamic provision of different commercial banks, instead of a one-size-fits-all regulatory model. While maintaining the safety of commercial banks, it also takes into account differences and profitability.

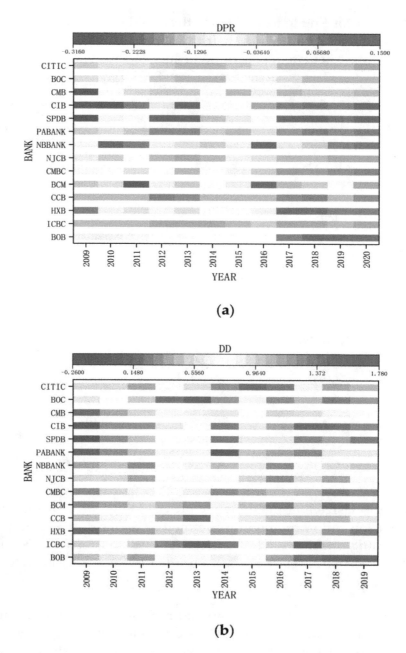

Figure 2. (**a**) Dynamic provisioning rate based on the model presented in this paper; (**b**) default distance of listed commercial banks.

According to the theoretical analysis in Chapter 3, macroeconomic and systemic financial risks are transmitted to the default risk of commercial banks through the two channels of asset return rate and asset volatility in the process of financial cycle changes, thus affecting the bank's leverage ratio adjustment and credit behavior. Therefore, it is possible to simulate the changes of default risk prediction of commercial banks to examine their credit behavior in the economic and financial cycle. After commercial banks are required to take dynamic provision based on the CCA–Probit–Copula model, the fixed index of default risk is changed from the default distance in CCA model to the modified default distance in formula (23). As shown in Figure 3, the modified default distance has a significant improvement in cross-cycle stability compared to the default distance in the CCA model. This indicates that the dynamic provisioning rate in this paper can make the risk prediction of commercial banks appear with less fluctuation, thus making the credit operation more stable and realizing the goal of counter-cyclical regulation of macro-prudential policy.

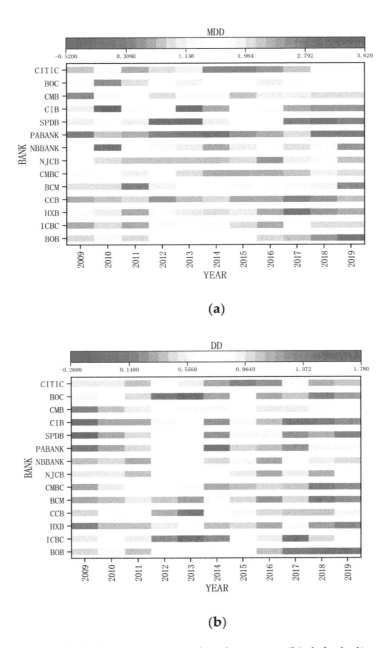

Figure 3. (**a**) Modified default distance presented in this paper; (**b**) default distance in CCA model.

5. Conclusions

In China, under an economic system dominated by indirect financing, maintaining the continuity of commercial bank credit is the key to ensuring the sustained development of the national economy. Therefore, counter-cyclical credit adjustment is an inevitable requirement for maintaining the sustainable development of China's economy. Establishing a forward-looking dynamic provisioning system is a key step to improve the macro-prudential supervision system and curb cyclical fluctuations in bank credit. After reading and summarizing relevant literature, a dynamic provisioning model based on the CCA–Probit–Copula model is constructed in this paper to achieve the policy goal of counter-cyclical adjustment of bank credit against the background of China's actual national conditions. The model measures the impact of China's systemic risks on the default risk of commercial banks and provides a counter-cyclical dynamic provisioning rate based on nine forward-looking indicators. According to the historical data of listed commercial banks in China, the empirical test proves that the dynamic provisioning requirements proposed in this model can effectively adjust the overall credit scale of the banking industry in counter-cyclical ways. Therefore, under the macro-prudential framework, policy goals of counter-cyclicality can be achieved, maintaining the security of China's financial system and sustainable development of the macroeconomy.

Research conclusions of this paper mainly include the following:

- Both the macroeconomic cyclical factors and the forward-looking factors of credit risk are taken into consideration. The effective way out of such dilemmas as insufficient historical credit data reserves of commercial banks, excessive reliance on subjective judgments, and conflicts with the current accounting system is the CCA–Probit–Copula dynamic provisioning model.

- On the basis of multiple forward-looking indicators, carrying out the CCA–Probit–Copula dynamic provisioning model can make it possible to propose matching differentiated dynamic provisioning requirements in accordance with the degree to which different commercial banks' default risks are affected by macro-cyclical factors. This not only considers the safety and liquidity of commercial banks, but also ensures their profitability and competitiveness.

- The dynamic provisioning rate based on the CCA–Probit–Copula model can respond sensitively to the cyclical changes in the overall commercial banking sector's default risk, which enables banks to accumulate provisions for high-risk periods at lower costs during low-risk periods. Moreover, the continuity and stability of bank credit operations can be significantly improved under the effect of this dynamic provisioning rate, so as to promote the sustainable development of China's economy.

Author Contributions: Conceptualization: X.H. and A.Z.; methodology: X.H. and A.Z.; software: A.Z.; validation: X.H. and A.Z.; formal analysis: X.H. and A.Z.; data curation: X.H. and A.Z.; writing—original draft preparation: X.H. and A.Z.; writing—review and editing: X.H. and A.Z.; funding acquisition: X.H. All authors have read and agreed to the published version of the manuscript.

Acknowledgments: The authors are grateful to the editors and anonymous reviewers for their valuable comments on earlier versions of the manuscript.

Appendix A

Because the A-share market has price limits, the daily return rates of listed commercial banks are all between −10% and 10%. According to the actual situation of the MES value of 14 listed commercial banks in China selected in this paper, 1%, 3%, 5%, 7%, and 9% are selected as the boundary values for defining Event 1 and Event 2, respectively. Regression analysis was performed on events with different value methods, and the optimal definition of Event 1 and Event 2 was determined based on the following three principles.

- In the regression analysis of events with different definition methods, the method with the most universally significant parameter estimation is selected.

- In regression analysis, the same forward-looking indicator should indicate the same direction for changes in the default risk of commercial banks, otherwise it will be regarded as a false regression.

- The emergence of extreme values in the regression parameters should be avoided, otherwise the regression results defined by this value method cannot be used to propose the dynamic provisioning ratio.

Due to space limitations, the regression results of other event definition methods are not presented in the paper. Those interested can contact the author's email at zhangaoran@sjtu.edu.cn.

References

1.   Borio, C. *Towards a Macroprudential Framework for Financial Supervision and Regulation*; BIS: Basel, Switzerland, 2003.

2. Kashyap, A.K.; Stein, J.C. Cyclical implications of the Basel II capital standards. *Econ. Perspect.* **2004**, *28*, 18–31.

3. Liu, Z. Research on the Quantity Selection of Regulatory Capital. *Financ. Regul. Res.* **2012**, *1*, 75–87.

4. Kashyap, A.K.; Rajan, R.G.; Stein, J.C. Rethinking capital Regulation. In Proceedings of the Economic Policy Symposium, Jackson Hole, WY, USA, 10 August 2020.

5. Hanson, S.; Kashyap, A.K.; Stein, J.C. A Macroprudential Approach to Financial Regulation. *J. Econ. Perspect.* **2011**, *25*, 3–28. [CrossRef]

6. Wezel, T.; Chan-Lau, J.A.; Columba, F. *Dynamic Loan Loss Provisioning Simulations on Effectiveness and Guide to Implementation*; IMF: Washington, DC, USA, 2012.

7. Kanagaretnam, K.; Lobo, G.J.; Yang, D. Determinants of signaling by banks through loan loss provisions. *J. Bus. Res.* **2005**, *58*, 312–320. [CrossRef]

8. Jin, J.Y.; Kanagaretnam, K.; Lobo, G.J.; Mathieu, R. Impact of FDICIA internal controls on bank risk taking. *J. Bank. Financ.* **2013**, *37*, 614–624. [CrossRef]

9. Balla, E.; McKenna, A. Dynamic provisioning: A countercyclical tool for loan loss reserves. *Econ. Q.* **2009**, *95*, 383–418.

10. López, M.; Tenjo, F.; Zárate, H. Credit Cycles, Credit Risk and Countercyclical Loan Provisions. *Ens. Sobre Política Econ.* **2014**, *74*, 9–17.

11. Jiménez, G.; Ongena, S.; Peydró, J.; Saurina, J. Macroprudential Policy, Countercyclical Bank Capital Buffers, and Credit Supply: Evidence from the Spanish Dynamic Provisioning Experiments. *J. Polit. Econ.* **2017**, *125*, 2126–2177. [CrossRef]

12. Fernández de Lis, S.; Garcia-Herrero, A. *Dynamic Provisioning: Some Lessons from Existing Experiences*; Asian Development Bank Institute: Manila, Philippines, 2010.

13. Fernández de Lis, S.; Garcia-Herrero, A. Dynamic Provisioning: A Buffer Rather Than a Countercyclical Tool. *Economía* **2013**, *2*, 387–398.

14. Huang, R.; Jiang, H.; Huang, J. Dynamic Provisioning, Financial Risk and Economic Cycle Based on DSGE Model. *Mod. Financ. Econ.* **2014**, *2*, 29–41.

15. Gao, J.; Fan, C.; Yang, D. The Synergistic Effect of Chattel Mortgage Financing for Enterprises and Macro-prudential Regulation. *J. Financ. Res.* **2017**, *39*, 111–125.

16. Zhang, X.; Yu, L. Spain's Dynamic Provisioning System and Its Enlightenment to China. *J. Financ. Res.* **2004**, *26*, 28–35.

17. Li, W. Discussion on Counter-cyclical Policies under the Framework of Macro-prudential Supervision. *J. Financ. Res.* **2009**, *31*, 7–24.

18. Li, H.; Hu, Y.; Si, Z. Research on the Implementation of Dynamic Provisioning in China's Banking Industry. *China Financ.* **2010**, *8*, 142–151.

19. Chen, C.; Wei, J.; Cao, L. Do China's Commercial Banks Use Loan Loss Provision for Income Smoothing? *J. Financ. Res.* **2015**, *37*, 46–63.

20. Zhang, R.; Li, D. An Analysis of Managerial Discretion Behavior Based on Discretionary Loan Loss Provision. *Financ. Forum* **2016**, *12*, 30–39.

21. Bushman, R.M.; Williams, C.D. Accounting discretion, loan loss provisioning, and discipline of Banks' risk-taking. *J. Account. Econ.* **2012**, *54*, 1–18. [CrossRef]

22. Li, Y.; Lu, J. A Study on Provisioning for Forward- looking Loan Loss in the Banking. *Financ. Forum* **2008**, *4*, 42–48.

23. Xu, Y.; Liu, Q.; Wang, Z. Research on the Appropriateness of Dynamic and Forward-looking Loan Loss Provision. *J. Financ. Res.* **2011**, *33*, 100–114.

24. Gray, D.F.; Merton, R.C.; Bodie, Z. A New Framework for Measuring and Managing Macrofinancial Risk and Financial Stability. 2007. Available online: https://www.researchgate.net/publication/43106070 (accessed on 3 February 2015).

25. Jobst, A.A.; Gray, D.F. Systemic CCA—A Model Approach to Systemic Risk. In Proceedings of the Beyond the Financial Crisis: Systemic Risk, Spillovers and Regulation, Dresden, Germany, 28 October 2010.

26. Merton, R.C. Pricing of corporate debt: The Risk Structure of Interest Rates. *J. Financ.* **1974**, *29*, 449–470.

27. Cox, J.C.; Ross, S.A. The valuation of options for alternative stochastic processes. *J. Financ. Econ.* **1976**, *3*, 145–166. [CrossRef]

28.   Acharya, V.V.; Pedersen, L.H.; Philippon, T.; Richardson, M. Measuring Systemic Risk. *Rev. Financ. Stud.*
      2016, *30*, 2–47. [CrossRef]
29.   Frankel, J.A.; Rose, A.K. Currency crashes in emerging markets: An empirical treatment. *J. Int. Econ.* **1996**,
      41, 351–366. [CrossRef]
30.   Behn, M.; Detken, C.; Peltonen, T.A.; Schudel, W. *Setting Countercyclical Capital Buffers Based on Early Warning
      Models: Would it Work*; European Central Bank: Frankfurt, Germany, 2013.
31.   Detken, C.; Weeken, O.; Alessi, L.; Bonfim, D.; Boucinha, M.M.; Castro, C.; Frontczak, S.; Giordana, G.; Giese, J.;
      Jahn, N.; et al. *Operationalising the Countercyclical Capital Buffer: Indicator Selection, Threshold Identification and
      Calibration Options*; European Systemic Risk Board: Frankfurt, Germany, 2014.
32.   Shen, Y.; Qi, L. Index System Design and Monitoring of Chinese Financial Bank Systemic Risks. *J. Southwest
      Univ. Soc. Sci. Ed.* **2008**, *34*, 139–143.
33.   Ma, J.; He, X.; Liu, S. *A Crisis Warning Model Based on Macro Variables*; National Institute of Finance, Tsinghua
      University: Beijing, China, 2019.
34.   Yi, G.; Wang, Z. Monetary Policy and Financial Assets Price. *Econ. Res. J.* **2002**, *48*, 13–20.
35.   Siwińska-Gorzelak, J.; Brzozowski, M. Sovereign default and the structure of private external debt. *Cent. Eur.
      Econ. J.* **2019**, *5*, 1–9. [CrossRef]
36.   Agarwal, J.P. Optimal Monetary Reserves for Developing Countries. *Weltwirtschaftliches Arch.* **1971**,
      107, 76–91. [CrossRef]

6

Digital Transformation and Knowledge Management in the Public Sector

Ana Alvarenga [1], Florinda Matos [2,*], Radu Godina [3] and João C. O. Matias [4,5]

[1] Department of Information Science and Technology, Instituto Universitário de Lisboa (ISCTE-IUL), 1649-026 Lisboa, Portugal; arcfa@iscte-iul.pt
[2] Centre for Socioeconomic and Territorial Studies (DINÂMIA'CET-ISCTE), Instituto Universitário de Lisboa (ISCTE-IUL), 1649-026 Lisboa, Portugal
[3] UNIDEMI, Department of Mechanical and Industrial Engineering, NOVA School of Science and Technology, Universidade NOVA de Lisboa, 2829–516 Caparica, Portugal; r.godina@fct.unl.pt
[4] DEGEIT—Departamento de Economia, Gestão, Engenharia Industrial e Turismo, Universidade de Aveiro, Campus Universitário de Santiago, 3810–193 Aveiro, Portugal; jmatias@ua.pt
[5] GOVCOPP—Unidade de Investigação em Governança, Competitividade e Políticas Públicas, Universidade de Aveiro, Campus Universitário de Santiago, 3810–193 Aveiro, Portugal
* Correspondence: florinda.matos@iscte-iul.pt

Abstract: Digitizing public services is, at the moment, an essential necessity for numerous governments around the world. An improved government through digitization will not only have a growing effect on businesses, but it will also be able to intensify citizen engagement and push for economic growth. During the last 10 years more countries have progressively begun to provide digital services to their citizens. Therefore, in order to address this development, the purpose of this paper is to analyze the evolution of the digital government literature in order to describe the aspects of digital transformation in the public sector and how it is related to knowledge management. In this study the methodology is quantitative and it is based on a review and a survey made with the main goal being the estimation from several collected data on how the digital transformation process in the Public Administration takes place and what its relationship is with knowledge management. The review study is based on articles found on Scopus database and it addresses the role that digital government research plays in the theory and practice of knowledge management. In the survey study, 54 employees working for the services of the two governmental areas of the Portuguese Ministry of the Environment were surveyed. The results show that the research on the theme is still at an exploratory stage due to the lack of studies relating digital government to knowledge management effectiveness in the public sector. The results also show that the success of digital government seems to be related with the quality of the organizations' knowledge management, complementing each other for significant improvements in the public sector. In terms of originality, this study aims to contribute and stimulate data-driven discussions regarding the impacts of the digital transformation in the public sector and their relation with the implementation of knowledge management practices. The results offer insights into future research needs.

Keywords: digital transformation; knowledge management; digital government; public sector; public administration

1. Introduction

Digital transformation is a necessity for the modern enterprise, whether public or private, due to the strength and vertiginous speed with which digitalization has entered and has taken over our lives, which has meant that many organizations have not been able to adapt to it yet. The main and most important reason for this state of affairs in organizations is the lack of knowledge or trained personnel, which could allow them to understand how to cope with this change. While many public administration services have made great progress, the full potential of digital adaptation remains untapped. The digital government panorama changes continually to reflect how the government tries to find innovative digital solutions in social, economic, and political areas and how it could transform the decision-making process [1–3].

The current rising necessity of organizational change is altering, through digital transformation, the way governments look at knowledge management practices to address social needs or improve service delivery effectively. Understanding and predicting these changes is extremely important for policymakers, government executives, researchers, and all those who prepare, devise, implement, or evaluate digital government decisions [4].

In [5], three benefits of knowledge management in digital governance were identified: the enhancement of government competence, the increase in quality of government service, and the promotion of a healthy government development. Thus, this supports the idea that the success of digital government depends heavily on knowledge management.

Knowledge management came to the forefront due to the need for public and private organizations to make more rational and effective use of their knowledge [6]. As the authors state in [7], knowledge management "may potentially offer a competitive advantage and help develop knowledge-intensive economies".

Therefore, knowledge management is an important and specific issue in the research context of the public sector. The authors in [8] affirm that "the public sector is influenced by a growing need for: competition, performance standards, monitoring, measurement, flexibility, emphasis on results, customer focus and control". It seems that "knowledge management for government is no longer a choice, but an imperative if economies are to survive in the era of privatization, liberalization, and globalization" [9]. According to the authors in [10], knowledge management "has the potential to greatly influence and improve public sector renewal processes". Indeed, within the public sector, knowledge management "is a powerful facilitator in the current push for greater efficiency in all areas" [11].

Nevertheless, in [10] it is argued that "the development of a knowledge management culture within the public sector is more challenging than in the private sector". The study in [12] supports this argument by highlighting that "organizational goals in public organizations are typically more difficult to measure and more conflicting than in private organizations and are affected differently by political influences".

According to [13], knowledge management has been an object of attention of the academic community, public decision-makers, consultants, and business people since the beginning of the 1990s. A study published in the Journal of Knowledge Management, reports that the importance of knowledge management in the public sector is growing as a research area. It points out that the low level of international cooperation between the authors and the small number of comparative case studies show that the literature is fragmented [14].

Deliberately, systematically, and holistically managing knowledge can increase awareness of the benefits to individuals and organizations. However, there seems to be a lack of knowledge management awareness in the public sector. This can be severely detrimental in the process of digital transformation and in the effective implementation of knowledge management initiatives in organizations seeking to increase performance.

One of the purposes of this paper is to present a structured literature review of the digital government and knowledge management in public administration. In addition, as this article consolidates a body representative of the digital government literature, it can also be used to define and integrate future research in the area. The scientific literature review was carried out in support of an exploratory research, which consisted of analyzing the effect of digital transformation on knowledge management practices in Portuguese Public Administration.

Thus, the study has the following objectives: to verify if the digital transformation has changed the way the public organization carries out the knowledge management processes and to effectively identify knowledge management practices related to the digital transformation process. Therefore, the research question was: what is the relationship between the implementation of digital transformation and the use of knowledge management practices in public organizations?—and the research hypothesis is: the digital transformation process has an impact on knowledge management practices and, knowledge management, in turn, is a critical factor in the success of digital transformation.

Furthermore, to fulfill the objectives and hypothesis defined by the exploratory research, in the literature review are analyzed several studies in order to understand the definitions, origins, and peculiarities of digital transformation and knowledge management in the public sector. The literature review reveals who has already written and what has been published on the subject, what aspects have already been addressed, and which aspects are least addressed on the research topic.

This paper is composed of several sections: Section 2 presents the literature review methodology and Section 3 addresses the questionnaire methodology; Section 4 presents the literature review results and their analysis. Section 5 presents the results and the analysis of the survey and, finally, in Section 6 a conclusion that offers a future research agenda and limitations is presented.

2. Literature Review Methodology

2.1. The Structured Literature Review

This article employs a variant of a structured literature review to answer the research question addressed in the introduction. The methodology is similar to other recent reviews of the literature [14–18]. A structured review of the literature critically identifies, selects, and evaluates the research in order to answer a formulated question [19]. Performing a literature review is a formal way of synthesizing available information from available primary studies relevant to a set of research questions. It involves planning a well-thought-out research strategy that has a specific focus and answers those questions.

The literature review follows a clearly defined protocol where the criterion is prominently stated before the review is made. It is a comprehensive and transparent survey based on databases and grey literature that can be replicated and reproduced by other researchers. The review identifies the type of information researched, criticized, and reported within known time frames. Search terms, search strategies (including database names, platforms, search dates), and thresholds are all included in the review. As stated in [20], "greater clarity about the terminology and methods surrounding literature reviews will help researchers identify when and how such revisions can be made".

In this article the methodology of structured literature review is applied in order to share the results of other studies that are within the scope of the research, relate a study to the broader current dialogue in the literature on a topic, filling gaps and expanding previous studies, and finally, provide a framework to establish the importance of the study and an indicator to compare the results of the study with other outcomes.

According to the methodology of structured literature review, several authors [15,17,18] formulated the following main steps:

1. Define the research questions.
2. Write a research protocol for the review.
3. Determine the articles to include and carry out a comprehensive bibliographic search.
4. Develop a coding framework.
5. Code the articles and ensure reliability.
6. Analyze critically and discuss results.

Therefore, this article presents a comprehensive review of digital government articles published in the Scopus database from 2000 until the beginning of 2019. The following subsections describe the methods applied to the development of the literature review.

2.2. Research Protocol

A research protocol provides a step-by-step guide for conducting literature reviews, which may include systematic reviews, scope reviews, and meta-analyses. According to the authors in [21], "it is essential to write a protocol stating the review question, the methods to be used, the types of study and projects that the reviewer intends to find, and by what means and how studies will be evaluated and synthesized".

Therefore, research protocols are essential to ensure high-quality literature reviews. However, defining a protocol comprises many aspects, such as the formulation of research questions, definition of a search strategy and the adequate sources where to find primary studies, specification of the inclusion and exclusion criteria to be used in the selection of studies, and characterization of the process to be used to extract, synthesize, describe, and categorize the selected studies, extracting data and making quality evaluations.

The protocol should contain specific guidelines for identifying and selecting articles relevant to the review as well as outlining review methods for the entire process.

Following these suggestions, a written protocol was developed, describing the identification of the keywords, the source of information, the support tools and the main information searched in the documents. In this way, steps were defined in the research protocol, such as the construction of the collection of articles (Sample I); filtration process; scientometric analysis; content analysis (Sample II), and finally, the construction of gaps and research opportunities. A manual coding procedure was also developed, which indicated which information to recover from each paper, since "manual coding has advantages compared to computer-aided coding because when words with similar meanings like 'human capital' and 'employees' are found, they can be understood in their real sense and encoded accordingly" [15].

Thus, the review protocol is essential to reduce bias in the review process and limit overlap with existing reviews. It also provides an outline for the review process that helps plan and anticipate challenges that may arise during the review.

2.3. Literature Research

For the paper selection, a bibliographic research methodology was adopted based on the analysis of the already published literature, in the form of books, articles, and grey literature, which included knowledge management, digital government, and public administration as the primary research areas.

For the identification of the keywords, several attempts and searches were made in advance until the correct constructions could be chosen. More than 15 research builders were researched and interrelated. It was verified that with the term "digital transformation" the research in the databases returns few studies, detecting a gap in the literature. Alternatively, constructions with terms with similar meaning as "e-government" and "Digital Government" were made.

Regarding the search through keywords, it was carried out in January 2019 in the Scopus database, and a manual coding procedure was adopted to ensure that no articles were lost during the research. Based on the data set, the titles, abstracts, and keywords of all articles published in the periods from 2000 to the beginning of 2019 were examined, and articles containing knowledge management and digital government aspects from a public administration perspective were selected. During the search of documents in the database, a low number of results were observed. Only articles published in the English language were selected.

From this research, an initial group of 69 relevant articles was selected and, of these articles, a final group of 30 articles was used, which are depicted in Table 1.

Table 1. The 30 found articles addressing digital transformation.

Reference	Title
[22]	A multi-methods study exploring the role of stakeholders in the digital preservation environment: The case of Ghana.
[23]	Preserving the digital heritage of public institutions in Ghana in the wake of electronic government.
[24]	What lessons can be learned from the US archivist's digital mandate for 2019 and is there potential for applying them in lower resource countries?
[25]	The issues and considerations associated with BIM integration.
[26]	Transnational digital government research collaborations: Purpose, value, challenges.
[27]	Public sector readiness for digital preservation in New Zealand: The rate of adoption of an innovation in records management practices.
[28]	Information sharing in and across government agencies: The role and influence of scientist, politician, and bureaucrat subcultures.
[29]	Technology as a tool of transformation: E-cities and the rule of law.
[30]	Document logistics in the public sector: Integrative handling of physical and digital documents.
[31]	Digital government and public management research: Finding the crossroads
[32]	Archivists 2.0: Redefining the archivist's profession in the digital age.
[33]	Government workers say goodbye to paper
[34]	Creating value through managing knowledge in an e-government to constituency (G2C) environment
[35]	Success factors for public sector information system projects: Qualitative literature review
[36]	Solon: A holistic approach for modelling, managing, and mining legal sources
[37]	Knowledge brokering in the web 2.0 era: Empirical evidence of emerging strategies in government agencies
[38]	The fourth industrial revolution, agricultural, and rural innovation, and implications for public policy and investments: A case of India
[39]	Exploitation and exploration strategies to create data transparency in the public sector
[40]	Ensuring interoperability of geographic information in local government and inspire
[41]	Knowledge management in the public sector: Communication issues and challenges at local government level
[42]	E-governance in agriculture: Digital tools enabling Filipino farmers.
[43]	Digital records keeping to information governance in Estonian local governments
[44]	Integrating knowledge management tools for government information
[32]	Organizational learning from service innovation in the public sector of Dubai
[45]	Case studies on digital government
[46]	Knowledge management system for governance: Transformational approach creating knowledge as product for governance
[47]	A conceptual framework for effective appropriation of proactive public e-services
[48]	E-government initiatives and information management in two local government authorities
[49]	The e-governance concerns in information system design for effective e-government performance improvement
[50]	ICT and PA: A marriage made in heaven?

According to [20], "rapid growth literature reviews have resulted in an infinity of terminology to describe approaches that, despite their different names, share certain characteristics, namely, collecting, evaluating, and presenting evidence of available research".

According to this research, the term "digital transformation" consists of organizational change that uses digital technologies and business models to improve the organization's performance and customer experience. The term e-government consists of the use of information technologies in the internal processes of government, in the delivery of state products and services to both citizens and industry, and in the use of electronic tools and information technologies to approximate government and citizens. The view of e-government as a resource rationalizer seems to be linked to an older, more generalist conception of what digital government is today. For this reason, the search strategy used the terms "Digital Government", "Knowledge Management", and "Public Sector" as keywords.

From the search of those keywords in the Scopus database, 69 results showed up, 39 of which were excluded: 6 because they were in duplicate and 33 because they were outside the scope of the investigation, as it can be seen in Figure 1. The filtering process resulted in sample I, which included 30 articles of studies on digital government, and in sample II, which is composed of 10 articles that were analyzed according to the criterion of the existence of a relationship with knowledge management. In order to obtain sample II, the final 30 selected articles from the databases were filtered using a scientometric analysis, followed by a detailed analysis of the content of the articles by categories, selecting those that were within the scope of the investigation. This sample is composed of 10 articles that contain aspects of knowledge management within the digital government studies.

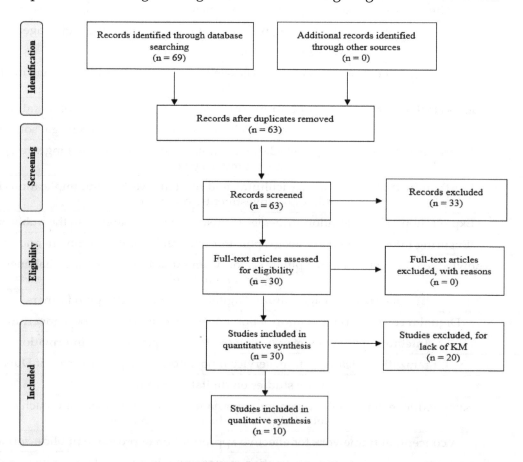

Figure 1. Flow diagram representing the collection of articles in databases and filtering process.

2.4. Developing a Coding Framework

The coding framework is based on advanced research frameworks developed by several authors [14–16,18,51]. A formal and systematic approach was adopted by adapting the analytical framework to the data set in order to extract the relevant information. As a result, seven categories were created to systematize the coding, as it can be observed in Table 2.

Table 2. Research framework and main results.

Category	Variables	Articles	%
Authors, institution, year	Authors	61	
	Institution	40	
	Years	2000–2019	
Document type	Conference Paper	15	50.0
	Article	10	33.3
	Review	2	6.7
	Book	1	3.3
	Book Chapter	1	3.3
	Editorial	1	3.3
	Totals	30	100.0
Jurisdiction	Central government	19	63.3
	State/regional	2	6.7
	Local government	7	23.3
	Public business enterprise (PBE)	1	3.3
	Other	1	3.3
	Totals	30	100.0
Location	Europe/UK	14	46.6
	Australasia	1	3.3
	North America	7	23.3
	South America	0	0.0
	Africa	2	6.7
	Asia/China	4	13.3
	Other	2	6.7
	Totals	30	100.0
Research method	Quantitative cross-sectional	1	3.3
	Case study	7	23.3
	Literature review–normative	3	10.0
	Action research	1	3.3
	Qualitative study	9	30.0
	Quantitative study	2	6.7
	Mixed methods	4	13.3
	Other	3	10.0
	Totals	30	100.0
Framework	No framework-model used	2	6.7
	Applies or considers previous framework-model	27	90.0
	Proposes a new framework-model	1	3.3
	Totals	30	100.0
Theme	Digital preservation	3	10.0
	Information technology	8	26.7
	knowledge management strategy	4	13.3
	Knowledge innovation	3	10.0
	Management of elements and processes	3	10.0
	Personal and organizational learning	1	3.3
	Organizational culture	1	3.3
	Information management	6	20.0
	Other	1	3.3
	Totals	30	100.0

By looking at Table 2 it is possible to observe that the first category classifies them by journal. The main goal is to analyze the evolution of literature: citation scores were used to measure the impact of articles, authors, and journals.

The second category is a division of the sample by type of document that has been most used in the digital government literature since the year 2004.

The third category is jurisdiction based on different levels of government, rather than the broader organizational types found in [15]. In general terms, government jurisdictions are country-specific, while public organizations are comparable across countries. Therefore, by analyzing government jurisdictions, the goal is to understand publication standards and find out if differences in national contexts and data accessibility exist.

The fourth category is the location. Thus, when analyzing a location, the objective is to understand the extent to which the literature supports the development of digital evolution as well as knowledge-intensive economies.

The fifth category is the search method used. Digital government research is still reaching an epistemological consensus among the authors since the main strategies lead to the development of multiple research methods. The goal is to understand what methods have been used in digital government research.

The sixth category is framework-model. This category is derived from [52]. The main objective of the analysis of the framework used is to understand if the literature is proposing new specific models and if it applies or considers the previous framework-models, or if it does not use framework-models for the public sector at all.

The seventh category is the research theme. By analyzing the themes of the selected articles, it was possible to identify areas of interest for other scholars, new research opportunities, and to better understand the scientific dialogue.

After analyzing the articles in sample I and, according to the objective of the development of the review, the category "Focus" used by [14] was removed and the category "Research Theme" was added, giving a clearer information on the evolution and focus of the digital government literature. The classification for this category is similar to that of [52].

3. Results of the Literature Review and Discussion

The following subsections present results that attempt to answer the following research questions: the first—research question 1—"What is the evolution and focus of the digital government literature?"; the second—research question 2—"What is the future of research in digital government?"; and, the third,—research question 3—"How does digital government literature relate to knowledge management?".

To do this, gross counts were used, as shown in Table 2. In addition, when issues were found that needed more research and criticism, a more in-depth analysis was conducted based on the combination of the descriptive results, deepening specific questions found in the articles.

3.1. Authors, Institution, Year

Analyzing the evolution of articles on digital government in public administration, the results show an increase. The literature search identified 30 relevant articles, of which 73.3% were published after 2010, suggesting a growing trend. The years included ranged between 2000 and 2019, but in the interval 2000–2003, as well as for the years 2006, 2008, 2013, and 2015, no relevant articles were found for the study as shown in Figure 2. The year that has the highest number of publications is 2018 (5 articles) and it is also worth mentioning the years 2017 (3 articles) and 2016 (4 articles). This shows, once again, the growing tendency for studies on digital government. Nevertheless, despite the increase in the number of publications per year, the reduced number of documents and a significant shortage of literature about digital government is still evident.

Thus, by observing Figure 2, some of the more recent articles are from 2018 to 2019 [22,31,42,53] and some of the oldest are from 2004 to 2007 [28,33,44].

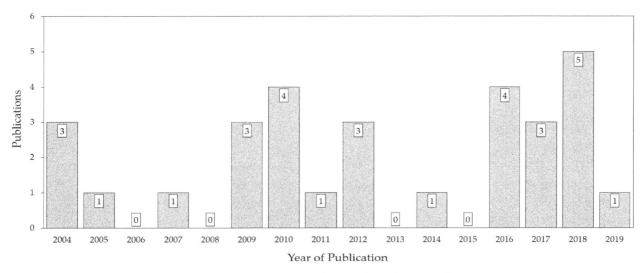

Figure 2. Representation of the total publications by year.

Regarding the analysis of authors, as shown in Table 2, in 30 articles, there are a total of 61 authors/coauthors, showing a significant number of authors who participated in the digital government literature. However, according to Table 1, only two of these authors have more than one publication, showing few dominant authors in the digital government research. The most prolific ones are Kofi Koranteng Adu [22], with two articles published in 2016 and 2018, and Gil-García et al. [31], with two articles published in the years 2011 and 2018.

The main reason for examining these authors and their citations is to verify the superstar effect that sometimes occurs when a small fraction of researchers or institutions produce the highest number of studies and attract a disproportionate number of quotations [54–56]. Although there is a significant fraction of 61 researchers and 40 institutions, there is not a large number of studies led by the same authors or institutions. Thus, in this analysis, the evidence of disproportionately influential individuals was not studied. As an alternative, it opted for the articles with the highest number of publications and their respective authors, according to Table 3.

Table 3. The 12 most cited public sector digital government articles.

Paper	Title	Citations
[34]	Creating value through managing knowledge in an e-government to constituency (G2C) environment	65
[28]	Information Sharing in and Across Government Agencies: The Role and Influence of Scientist, Politician, and Bureaucrat Subcultures	40
[44]	Integrating knowledge management tools for government information	25
[27]	Public sector readiness for digital preservation in New Zealand: The rate of adoption of an innovation in records management practices	13
[29]	Technology as a tool of transformation: e-Cities and the rule of law	11
[43]	Digital records keeping to information governance in Estonian local governments	9
[32]	Archivists 2.0: Redefining the archivist's profession in the digital age	8
[45]	Case studies on digital government	6
[31]	Digital government and public management research: finding the crossroads	4
[24]	What lessons can be learned from the US archivist's digital mandate for 2019 and is there potential for applying them in lower resource countries?	3
[23]	Preserving the digital heritage of public institutions in Ghana in the wake of electronic government	3
[25]	The Issues and Considerations Associated with BIM Integration	2

The article with the most significant number of citations (65) was written by Koh, C.E. et al. [34] and was published in the Journal of Computer Information Systems in 2005. This article, from the University of North Texas, uses as research method a case study about central government focused on information technology and knowledge management. The case study focuses on government agencies due to their challenges in the progression of digitalization, caused by the size and complexity of government structures and the large amount of information these government agencies maintain. Thus, the article proposes that government agencies should go through an evolutionary path as they progress from an introductory digital presence to more complex forms of interaction with constituents. It highlights key facilitators that enable a steady progress by changing how citizens interact with government, increase accessibility to information, and increase efficiency in the public sector.

The article with the second highest number of citations (40), written by Drake, D.B. et al. [28], was published in the Social Science Computer Review in 2004. This article uses an exploratory method and an interdisciplinary study on central government, focusing on issues related to information sharing within and between three public bodies. The study illustrates key points about information sharing among subcultures and some implications for research and practice.

The article written by Prokopiadou, G., et al. [44] has the third highest number of citations (25) and was published in the Government Information Quarterly in 2004. This article uses as research method a qualitative study regarding central government in which it introduces a digital library architecture for the management and delivery of information produced or disseminated through public services. The study notes the lack of advanced information standards and tools and emphasizes public sector challenges such as the presence of fragmented and dispersed information, legislative and administrative diversity, administrative hierarchy, and discrepancies in the implementation of policies at central, regional, and local levels. Furthermore, the study aims to highlight the importance of government information for business transactions, decision-making, and for providing information about organizations to citizens.

The articles with a number of citations ranging between 10 and 15 can be found in [27,29] and were published in Government Information Quarterly and Information Systems: People, Organizations, Institutions, and Technologies, respectively. These articles use, as a qualitative research method, studies about central government and local government, with a focus on digital preservation, information technology, and information and knowledge sharing.

With less than 10 citations, there were seven documents published between 2007 and 2018.

The article of [43], through a qualitative study, provides an overview of the developments in local governments of Estonia in the last 10 years with the objective of introducing the Electronic System of Document and Records Management as the central governance system. This article describes the development of the digital governance model, the first results in terms of implementation of its modules, and other plans on the introduction of information governance in local governments.

In addition, the articles of [24,32], both published in the Records Management Journal, study local and central government in Sweden and in the USA and their focus is on the professional practice of archivists involving information technology and the archivist's digital mandate. The research methods used were mixed and included empirical studies, interviews, literature review, and case studies.

The article in [31], published in the Public Management Review in 2018, is the most recent article appearing in Table 3 of the most cited in sample I. This article analyzes previous studies on the digital government community along with a systematic review of recent articles, published in leading US and European public administration journals, in order to identify and compare the key characteristics of these academic communities, including their top researchers, theories, topics, and methods. From a perspective of public management, digital government could be considered an essential aspect of innovation, coproduction, transparency, and the generation of public value.

From the remaining articles, several research methods were identified, such as case studies, literature review, quantitative cross-sectional, and mixed methods. The studies involve, mostly, central governments and focus on information technology and information management, covering a several number of themes, such as project management, which studied the Building Information Modeling (BIM) methods for storing data and asset information using object-oriented modelling of infrastructure [25], digital preservation, and digital community.

Additionally, after the analysis, it was also possible to conclude that six of the documents in Table 3 are conference papers, and some of them were published in the same papers: two articles, written by [27,44], were published in the Government Information Quarterly and another two articles, written by [24,32], were published in the Records Management Journal.

Regarding the summation of the number of citations per year, the years from 2015 to 2019 were considered. It was verified that the number of citations of sample I has a higher incidence in the years 2017 and 2018 with 20 citations in each of the years. In addition, 2019 already has three citations, showing that since 2017 there seems to have been a growing interest in the research of digital government. The years 2015 (14 citations) and 2016 (16 citations) have a similar number of citations. The set of articles contain 73 citations in total since 2015, as it can be seen in Figure 3.

Figure 3. Citations by year (2015–2019) of most cited public sector DG articles.

3.2. Document Types

The documents selected in sample I have different types: 15 are conference papers, 10 are articles, 2 are books or book chapters, and 1 is an editorial. As shown in Figure 4, the most significant percentage belongs to conference articles (50%), followed by articles (33.3%), both of which show a trend in the type of documents of the digital government literature.

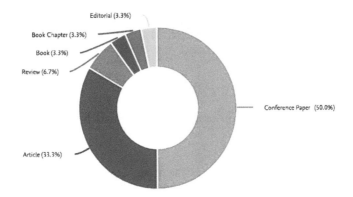

Figure 4. Classification of documents by type.

3.3. Jurisdiction

According to Table 2, the main focus of the digital government literature is central governments (63.3%), followed by the local governments (23.3%). There are also other attributes such as state/regional and public business enterprise (PBE) in 10% of documents. However, in coding the articles, the lines between what is a central government function and a state/regional function are sometimes blurred or nonexistent because different countries have different structures.

3.4. Location

Analyzing the criterion location, the results show that Europe/UK is the most studied region, with 19 articles representing 46.6% of the studies, followed by the North American region with 7 articles representing 23.3% of the studies. The Asia/China region, with 4 articles, represents 13.3% of the sample. No articles were found regarding South America. Digital government research articles include various countries, such as the Philippines, Estonia, Australia, China, USA, Greece, India, Ghana, Sweden, Germany, Norway, and New Zealand. According to this analysis, a great variety of countries that study digital government in different contexts can be highlighted. With the emergence of articles from several countries, the possibility of international comparisons regarding differences and common guidelines of digital government research is growing.

The most significant number of articles was identified in the Europe/UK region, covering the years 2009 to 2018, with Sweden being the most analyzed country. The US is also the country that continues to produce more articles regarding the North American region. The results also show that, since 2017, the Asia/China region is growing in published studies (13.3%), which may be due to the growing importance of Asia in terms of the global economy. In addition, studies about India are increasing and focus mainly on universities and research centers. Locations like Australia, where one study was found in 2018, South America, which has no studies and Africa, with studies from 2016 and 2018, are under-represented and under-researched. Finally, a study from New Zealand addressing Oceania region was published in 2009. Figure 5 represents the articles published per location. However, nine studies were left out of this classification, due to the fact that they were either theoretical or the location was not disclosed.

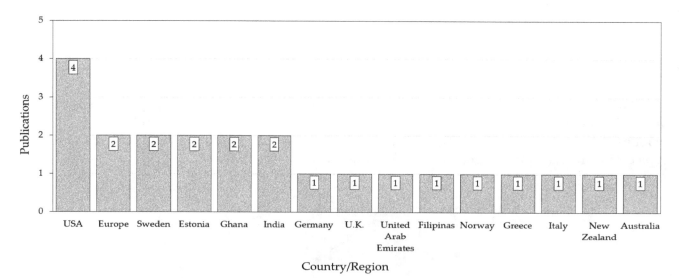

Figure 5. Classification of the published articles by location.

3.5. Research Methodology

Qualitative approaches represent 30.0% of sample I (9 articles) and are the most used and representative approaches in digital government research. The case studies are the second most used approach, with seven articles representing 23.3% of the sample. In the analysis of the research method of the articles, it was difficult to classify them by specific attributes due to the existence of a mixture of methods. From 2009 until 2018, the articles contained four mixed methods and three other methods, highlighting the existence of a significant fraction of studies that do not use a specific research method.

According to Table 2, approaches such as quantitative cross-sectional and action research represent only 6.7% of the sample (only 1 article per research method). The quantitative studies represent 6.7% with two articles, and the literature review represents 10% with three articles.

3.6. Framework

The digital government literature focused mainly on the use of existing frameworks (90%). The development of new frameworks concentrated only 3.3% of the studies and 6.7% of the articles did not use specific frameworks. Thus, this can be an evidence of the interest of researchers in the issue of digital government.

3.7. Themes

The analysis of the results of the research themes shows that eight articles (26.7% of the sample) focus on information technology and six articles (20% of the sample) focus on information management. The third most analyzed issue is the knowledge management strategy, with four articles representing 13.3% of the sample. The subjects "digital preservation", "knowledge innovation", and "management of elements and processes" have three articles each and together represent 10.0% of the sample. Less analyzed themes, like "organizational learning" and "organizational culture", represent the remaining 10% of the studies.

The distribution of themes shows that the topics are scattered. Analyzing the evolution over time, the results show that the theme of "information technology" has been approached between the years 2004 to 2019 with a higher incidence in the articles from the year 2018. This growing trend is due to the importance of information technology in the process of transformation in the public sector. From 2012 until 2017, the research focused more on the theme of "knowledge management strategy".

To complement the themes of the selected articles, the articles of the sample were also analyzed according to the research areas addressed. Table 4 and Figure 6 show that the areas of research "Computer Science" and "Social Sciences" were included 27 times representing 44% of the sample, followed by "Business, Management and Accounting" and "Decision Sciences", which were included 14 times, representing 28%. The remaining areas were included eight times, representing 18% of the sample.

Table 4. Documents by subject area.

Subject Area	Number
Computer Science	15
Social Sciences	12
Business, Management and Accounting	8
Decision Sciences	6
Engineering	3
Agricultural and Biological Sciences	1
Chemistry	1
Earth and Planetary Sciences	1
Economics, Econometrics and Finance	1
Mathematics	1

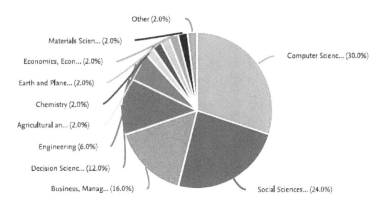

Figure 6. Documents by subject area.

3.8. Content Analysis (Sample II)

Sample II, as seen in Table 5, was constructed with 10 studies from the content analysis of sample I, in order to answer the third question in the study—How does digital government literature relate to knowledge management?

Table 5. Documents by keyword "knowledge management".

Year	Author(s)	Title	Jurisdiction	Location	Research Method	Themes	Ref.
2018	Rahman and Al Joker	Organizational learning from service innovation in the public sector of Dubai	Local government	Asia/China (Dubai)	Case study	Organizational learning, organizational culture, service innovation, transformation, intelligent government, politics, strategic learning	[53]
2017	Shilohu Rao, Goswami and Chaudhary	Knowledge Management system for Governance: Transformational approach creating knowledge as product for Governance	Central government	Asia/China (India)	Qualitative study	knowledge management strategy, knowledge management, transformational growth, multidimensional aspects, transformation	[46]
2016	Matheus and Janssen	Exploitation and exploration strategies to create data transparency in the public sector	Central government	Other	Case study	Innovation, Ambidexterity, data transparency, efficiency	[39]
2016	Bataw, Kirkham and Lou	The Issues and Considerations Associated with BIM Integration	Central government	Europe/UK (United Kingdom)	Mixed methods	Information Technology, Methods Building Information Modeling (BIM), Storage, Information Management, Project Management	[25]
2012	Lamari and Belgacem	Knowledge brokering in the web 2.0 era: Empirical evidence of emerging strategies in government agencies	Public business enterprise (PBE)	North America (EUA)	Mixed methods	knowledge innovation, digital innovation, knowledge brokers, government agencies, knowledge management strategies	[37]
2012	Pappel and Saarmann	Digital records keeping to information governance in Estonian local governments	Local government	Europe/UK	Qualitative study	Information Technology, Electronic Document and Records Management System, process and workflow management, knowledge management, effectiveness	[43]
2010	Ndlela	Knowledge management in the public sector: Communication issues and challenges at local government level	Local government	Europe/UK (Norway)	Qualitative study	Knowledge management, communication, knowledge transfer, organizational culture	[41]
2010	Eiermann and Walter	Document logistics in the public sector: Integrative handling of physical and digital documents	Local government	Europe/UK (Germany)	Quantitative study / qualitative approach / Case study	Document logistics, information management, communication	[30]
2005	Koh, Ryan and Prybutok	Creating value through managing knowledge in an e-government to constituency (G2C) environment	Central government	North America (EUA)	Case study	Digital presence, accessibility to information, government agencies, key facilitators	[34]
2004	Drake, Steckler and Koch	Information Sharing in and Across Government Agencies: The Role and Influence of Scientist, Politician, and Bureaucrat Subcultures	Central government	Other	Exploratory and interdisciplinary study	Organizational culture, information sharing, communication, organizational culture	[28]

For the article selection, criteria for title and abstract analysis was used along with the application of keyword filtering to knowledge management. The objective was to analyze the content by verifying how knowledge management is present in studies of digital government and how they are related, comparing the main characteristics of knowledge management approach in digital government research, theories, topics, and methods. Their similarities and differences present opportunities for more dialogue between digital government and knowledge management scholars, who can produce synergies to increase the production and dissemination of knowledge.

From this analysis, it was verified that the authors in [53] have published a study that addresses organizational learning and citizen-centered service innovation in the federal and local governments of Dubai. This case is presented in the context of the rapid transformation of the Dubai eGovernment into a smart government that began in 2013. The goal was to outline possible policy and strategic learning more driven by demand and service improvement initiatives.

The authors in [46] have published an article that addresses knowledge management as a phenomenon established and applied in various disciplines for transformational growth. The study focuses on the India Digital Program, launched in 2015, which had the vision of "turning India into a digitally empowered society and knowledge economy". The document highlights the multidimensional aspects of the implementation of knowledge management for digital government, such as the need for knowledge management in a Federal Government system, along with its main objectives, with the main resources moving from structure to implementation.

The article of [39] analyses ambidexterity, which is the ability of an organization to be able to develop new products and innovate while continuing to provide and update its existing services. A case study, to understand better how the combination of exploitation and exploration can enable data transparency, was used.

In [25] the Building Information Modeling (BIM) methods in the UK government are studied as a critical aspect in the notion of "interoperability" between various software applications used in the design process and construction and a common data format for the efficient exchange of information. A mixed methods approach was used: questionnaire analysis and a secondary case study analysis.

The research presented in [37] is based on a representative sample of knowledge brokers from government agencies. The study goes beyond the rhetorical and hermeneutical analyses on this subject, to outline an empirical and factual view of emerging practices and strategies in knowledge intermediation within Québec's government agencies known for their wide use of Web 2.0 platforms and digital innovation.

The authors in [43] conducted a study that provides an overview of developments in local governments in Estonia over the last 10 years intending to introduce the Electronic Records and Records Management System as the central system of governance. It is emphasized that information systems have as their main objective in the public sector to store, manipulate, diffuse, and preserve knowledge to achieve the effectiveness of electronic governance.

In [41] the authors examined the major communication challenges, namely those faced by small municipalities in their efforts to implement knowledge management programs. The study data was extracted from a survey collected in a small municipality of Norway. The article highlights the role of appropriate and inadequate communication behavior patterns for knowledge transfer at local government levels.

In [30] the authors address the current state of document logistics in the public sector and identified current needs and potential trends for the near future using a quantitative study. In addition, a qualitative approach was chosen to further examine the findings of the study, gaining greater insight by conducting a case study with the federal state of Bremen, Germany. The related documents and information are considered an essential basis for communication in the public sector.

In [34] the authors propose that government agencies should go through an evolutionary path as they progress from an introductory digital presence to more complex forms of interaction with constituents. A path of progression is described, and its key facilitators are highlighted.

Finally, the authors in [28] present an exploratory and interdisciplinary study of issues related to information sharing within and between three public bodies, to illustrate the key points about information sharing among subcultures and some of its implications for research and practice.

After this analysis, it was verified that most of the articles do not present a research approach directly related to knowledge management but approach themes that can indirectly improve knowledge management practices within the public sector. The success of digital government depends on the quality of the organization's knowledge management and how they simultaneously complement each other. There is a lack of studies that relate digital government to the direct or strategic effect of knowledge management effectiveness in the public sector.

4. Quantitative Research Questionnaire Methodology

In the first phase of the research, an analysis of the literature was carried out, with the purpose of analyzing the digital transformation process and its relationship with knowledge management in public administration. To support the research hypothesis and meeting what is intended with this research, the choice of the scientific method fell on a quantitative study, which the authors considered more appropriate to answer the problem. Thus, through quantitative research the problem was quantified by generating numerical data, which can be transformed into usable statistics, to understand the behaviors, attitudes, opinions, and other actions of the sample and to generalize the results to a population. Therefore, with this quantitative method, it was intended to verify the effect of digital transformation on knowledge management practices in Portuguese public administration.

4.1. Sample

The research was carried out in two governmental areas, the General Secretariat of the Ministry of Environment (SGMAMB) and the Office of the Minister for the Environment and Energy Transition (MATE) belonging to the Ministry of the Environment of the Portuguese Government, which was chosen because it is part of the project Fujitsu's SmartDOCS® in the Portuguese Public Administration, which consists of the implementation and procedural management platform.

In the selection of the target audience, characteristics considered interesting within the scope of this study were analyzed. Collaborators directly involved in the process of implementing the digital transformation were selected, as this is a probabilistic convenience sample.

The target population has a total of 213 employees belonging to the services of the two governmental areas of the Ministry of the Environment, of which 54 employees constitute the sample of the study, which represents 25.35% of the target population.

At SGMAMB, comprising 113 employees, questionnaires were distributed to 37 employees, and at MATE, comprising 101 employees, questionnaires were distributed to 17 employees, corresponding to a percentage of 33.04% and 16.83% of the target population of each of the respective government areas. Questionnaire respondents were asked to indicate their gender, age, educational qualifications, years of work, function, and areas of work, in order to use these elements as characteristics of the sample, as it can be seen in Table 6.

The sample presented in Table 6 is composed of mainly females (75.93%), aged between 35 and 49 years (48.15%), and with more than 30 years of work in the studied organization (33.33%). The most frequent educational qualifications correspond to secondary education (10th to 12th years, 42.59%) and graduation (42.59%). SGMAMB integrates a greater number of employees (68.42%), the "administrative" function is the most frequently performed (46.30%), and, finally, the work areas with the highest incidence correspond to the advisory area (20.37%) and the administrative support area (18.52%).

Table 6. Research framework and main results.

Government Areas		SGMAMB		MATE		Total	
		Nr	%	Nr	%	Nr	%
Gender	Male	9	24.32%	4	24.53%	13	24.07%
	Female	28	75.68%	13	76.47%	41	75.93%
Age	From 18 to 24 years	0	0.00%	1	5.88%	1	1.85%
	From 25 to 34 years	0	0.00%	2	11.76%	2	3.70%
	From 35 to 49 years	18	48.65%	8	47.06%	26	48.15%
	From 50 to 64 years	18	48.65%	5	29.41%	23	42.59%
	Over 65 years	1	2.70%	1	5.88%	2	3.70%
Literary abilities	1st to 4th year of EB	0	0.00%	0	0.00%	0	0.00%
	5th to 6th year of EB	0	0.00%	0	0.00%	0	0.00%
	7th to 9th year of EB	1	2.70%	0	0.00%	1	1.85%
	High school (10th to 12th year)	13	35.14%	10	58.82%	23	42.59%
	Bachelor	1	2.70%	0	0.00%	1	1.85%
	Graduation	19	51.35%	4	24.53%	23	42.59%
	masters	2	5.41%	2	11.76%	4	7.41%
	PhD/Post Doc	1	2.70%	1	5.88%	2	3.70%
Years of work	Less than 1 year	0	0.00%	1	5.88%	1	1.85%
	Between 1 and 5 years	1	2.70%	1	5.88%	2	3.70%
	Between 5 and 10 years	2	5.41%	2	11.76%	4	7.41%
	Between 10 and 15 years	4	10.81%	3	17.65%	7	12.96%
	Between 15 and 20 years	7	18.92%	1	5.88%	8	14.81%
	Between 20 and 25 years	5	13.51%	2	11.76%	7	12.96%
	Between 25 and 30 years	6	16.22%	1	5.88%	7	12.96%
	More than 30	12	32.43%	6	35.29%	18	33.33%
Function	Administrative	14	37.84%	11	64.71%	25	46.30%
	Advisor	2	5.41%	4	24.53%	6	11.11%
	Senior Technician	13	35.14%	2	11.76%	15	27.78%
	Computer Specialist	4	10.81%	0	0.00%	4	7.41%
	Computer Technician	1	2.70%	0	0.00%	1	1.85%
	Division Supervisor	3	8.11%	0	0.00%	3	5.56%
Areas of job	Administrative-financial area	12	32.43%	0	0.00%	12	22.22%
	Advisory area	3	8.11%	8	47.06%	11	20.37%
	Training area	1	2.70%	0	0.00%	1	1.85%
	International Relations Area	4	10.81%	0	0.00%	4	7.41%
	IT area	5	13.51%	0	0.00%	5	9.26%
	Human resources area	7	18.92%	0	0.00%	7	12.96%
	Legal Advisory Area	4	10.81%	0	0.00%	4	7.41%
	Administrative support area	1	2.70%	9	52.94%	10	18.52%

4.2. Questionnaire

After the literature review and with a better perception of the state of the art and the importance of digital transformation and knowledge management in public organizations, next is the design phase of the issues that would be the basis of the questionnaires that were made available to a group of employees of the Ministry of the Environment.

The questionnaire focuses on estimating, from the collected data, how the digital transformation process in the Portuguese Public Administration takes place and what its relationship is with knowledge management.

In the elaboration of the questionnaire, an introductory note was added which displays the context of the request for collaboration, the guarantee of anonymity of participation, and the confidentiality of the provided information.

The questionnaire consists of 47 closed-answer questions constructed and organized in two groups allowing the assessment of the perceptions, opinions, attitudes, and behaviors of employees concerning the process of digital transformation and concerning knowledge management in the organization. Therefore, the questionnaire structure consists of two parts, the first consisting of seven questions regarding the characterization of the sample and the second with 47 questions regarding digital transformation and knowledge management.

The questions address issues such as the state of knowledge management or how the organization fosters the importance of digital transformation and knowledge management. Questions were also elaborated to show the relationship between digital transformation and knowledge management.

The choice of the most appropriate response format considered its advantages, such as ease of application, process, and analysis; ease and speed in the act of responding; presenting a low possibility of errors and working with several alternatives.

Thus, the answer to this questionnaire is based on a 5-point psychometric scale—the Likert scale. A response rate was applied that varies consecutively using scores from 1 to 5. The scale used in the questionnaire presents a series of five answer options, of which the respondent must select one of the following:

1.   Totally disagree,
2.   Disagree,
3.   Neither Agree nor Disagree,
4.   Agree,
5.   Totally agree.

Additionally, in order to safeguard the bias of the collected responses, an option of "0–Don't Know" was created and added.

For the analysis and validation of the items, considering the respective meaning of each of the identified issues, they were structured in two representative groups of each of the identified dimensions:

1.   Issues regarding digital transformation
2.   Issues related to Knowledge Management practices

The data collection procedure was carried out in June 2019, and the questionnaire was made available in person at the organization's facilities and a response rate of 25.35% of the target population was obtained.

4.3. Methods

The data were treated using descriptive and inferential statistics, using the SPSS program (Statistical Package for the Social Sciences, Version 26.0; SPSS Inc., Chicago, IL, USA) and the effects with $p < 0.05$ were considered statistically significant.

In the first phase, the set of collected data was submitted and transformed operationally to a basic uniformly varied descriptive analysis.

The results obtained regarding the dimensions of Minimum, Maximum, Average, Standard Deviation, and Asymmetry regarding the totality of the variables observed in the two groups considered were analyzed: Digital Transformation and Knowledge Management.

The homogeneity of the basic variables of each of the groups of identified questions was analyzed to validate whether they demonstrate significant correlations with each other to proceed with the representation of this set of variables by a single variable, that is, one variable for each one of the groups—calculation of Cronbach's alpha index.

After validating the internal coherence expression of the set of responses for the variables in each group, the average response was calculated for all the variables in that group, in order to present, in a first approximation, the unit value underlying that group.

In addition, the main component analysis was carried out by calculating for each group the main component analysis in order to validate whether, with a variability of approximately 50%, it will make sense to represent the group of variables by the first component.

Additionally, the linear regression methodologies were applied to verify the existence of relationships between the created average variables.

5. Result Analysis

5.1. Statistical Characterization of Groups of Variables

After applying basic descriptive analysis methodologies to the two conceptual groups of variables that make up the questionnaire, taking into account their meaning, it was intended to validate the possibility of replacing each of these groups by a single variable, that is, one variable for every group, expressing their meaning.

However, as for the dispersion around the averages, only in exceptional cases does this value exceed 1, so it is possible to infer a remarkable homogeneity in terms of the obtained responses. The correlations between pairs of variables in the two groups were positive, although some of these values are not significant.

Therefore, it was possible to verify the high values of Cronbach's alpha coefficient (>0.7) for both groups of variables, which could improve if some variables were eliminated. These values are also supported by the percentage of total variance obtained for the global variables of each conceptual group, expressed in the analyzes of the first and second main components. It was also found that in both groups, the first component absorbs a large part of the total variability, as depicted in Table 7.

Table 7. Analysis of internal coherence and variance, explained by the first two main components, for each group.

Variable Group	Cronbach Alfa	% of Variance	
		1st CPP	2nd CPP
Digital Transformation	0.878	27.0	15.9
Knowledge Management	0.785	27.6	19.0

Thus, it was possible to verify that, underlying each of the two groups of variables, there is a variable that these observed variables are manifestations, which can be approximated either by the average value of the variables of each group (in the first approximation) or by the first main component respectively—both are linear combinations of group variables.

Furthermore, for reasons of interpretation, it was chosen to proceed with the representation of groups of variables by calculating the average.

5.2. Study by Regression of the Relationships Between Groups of Variables

Therefore, after validating the behavior of each of the groups of variables through a linear combination in order to represent each of the groups, the mean was used to represent the groups.

Thus, in this study it is attempted to estimate by linear regression, the possible linear relationships between the two mean variables representative of the respective groups of questions: DT_med and KM_med, as depicted by Table 8.

Table 8. Analysis of linear relationships, for each group.

Model	Explanatory Variables		Cte.	B_1	B_2	R^2
	KM_med	DT_med				
1		X	(N.S)	0.510 (S)	-	0.66
2	X		(N.S)	0.856 (S)	-	0.66

Legend: (N.S.)—Not significant, (S.)—Significant.

Therefore, it was possible to observe that both Digital Transformation (on average) and knowledge management (on average) present significant values (S.) of the respective coefficients.

The results show that R^2 values are reasonable, namely: 0.66 when considering the explanatory variable DT_med and also 0.66 when considering the explanatory variable KM_med. The regression model whose objective was to verify whether the model explains knowledge management as a function of Digital Transformation showed reasonable average results in the order of 60%, so it can be concluded that the introduction of digital transformation in the Ministry of the Environment has increased knowledge management.

5.3. Overall Discussion

The methodology applied in the exploratory research allowed us to prove the existence of a cause–effect relationship between variables related to digital transformation and variables related to Knowledge Management practices.

Based on the methods of multivariate data analysis, it was possible to validate the hypothesis of the work, in which, in the opinion of the respondents, the Digital Transformation process has a relevant effect on Knowledge Management practices. Furthermore, in turn, it was validated that knowledge management is a critical factor in the success of digital transformation.

For both groups of variables, it was possible to verify a positive asymmetry, meaning that respondents tend to choose high response values, generally above the central value (3), of the chosen Likert response scale—graded from 1 to 5, which corroborates this analysis.

Knowledge management proved to be a critical factor in the success of digital transformation in the public organization. According to literature, knowledge management is the process of creating, capturing, and using knowledge from an organization's intangible assets to improve [57]. Knowledge management, considering it as an intangible and precious asset of an organization, has gained relevance in the strategic positioning of organizations. Within Public Administration, knowledge management "is a powerful facilitator in the current drive for greater efficiency in all areas [11]". In this way, the authors in [10] states that knowledge management "has the potential to greatly influence and improve the renewal processes of the public sector".

Thus, it is concluded that the use of technology combined with the systematic use of knowledge increases efficiency, improves efficiency, and facilitates competence, creativity, and innovation in the studied public organization. In addition, knowledge management proved to be a process of leveraging and articulating the skills and knowledge of employees with the support of information technology [58].

The results of the study show the growing importance of digital government (DG) in the public administration, as measured by the increasing number of published papers and the identification of several key issues. However, there is low specialization because few authors write extensively about the public sector. This lack of cohesive literature is evidenced by the low citation rates.

Furthermore, the low levels of international cooperation between authors contribute to the fragmentation of literature. Some research themes and some geographic areas within the public sector theme are overanalyzed, and others are under-researched. Finally, researchers must rethink methodological approaches to make meaningful contributions to the literature to develop more critical approaches.

6. Conclusions

As a field of research, the digital government has emerged from several disciplines, including public administration, knowledge management and innovation, information technology, information management, element and process management, communication and organizational culture, among others. There have been several efforts in the last decade to outline this emerging academic community, assessing the growing body of research represented by new, revised publications each year.

In this study a review and survey were made with its main focus on estimating, from the collected data, how the digital transformation process in the Public Administration takes place and what its relationship is with knowledge management. The review study aimed to understand the role that digital government research plays in the theory and practice of knowledge management. In the survey study, 54 employees belonging to the services of the two governmental areas of the Portuguese Ministry of the Environment were surveyed.

Knowledge management could provide the overall strategy and techniques for eloquently managing digital government content in order to make knowledge more usable and accessible and keep it current. For the success of digital government, more studies should be carried out using appropriate methods and proposals for new research models, which include the knowledge management approach in the digital government literature. From a perspective of knowledge management, the digital government could be considered an essential aspect of innovation, coproduction, transparency, and the generation of public value.

With the intent to understand the relationship between the implementation of digital transformation and the use of knowledge management practices in public organizations and based on the methods of multivariate data analysis, it was possible to validate the hypothesis of the work, in which, in the opinion of the respondents, the digital transformation process has a relevant effect on knowledge management practices. Furthermore, in turn, it was validated that knowledge management is a critical factor in the success of digital transformation. The regression model disclosed that knowledge management as a function of digital transformation showed a reasonable average outcome in the order of 60%, so it can be concluded that the introduction of Digital Transformation in the Portuguese Ministry of the Environment increased Knowledge Management.

Furthermore, it has been found that the terms used in digital governance studies diverge from other terms that have the same meaning as e-government, which makes bibliographic research challenging. In addition, studies with the term digital transformation are scarce, so digital transformation studies and studies of the terms to be used in the digital government literature may be a possible direction for researchers.

As a result of this study, some research agenda topics were found, such as: studies on knowledge management in the process of digital transformation in public administration; case studies in public organizations that have a high impact on the improvement of public services; studies with methodological approaches that contribute significantly to the digital government literature; structured literature reviews on the topic, including research in more databases in order to perform a more in-depth analysis of the literature of digital government; and international comparative studies.

Several limitations can be highlighted. Firstly, the public sector documents were found only in the Scopus database, which could potentially ignore, involuntarily, some relevant articles on digital government and knowledge management studies. Nevertheless, the selection is a comprehensive and representative sample of the digital government literature.

In addition, this study was based on the analysis and interpretation of results, which can sometimes be subjective. Other researchers using the same data may present different interpretations and conclusions.

Author Contributions: Formal analysis, F.M. and R.G.; supervision, F.M. and J.C.O.M.; writing—original draft, A.A. and F.M.; writing—Review and editing, F.M., R.G. and J.C.O.M. All authors have read and agreed to the published version of the manuscript.

References

1. Al-Ruithe, M.; Benkhelifa, E.; Hameed, K. Key issues for embracing the cloud computing to adopt a digital transformation: A study of saudi public sector. *Procedia Comput. Sci.* **2018**, *130*, 1037–1043. [CrossRef]
2. Weerakkody, V.; Omar, A.; El-Haddadeh, R.; Al-Busaidy, M. Digitally-enabled service transformation in the public sector: The lure of institutional pressure and strategic response towards change. *Gov. Inf. Q.* **2016**, *33*, 658–668. [CrossRef]

3.   Omar, A.; Weerakkody, V.; Sivarajah, U. Digitally enabled service transformation in UK public sector: A case analysis of universal credit. *Int. J. Inf. Manag.* **2017**, *37*, 350–356. [CrossRef]

4.   Lee, J.; Kim, B.J.; Park, S.; Park, S.; Oh, K. Proposing a value-based digital government model: Toward broadening sustainability and public participation. *Sustainability* **2018**, *10*, 3078. [CrossRef]

5.   Zhou, Z.; Gao, F. E-government and knowledge management. *Int. J. Comput. Sci. Netw. Secur.* **2007**, *7*, 285–289.

6.   Araújo, R.P.; Mottin, A.P.; Rezende, J.F.D.C. Gestão do conhecimento e do capital intelectual: Mapeamento da produção acadêmica brasileira de 1997 a 2011 nos encontros da ANPAD. *Organ. Soc.* **2013**, *20*, 283–301. [CrossRef]

7.   Serenko, A.; Bontis, N.; Booker, L.; Sadeddin, K.; Hardie, T. "A scientometric analysis of (1994–2008)", knowledge management and intellectual capital academic literature. *J. Manag. Knowl.* **2010**, *14*, 3–23. [CrossRef]

8.   De Angelis, C.T. Models of governance and the importance of KM for public administration. *J. Knowl. Manag. Pr.* **2013**, *14*, 1–18.

9.   Misra, D.C. Ten guiding principles for knowledge management in e-government in developing countries. In *First International Conference on Knowledge Management for Productivity and Competitiveness*; National Productivity Council: New Delhi, India, 2007.

10. Edge, K. Powerful public sector knowledge management: A school district example. *J. Knowl. Manag.* **2005**, *9*, 42–52. [CrossRef]

11. Mcadam, R.; Reid, R. A comparison of public and private sector perceptions and use of management. *J. Eur. Ind. Train.* **2000**, *24*, 317–329. [CrossRef]

12. Amayah, A.T. Determinants of knowledge sharing in a public sector organization. *J. Manag. Knowl.* **2013**, *17*, 454–471. [CrossRef]

13. Hislop, D. *Knowledge Management in Organizations: Acritical Introduction*; Oxford University Press: Oxford, UK, 2013.

14. Massaro, M.; Dumay, J.; Garatti, A. Public sector knowledge management: A structured literature review. *J. Knowl. Manag.* **2015**, *19*, 530–558. [CrossRef]

15. Guthrie, J.; Ricceri, F.; Dumay, J. Reflections and projections: A decade of intellectual capital accounting research. *Br. Account. Rev.* **2012**, *44*, 68–82. [CrossRef]

16. Dumay, J.; Garanina, T. Intellectual capital research: A critical examination of the thirdstage. *J. Intellect. Cap.* **2013**, *14*, 10–25. [CrossRef]

17. Dumay, J. 15 years of the journal of intellectual capital and counting: A manifesto for transformational IC research. *J. Intellect. Cap.* **2014**, *15*, 2–37. [CrossRef]

18. Dumay, J.; Cai, L. A review and critique of content analysis as a methodology for inquiring into IC disclosure. *J. Intellect. Cap.* **2014**, *15*, 264–290. [CrossRef]

19. Dewey, A.; Drahota, A. Introduction to systematic reviews: Online learning module Cochrane Training. Available online: https://training.cochrane.org/interactivelearning/module-1-introduction-conducting-systematic-reviews (accessed on 16 July 2020).

20. Arksey, H.; O'Malley, L. Scoping studies: Towards a methodological framework. *Int. J. Soc. Res. Methodol.* **2005**, *8*, 19–32. [CrossRef]

21. Petticrew, M.; Roberts, H. *Systematic Reviews in the Social Sciences: A. Practical Guide*; John Wiley & Sons: Hoboken, NJ, USA, 2008; p. 354.

22. Adu, K.K. A multi-methods study exploring the role of stakeholders in the digital preservation environment: The case of ghana. *Electron. Libr.* **2018**, *36*, 650–664. [CrossRef]

23. Adu, K.K.; Ngulube, P. Preserving the digital heritage of public institutions in Ghana in the wake of electronic government. *Libr. Hi Tech* **2016**, *34*, 748–763. [CrossRef]

24. Baron, J.R.; Thurston, A. What lessons can be learned from the US archivist's digital mandate for 2019 and is there potential for applying them in lower resource countries? *Rec. Manag. J.* **2016**, *26*, 206–217. [CrossRef]

25. Bataw, A.; Kirkham, R.; Lou, E. The issues and considerations associated with BIM integration. In *MATEC Web of Conferences*; EDP Sciences: Les Ulis, France, 2016; Volume 66.

26. Dawes, S.S.; Burke, G.B.; Gharawi, M. Transnational digital government research collaborations: Purpose, value, challenges. In Proceedings of the 12th Annual International Digital Government Research Conference on Digital Government Innovation in Challenging Times, College Park, MD, USA, 12–15 June 2011.

27. Dorner, D. Public sector readiness for digital preservation in New Zealand: The rate of adoption of an innovation in records management practices. *Gov. Inf. Q.* **2009**, *26*, 341–348. [CrossRef]

28. Drake, D.B.; Steckler, N.A.; Koch, M.J. Information sharing in and across government agencies: The role and influence of scientist, politician, and bureaucrat subcultures. *Soc. Sci. Comput. Rev.* **2004**, *22*, 67–84. [CrossRef]

29. Eger, J.M.; Maggipinto, A. Technology as a tool of transformation: E-cities and the rule of law. In *Information Systems: People, Organizations, Institutions, and Technologies*; AD'Atri, S., Ed.; Physica-Verlag HD: Berlin/Heidelberg, Germany, 2010; pp. 23–30.

30. Eiermann, L.; Walter, S. Document logistics in the public sector: Integrative handling of physical and digital documents. *Int. J. Netw. Virtual Organ.* **2010**, *7*, 240–256. [CrossRef]

31. Gil-García, J.R.; Dawes, S.S.; Pardo, T.A. Digital government and public management research: Finding the crossroads. *Spec. Issue Digit. Gov. Public* **2018**, *20*, 633–646. [CrossRef]

32. Rahman, M.H.A.A.J. Archivists 2.0: Redefining the archivist's profession in the digital age. *Rec. Manag. J.* **2012**, *22*, 98–115.

33. Kammerer, S.C. Government workers say goodbye to paper. *DB2 Mag.* **2004**, *9*, 38–40.

34. Koh, C.E.; Ryan, S.; Prybutok, V.R. Creating value through managing knowledge in an e-government to constituency (G2C) environment. *J. Comput. Inf. Syst.* **2005**, *45*, 32–41.

35. Kolasa, I. Success factors for public sector information system projects: Qualitative literature review. In Proceedings of the European Conference on e-Government, ECEG, Lisbon, Portugal, 12–13 June 2017; Volume Part F129463, pp. 326–335.

36. Koniaris, M.; Papastefanatos, G.; Anagnostopoulos, I. Solon: A holistic approach for modelling, managing and mining legal sources. *Algorithms* **2018**, *11*, 196. [CrossRef]

37. Lamari, M.; Belgacem, I. Knowledge brokering in the web 2.0 era: Empirical evidence of emerging strategies in government agencies. In Proceedings of the 2012 International Conference on Education and e-Learning Innovations, Sousse, Tunisia, 1–3 July 2012.

38. Lele, U.; Goswami, S. The fourth industrial revolution, agricultural and rural innovation, and implications for public policy and investments: A case of India. *Agric. Econ.* **2017**, *48*, 87–100. [CrossRef]

39. Matheus, R.; Janssen, M. Exploitation and exploration strategies to create data transparency in the public sector. In Proceedings of the ACM International Conference Proceeding Series, Delft, The Netherlands, 1–3 March 2016; pp. 13–16.

40. Müller, H.; Würriehausen, F. Ensuring interoperability of geographic information in local government and inspire. In Proceedings of the 14th International Multidisciplinary Scientific GeoConference SGEM 2014, Albena, Bulgaria, 17–26 June 2014; Volume 3, pp. 559–566.

41. Ndlela, M.N. Knowledge management in the public sector: Communication issues and challenges at local government level. In Proceedings of the 11th European Conference on Knowledge Management, Famalicão, Portugal, 2–3 September 2010; Volume 2, pp. 711–716.

42. Panganiban, G.G.F. E-governance in agriculture: Digital tools enabling filipino farmers. *J. Asian Public Policy* **2019**, *12*, 51–70. [CrossRef]

43. Pappel, I.; Pappel, I.; Saarmann, M. Digital records keeping to information governance in Estonian local governments. In Proceedings of the International Conference on Information Society (i-Society 2012), London, UK, 25–28 June 2012; pp. 199–204.

44. Prokopiadou, G.; Papatheodorou, C.; Moschopoulos, D. Integrating knowledge management tools for government information. *Gov. Inf. Q.* **2004**, *21*, 170–198. [CrossRef]

45. Rocheleau, B. *Case Studies on Digital Government*; IGI Global: Hershey, PA, USA, 2007; ISBN 978-1-59904-177-3.

46. Shilohu Rao, N.J.P.; Goswami, D.; Chaudhary, R. Knowledge management system for governance: Transformational approach creating knowledge as product for governance. In *Crowdsourcing and Knowledge Management in Contemporary Business Environments*; IGI Global: Hershey, PA, USA, 2017; Volume 2, pp. 742–751.

47. Sirendi, R.; Mendoza, A.; Barrier, M.; Taveter, K.; Sterling, L. A conceptual framework for effective appropriation of proactive public e-services. In Proceedings of the 18th European Conference on Digital Government, Santiago, Spain, 25–26 October 2018; Volume 2018, pp. 213–221.

48. Svärd, P. *E-Government Initiatives and Information Management in Two Local Government Authorities*; Academic Publishing International: Cambridge, MA, USA, 2010; pp. 429–436.

49.   Vat, K.H. The E-governance concerns in information system design for effective e-government performance improvement. In *Handbook of Research on E-Government Readiness for Information and Service Exchange: Utilizing Progressive Information Communication Technologies*; IGI Global: Hershey, PA, USA, 2010; Chapter 3, pp. 48–69.

50.   Vivo, M.C.D.; Polzonetti, A.; Tapanelli, P. ICT and PA: A marriage made in heaven? In Proceedings of the European Conference on Information Systems Management, Verona, Italy, 8–10 June 2009; pp. 119–125.

51.   Jane Broadbent, J.G. Public sector to public services: 20 years of 'contextual' accounting research. *Account. Audit. Account. J.* **2008**, *21*, 129–169. [CrossRef]

52.   Alexander Serenko, J.D. Knowledge management journal. Part II: Studying research trends and discovering the Google Scholar Effec. *J. Knowl. Manag.* **2015**, *19*, 1335. [CrossRef]

53.   Rahman, M.H.; Al Joker, A.S. Organizational learning from service innovation in the public sector of Dubai. In Proceedings of the 15th International Conference on Intellectual Capital, Knowledge Management & Organisational Learning, Cape Town, South Africa, 29–30 November 2018; Volume 2018, pp. 261–267.

54.   Merton, R.K. *Social Structure and Social Theory*; Free Press: New York, NY, USA, 1968.

55.   Merton, R.K. The Matthew Effect in Science, II: Cumulative Advantage and the Symbolism of Intellectual Property. *Isis* **1988**, *79*, 606. [CrossRef]

56.   Merton, R.K. On market timing and investment performance. I. An equilibrium theory of value for market forecasts. *J. Bus.* **1981**, *54*, 363–406.

57.   Liao, S. Knowledge management technologies and applications—Literature review from 1995 to 2002. *Expert Syst. Appl.* **2003**, *25*, 155–164. [CrossRef]

58.   Bennet, A.; Bennet, D. The Partnership between Organisational Learning and Knowledge Management. In *International Handbooks on Information Systems*; Springer: Berlin/Heidelberg, Germany, 2004.

7

Do Corporate Social Responsibility Disclosures Improve Financial Performance? A Perspective of the Islamic Banking Industry in Pakistan

Zia Ur Rehman [1], Muhammad Zahid [1,*], Haseeb Ur Rahman [2], Muhammad Asif [1],
Majed Alharthi [3], Muhammad Irfan [4,*] and Adam Glowacz [5]

[1] Department of Management Sciences, City University of Science and IT, Peshawar 25000, Pakistan; obaid3915@gmail.com (Z.U.R.); asifbaloch@cusit.edu.pk (M.A.)
[2] Institute of Management Sciences, University of Science and Technology, Bannu 28100, Pakistan; drhaseeb@ustb.edu.pk
[3] Finance Department, College of Business, King Abdulaziz University, Rabigh 21911, Saudi Arabia; mdalharthi@kau.edu.sa
[4] Electrical Engineering Department, College of Engineering, Najran University Saudi Arabia, Najran 61441, Saudi Arabia
[5] Department of Automatic, Control and Robotics, AGH University of Science and Technology, 30-059 Krakow, Poland; adglow@agh.edu.pl
* Correspondence: zahid@cusit.edu.pk (M.Z.); irfan16.uetian@gmail.com (M.I.)

Abstract: This study aims to investigate the impact of corporate social responsibility disclosures (CSRD) on the financial performance of the Islamic banking industry of Pakistan. The study employed the method of content analysis for collecting the required data from annual reports of all four full-fledged Islamic banks operating in Pakistan from 2012 to 2017. The study developed a novel comprehensive CSRD index by using the "Global Reporting Initiative" (GRI) and "Accounting and Auditing Organization of Islamic Financial Institutions" (AAOIFI). This index consists of five dimensions and 105 sub-dimensions of CSRD. The use of Ordinary Least Squares (OLS), Panel Corrected Standard Errors (PCSEs), and Generalized Least Squares (GLS) using random-effect (RE) and fixed-effect (FE) estimators revealed a significant negative relationship between CSRD and the financial performance of the sample firms. Regarding separate dimensions, the relationship of the Environmental and Economic dimensions of CSRD is significantly positive with current performance, but it is insignificant for the relationships of Legal, Philanthropic, and Ethical dimensions of CSRD with the current financial performance. In addition to contributing to the scarce literature in the Islamic banking industry of a developing country like Pakistan, the study will also help the policymakers and other stakeholders, including the AAOIFI, to develop a comprehensive CSRD policy or index and further improve the already established standards for CSRD.

Keywords: corporate social responsibility disclosure (CSRD); financial performance; Islamic Banking Industry of Pakistan; GRI; AAOIFI; CSRD index

1. Introduction

Adam Smith noted in his book "The Theory of Moral Sentiments" that capitalism would not sustain if not based on integrity and honesty. He suggested that the self-interests of the owners and the managers could be countered by first establishing and then following the moral and ethical values [1]. Most of the recent studies in corporate governance have focused on certain specific issues like corporate fraud, the misuse of managerial powers, and social irresponsibility in business. In response to the changing and challenging market and managerial behavior, the business firms are compelled to take externalities into account. Business ethics and corporate social responsibilities (CSR) are now crucial for being competitive; firstly, these help firms to maintain excellent and trained staff, and secondly, these assist firms in addressing and meeting the customer's expectations [2]. CSR is a corporate move for the betterment of the whole society apart from the compulsions of law and the primary objective that firms are supposed to perform for the wellbeing of shareholders only [3]. Unlike the Western approach, the Islamic perception of CSR is different; it is considered a holy concept. Islam explains CSR in a more religious context that has its roots in both the Quran and Sunnah, which provides a better substitute or framework for the philosophy of the human's interaction with its fellow humans and nature as a whole. The ethical and the moral principles originating from the revelations are greatly eternal, enduring, and absolute; one can perform better by exercising the social and the business responsibilities simultaneously [4].

The Holy Quran has emphasized the CSR activities and declares these for those who are the believers, such as: "Ye cannot attain righteousness unless ye donate to charity from possessions ye love. What ye donate to charity, ALLAH is aware of" Quran, surah 3 Ayahs 92 [3:92]. The financial contributions under CSR are emphasized by the Holy Quran and the Sunnah in the shape of Sadqat and Zakat. Zakat means purification. It is a yearly contribution that is mandatory for the rich and paid to the poor, especially to the widows, orphans, and the elderly people who are no longer able to work or earn for themselves. Islam as a religion offers a complete code of life, including instructions about faith, ethics, morality, prayers, and belief in Allah in every walk of life, such as political, business, social, economic, and religious affairs [5]. The primary purpose of Islam is holistic welfare. The ethical and moral teachings of Islam produce complete and everlasting principles that set guidelines for individuals, society, and economic and business interactions [6].

However, in modern corporations, corporate social responsibility disclosure (CSRD) refers to the improvement of financial performance by bringing significant and positive outcomes through customers' loyalty and commitment to paying high prices and the reduction of the risk directed towards their reputation, especially in times of unfavorable economic conditions [7]. The journey towards CSR has started for the last few centuries and is still moving forward, with no signs of slowing down its pace [8,9]. CSR has much importance in the success of an organization, as customers prefer for the organizations to be responsible economically as well as socially. In Pakistan, the majority of the CSR activities are performed in the light of corporate philanthropy. Corporate financial contributions in the form of donations are considered an authentic tool to improve a corporation's image in an extremely competitive environment [10]. For the last few years, many financial institutions have started introducing CSR practices in their operational and organizational strategies. The banking industry is relatively different, especially regarding corporate governance and other reforms and regulations, including CSR. The banking industry has a central role in society due to its higher level of social interaction; therefore, banks are expected to be socially responsible [11]. Substantial research has examined the relationship between CSRD and the financial performance of conventional financial institutions, which produced inconsistent results. The majority of these studies used the global reporting initiative (GRI) as a benchmark for developing the CSRD index. Some studies on whether CSRD has any contribution towards the financial performance of Islamic banks have also been conducted throughout the world, bearing positive, negative, and neutral results. The majority of these studies relied on the standards established by the Accounting and Auditing Organization of Islamic Financial Institutions (AAOIFI) for developing the CSRD index. Therefore, the motivation of this study is to bridge the gap between these two standards by merging them and developing a more comprehensive index. The AAOIFI standards will help cover the issues related to Shariah compliance, such as Riba, Zakat and Sadqat, Qard-E-Hassana, Shariah Supervisory Board (SSB) approvals, attestation, and other ethical issues. The GRI standards will cover the issues related to conventional aspects, such as community, employees, environment, human rights, and other legal issues.

As far as the Islamic banking industry in Pakistan is concerned, minimal work has been done on the subject matter of CSRD. The Islamic banking industry has a good market share in the overall existing banking industry of Pakistan. Due to the increasing importance of CSR and its disclosures in the banking industry in general and in the Islamic banking industry in particular, it is vital to find out whether or not the increasing market share and financial performance have any relevance to CSR practices and their disclosures in Pakistan. Hence, this study aims to answer the research questions: What is the level of exposure of CSR of the Islamic banking industry in Pakistan? What is the impact of CSR disclosure on the financial performance of the Islamic banking industry in Pakistan? What are the impacts of dimensions of CSR disclosure on the financial performance of the Islamic banking industry in Pakistan?

After answering the above research questions, the study offers several theoretical, methodological, and practical contributions. Firstly, the study contributes to the literature on Islamic banking in Pakistan, as there were limited studies in the past [9,12]. Secondly, the study has a theoretical contribution in the application of the crux of stakeholder theory in the literature of Islamic banking, which may further assist the industry in understanding the demand of multiple stakeholders and legitimizing their license to operate on the larger canvas of the society [13–15]. Thirdly, the study extends the existing CSRD index, which is based on the Global Reporting Initiative (GRI) framework and "Accounting and Auditing Organization of Islamic Financial Institutions" (AAOIFI); it consists of five dimensions and 105 sub-dimensions of CSRD. The study claims that the novel index is more comprehensive than those of previous studies [9,16] and has a methodological contribution in measuring CSRD in developing countries like Pakistan. Likewise, the study applied a panel data longitudinal analysis approach from 2012 to 2017, as the focus of the previous studies was limited in the period and dimensions of CSRD. The study period is important, as many environmental, social, and governance reforms (ESG), along with the concept of green banking, its regulations, and the codes of corporate governance of 2012 and 2017, were introduced during this time in Pakistan. Finally, this study provides practical implications for management and policymakers of the Islamic banking industry to understand the importance of CSRD reporting and its impact on overall firm performance. Furthermore, it would add to the systematic presentation of CSRD in developing an international attitude towards CSRD, especially in developing countries.

The rest of the paper consists of a literature review where the theoretical framework and hypothesis development followed by the conceptual framework are discussed. The data sample, measurement of financial performance and CSRD with the research model, and the estimations are discussed in the methodology section. Finally, the results and discussions with conclusions, limitations of the study, and future directions are reported.

2. Literature Review

2.1. CSRD and Financial Performance of Islamic Banks

Prior studies noted a positive and considerable association between firms' profitability and the magnitude of their CSRD [9,17,18]. Most profitable organizations disclose their CSR information to show their social role in the wellbeing of the community and ensure their survival in the industry. A study found a significant positive relationship between the practices of CSR disclosed in the annual reports and performance of the selected Islamic banks regarding the goodwill in Malaysia [19]. In another study, the possible link between CSRD and financial performance of the Islamic banks selected from different countries from 2010 to 2011 was investigated. The analyses indicated a significant positive relationship between the CSRD and financial performance [20]. Another study investigated the information that is crucial for ethical issues in Islamic business [21]. They designed a moral benchmark that is considered vital to differentiate Islamic banks from conventional banks. Using content analyses, they collected data from annual reports and noted a significant gap between the expected and actual disclosures. They concluded that the expected gap may have originated from the indifferent behavior of the stakeholders or the Arab culture where the sample banks were located. In the end, they summarized that if the Islamic banks intend to remain in competition with conventional banks, their communication should be even more useful to improve their overall reputation in the society in which they operate. Another dimension of the study examined the degree and the nature of CSRD and its impact on the firms' performance in a study of 90 Islamic banks from 13 countries for a period from 2010 to 2011 [20]. The study constructed a comprehensive CSRD index for the Islamic banks where the AAOIFI standard No. 7 was used to collect data. The study reported a direct link between CSRD, the financial performance of Islamic banks, and the level of CSRD for different countries. Among them, Indonesia stood first with the highest score of 54%, while Pakistan was the last with the lowest score, i.e., 30.4%. The researchers investigated CSRD in the Islamic banks of Malaysia and found that the volume and quantity of CSRD have improved with time [22]. Another study [23] noted a regular sequence in the CSRD in three phases in the Islamic banking industry of Bangladesh, i.e., the pre-1990s, 1990–2001, and post-2001. Similarly, they divided the moral and the ethical reporting of CSR into two categories, i.e., the particular style of reporting that is related to the Islamic banks, especially those practicing Shariah compliance, and the universal standards of reporting practices that mostly account for shareholders' communities, customers, and the employees. They noticed an overall positive increase in both the particular and the universal standards of disclosures over the corresponding period, but an upward shift in the universal disclosures after 2006. However, in contrast, some studies found a negative association between CSRD dimensions and financial performance. For example, a study found a negative impact of the environmental and social dimensions of CSRD on the financial performance of Malaysian Islamic banks [9].

2.2. Theoretical Framework and Hypothesis Development

The stakeholder's theory states that the main objective of organizations is the creation and maximization of stakeholders' value. Whenever the firms meet the expectations of more than a single stakeholder, they come into a position to improve their performance [13,24]. Given this, the theory that explains the disclosure of CSR and its impact on the firm's performance is the stakeholder theory. As per this theory, if an organization wants to be more efficient, it has to pay greater attention to all of the relationships, especially to those that affect or are affected by the organization's objectives. The stakeholder management assumption of the theory is a useful tool to gain the results which are already predicted, especially the profitability. This aspect of the said theory signals a link between the stakeholders and the performance of the corporation [13]. To summarize the stakeholders' theory, the stakeholders are assets and the managers are expected to manage them effectively. Similarly, the social responsibilities of the business organizations are to accomplish the needs of their stakeholders for which they are legally and socially responsible [25]. From a CSR perspective, society expects firms to run their operations responsibly regardless of their economic and commercial interests. The main crux of this theory is that the organization's goals must be in line with the goals of society. The theory further supports the goals of the Islamic banks to satisfy the demand of multiple stakeholders in the normative approach and avail instrumental benefits in the shape of better financial performance [13,26]. All of these arguments and assumptions are also compatible with the teachings of Islam regarding CSR. In addition to compliance with the governmental policies and reforms, Islam also necessitates the welfare of the individuals, society, environment, and all other creatures in the universe. Most of the prior empirical studies found a positive link between the individual dimension of CSRD and financial performance [9,27]. These positive impacts are mainly attributed to the competitive advantage, which improves customers' relations and retention and thus recognizes better financial performance. Competitive advantage is closely related to firms' financial performance. The conventional concept of competitiveness is widely used in a business strategy, which means that a firm becomes competitive when it gains higher financial returns than the average of its industry peers [28]. Similarly, the authors further argued that the individual dimension of the CSRD is equally important, as certain information may be lost while using the aggregate CSRD against financial performance. Thus, it is necessary to find a link between the individual dimensions of CSRD and financial performance. The detailed literature review and the previous discussion hint at a positive association of the particular dimensions of CSRD, i.e., Ethical, Legal, Environmental, Economic, and Philanthropic, with financial performance. Therefore, the following hypotheses are developed.

Hypothesis 1. *The CSRD has a positive impact on the financial performance of the Islamic banking industry in Pakistan.*

Hypothesis 2. *The ethical dimension of CSRD has a positive impact on the financial performance of Islamic banks.*

Hypothesis 3. *The legal dimension of CSRD has a positive impact on the financial performance of Islamic banks in Pakistan.*

Hypothesis 4. *The economic dimension of CSRD has a positive impact on the financial performance of Islamic banks in Pakistan.*

Hypothesis 5. *The environmental dimension of CSRD has a positive impact on the financial performance of Islamic banks in Pakistan.*

Hypothesis 6. *The philanthropic dimension of CSRD has a positive impact on the financial performance of Islamic banks in Pakistan.*

2.3. Conceptual Framework

The conceptual framework of the study is based on Carroll's CSR model and the two approaches, namely normative and instrumental, of the stakeholder theory. The Carroll CSR model supports the ethical, legal, economic, environmental, philanthropic, and financial performance [29]. The approaches of stakeholder theory further underpin the relationships among these variables; the Islamic banks try to satiate the demand of multiple stakeholders in the normative approach and avail instrumental benefits in the shape of better financial performance [13,26]. These relationships are depicted in Figure 1.

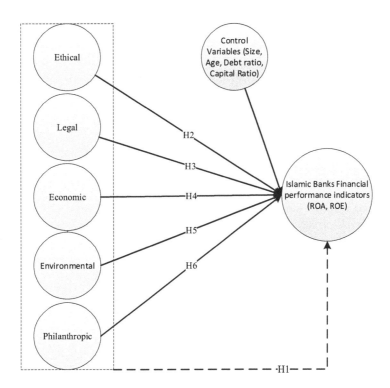

Figure 1. Conceptual framework.

3. Materials and Methods

3.1. Sample for the Research

In Pakistan, the total population of Islamic Banks registered with the State Bank of Pakistan (SBP) was five banks, namely the MCB Islamic Bank Limited, Bank Al Meezan Limited, Bank Al Baraka Limited, Bank Islami Limited, and Dubai Islamic Bank Limited [30]. However, the study excluded MCB Bank Limited, as it operates in both the Islamic and conventional or commercial banking, and had no separate annual report on Islamic banking and CSRD. The study selects the data collection period from 2012 to 2017, as many reforms regarding the environment, society, and governance (ESG), along with the concept of green banking, its regulations in Pakistan, and the codes of corporate governance of 2012 and 2017, were introduced during this period.

3.2. Measurement of Financial Performance

Most of the previous studies that investigated the association between CSRD and financial performance mainly relied on the accounting aspect of firms' performance [31]. These studies used return on assets (ROA), which is a key indicator of the firms' financial performance showing managerial efficiency, ability, and competency to generate profits by using the assets of the banks. Some studies also used the accounting measure of Return on equity (ROE) for measuring firm performance as an additional indicator or robustness check. It is also necessary to mention that ROE is strongly linked with the ROA, and, therefore, it is important to use this ratio as an extra measure of a bank's performance. Hence, this study uses ROA to measure the financial performance of the Islamic banks and employs ROE for further validation of the results.

3.3. Measurement of CSR Disclosure

For data collection, the study relied on the annual reports of Islamic banks of Pakistan. The procedure of content analysis was adopted for data collection from the annual reports of the sample banks. The content analysis procedure is considered less expensive and unmistakable as compared to some other methods. Hence, it is frequently used in previous studies related to CSRD [32,33]. Following prior studies, an unweighted scoring method was applied to record the data for the CSRD index by using a dichotomous procedure, where disclosure is assigned a value of 1 if an item is disclosed in the report of a bank, and 0 otherwise [26,34]. The study used five dimensions of CSRD, namely Ethical, Legal, Environmental, Economic, and Philanthropic, which constitute composite CSRD. The sub-dimensions of each dimension are marked as 1 in the case that the sub-dimension is reported in the annual report, and 0 otherwise, by using the content analysis technique for the respective bank. Finally, adding these scores contributes to the total disclosure of CSRD for each sample bank. For each dimension of CSRD, this procedure is summarized by the equation as $\frac{\sum di}{N}$, where d = 1 if the CSRD exists and 0 if not, while N is the total number of maximum possible disclosures for the given dimension. Similarly, the whole equation for the composite CSRD is given as:

$$\mathrm{CSRD} = \frac{\sum_{i=1}^{n} X_{ikt}}{N}$$

where the CSRD index $_{kt}$ represents the disclosure index for dimension k and time t, while X is a variable starting from 1 to n (1 ... n) for the given dimension k and the time t.

ROA represents a return on assets, which is measured by dividing the net income by the total assets, while the CSRD is the total CSR disclosure score, which can be calculated as dividing the total disclosures of the sub-dimensions by the maximum number of sub-dimensions possibly reported by a bank. The CSR dimensions consist of the Ethical, Legal, Environmental, Economic, and Philanthropic dimensions, which compose the CSR aggregate, i.e., CSRD. The capital ratio, represented by Cap Ratio, is calculated as the equity capital divided by total assets for the respective year. Size represents the size of the bank, which will be calculated as the log of total assets. The debt ratio will be calculated as the ratio of long-term debt to the total assets. Similarly, the firm's age can be calculated by taking the years since the bank was registered or started its operations. Here, ε represents the error factor, and α is the intercept in the regression model. Return on equity (ROE), used as a robustness check, is measured as the net income divided by shareholders' equity.

3.4. Estimation

The random-effect (RE) and fixed-effect (FE) models of Generalized Least Squares (GLS) were applied to the panel data to investigate the impact of CSRD on the financial performance of Islamic banks. In addition, the study used the Ordinary Least Squares (OLS) regression and Panel-Corrected Standard Errors (PCSEs) estimators for the robustness of the GLS estimations. However, the study claims the results of GLS, as these are more robust than other estimators for panel data analyses. The GLS random-effect model assumes the variation across the entities to be random and uncorrelated with the predictor or independent variables included in the model. In contrast, the fixed-effect model of GLS controls is for all of the time-invariant differences between the cross-sections; hence, the estimated coefficients of the fixed-effect models cannot be biased because of omitted time-invariant characteristics. The author explains the difference as " ... the crucial distinction between fixed and random effects is whether the unobserved individual effect embodies elements that are correlated with the regressors in the model, whether these effects are stochastic or not" [35]. In GLS, the Hausman test was employed to decide between the random-effect and fixed-effect models. If the result of the Hausman test is significant (Chi 2, Prob. > Chi 2), then the fixed-effect model is appropriate; if not, then the random-effect model is selected. Most of the previous studies related to CSR and financial performance employed the same methodology [36,37]. The results of the Hausman test in this study are reported below. The research models are shown as follows.

Model I

$$ROA = \alpha + \beta1 CSRD + \beta2 SIZE + \beta3 Cap\ Ratio + \beta4\ Age + \beta5\ Debt\ Ratio + \varepsilon$$

Model II

$$ROA = \alpha + \beta1 Dimensions + \beta2 SIZE + \beta3 Cap.ratio + \beta4\ Age + \beta5\ Debt\ Ratio + \varepsilon$$

4. Results and Discussion

The descriptive statistics with the Skewness and Kurtosis show that some variables were not normally distributed, which might be due to outliers. Thus, the data were normalized by using the Van der Waerden data distribution method. The Kurtosis statistics are in a range of ±3 and the Skewness in a range of ±1.96 [21], as reported in Table 1. In addition, the mean and the standard deviation, the minimum statistics, and the maximum statistics with the mean statistics are also reported in Table 1. To check the heteroscedasticity, the Breusch–Pagan/Cook–Weisberg test and White's test were conducted on both the composite CSRD model and the dimension model. In both the models, there was no issue of heteroscedasticity, as the probability of both the tests (Breusch–Pagan/Cook–Weisberg and White's tests) was less than 0.5. Therefore, the data are fit for regression.

The descriptive statistics for all of the variables of the study from the given sample of 24 observations over 6 years from all four full-fledged Islamic banks across the country are reported in Table 1. The findings show that the lowest value is −0.140 and the highest value is 0.950, with a standard deviation of 0.273 for ROA. The mean for ROA is 0.202, which indicates that return on assets at the given period, i.e., 2012–2017, remained stable. However, as far as the CSRD index is concerned, the minimum statistic is 35, while the maximum value is 78, along with the mean value of 57.38. These statistics indicate that the banks have increased their disclosures during the given period, which shows their confidence and belief in CSR practices and CSRD. This also provides a clear indication of the Islamic banks' commitment towards increasing their interaction with the customers and the investors, as well as the society at large, to reduce the communication gap and improve the overall image of the Islamic banking industry. The positive increase in the CSRD can be interpreted as: The banks consider socially responsible activities very crucial for shaping the public opinion in favor of the banks. The average size of the bank has a lowest value of 0.103 and a highest value of 11.81, with a mean value of 8.46. This shows an overall expansion in the size of the banks and their assets over the given period. Similarly, the capital ratio has a lowest value of 0.035 and a highest statistic of 0.172, with a mean value of 0.116 and a standard deviation of 0.033. The lowest statistics for debt ratio are 2.780, while the highest statistics are 20.580, with mean statistics of 11.59, which shows an increase in the level of debt. This indicates that banks increasingly dependent on debt to finance their operations. The firm's age has a minimum statistic of 2 and a maximum statistic is 14, with a mean value of 8.25, showing that most of the sample banks have an average age of less than 10 years. The minimum statistic for the individual dimension of CSRD, i.e., the environmental dimension, is 2, and the maximum is 10, while the mean score is 5.21. The minimum number for the legal dimension is 3 and the maximum is 9, with a mean value of 6.71. The minimum statistic for the ethical dimension of CSRD is 2, while the maximum is 13 and the mean score is 7.88. The minimum value for the economic dimension of CSRD is 5, while the maximum is 10. The mean value is 7.04 with a standard deviation of 1.68, which is pretty handsome, showing a strong and growing commitment of the banks towards the disclosure of this dimension. The minimum value for the philanthropic/social dimension of CSRD is 18 and the maximum value is 37, with a mean score of 26.46.

Table 1. Descriptive statistics.

	Minimum Statistic	Maximum Statistic	Mean Statistic	Std. Deviation Statistic	Skewness		Kurtosis	
					Statistic	Std. Error	Statistic	Std. Error
ROA	−0.14	0.95	0.20	0.27	1.21	0.47	0.93	0.91
ROE	0.02	0.28	0.12	0.07	0.45	0.47	0.41	0.91
Firm Size	0.10	11.81	8.46	4.93	−1.22	0.47	−0.54	0.91
Capital ratio	0.03	0.17	0.11	0.03	−0.83	0.47	0.66	0.91
Debt ratio	2.78	20.5	11.59	5.61	−0.32	0.47	−1.08	0.91
Age	2	14	8.25	3.08	−0.17	0.47	−0.42	0.91
CSRD	35	78	57.38	14.26	−0.19	0.47	−1.36	0.91
Environmental	2	10	5.21	2.58	0.25	0.47	−1.04	0.91
Legal	3	9	6.71	1.45	−0.26	0.47	0.37	0.91
Ethical	2	13	7.88	3.71	−0.37	0.47	−1.33	0.91
Economic	5	10	7.04	1.68	0.40	0.47	−0.81	0.91
Philanthropic/social	18	37	26.46	6.15	0.24	0.47	−1.14	0.91

From Table 2, as shown, the Pearson correlation matrix does not detect any multicollinearity, i.e., above 0.8 between two predictors. So, the predictors that are to be tested for regression are not highly correlated and are, therefore, fit for further analysis.

Figure 2 shows a relation between the average percentages for CSRD over the period 2012–2017. The figure indicates that the average CSRD in 2012, 2013, and 2014 is 49%, while from 2015, there is an abrupt change in percentage, reaching a score of 53%. It falls back to 51% and 50.8% in 2016 and 2017, respectively. During the corresponding period, the average percentage score for the industry remained at 51%.

Table 2. Correlation matrix.

	(1)	(2)	(3)	(4)	(5)	(6)	(7)	(8)	(9)	(10)	(11)	(12)
ROA (1)	1											
Size (2)	−0.03	1										
Age (3)	−0.01	0.90 *	1									
Capital Ratio (4)	−0.08	0.04	−0.09	1								
Debt Ratio (5)	−0.06	0.72 **	0.88 **	0.11	1							
Environment (6)	0.02	0.80 *	0.79 **	−0.09	0.87 *	1						
Legal (7)	−0.647 **	0.16	0.10	0.23	0.20	0.11	1					
Ethical (8)	−0.70 *	0.33	0.27	0.33	0.33	0.28	0.81 **	1				
Economic (9)	0.55 **	0.29	0.17	0.31	0.31	0.19	0.78 **	0.73 **	1			
Philanthropic (10)	0.73 **	0.36	0.27	0.27	0.36	0.29	0.77 **	0.88 **	0.78 **	1		
CSRD (11)	0.56 **	0.33	0.31	0.10	0.26	0.33	0.80 **	0.81 **	0.63 **	0.68 **	1	
Lag ROA (12)	0.41	0.89 **	0.10	0.04	−0.11	0.09	0.06	0.63 **	0.69 **	0.61 **	0.78 **	1

Note: Standard errors are in parentheses. ** $p < 0.05$, * $p < 0.1$.

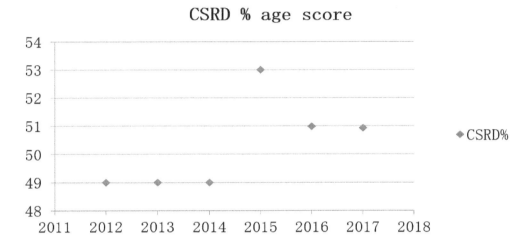

Figure 2. Trend of percentage corporate social responsibility disclosure (CSRD) score for the Islamic banking industry.

The results of the Hausman test for all of the models are reported at the ends of Tables 3 and 4. In all of the models, the results indicated that the random-effect model was an appropriate choice, as it is believed that the omitted variables only vary over time or between cases. Likewise, when such a situation exists, the random-effect model can give relatively more robust results [38]. Furthermore, endorsing our results, it is also acknowledged that Islamic banks in Pakistan are limited in number; hence, they keep a close eye on each other, especially regarding CSR activities and market strategies for the satisfaction of multiple stakeholders. Table 3 explains 54.2% of the variation in ROA and 52.1% variation in ROE due to change in the predictors. The model is significant at $p < 0.01$. The results indicate that CSRD has a significant negative relationship with financial performance (ROA) at $p < 0.01$. These results, which endorse prior studies, noted a significant negative relationship between CSR and financial performance [31,39]; this may have a plausible explanation in that increases in CSR activities and their financial cost have negatively affected the financial performance of the banks by decreasing their profitability. However, these findings are contradictory to the first hypothesis, H_1, of the study; thus, it is rejected. The significantly negative coefficient (instead of positive) for CSRD with financial performance is also contrary to the suppositions of the stakeholders. Nevertheless, the findings are consistent with the postulations of the tradeoff hypothesis presented by Friedman, that the firms' prime responsibility is to maximize the profits of the stakeholders [39]. Hence, managers and firms involved in social activities could cause extra costs to the firms that ultimately decrease their profits. In short, the theory suggests that the greater the level of CSRD, the smaller would be the financial performance of the firm [37,40].

Table 3. CSRD and financial performance.

	(1)	(2)	(3)	(4)	(5)	(6)
	ROA OLS	ROA GLS Random	ROA GLS Fixed	ROE OLS	ROE GLS Random	ROE GLS Fixed
CSRD	−0.587 **	−0.587 ***	−0.053	0.022	0.022	0.009
	(0.201)	(0.201)	(0.286)	(0.146)	(0.146)	(0.109)
Firm size	−1.331	−1.331	0.396	0.667	0.667	1.094 *
	(1.344)	(1.344)	(1.341)	(0.740)	(0.740)	(0.524)
Capital ratio	0.028	0.028	0.725	−0.050	−0.050	0.410 **
	(0.254)	(0.254)	(0.481)	(0.136)	(0.136)	(0.179)
Debt ratio	−0.502	−0.502	−0.331	−0.365	−0.365	−0.322
	(0.492)	(0.492)	(0.514)	(0.265)	(0.265)	(0.193)
Age	2.303	2.303 *	0.876	−0.279	−0.279	−1.630
	(1.332)	(1.332)	(3.792)	(0.730)	(0.730)	(1.438)
Lag ROA	0.130	0.130	−0.067	-	-	-
	(0.250)	(0.250)	(0.261)	-	-	-
Years	−0.356 *	−0.356 *	−0.215	0.015	0.015	0.344
	(0.184)	(0.184)	(1.090)	(0.099)	(0.099)	(0.400)
Lag ROE	-	-	-	0.787 ***	0.787 ***	0.164
	-	-	-	(0.144)	(0.144)	(0.199)
_cons	716.232 *	716.232 *	433.129	−31.300	−31.300	−693.116
	(370.697)	(370.697)	(2195.810)	(199.219)	(199.219)	(806.422)
Obs.	24	24	24	24	24	24
R−squared	0.542	0.542	0.344	0.837	0.837	0.521
Hausman Test (Chi2)	-	8.3	-	-	-	34.82 ***
Prob. > Chi 2	-	0.307	-	-	-	0.000

Note: Standard errors are in parentheses. *** $p < 0.01$, ** $p < 0.05$, * $p < 0.1$.

Figure 2 indicates that the Islamic banking industry has increased CSRD, but, still, the stakeholders' perception in this regard is not positive, which, on one hand, shows a strong commitment of the industry towards CSRD, but, on the other hand, a poor public or customer response. This might be due to the rationale that "Pakistanis are the most generous people. Pakistan's contribution to charity is almost 1% of its GDP, which distinguishes it in the list of top-ranked countries with respect to charitable activities, like the United Kingdom contributing 1.3% of GDP and Canada contributing 1.2% of its GDP to charity; Pakistan gives about twice what India gives to charity" [41]. Despite all of these facts, the significantly negative coefficient of CSRD may also signal that the message of the Islamic banking industry has not been properly communicated to the stakeholders. As a plausible explanation for this, the annual reports published by Islamic banks are not well organized. Except for Bank Al Meezan Limited, the rest of these reports could not properly showcase the CSR-related information, which might affect the behavior of the potential customers. The average industrial age reveals that the Islamic banking industry is in the emerging stage; therefore, it would take time to acquire a stage of maturity. The country has also passed through an intense wave of terrorism and extremism starting from 2002 onward, which has affected business activities, the overall economy in general, and the banking industry in particular. However, the average CSRD shows a slight increase in the average CSRD for the last couple of years, while an average decrease has been reported in the financial performance (ROA). The findings for ROA are also consistent with those of ROE, which is used as an additional measure to gauge performance and validate the results.

The regression results reported in Table 4 explain 83% of the variation in ROA and 92.8% variation in ROE due to change in the predictors. These results show that all of the dimensions of CSRD are statistically insignificant with the firm's current financial performance (ROA), except the environmental and economic dimensions. These results also indicate that the ethical dimension of CSRD is insignificant with the firm's financial performance, which rejects hypothesis H_2 of the study. It is to be noted that the ethical dimension of CSRD is statistically significant with the ROE at significance level $p < 0.05$. The ROE, which is used as a robustness check throughout the analysis, is mostly associated with the owners of the banks. Therefore, the owners of the banks are comparatively more attracted to the ethical issues, as these are worthy of the goodwill of the banks without incurring any direct cost to them. Similarly, the legal dimension of CSRD is also statistically insignificant with the firm's financial performance, so hypothesis H_3 is also rejected. These results endorse a previous study showing that most of the developing countries have a lower priority for the legal dimensions [42]. This does not necessarily mean that firms in the developing countries flaunt the laws, but they are under minor pressure to operate responsibly. In these countries, there are certain issues in the legal systems that do not pressure the firms to operate in full compliance with the relevant laws. These countries are also far behind the developed countries in practicing issues like human rights and others such as the CSR in their legislation [34].

Table 4. Dimensions of CSRD and financial performance.

	(1)	(2)	(3)	(4)	(5)	(6)
	ROA (OLS)	ROA (GLS Random)	ROA (GLS Fixed)	ROE (OLS)	ROE (GLS Random)	ROE (GLS Fixed)
Environmental	0.821 **	0.821 **	0.723	0.283	0.283	0.142
	(0.324)	(0.324)	(0.411)	(0.204)	(0.204)	(0.200)
Legal	−0.011	−0.011	0.364	−0.102	−0.102	0.364
	(0.304)	(0.304)	(0.394)	(0.176)	(0.176)	(0.205)
Ethical	−0.436	−0.436	−1.052 *	0.472*	0.472 **	−0.347
	(0.370)	(0.370)	(0.548)	(0.232)	(0.232)	(0.320)
Economic	0.645 *	0.645 *	0.384	0.583 **	0.583 ***	0.062
	(0.339)	(0.339)	(0.376)	(0.203)	(0.203)	(0.222)
Philanthropic	−0.598	−0.598	−0.675	0.009	0.009	0.056
	(0.399)	(0.399)	(0.583)	(0.230)	(0.230)	(0.289)
Firm size	−0.799	−0.799	−0.287	0.556	0.556	1.244 *
	(1.067)	(1.067)	(1.181)	(0.631)	(0.631)	(0.575)
Capital ratio	0.086	0.086	0.926	−0.238	−0.238	0.698 *
	(0.195)	(0.195)	(0.686)	(0.157)	(0.157)	(0.356)
Debt ratio	0.005	0.005	0.325	−0.326	−0.326	−0.285
	(0.371)	(0.371)	(0.487)	(0.218)	(0.218)	(0.237)
Firm age	1.821	1.821 *	3.936	0.119	0.119	−1.432
	0.821 **	0.821 **	0.723	0.283	0.283	0.142
Lag ROA	0.087	0.087	0.042	-	-	-
	(0.216)	(0.216)	(0.217)	-	-	-
Years	−0.509 **	−0.509 ***	−0.973	−0.269 *	−0.269 *	0.328
	(0.186)	(0.186)	(1.169)	(0.139)	(0.139)	(0.571)
Lag ROE	-	-	-	0.722 ***	0.722 ***	0.018
	-	-	-	(0.203)	(0.203)	(0.278)
_cons	1026.163 **	1026.163 ***	1959.252	542.467 *	542.467 *	−660.113
	(374.915)	(374.915)	(2355.501)	(279.282)	(279.282)	(1151.203)
Obs.	24	24	24	24	24	23
R-squared (Overall)	0.830	0.830	0.752	0.928	0.928	0.715
Hausman Test (Chi2)	-	5.000	-	-	11.25	-
Prob. > Chi 2	-	0.931	-	-	0.423	-

Note: Standard errors are in parentheses. *** $p < 0.01$, ** $p < 0.05$, * $p < 0.1$.

However, the environmental dimension of CSRD has a positive and significant relationship with the financial performance of the sample Islamic banks at a significance level of $p < 0.05$. Therefore, the hypothesis H_4 is accepted. This shows that the customers and other stakeholders pay greater attention to environmental issues. The previous studies indicate inconsistent results for the relationship between the environmental dimension and financial performance. Some of these studies found a negative or neutral association [43,44]. However, the results of the current study are in line with many previous studies showing a significant positive relationship between the environmental dimension of CSRD and the financial performance [31,45–48]. The economic dimension of CSRD has a positive and statistically significant relationship with the financial performance (ROA) at a significance level $p < 0.10$, which confirms hypothesis H_5 of the study. Similarly, the economic dimension of CSRD is also statistically significant and positive with the ROE at a significant level $p < 0.01$. The findings which support H_6 are compatible with a prior study showing a positive and significant relationship between the economic dimension of CSRD and financial performance [49]. The Islamic banking industry has flourished for the last couple of years, especially in Pakistan, with a high profit margin, based on Shariah; therefore, the customers are increasingly inclined towards Islamic banking due to the economic transparency and other benefits offered. The customers are attracted to the Islamic banking industry due to its operations based on the principles of profit and loss. As indicated by Figure 2, these banks are more inclined towards publicizing the economic information because, economically, they are considered to be more transparent, committed, and ethically responsible.

The philanthropic dimension of CSR also has an insignificant relationship with ROA, which rejects hypothesis H_6 of the study. As we know, Islam has a social and legal code of conduct, which is its beauty. The philanthropic aspect of CSRD is what the customers expect from an Islamic bank. The negative and insignificant relationship of the philanthropic dimension with financial performance could be possibly explained in that Islam discourages disclosing the philanthropic efforts due to ethical considerations [50]. Islam discourages both individuals and groups from disclosing the philanthropic and social practices they carry, as this may hurt the ego, dignity, and self-esteem of those who receive Zakat, Sadqat, Qard-e-Hassana, donations, charity, etc. Islam also warns that the publicity of philanthropic activities may hurt the true sense of giving (or welfare), which affects its promised return in the eternal world. Hence, philanthropic practices are usually kept hidden and undisclosed in an Islamic society; if they are not, or are reported, the customers may perceive these negatively. In addition, the study also estimated all models through Panel-Corrected Standard Error (PCSE), which is considered an appropriate estimator for micro-panel datasets where N is small and T is large [51–55]. The findings reported in Table 5 under the PCSEs are consistent with those of OLS and GLS, which further authenticates the accuracy and reliability of all of the estimations in the current study.

Table 5. Panel-Corrected Standard Errors.

	(PCSEs)	(PCSEs)	(PCSEs)	(PCSEs)
	ROA	ROE	ROA	ROE
CSRD	−0.587 ***	0.022	-	-
	(0.198)	(0.072)	-	-
Firm size	−1.331	0.667	−0.799	0.556
	(1.017)	(0.545)	(0.869)	(0.523)
Capital ratio	0.028	−0.050	0.086	−0.238 **
	(0.239)	(0.104)	(0.202)	(0.119)
Debt ratio	−0.502	−0.365 ***	0.005	−0.326 **
	(0.481)	(0.132)	(0.243)	(0.159)
Firm age	2.303 **	−0.279	1.821 **	0.119
	(0.921)	(0.494)	(0.790)	(0.492)
Lag of ROA	0.130	-	0.087	-
	(0.241)	-	(0.198)	-
Lag of ROE	-	0.787 ***	-	0.722 ***
	-	(0.102)	-	(0.165)
Environmental	-	-	0.821 ***	0.283
	-	-	(0.262)	(0.179)
Legal	-	-	−0.011	−0.102
	-	-	(0.189)	(0.131)
Ethical	-	-	0.436	0.472 ***
	-	-	(0.339)	(0.156)
Economic	-	-	0.645 **	0.583 ***
	-	-	(0.306)	(0.181)
Philanthropic	-	-	−0.598	0.009
	-	-	(0.382)	(0.111)
Years	−0.356 ***	0.015	−0.509 ***	−0.269 **
	(0.115)	(0.062)	(0.140)	(0.106)
Constant	716.232 ***	−31.300	1026.163 ***	542.467 **
	(232.074)	(124.751)	(281.519)	(213.381)
Obs.	23	23	23	23
R-squared	0.542	0.837	0.830	0.928

Standard errors are in parentheses. *** $p < 0.01$, ** $p < 0.05$, * $p < 0.1$.

5. Conclusions and Recommendations

This study aimed to examine the relationship between CSRD and the financial performance of the Islamic banks in Pakistan. The findings indicate that the overall level of CSRD for the given sample is 51%, which is slightly different from the CSRD reported by a previous study [20]. The prior study shows that Islamic banks in Pakistan disclose around 30.4% of CSR in their annual reports. This indicates that CSRD increased from 2014 onward. The findings also reveal a significant negative relationship between the CSRD and financial performance of the Islamic banks in Pakistan. Concerning separate dimensions, the legal, philanthropic, and ethical dimensions also have no significant or positive associations with the financial performance of these banks. Though these findings are not in line with most of the established hypotheses (H1, H2, H3, and H6) of the study and postulations of stakeholder theory, still, these results are compatible with Friedman, who argued that CSRD may cause extra costs to the firms that ultimately decrease their profits. In short, the theory suggests that the greater the level of CSR, the smaller the financial performance of the firm will be. Hence, the results are contrasted with the theoretical argument of stakeholder theory, which posits that CSRD improves firms' financial performance by increasing their goodwill. In addition, Islam supports and encourages carrying out CSR activities, but at the same time discourages their disclosure (CSRD), especially when it is related to the social and philanthropic activities for individuals and society. The discouragement has a rationale that reporting or publicizing these activities may hurt the ego, self-esteem, and respect of the individuals at the receiving end. Because of this, CSRD of the Islamic banks might have created a negative perception in the minds of customers, especially in the cultural context of Pakistan, that could not yield the desired results, i.e., improving firm performance.

Unlike the others, the economic dimension has a significant positive association with financial performance, which may be due to the customers' confidence in the merit and transparency of financial matters of the Islamic banks. The findings might also show the rationale that customers express trust in the profit and loss sharing mechanisms of Islamic banks, as they function per the Shariah principles of Islam. The average percentage score also suggests that priority has been given to the economic dimension in the average CSRD. Similarly, the environmental dimension also shows a significant positive relationship with financial performance, while the ethical dimension shows a significant positive association with the financial performance—the ROE shows a strong commitment of the banking industry towards disclosing information regarding these dimensions, causing a positive impact on the financial performance of the Islamic banking industry. These dimension-wise results support the stakeholder theory, but contradict the Friedman theory.

These results indicate that most of the Islamic banks, as expected, disclosed comparatively high levels of composite CSR practices, but lack a balanced disclosure of the individual dimensions of these practices. It is noted that priority is given to disclosing information related to financial obligations as compared to other dimensions. Except for Bank Al Meezan Limited, the annual reports published by Islamic banks were also found to be non-systematic, as the required information was scattered throughout these reports, making it difficult for the potential customers to access it, which may be one of the reasons for the unexpected results, especially H1, H2, H3, and H6. Being based on the principles of Shariah, Islamic banks are expected to be socially, ethically, and morally responsible, and to publish their CSR at the top to justify their moral and socially friendly nature. These institutions cannot be called true Islamic banks if they do not meet the criteria set by the principles of Shariah.

The standards of the AAOIFI, with which compliance is voluntary, aim to regulate the CSRD in Islamic banks. Likewise, the GRI reporting guidelines for CSRD in conventional banks or other business firms are also voluntary. By merging both the standards of AAOIFI and GRI, this study develops a novel index to standardize and unify the reporting of CSRD according to internationally acceptable standards in the framework of Shariah for Islamic banks. This index may be mandated for increasing CSRD, as the voluntary nature of compliance with both indexes might be a reason for low CSRD. Furthermore, the Islamic banking industry may focus on channels of communication like print and electronic media, along with using simple local languages, so that the messages can be effectively communicated to the target customers/stakeholders. The industry may also follow a comprehensive CSR policy that could counter the propaganda and increase its goodwill. The AAOIFI, a regulating authority, may also revisit its standards for CSR and CSRD in light of the new index (Appendix A, Table A1) to meet the upcoming challenges of the Islamic banking industry. In addition, to locate CSR-related information easily, the Islamic banks are also required to publish their annual reports in Urdu and other local languages to minimize the communication gap in countries like Pakistan, where the literacy rate is not high and the general public has a low understanding of the English language.

This study investigated the impact of both the composite CSRD and its dimensions on the financial performance of the Islamic banks in Pakistan from 2012 to 2017. By using the index of this study, studies in the future may work on the data of 2017 onward in Pakistan, as well as on large sample sizes in other countries with Islamic banks. In the future, moderation and mediation of integrated strategies and corporate governance could also be explored in the model of CSRD and financial performance of the Islamic banks. Likewise, for a clearer picture, the qualitative aspect, along with newsletters and websites of the respective banks, could also be considered by future studies. Last but not least, the new green banking regulations of 2017 may also be considered from the perspective of the Islamic banking industry of Pakistan in the future.

Author Contributions: All authors contributed equally. All authors have read and agreed to the published version of the manuscript.

Appendix A

Table A1. Comprehensive Corporate Social Responsibility Disclosure Index.

Dimension of CSRD	Sub-Dimensions of CSRD
1. Environment	• Introduction to greenhouse products • Definition of greenhouse products • Controlling measures for the emission of greenhouse gases (CO_2, CO) • Energy conservation • Measures for water consumption/availability • Biodiversity • Transportation • Supplier environmental assessment • Conferences on environment-related issues • Amount of donations to environmental protection • Investments in sustainable developmental projects • Investment in environmentally friendly projects • Focus on risk-based corrective actions • Measures for the restoration and protection of natural resources • Stakeholders' involvement in environmental issues • Environmental grievances mechanism • Climate change policy • Any award for environmental achievement
2. Legal	• Follow the Shariah and accounting rules • Whether the principles of Shariah are followed • Whether the human rights labor laws are followed • Whether the bank is dealing with legal products • Whether the bank observes anti-money-laundering laws • Provides secure transaction facility to customers • Tax payment • Any internal legal advisory committee • Any legal Shariah committee • Training on anti-corruption and other legal issues

Table A1. *Cont.*

Dimension of CSRD	Sub-Dimensions of CSRD
3. Ethical	▪ Any anti-money-laundering policy ▪ Whether the transactions are free of Riba ▪ Whether the fund's sources are disclosed for its customers ▪ Provides the correct information to its customers ▪ Prevents corruptions and irregularities in the banking system ▪ Any internal regulating body dealing with fraud and anti-corruption ▪ Any internal regulating body dealing with sexual harassment and workplace violence ▪ Policies regarding sexual harassment and workplace violence ▪ Non-discriminative policies regarding sex, age, and ethnicity ▪ Dealing with legal items only ▪ A proper code of ethics for the accountants ▪ A proper code of ethics for the internal auditors ▪ Disciplinary action committee ▪ Code of ethics for the employees ▪ Any grievances mechanism regarding ethical issues
4. Economic	▪ Whether the revenues generated are disclosed ▪ Employees' wages and benefits are reported ▪ Whether the paid taxes are reported ▪ Whether profit and loss statements are reported ▪ Payments to the equity/capital owners reported ▪ Any community investment reported ▪ Economic value distributed in the form of operating cost reported ▪ Procurement policy ▪ Any economic Achievement Award ▪ Any economic award ▪ Economic grievances mechanism ▪ International economic appreciation award
5. Philanthropic/social	❖ Community and Social Development ▪ Donations for health issues ▪ Donations for sports activities ▪ Participating in relief and disaster management issues ▪ Donations for education ▪ Microfinance ▪ Funding other organizations for social activities ▪ Establishing a comprehensive link with the public industry/society ▪ Involvement in government-sponsored social activities ▪ Creating job opportunities ▪ Job opportunities for special persons ▪ Women branches ▪ Amount of zakat paid ▪ Those who receive the amount of zakat/zakat beneficiaries ▪ SSB attestation that the amount of zakat has been computed according to sharia ▪ SSB attestation that the sources and uses of zakat are according to ▪ Shariah ▪ Amount of Sadaqah paid ▪ Sadaqah beneficiaries ▪ Qard e Hassana paid ▪ Beneficiaries of Qard e Hassana ▪ Policy regarding debt ▪ Amount of debt written off ▪ Any public policy ▪ Credit committee ▪ Whether local communities are taken on board in social activities

Table A1. *Cont.*

Dimension of CSRD	Sub-Dimensions of CSRD
5. Philanthropic/social	❖ Product and Service Responsibilities ▪ Definition or glossary for a new product ▪ Introduction of SSB-approved new products ▪ Whether the new product is based on the concept of Shariah ▪ Any external or internal communication channel with stakeholders ▪ Regarding product ▪ Zero investment in non-permissible product or services ▪ Market survey and feasibility report ▪ Efforts for research and development promotion ▪ Products with customers' health and safety ▪ Riba-free products ▪ Ensuring the customers' privacy ▪ Whether customers are provided with access to the online banking services ❖ Commitment towards Employees ▪ Efforts for a diversified staff ▪ Employees' health and safety ▪ Providing equal employment opportunities ▪ Provide training on Shariah awareness ▪ Provide training on professional skills and challenges ▪ Providing higher education opportunities to employees ▪ Employee appreciation ▪ Employees' safety and protection ▪ Equal remuneration for men and women ▪ Proper promotion mechanism/promotion policy ▪ Remuneration committee ▪ Standard labor practices policy ▪ Employee management interaction ▪ Secure internet facilities for the employees ▪ Grievances mechanism for employees

Data Source: Authors.

References

1. Smith, A.; Adam, S. Theory of Moral Sentiments. In *Cambridge Texts in the History of Philosophy*; Cambridge University Press: Cambridge, UK, 1759; pp. 1–244.

2. Gardiner, L.; Rubbens, C.; Bonfiglioli, E. Research: Big business, big responsibilities. *Corp. Gov.* **2003**, *3*, 67–77. [CrossRef]

3. Pearce II, J.A.; Doh, J.P. The high impact of collaborative social initiatives. *MIT Sloan Manag. Rev.* **2005**, *46*, 29–39.

4. Dusuki, A.W. What Does Islam Say about Corporate Social Responsibility? *Rev. Islam. Econ.* **2008**, *12*, 5–28.

5. Khan, M.M.; Usman, M. Corporate Social Responsibility in Islamic Banks in Pakistan. *J. Islam. Bus. Manag.* **2016**, *6*, 179–190.

6. Norafifah, A.; Sudin, H. Perceptions of Malaysian corporate customers towards Islamic banking products and services. *Int. J. Islam. Financ. Serv.* **2002**, *3*, 13–29.

7. Peloza, J.; Shang, J. Investing in CSR to Enhance Customer Value. In *Director Notes No. 3*; The Conference Board of Canada: Ottawa, ON, Canada, February 2011; Volume 3.

8. Quazi, A.; Amran, A.; Nejati, M. Conceptualizing and measuring consumer social responsibility: A neglected aspect of consumer research. *Int. J. Consum. Stud.* **2016**, *40*, 48–56. [CrossRef]

9. Jan, A.; Marimuthu, M.; Pisol, M. The nexus of sustainability practices and financial performance: From the perspective of Islamic banking. *J. Clean. Prod.* **2019**, *1*, 1–25. [CrossRef]

10. Lodhi, S.; Makki, M. Determinants of Corporate Philanthropy in Pakistan. *Pakistan J. Commer. Soc. Sci.* **2008**, *1*, 17–24.

11. Agus, M.; Indrarini, H.; Lee, L.R.; Martinov-Bennie, N.; Soh, D.S.B.; Al, A.; Ahmed, A.; Hossain, M.A.M.S.; Alkhatib, K.; Marji, Q.; et al. Enforcement Rules of the University Act. *Int. J. Bus. Soc. Sci.* **2012**, *4*, 1–21.

12. Aliyu, S.; Hassan, M.K.; Mohd Yusof, R.; Naiimi, N. Islamic Banking Sustainability: A Review of Literature and Directions for Future Research. *Emerg. Mark. Financ. Trade* **2017**, *53*, 440–470. [CrossRef]

13. Donaldson, T.; Preston, L.E. The Stakeholder Theory of the Corporation: Concepts, Evidence, and Implications. *Acad. Manag. Rev.* **1995**, *20*, 65–91. [CrossRef]

14. Dowling, J.; Pfeffer, J. Organizational Legitimacy: Social Values and Organizational Behavior. *Pac. Sociol. Rev.* **1975**, *18*, 122–136. [CrossRef]

15. Suchman, M.C. Managing Legitimacy: Strategic and Institutional Approaches. *Acad. Manag. Rev.* **1995**, *20*, 571–610. [CrossRef]

16. Amran, A.; Fauzi, H.; Purwanto, Y.; Darus, F.; Yusoff, H.; Zain, M.M.; Malianna, D.; Naim, A.; Nejati, M. Social Responsibility Disclosure in Islamic Banks: A Comparative Study of Indonesia and Malaysia. *J. Financ. Rep. Account.* **2017**, *15*, 99–115. [CrossRef]

17. Haniffa, R.M.; Cooke, T.E. The impact of culture and governance on corporate social reporting. *J. Account. Public Policy* **2005**, *24*, 391–430. [CrossRef]

18. Said, R.; Zainuddin, Y.H.; Haron, H. The relationship between corporate social responsibility disclosure and corporate governance characteristics in Malaysian public listed companies. *Soc. Responsib. J.* **2009**, *5*, 212–226. [CrossRef]

19. Arshad, R.; Othman, S.; Othman, R. Islamic Corporate Social Responsibility, Corporate Reputation and Performance. *Proc. World Acad. Sci. Eng. Technol.* **2012**, *6*, 1070.

20. Farag, H.; Mallin, C.; Ow-Yong, K. Corporate social responsibility and financial performance in Islamic banks. *J. Econ. Behav. Organ.* **2014**, *103*, 1–18.

21. Haniffa, R.; Hudaib, M. Exploring the ethical identity of Islamic Banks via communication in annual reports. *J. Bus. Ethics* **2007**, *76*, 97–116. [CrossRef]

22. Abdul Rahman, A.; Md Hashim, M.F.A.; Abu Bakar, F. Corporate Social Reporting: A Preliminary Study of Bank Islam Malaysia Berhad (BIMB). *Issues Soc. Environ. Account.* **2010**, *4*, 18–39. [CrossRef]

23. Belal, A.R.; Abdelsalam, O.; Nizamee, S.S. Ethical Reporting in Islami Bank Bangladesh Limited (1983–2010). *J. Bus. Ethics* **2015**, *129*, 769–784. [CrossRef]

24. Ararat, M. A development perspective for "corporate social responsibility": Case of Turkey. *Corp. Gov.* **2008**, *8*, 271–285. [CrossRef]

25. Jamali, D.; Mirshak, R. Corporate Social Responsibility (CSR): Theory and Practice in a Developing Country Context. *J. Bus. Ethics* **2006**, *72*, 243–262. [CrossRef]

26. Gao, J.; Bansal, P. Instrumental and Integrative Logics in Business Sustainability. *J. Bus. Ethics* **2013**, *112*, 241–255. [CrossRef]

27. Bingham, T.; Walters, G. Financial Sustainability Within UK Charities: Community Sport Trusts and Corporate Social Responsibility Partnerships. *Int. J. Volunt. Nonprofit Organ.* **2012**, *24*, 606–629. [CrossRef]

28. Aigner, D.J.; Lloret, A. Sustainability and competitiveness in Mexico. *Manag. Res. Rev.* **2013**, *36*, 1252–1271. [CrossRef]

29. Carroll, A.B.; Shabana, K.M. The Business Case for Corporate Social Responsibility: A Review of Concepts, Research and Practice. *Int. J. Manag. Rev.* **2010**, *12*, 85–105. [CrossRef]

30. SBP. *Islamic Banking Bulletin December 2017 Islamic Banking Department State Bank of Pakistan*; 2017. Available online: http://www.sbp.org.pk/ibd/bulletin/2017/Dec.pdf (accessed on 8 April 2020).

31. Griffin, J.J.; Mahon, J.F. The Corporate Social Performance and Corporate Financial Performance Debate: Twenty-Five Years of Incomparable Research. *Bus. Soc.* **1997**, *36*, 5–31. [CrossRef]

32. Zahid, M.; Rehman, H.U.; Ali, W.; Khan, M.; Alharthi, M.; Qureshi, M.I.; Jan, A. Boardroom gender diversity: Implications for corporate sustainability disclosures in Malaysia. *J. Clean. Prod.* **2019**, *244*, 1–24. [CrossRef]

33. Delai, I.; Takahashi, S. Corporate sustainability in emerging markets: Insights from the practices reported by the Brazilian retailers. *J. Clean. Prod.* **2013**, *47*, 211–221. [CrossRef]

34. Zahid, M.; Rahman, H.U.; Muneer, S.; Butt, B.Z.; Isah-Chikaji, A.; Memon, M.A. Nexus between government initiatives, integrated strategies, internal factors and corporate sustainability practices in Malaysia. *J. Clean. Prod.* **2019**, *241*, 118329. [CrossRef]

35. Greene, W.H. *Econometric Analysis*, 8th ed.; Pearson Education: London, UK, 2017.

36. Musibah, A.S.; Alfattani, W.S.B.W.Y. The Mediating Effect of Financial Performance on the Relationship between Shariah Supervisory Board Effectiveness, Intellectual Capital and Corporate Social Responsibility, of Islamic Banks in Gulf Cooperation Council Countries. *Asian Soc. Sci.* **2014**, *10*, 139–164. [CrossRef]

37. Saleh, M.; Zulkifli, N.; Muhamad, R. Looking for evidence of the relationship between corporate social responsibility and corporate financial performance in an emerging market. *Asia-Pac. J. Bus. Adm.* **2011**, *3*, 165–190. [CrossRef]

38. Rothenberg, S.; Hull, C.E.; Tang, Z. The Impact of Human Resource Management on Corporate Social Performance Strengths and Concerns. *Bus. Soc.* **2017**, *56*, 391–418. [CrossRef]

39. Friedman, M. The Social Responsibility of Business Is to Increase Its Profits. *New York Times Magazine*, 13 September 1970; 122–124.

40. Salzmann, A. Is there a moral economy of state formation? Religious minorities and repertoires of regime integration in the Middle East and Western Europe, 600-1614. *Theory Soc.* **2010**, *39*, 299–313. [CrossRef]

41. Amjad, S.M.; Ali, M. *Stanford Social Innovation Review*; 2018. Available online: https://ssir.org/articles/entry/philanthropy_in_pakistan# (accessed on 8 April 2020).

42. Kiarie, M. Corporate citizenship: The changing legal perspective in Kenya. In Proceedings of the Interdisciplinary CSR Research Conference, Nottingham, UK, 22–23 October 2004; International Centre for Corporate Social Responsibility (ICCSR): Nottingham, UK.

43. Chen, K.H.; Metcalf, R.W. The Relationship between Pollution Control Record and Financial Indicators Revisited. *Account. Rev.* **1980**, *55*, 168–177.

44. Jaggi, B.; Freedman, M. An examination of the impact of pollution performance on economic and market performance: Pulp and paper firms. *J. Bus. Financ. Account.* **1992**, *19*, 697–713. [CrossRef]

45. Mahoney, L.; Roberts, R.W. Corporate social performance, financial performance and institutional ownership in Canadian firms. *Account. Forum* **2007**, *31*, 233–253. [CrossRef]

46. Taman, S. The concept of corporate social responsibility in Islamic law. *Indiana Int. Comp. Law Rev.* **2011**, *21*, 481–508. [CrossRef]

47. Ullmann, A.A. Data in Search of a Theory: A Critical Examination of the Relationships Among Social Performance, Social Disclosure, and Economic Performance of U.S. Firms. *Acad. Manag. Rev.* **1985**, *10*, 540–557.

48. Pava, M.L.; Krausz, J. The association between corporate social-responsibility and financial performance: The paradox of social cost. *J. Bus. Ethics* **1996**, *15*, 321–357. [CrossRef]

49. Crane, A.; Matten, D. Questioning the domain of the business ethics curriculum. *J. Bus. Ethics* **2004**, *54*, 357–369. [CrossRef]

50. Platonova, E.; Asutay, M.; Dixon, R.; Mohammad, S. The Impact of Corporate Social Responsibility Disclosure on Financial Performance: Evidence from the GCC Islamic Banking Sector. *J. Bus. Ethics* **2018**, *151*, 451–471. [CrossRef]

51. Beck, N.; Katz, J.N. Time-series–cross-section data: What have we learned in the past few years? *Annu. Rev. Polit. Sci.* **2001**, *4*, 271–293. [CrossRef]

52. Beck, N.; Katz, J.N. What to do (and not to do) with time- series cross-section data. *Am. Polit. Sci. Rev.* **1995**, *89*, 634–647. [CrossRef]

53. Hoechle, D. Robust standard errors for panel regressions with cross-sectional dependence. *Stata J.* **2007**, *7*, 281. [CrossRef]

54. Rahman, H.U.; Ibrahim, M.Y.; Che-Ahmad, A. Physical characteristics of the chief executive officer and firm accounting and market based performance. *Asian J. Account. Gov.* **2017**, *8*, 27–37. [CrossRef]

55. Rahman, H.U.; Rehman, S.; Zahid, M. The impact of boardroom national diversity on firms' performance and boards' monitoring in emerging markets: A case of Malaysia. *City Univ. Res. Journa* **2018**, *18*, 1–15.

8

The Influence of IFRS Adoption on Banks' Cost of Equity: Evidence from European Banks

Sang-Giun Yim

School of Finance and Accounting, Kookmin University, Kookmin University, 77, Jeongneung-ro, Seongbuk-gu, Seoul 02707, Korea; yimsg@kookmin.ac.kr.

Abstract: This study examines how mandatory adoption of International Financial Reporting Standards (IFRS) in European countries affects banks' cost of equity. Supporters of IFRS argue that its adoption improves the quality of accounting information, which in turn decreases the cost of equity. However, banking regulators could intervene in the implementation of new accounting standards to protect the stability of the banking system, which would deteriorate banks' information environment and thereby increase the cost of equity. Using a regression analysis of European listed bank data, I find that banks' cost of equity increases after the adoption of IFRS in countries with strong bank supervisory offices. I also find that strong legal enforcement and additional disclosure requirements jointly reduce banks' cost of equity, but pre-IFRS inconsistencies between local accounting standards and regulatory standards jointly increase banks' cost of equity. This study contributes to the literature on market discipline in banking and has policy implications: The findings suggest that, when implementing new accounting standards, potential conflicts between financial reporting and banking regulations should be considered.

Keywords: cost of equity; IFRS adoption; European banks; corporate governance; banking regulation

---

1. Introduction

The 2007 US subprime mortgage crisis shows the importance of the banking system for sustainable economic growth. The adverse effects of this crisis not only impacted the banks and debtors as parties to the mortgage loan contracts, but it also spread across the entire financial system and the real economy. As a result, despite the US government's efforts to stabilize the financial system, real domestic production per capita in the United States decreased by more than 5% from the fourth quarter of 2007 to the second quarter of 2009. This shows how the soundness of the banking system is critical to sustainable economic growth.

While several government regulations have been adopted to maintain the stability of the banking industry, innovations in financial instruments have been developing quickly, and regulatory bodies are playing catch up with the financial market. Consequently, the role of market discipline is crucial because market mechanisms can adapt more flexibly and promptly to change.

Unlike government regulators, market participants are not authorized to access banks' private information. Therefore, the public information environment is critical for the market discipline of banks. Financial statements are a reliable and comprehensive source of public information. Hence, this study investigates the influence of changes in accounting standards on European banks' financial statements post-International Financial Reporting Standards (IFRS) adoption.

Researchers argue that IFRS adoption improves accounting quality because it requires more disclosure than most local European accounting standards pre-IFRS. They suggest that IFRS adoption improves both earnings quality and the information environment. Consequently, post-IFRS, security trading by foreign investors increased, and equity values increased. These studies mainly focus on the impact of IFRS adoption on non-financial firms and equity market characteristics, however, and pay little attention to the banking industry or to the use of accounting information in contracts [1].

IFRS adoption impacts banks differently from non-financial firms because banks possess financial assets. IFRS requires financial assets to be recorded at fair market value, which is a noisy measure of future cash flow. Hence, increased use of this measure post-IFRS could increase the noise in the prediction of cash flow from bank assets, which could increase banks' information risks. Furthermore, unlike the cost of equity for non-financial firms, that for banks could increase post-IFRS.

Furthermore, IFRS as a principle-based accounting system is more flexible than most of the pre-IFRS local accounting standards. In contrast to a rule-based accounting system, a principle-based accounting system allows managers more accounting choices. Thus, accounting information can vary depending on choices made during the preparation of the information. This could enhance decision-making because information selection could be tailored. However, the verifiability of the accounting information could suffer post-IFRS, as the same accounting information can be presented in different ways. Verifiability is critical in contracts [2] because low verifiability provides room for moral hazard regarding debt contracts using accounting information in the debt covenants. Thus, IFRS adoption could reduce the contractibility of accounting information [1]. In sum, although IFRS adoption could improve the information environment for equity markets, it could also have a negative impact on debt markets.

In most countries, the banking industry is regulated by a governmental or a non-governmental organization to protect the stability of the financial system. Should IFRS adoption increase the instability of debt markets, bank supervisors can intervene. When bank supervisors have especially strong power, they have great influence on banks' financial reporting. The bank supervisors' main concern is the stability of financial markets; therefore, if necessary, they could intervene in the financial reporting by managing the law or the implementation of accounting standards, as Skinner [3] reported using a Japanese case. Although the supervisors' intervention stabilizes the lending system of the country, the distortion in the adoption of new accounting standards damages the transparency of the accounting information. Consequently, banks' information risks increase, which increases banks' cost of equity.

Based on the argument above, I hypothesize that IFRS adoption increases banks' cost of equity in countries with strong banking regulations. I also conjecture that IFRS adoption decreases banks' cost of equity in countries with strong investor protection.

Using European listed bank data, I test my hypotheses through a multivariate regression analysis. The results show that IFRS adoption increases banks' cost of equity in countries with strong banking supervision, supporting my conjecture. In examining the effect of additional disclosure requirements, I find that strong legal enforcement and additional IFRS disclosure requirements jointly reduce banks' cost of equity. However, banks' cost of equity is increased by the joint effect of the improvement of comparability by IFRS adoption and banking regulatory power.

This study contributes to the literature in several ways. First, this is one of the few studies that examines how IFRS adoption affects the valuation of the banking sector. Armstrong et al. [4] report that the market reaction of banks' stock prices to IFRS adoption is stronger than that of other industries. Meanwhile, Daske et al. [5] and Li [6] examine the effect of IFRS adoption on market reaction, but they do not examine the banking industry.

Second, this study has policy implications. The importance of market discipline in banking increases as financial instruments become more complex [7]. As seen in the 2007 Mortgage Crisis in the United States, financial instruments have recently been innovated at a rapid pace, and government regulations are not keeping up with the pace of innovation in financial instruments. However, market participants can respond quickly to market innovation, unlike government regulations. Thus, market discipline can supplement government regulation. Since investors rely on public information, high-quality accounting information is important in the market discipline of banks [8]. As this research suggests, in addition to high-quality accounting information, country-level banking governance is necessary for the efficient market discipline of banks.

Third, this study shows the interaction between the institutional environment of banks and changes in accounting standards. Researchers have pointed out that the institutional environment influences financial reporting [9–11]. Supporting this argument, studies on mandatory IFRS adoption suggest that investor protection facilitates IFRS adoption [6,12]. However, few studies have examined the role of bank regulation in adopting new accounting standards.

The remainder of this paper proceeds as follows. Section 2 summarizes prior studies regarding the effect of IFRS adoption on the cost of equity, institutional environments of the banking industry, and the economic consequences of IFRS adoption. Section 3 documents hypothesis development. Section 4 presents the research design, sample selection, and descriptive statistics. Section 5 documents the results of regression analyses. Section 6 concludes the paper.

2. Literature Review and Background

2.1. The Effect of IFRS Adoption

Prior studies argue that IFRS adoption improves several aspects of financial reporting, the information environment, and capital markets. Empirical studies find that earnings quality [13,14] and the information environment [12,15,16] are improved following IFRS adoption. Consequently, security trading [5,17,18] and equity valuation [5,6] improve post-IFRS.

Theory expects that the quality of disclosure is negatively related to the cost of equity [19–21], which is backed by empirical evidence [22,23]. Since IFRS adoption improves the transparency of accounting information and the information environment, researchers expect that IFRS adoption decreases the cost of equity. Li [6] finds evidence supporting this using European non-financial firm data.

However, IFRS adoption also has a negative consequence because it increases a manager's choice of accounting policy, which reduces the contractibility of the accounting information. Supporting this argument, Ball et al. [1] report that IFRS adoption reduces accounting-based debt covenants. This study implies that IFRS adoption is not welcomed by bank regulators because it reduces the contractibility of debt contracts, which results in instability in the financial markets. In addition, the findings of Ball et al. [1] also suggest that banks' risks increase post-IFRS because banks' lending contracts that utilize accounting information in debt covenants become inefficient.

2.2. The Institutional Environment of Listed Banks

This study focuses on the equity capital in European listed banks, which are exposed to two different types of institutional environments: Bank supervision and disclosure regulation. Listed banks are regulated by banking supervisory offices. Although the detailed structures of bank supervisory systems vary by country [24], the ultimate goal of supervisory offices is the same, namely, to safeguard the stability of the financing system because the stability of financial markets plays a critical role in the economic growth of the country. As a publicly listed firm, listed banks are also bound to the disclosure requirements of investors, whose main concern is not in protecting the stability of the markets, but in protecting investors' private interests.

The difference in policy objectives between bank regulation and corporate disclosure creates conflicts between accounting policy and bank regulation. Skinner [3] investigates the adoption of deferred tax accounting in Japan in 1998, during which Japanese banks' regulatory capital was insufficient. Thus, to maintain banks' solvency, the Japanese government and bank regulators decided to use a deferred tax asset as regulatory capital. Because maintaining the solvency of banks is more important for the country's economy, the quality of accounting information was sacrificed during the adoption of deferred tax asset accounting. Skinner [1] implies that banking regulations limit or distort the adoption of new accounting standards if the standards negatively affect the solvency of banks. IFRS adoption could necessitate regulatory intervention, as in the case investigated by Skinner [3]. Bischof [25] also pointed out that there are incentives to prevent European bank regulators from introducing new accounting standards that affect banks' financial statements, which means that the intervention of bank supervisory offices in the adoption of new accounting standards is not limited to a specific country.

To implement accounting standards, support of institutional environments is necessary [9]. However, as prior studies show [3,25], listed banks face a potential conflict between bank regulation and financial disclosure; therefore, how IFRS adoption influences listed banks is unclear.

Basel II is a set of guidelines that shaped the mandatory adoption of IFRS in European counties. Although replaced by Basel III, Basel II is still useful in understanding the mechanism of the banking regulations. Basel II is based on the following three pillars: (1) Minimum capital requirement that requires safer capital as banks' risky assets increase; (2) review process by a government supervisory office; (3) market discipline that relies on sophisticated investors' monitoring. For the first and second pillars, private information can be required from banks or banks' auditors. Frequently, these two pillars have priority over accounting standards [3,25]. For the third pillar, market discipline penalties include direct penalty by investor activism and indirect penalties through market prices of securities, including stock prices. Due to the high information efficiency of market prices, market discipline can reflect the bank's health information at a rate that bank supervisors cannot follow. This means that market discipline is superior to bank supervisors in reflecting the consequences of financial instruments, which are rapidly becoming increasingly complex as they undergo innovation, on the health of banks. Therefore, the importance of market discipline is in an increasing trend [7].

Banking regulations affect banks' financial reporting. Bank supervisors can require banks to disclose private information found during the review process [26,27]. Furthermore, regulatory capital requirements enhance disclosure by providing timely and extensive information that is not required by accounting standards [28]. Stringent banking regulations could conflict with accounting information in that the regulations safeguard the banking system, whereas the accounting information focuses on capital providers. Moreover, banking regulators could sacrifice the quality of accounting information to stabilize the financial system [3,28] or to avoid rapid changes in the accounting numbers to minimize the negative impact on debt contracts based on accounting information [1,25].

The influence of investor protection is the same for banks and non-financial firms. Strong investor protection provides incentives to managers to provide transparent accounting information [10,11,29]. Consequently, IFRS adoption reduces banks' cost of equity [6,30,31].

2.3. IFRS Adoption in the Banking Sector

Compared with the previous local accounting standards, IFRS adoption brought several changes. The two most important changes for this study [2,14] include an increase in fair value measurement and an increase in accounting choices.

As the fair value measure increases, the statement of financial position (balance sheet in US Generally Accepted Accounting Principles terminology) increases in relevance for equity valuation. However, the market volatility included in fair value increases the noise in measuring banks' future cash flows. Even though fair value measures do not directly rely on level 1 inputs, which are market values, level 2 or level 3 inputs of fair value measures do not alleviate the information risk because they discretionary. In sum, extended use of fair value measures increases information risks, which are unfavorable for both investors and bank regulators.

In addition, although the increase in accounting choices enhances the relevance of the statement of financial position to equity valuation, this increase could influence the banking industry negatively. The increase in accounting choices complicates verification of compliance with the debt covenants. This provides opportunities for moral hazard for both parties of the debt contract. The reduction of contractibility of accounting information could have a significant impact on capital markets, which necessitates intervention by banking regulators [3,25].

3. Hypothesis Development

Regarding IFRS adoption and banks' cost of equity, two risks should be considered. The first risk is banks' business risks, which come from operating characteristics; for example, borrowers' credit risks. The second is information risk [19,20]. Both risks increase banks' cost of equity.

Because the minimum capital regulation is applied stringently, the regulatory capital ratio efficiently reduces banks' risk [28]. This risk reduction decreases banks' cost of equity. If banks' risk is already lowered by banking regulations, IFRS adoption has little impact on the disclosure of information about banks' risks. Therefore, IFRS adoption has little impact on the cost of equity if capital regulation is strong. Based on this conjecture, I suggest the following hypotheses:

H1: *Banks' cost of equity decreases as the minimum capital regulation strengthens.*

H2: *Strong capital regulation weakens the impact of IFRS adoption on banks' cost of equity.*

If banking regulatory agencies have strong power, they can require private information directly from banks or banks' auditors for regulatory actions [1,28]. Therefore, bank regulation strength reduces banks' cost of equity because strong banking regulators can monitor and discipline banks.

Banking regulations have priority over financial reporting in most countries; therefore, these regulations could interfere with IFRS adoption if new accounting standards have a negative effect on the banking system. IFRS adoption increases choice among accounting rules; therefore, using accounting information for debt covenants allows for moral hazard for any one of the contracting parties in debt contracts [1]. Several banks' contracts use accounting information for debt covenants; hence, changes in accounting standards could affect banks' existing contracts. Therefore, bank supervisors have the incentive to intervene in the adoption of new accounting standards to prevent potential turmoil, which would interfere with the faithful implementation of IFRS [3,25]. The intervention of bank supervisors increases information risk of banks, which would increase bank supervisors' power. Based on this conjecture, I suggest the following hypotheses:

H3: *Banks' cost of equity decreases as the bank supervisors' power strengthens.*

H4: *IFRS adoption increases banks' cost of equity in the countries with strong banking supervisors.*

Market discipline needs a good information environment including high-quality accounting information. Country-level investor protection improves accounting quality by helping faithful financial reporting [9,29], which leads to a reduction in the cost of equity [11,30,31]. Thus, in countries with strong investor protection, IFRS adoption reduces banks' cost of equity. In relation to the institutional aspects of the banking sector, I therefore suggest the following hypothesis:

H5: *The influence of IFRS adoption on banks' cost of equity is weakened when investor protection is strengthened.*

The impact of IFRS adoption varies with the extent of changes that occur in IFRS adoption [32]. In most European countries, IFRS adoption requires more disclosure. Thus, the impact of IFRS adoption increases additional disclosure requirements. Moreover, the impact of IFRS adoption varies with the inconsistencies between IFRS and the local accounting standards implemented before IFRS adoption. Accordingly, I propose the following hypotheses.

H6: *The influence of IFRS adoption increases when IFRS adoption requires additional disclosures.*

H7: *The influence of IFRS adoption increases when inconsistencies exist between IFRS and the local accounting standards implemented before IFRS adoption.*

4. Research Design

4.1. Regression Model

I use the implied cost of equity as my proxy for expected returns because it has fewer errors than realized-return-based proxies [30,31,33] from information shocks. I average four estimates calculated using the models of Easton [34], Gode and Mohanram [35], Gebhardt et al. [36], and Claus and Thomas [37] to mitigate error in each measurement [30,31].

Studies on the effect of IFRS adoption frequently use a difference-in-differences model using voluntary adopters as the control group. This model controls for the influence that occurs simultaneously with IFRS adoption. However, except the treatment, the control group of the difference-in-differences model should be identical to the treatment group. Furthermore, only three countries have banks that adopted IFRS voluntarily. Most European banks adopt IFRS mandatorily, which means that IFRS adoption was an exogenous event for most European banks. Hence, I do not use the difference-in-differences design.

To test H1 to H5, I use the following model (1):

$$CoC = \alpha + \beta_1 POST + \beta_2 ENFORCE + \beta_3 OFFICE + \beta_4 CAPITAL + \beta_5\ POST*ENFORCE \\ + \beta_6\ POST*OFFICE + \beta_7\ POST*CAPITAL + CONTROLS + \varepsilon \tag{1}$$

Variable definitions are in the Appendix A. *POST* is the variable of interest. I include measures for the strength of capital regulation (*CAPITAL*), the power of bank supervisors (*OFFICE*), and the efficiency of legal enforcement (*ENFORCE*) in the regression model. *CAPITAL* and *OFFICE* are measured by The Bank Regulation and Supervision Survey 2003 conducted by the World Bank [28,38]. I centered *CAPITAL*, *OFFICE*, and *ENFORCE* by the sample mean of each variable to mitigate multicollinearity problems from biases of spurious correlations [39].

I control firm-level risks using proxies of size, return volatility, financial leverage, total capital ratio, and book-to-price ratio. Size, return volatility, and leverage are measured by the decile rank of each variable to mitigate measurement errors. I include variables to control for cross-listing on the US stock market because investor protection in the US market is stronger than it is in most European countries, but it is not affected by mandatory IFRS adoption. I also control for the annual inflation rate and the indicator variable for the adoption of IFRS 7, which could affect banks. I include the bias and dispersion of analyst forecasts to mitigate the effect of biases and the nonlinearity of the models for the implied cost of equity [37,40]. Many bank-year observations have only one one-year-ahead earnings forecast; hence, I include an indicator variable for the observations to control for potential bias and replace the dispersion of analyst forecasts with zero. I adjust the influence of the firm-level serial correlation using a firm-clustered standard error in all of the regression results in this study [41].

To test H6 and H7, I revise model (1) by including additional disclosure requirements (*ADD*) and inconsistencies between IFRS and the local accounting standards (*INC*). I use the survey of Nobes [42] to measure *ADD* and *INC*. Nobes [42] did not focus on banks; thus, items irrelevant to banks, for example, inventory or plant assets, are included. To avoid potential measurement errors from irrelevant items, I exclude items irrelevant to bank operations from *ADD* and *INC*. I centered *ADD* and *INC* by their sample means to avoid multicollinearity problems [39]. The following are the models for H6 and H7, respectively. Model (2) and model (3) are models for testing the effects of *ADD* and *ICC*, respectively.

$$CoC = \alpha + \beta_1 POST + \beta_2 ENFORCE + \beta_3 OFFICE + \beta_4 CAPITAL + \beta_5 POST*ENFORCE \\ + \beta_6 POST*OFFICE + \beta_7 POST*CAPITAL + \beta_8 ADD + \beta_9 POST*ADD \\ + \beta_{10} POST*ENFORCE*ADD + \beta_{11} POST*OFFICE*ADD + \beta_{12} POST*CAPITAL*ADD + \\ CONTROLS + \varepsilon \tag{2}$$

$$CoC = \alpha + \beta_1 POST + \beta_2 ENFORCE + \beta_3 OFFICE + \beta_4 CAPITAL + \beta_5 POST*ENFORCE + \\ \beta_6 POST*OFFICE + \beta_7 POST*CAPITAL + \beta_8 INC + \beta_9 POST*INC + \beta_{10} POST*ENFORCE*INC + \\ \beta_{11} POST*OFFICE*INC + \beta_{12} POST*CAPITAL*INC + CONTROLS + \varepsilon \tag{3}$$

4.2. Sample Selection

Mandatory IFRS adoption by the European Union provides the setting for a natural experiment. Therefore, I use data from listed banks of European countries from 1995 to 2009. The observations are required to have the Standard Industry Code between 6020 and 6099. Analyst forecast data and financial data are obtained from I/B/E/S and Compustat Global, respectively. I match the stock prices and analyst forecasts of seven months after the previous fiscal-year end to make sure that precious accounting information is fully incorporated. Non-positive earnings forecasts were excluded. If three-year-ahead to five-year-ahead analyst forecasts are missing, I fill in missing values using long-term earnings growth rate forecasts. I use the average of a historical three-year payout ratio to calculate the expected dividend payout ratio. If the payout ratio is missing, or smaller (larger) than 0 (1), I use the country-median value instead. I exclude banks that do not have observations both before and after the mandatory IFRS adoption in 2005. I classify years before 2004 as the pre-mandatory adoption period and years from 2005 as the post-mandatory adoption period [6,30,31].

Table 1 presents the composition of the final sample, which has 376 observations from 52 banks in 12 countries having 7 voluntary adopters and 45 mandatory adopters. Among the 376 observations, 52 and 324 observations are obtained from voluntary and mandatory adopters, respectively. Only three countries, namely, Germany, Greece, and Poland, have voluntary adopters. However, voluntary adopters could not provide a good benchmark for difference-in-differences tests, because they are not evenly distributed. The sample selection did not drive this result. By examining the entire Compustat Global database, I confirm that only three countries have banks that voluntarily adopted IFRS. This result implies that IFRS adoption is more like an exogenous event than an endogenous one. Furthermore, this also implies that financial reporting and banking regulations could have conflicting goals.

Table 1. Sample composition.

Panel A: Number of observations				
	Voluntary adopters	Mandatory adopters	Pre-mandatory adoption period (Before 2005)	Post-mandatory adoption period (From 2005)
Belgium	0	11	7	4
Denmark	0	17	8	9
Finland	0	6	1	5
France	0	34	16	18
Germany	33	4	23	14
Greece	7	29	17	19
Ireland	0	21	15	6
Netherland	0	17	10	7
Poland	12	28	16	24
Spain	0	38	18	20
Sweden	0	37	26	11
UK	0	82	53	29
Sum	52	324	210	166

Panel B: Number of banks		
	Voluntary adopters	Mandatory adopters
Belgium	0	1
Denmark	0	3
Finland	0	1
France	0	5
Germany	4	1
Greece	1	4
Ireland	0	3

Table 1. *Cont.*

Netherland	0	2
Poland	2	6
Spain	0	5
Sweden	0	4
UK	0	10
Sum	7	45

Panel C: Number of mandatory adopter observations		
	Pre-adoption	Post-adoption
Belgium	7	4
Denmark	8	9
Finland	1	5
France	16	18
Germany	2	2
Greece	14	15
Ireland	15	6
Netherland	10	7
Poland	11	17
Spain	18	20
Sweden	26	11
UK	53	29
Sum	181	143

4.3. Descriptive Statistics

Panel A in Table 2 shows the means of the main variables for regression analyses by country. Means of implied cost of equity are from 10% to 14%, whereas means of the regulatory capital ratio are larger than 10% and lower than 14.5%. Only three countries, namely, Germany, Greece, and Poland, have banks that voluntarily adopted IFRS. This implies that, unlike non-financial industries, European banks' IFRS adoption might be regulated by banks [6,25]. Voluntary adopters have a higher regulatory capital ratio than mandatory adopters in the same countries, suggesting the possibility that sound banks choose to adopt IFRS voluntarily to indicate their financial stability. Panel B presents the descriptive statistics for the full sample.

Table 2. Descriptive statistics.

Panel A: Country mean value of the cost of equity, market value, and regulatory capital ratio				
	N	CoC	Market value of equity	Total regulatory capital ratio
Belgium	11	0.1088	21,299	13.20%
Denmark	17	0.1386	10,351	11.25%
Finland	6	0.1039	2,270	12.23%
France	34	0.1282	41,695	11.00%
Germany	37	0.1086	23,640	11.57%
(Mandatory adopters)	4	0.1011	2,355	13.07%
Greece	36	0.1288	8,335	13.10%
(Mandatory adopters)	29	0.1285	8,133	13.06%
Ireland	21	0.1228	12,645	12.29%
Netherland	17	0.1146	21,282	11.83%
Poland	40	0.1250	4,356	14.47%
(Mandatory adopters)	28	0.1285	4,701	14.01%
Spain	38	0.1116	36,571	11.65%
Sweden	37	0.1017	13,381	10.44%
UK	82	0.1037	109,912	13.19%

Table 2. *Cont.*

Panel B. Summary statistics of the main variables for the regression analyses					
Variable	Mean	STD	25%	50%	75%
CoC	0.1150	0.0306	0.0960	0.1093	0.1270
SIZE (=logTA)	12.5453	2.5862	10.9217	12.2901	13.4738
OTC	0.1649	0.3716	0	0	0
EXCH	0.1383	0.3457	0	0	0
PP	0.0559	0.2299	0	0	0
INFLA	2.7212	2.3848	0.69565	2.134	4.2124
RETVOL	0.0891	0.0592	0.0501	0.0717	0.1087
LEV	0.9418	0.0311	0.9312	0.9510	0.9625
CAP Ratio	12.2579	4.5377	10.8	11.7	13.1
CAPR_DUM	0.3431	0.4754	0	0	1
FBIAS	0.0081	0.0395	−0.0090	−0.0010	0.0115
BPR	0.6449	0.5156	0.3877	0.5368	0.7352
DISP	0.0041	0.0164	0	0	0.0048
FOLLOW	3.6170	4.1617	1	1	5

Table 3 presents the differences in bank characteristics before and after IFRS adoption. The variables in Table 3 are chosen differently from those in Panel B of Table 2, because the purpose of Table 3 is to present the changes in bank characteristics intuitively. *CoC* significantly changes after the mandatory IFRS adoption. However, this univariate test does not confirm that the difference is due to IFRS adoption.

Table 3. Differences in bank characteristics before and after the mandatory International Financial Reporting Standards (IFRS) adoption.

Variable	Pre-Adoption (A)	Post-Adoption (B)	Difference (B−A)	t-Value	p-Value	
CoC	0.104	0.130	0.026	7.87	0.000	***
TA	243,865	581,665	337,800	5.10	0.000	***
MKT	16,309	31,747	15,438	3.64	0.000	***
RETVOL	0.089	0.084	−0.005	−0.72	0.470	
BPR	0.493	0.815	0.322	5.07	0.000	***
LEV	0.943	0.943	0.000	−0.01	0.993	
CAP Ratio	12.474	11.784	−0.690	−1.44	0.151	
FBIAS	0.003	0.010	0.007	1.74	0.083	*
DISP	0.005	0.003	−0.001	−0.68	0.497	
Follow	4.039	2.902	−1.137	−2.48	0.014	**
ONEFORECAST	0.475	0.601	0.126	2.27	0.024	**

*, **, and *** indicate significance at the 10%, 5%, and 1% levels by two-tailed tests, respectively.

5. Analysis Results

5.1. The Influence of IFRS Adoption and Institutional Environment on the Cost of Equity

Table 4 documents variables for institutional environments, and Table 5 presents the estimation results of model (1). *ENFORCE, OFFICE,* and *CAPITAL* have negative coefficients in both full and partial sample analyses. However, the coefficient on *CAPITAL* is insignificant in the partial sample analysis. These results imply that investor protection and bank regulation reduce banks' risk in general.

Table 4. Country characteristics.

Country	Legal enforcement (ENFORCE)	The index of official supervisory power of bank regulators (OFFICE)	Regulatory restrictions on bank capital (CAPITAL)	Additional disclosure required by IFRS adoption for banks (ADD)	Total no. of inconsistencies between local standardsand IFRS for banks (INC)
Panel A: Country means of variables					
Belgium	9.44	—	—	7	13
Denmark	10	8	2	5	13
Finland	10	8	4	7	13
France	8.68	7	2	5	15
Germany	9.05	10	1	6	16
Greece	6.82	10	3	8	14
Ireland	8.36	9	1	0	15
Netherland	10	8	3	2	5
Poland	—	—	—	3	14
Spain	7.14	9	4	8	18
Sweden	10	6	3	4	9
UK	9.22	11	3	0	15

Variable	Mean	STD	25%	50%	75%
Panel B: Summary statistics of the full sample					
CoC	0.1150	0.0306	0.0960	0.1093	0.1270
SIZE	12.5453	2.5862	10.9217	12.2901	13.4738
OTC	0.1649	0.3716	0	0	0
EXCH	0.1383	0.3457	0	0	0
PP	0.0559	0.2299	0	0	0
INFLA	2.7212	2.3848	0.69565	2.134	4.2124
RETVOL	0.0891	0.0592	0.0501	0.0717	0.1087
LEV	0.9418	0.0311	0.9312	0.9510	0.9625
CAP Ratio	12.2579	4.5377	10.8	11.7	13.1
CAPR_DUM	0.3431	0.4754	0	0	1
FBIAS	0.0081	0.0395	−0.0090	−0.0010	0.0115
BPR	0.6449	0.5156	0.3877	0.5368	0.7352
DISP	0.0041	0.0164	0	0	0.0048
FOLLOW	3.6170	4.1617	1	1	5

Table 5. Basic regression analysis.

Parameter	(A) Full Sample Period Coef	t-Value		(B) From 2003 to 2006 Coef	t-Value	
Intercept	0.0852	(14.18)	***	0.2003	(5.70)	***
POST	0.0061	(2.20)	**	−0.0177	(−0.60)	
ENFORCE	−0.0054	(−2.73)	***	−0.0076	(−3.49)	***
OFFICE	−0.0023	(−1.81)	*	−0.0049	(−1.96)	*
CAPITAL	−0.0078	(−3.24)	***	−0.0021	(−0.86)	
POST*ENFORCE	0.0010	(0.39)		−0.0024	(−0.88)	
POST*OFFICE	0.0037	(2.75)	***	0.0044	(2.53)	**
POST*CAPITAL	−0.0016	(−0.50)		0.0012	(0.40)	
IFRS7	0.0226	(3.04)	***			
SIZE_DEC	−0.0007	(−1.43)		−0.0007	(−0.64)	
OTC	−0.0049	(−0.89)		−0.0036	(−0.68)	
EXCH	0.0100	(3.06)	***	0.0082	(1.47)	
INFLA	0.0023	(2.51)	**	0.0000	(0.01)	
RETVOL_DEC	0.0000	(−0.03)		−0.0006	(−0.88)	
LEV_DEC	0.0011	(1.56)		0.0007	(0.93)	
CAPR	−0.0001	(−0.83)		0.0014	(1.62)	
CAPR_DUM	−0.0041	(−0.83)		0.0075	(0.70)	
FBIAS	0.2182	(1.90)	*	0.3136	(1.68)	
DISP	0.0780	(2.72)	***	0.2251	(0.42)	
ONEFORECAST	0.0029	(1.29)		0.0047	(1.16)	
BPR	0.0188	(2.77)	***	0.0155	(1.84)	*
# of OBS	285			131		
ADJ R2	0.572			0.3528		

*, **, and *** indicate significance at the 10%, 5%, and 1% levels by two-tailed tests, respectively. t-values are adjusted by firm cluster.

The interaction term of *POST* and *OFFICE* has positive coefficients, suggesting that banks in countries with strong regulations experience an increase in the cost of equity. Financial reporting and banking regulations conflict regarding IFRS adoption. In this case, banking regulations have priority over financial reporting [26]. Therefore, bank supervisors intervene in the IFRS adoption to suppress the negative impact of IFRS on the banking system, at least temporarily [3,25]. The intervention in IFRS adoption reduces the quality of accounting information and increases the uncertainty of banks and the cost of equity. This supports H4. However, the interaction terms of *ENFORCE* or *CAPITAL* with *POST* are insignificant; thus, H2 and H5 are not supported. The results are qualitatively consistent with the results for non-financial firms. Listed banks are also exposed to disclosure requirements; therefore, the results should be consistent with prior study [6].

5.2. The Changes in Disclosure Requirements by IFRS Adoption on Cost of Equity

Panel A of Table 6 documents the regression result of model (2). In column (A), the sign of the three-way interaction term of *ENFORCE* shows that legal enforcement facilitates the implementation of additional disclosure requirements by mandatory IFRS adoption, resulting in the decrease in banks' cost of equity. However, the coefficients on the three-way interaction terms of *CAPITAL* and *OFFICE* are insignificant. The result of the subsample period test presented in column (B) is qualitatively the same, except that the significance and magnitude are weaker. The results support the conjecture that the institutional environment for investor protection supports the implementation of IFRS adoption because it improves the relevance of accounting information on the equity valuation.

Table 6. The effect of changes in bank disclosures on cost of equity.

	Panel A: Effect of additional disclosures					
	(A) Full sample period			(B) From 2003 to 2006		
Parameter	Coef	t-Value		Coef	t-Value	
Intercept	0.0869	(10.33)	***	0.0794	(6.17)	***
POST	−0.0147	(−1.53)		−0.0082	(−0.82)	
ENFORCE	−0.0046	(−0.97)		−0.0050	(−1.03)	
OFFICE	−0.0023	(−1.12)		−0.0031	(−1.26)	
CAPITAL	−0.0081	(−2.23)	**	−0.0035	(−0.92)	
ADD	0.0002	(0.08)		0.0015	(0.70)	
POST*ENFORCE	0.0163	(1.10)		0.0041	(0.38)	
POST*OFFICE	0.0009	(0.27)		0.0002	(0.05)	
POST*CAPITAL	−0.0160	(−1.49)		−0.0033	(−0.36)	
POST*ADD	0.0009	(0.25)		−0.0031	(−1.04)	
POST*ENFORCE*ADD	−0.0069	(−2.16)	**	−0.0050	(−1.71)	*
POST*OFFICE*ADD	−0.0026	(−1.69)		−0.0001	(−0.06)	
POST*CAPITAL*ADD	0.0031	(1.47)		0.0019	(1.09)	
IFRS7	0.0232	(2.81)	***			
SIZE_DEC	−0.0011	(−1.59)		−0.0005	(−0.48)	
OTC	−0.0038	(−0.67)		−0.0030	(−0.58)	
EXCH	0.0103	(2.96)	***	0.0074	(1.41)	
INFLA	0.0024	(2.24)	**	−0.0001	(−0.10)	
RETVOL_DEC	0.0002	(0.37)		−0.0002	(−0.28)	
LEV_DEC	0.0009	(1.35)		0.0006	(0.77)	
CAPR	−0.0001	(−0.68)		0.0016	(1.79)	*
CAPR_DUM	−0.0049	(−0.94)		0.0089	(0.84)	
FBIAS	0.2212	(1.94)	*	0.3116	(1.77)	*
DISP	0.0766	(2.75)	***	−0.0595	(−0.12)	
ONEFORECAST	0.0016	(0.71)		0.0013	(0.33)	
BPR	0.0186	(2.50)	**	0.0231	(2.16)	**
No. of OBS	285			131		
ADJ R2	0.5772			0.3757		

Table 6. *Cont.*

Parameter	(A) Full sample period			(B) From 2003 to 2006		
	Coef	t-Value		Coef	t-Value	
Intercept	0.0882	(14.92)	***	0.0775	(7.01)	***
POST	0.0073	(1.29)		−0.0001	(−0.03)	
ENFORCE	−0.0078	(−3.12)	***	−0.0110	(−4.40)	***
OFFICE	−0.0015	(−1.04)		−0.0041	(−1.43)	
CAPITAL	−0.0085	(−3.87)	***	−0.0016	(−0.63)	
INC	−0.0013	(−2.16)	**	−0.0013	(−1.50)	
*POST*ENFORCE*	0.0018	(0.50)		−0.0057	(−1.54)	
*POST*OFFICE*	0.0031	(1.85)	*	0.0061	(3.01)	***
*POST*CAPITAL*	−0.0094	(−2.20)	**	−0.0087	(−3.41)	***
*POST*INC*	−0.0016	(−0.83)		−0.0012	(−1.01)	
*POST*ENFORCE*INC*	0.0018	(1.59)		0.0011	(1.18)	
*POST*OFFICE*INC*	0.0009	(1.15)		0.0024	(3.43)	***
*POST*CAPITAL*INC*	0.0064	(2.04)	**	0.0051	(2.93)	***
IFRS7	0.0233	(3.12)	***			
SIZE_DEC	−0.0010	(−1.81)	*	−0.0007	(−0.61)	
OTC	−0.0039	(−0.76)		−0.0036	(−0.83)	
EXCH	0.0108	(3.60)	***	0.0077	(1.46)	
INFLA	0.0019	(1.96)	*	−0.0009	(−0.81)	
RETVOL_DEC	−0.0002	(−0.40)		−0.0010	(−1.42)	
LEV_DEC	0.0010	(1.54)		0.0008	(1.08)	
CAPR	−0.0001	(−0.82)		0.0016	(1.99)	*
CAPR_DUM	−0.0038	(−0.78)		0.0107	(1.12)	
FBIAS	0.2151	(1.77)	*	0.3305	(1.77)	*
DISP	0.0752	(2.62)	**	0.1549	(0.37)	
ONEFORECAST	0.0021	(0.95)		0.0027	(0.75)	
BPR	0.0193	(2.69)	**	0.0330	(3.16)	***
No. of OBS	285			131		
ADJ R2	0.5814			0.4146		

*, **, and *** indicate significance at the 10%, 5%, and 1% levels by two-tailed tests, respectively. t-values are adjusted by firm cluster.

Panel B of Table 6 shows the influence of the improved comparability on banks' cost of equity. I use model (3) for this test. *INC* indicates the differences between IFRS and the pre-IFRS local accounting standards. Therefore, *INC* also proxies for the improved comparability across countries. Unlike *ADD*, *INC* indicates disclosure requirement changes to the pre-existing accounting standards. Therefore, from the banking regulators' point of view, *INC* could be a threat to the debt market because it relates to compliance with debt covenants of the pre-existing debt contracts. By contrast, *ADD* is likely unrelated to the compliance with debt covenants because *ADD* indicates new disclosure requirements. The items related to *ADD* were not in the previous accounting standards; hence, those items have little impact on debt covenants. Thus, the effect of bank supervisors' intervention is related to *INC*, not to *ADD*.

The three-way interaction term of *CAPITAL* and *OFFICE* is positive. This means that mandatory IFRS adoption increases the cost of equity in countries with stringent banking regulations and where the pre-existing accounting standards change significantly. As *INC* increases, bank supervisors' incentive to intervene in the implementation of IFRS increases because the adoption decreases the contractibility of accounting information [1,3,25]. Moreover, changes in accounting standards impact the regulatory capital ratio, which potentially impacts the stability of the banking system. As a result of the intervention, accounting standards are implemented to minimize the potential negative influence on the debt markets, which increases information risks.

6. Conclusions

This study examines the effect of mandatory IFRS adoption on European banks' cost of equity. The empirical results of this study show that the impact of IFRS adoption on banks' cost of equity varies depending on institutional aspects. Strong investor protection is helpful in decreasing the cost of equity following IFRS adoption. However, banking regulation increases banks' cost of capital, especially when IFRS adoption has a strong impact on debt contracts. These results show that market monitoring and bank regulation are potentially at odds because of differences in policy objectives. Consequently, the cost of capital is affected differently by IFRS adoption in two institutional aspects.

The results of this study have policy implications. Unlike other industry sectors, the banking sector has a strong regulatory environment. Therefore, the incentives of banking regulators must be considered when designing a disclosure policy for the banking sector. If these incentives are ignored, a disclosure policy can be distorted; hence, the intended results cannot be obtained. Furthermore, this policy can yield results opposite to the intended ones. In addition, although market discipline is an important part of the banking regulatory system, factors that enhance market discipline can easily be weakened by bank supervisors. As market discipline has become more important because of rapid innovations in the finance sector, policy makers should carefully design policies related to the banking system.

This study also has several limitations. First, due to availability, some countries are not included in the analysis, which could cause a selection bias. Second, I incorporate only two aggregate measures of bank regulation, which are not enough to explain every detail of banking regulation. Third, the effects of specific regulatory events that occurred during my sample period are not totally addressed in this study. Fourth, this study focuses only on listed banks. Several banks are unlisted; hence, market discipline on unlisted banks should be addressed in future research settings. Finally, this study does not address the impact of IFRS adoption on several aspects other than stock price; for example, credit allocation activities. These could be examined separately in other studies.

Acknowledgments: This study is based on one essay of my dissertation. I thank my dissertation chair Woon Oh Jung and committee members Lee-seok Hwan, Jong Hag Choi, Kyung-Ho Park, and Seung Yeon Lim for the guidance and support.

Appendix A

Table A1. Variable definitions.

Name	Definition
ADD	Increase in disclosure requirements that are not related to assets with a tangible form, e.g., depreciable assets or inventory [42]
BPR	Ratio of book value of equity to market value of common shares outstanding
CAPITAL	Regulatory restrictions on bank capital from Caprio et al. [38]
Capital Ratio	Ratio of the sum of core and supplementary capital to risk weighted assets
CAPR	Ratio of core and supplementary capital to risk weighted assets. Missing value is replaced by zero
CAPR_DUM	1 if CAPR is not available, 0 otherwise
CoC	Average of four estimates of implied cost of equity calculated by the models of Easton [33], Gode and Mohanram [34], Gebhardt et al. [35], and Claus and Thomas [36]
DISP	Standard variation of one-year-ahead earnings forecasts less actual earnings scaled by the forecast-period stock price if more than 1 one-year-ahead earnings forecasts exists, 0 otherwise
ENFORCE	Average of three indices for the efficiency of judicial system, rule of law, and corruption from La Porta et al. [43]

Table A1. *Cont.*

Name	Definition
EXCH	1 if a firm trades its shares in major stock markets (NYSE, NASDAQ, or Amex)
FBIAS	One-year-ahead earnings forecast less actual earnings scaled by the forecast-period stock price
FOLLOW	The number of analysts following
IFRS7	1 if the year of an observation is after 2007, 0 otherwise
INC	Total number of inconsistencies for banks between local accounting standards and IFRS measured by Nobes [42]
INFLA	Inflation rate measured by the wholesale price index
LEV	Total liabilities divided by total assets
LEV_DEC	Decile of *LEV*
MKT	Market value of equity in million US dollars
OFFICE	Index of official supervisory power of bank regulators from Caprio et al. [38]
ONEFORECAST	1 if only one analyst follows, and 0 otherwise
OTC	1 if a firm trades its shares in the US over-the-counter markets, and 0 otherwise
POST	1 if a firm-year observation falls in 2005 or later, and 0 otherwise
PP	1 if a firm trades its shares in a private placement under Rule 144A
RETVOL	Standard deviation of monthly stock returns for the last 12 months before the fiscal year end
RETVOL_DEC	Decile of *RETVOL*
SIZE	Natural log of the value of total assets in million US dollars
SIZE_DEC	Decile of the value of total assets
TA	Value of total assets in million US dollars
VOLUNT	1 if the bank adopted IFRS voluntarily, and 0 otherwise

References

1. Ball, R.; Li, X.; Shivakumar, L. Contractibility and Transparency of Financial Statement Information Prepared Uner IFRS: Evidence from Debt Contracts Around IFRS Adoption. *J. Account. Res.* **2015**, *53*, 915–963. [CrossRef]

2. Watts, R. Conservatism in Accounting Part I: Explanations and Implications. *Account. Horiz.* **2003**, *17*, 207–221. [CrossRef]

3. Skinner, D.J. The Rise of Deferred Tax Assets in Japan: The Role of Deferred Tax Accounting in the Japanese Banking Crisis. *J. Account. Econ.* **2008**, *46*, 218–239. [CrossRef]

4. Armstrong, C.S.; Jagolinzer, A.D.; Larcker, D.F. Chief Executive Officer Equity Incentives and Accounting Irregularities. *J. Account. Res.* **2010**, *48*, 225–271. [CrossRef]

5. Daske, H.; Hail, L.; Leuz, C.; Verdi, R. Mandatory IFRS Reporting around the World: Early Evidence on the Economic Consequences. *J. Account. Res.* **2008**, *46*, 1085–1142.

6. Li, S. Does Mandatory Adoption of International Financial Reporting Standards in the European Union Reduce the Cost of Equity Capital? *Account. Rev.* **2010**, *85*, 607–636. [CrossRef]

7. Greenbaum, S.I.; Thakor, A.V. *Contemporary Financial Intermediation*; Academic Press: Burlington, MA, USA, 2007.

8. Stephanou, C. *Rethinking Market Discipline in Banking: Lessons from the Financial Crisis. Policy Research working paper*; World Bank: Washington, DC, USA, 2010.

9. Ball, R.; Robin, A.; Wu, J.S. Incentives versus Standards: Properties of Accounting Income in Four East Asian Countries. *J. Account. Econ.* **2003**, *36*, 235–270. [CrossRef]

10. Bushman, R.M.; Piotroski, J.D.; Smith, A.J. What Determines Corporate Transparency? *J. Account. Res.* **2004**, *42*, 207–252. [CrossRef]

11. Leuz, C.; Nanda, D.; Wysocki, P.D. Earnings Management and Investor Protection: An International Comparison. *J. Financ. Econ.* **2003**, *69*, 505–527. [CrossRef]

12. Byard, D.; Li, Y.; Yu, Y. The Effect of Mandatory IFRS Adoption on Financial Analysts' Information Environment. *J. Account. Res.* **2011**, *49*, 69–96. [CrossRef]

13. Barth, M.E.; Landsman, W.R.; Lang, M.H. International Accounting Standards and Accounting Quality. *J. Account. Res.* **2008**, *46*, 467–498. [CrossRef]

14. Gebhardt, G.; Novotny-Farkas, Z. Mandatory IFRS Adoption and Accounting Quality of European Banks. *J. Bus. Financ. Account.* **2011**, *38*, 289–333. [CrossRef]

15. Chen, C.; Young, D.; Zhuang, Z. Externalities of Mandatory IFRS Adoption: Evidence from Cross-Border Spillover Effects of Financial Information on Investment Efficiency. *Account. Rev.* **2013**, *88*, 881–914. [CrossRef]

16. Yip, R.W.Y.; Young, D. Does Mandatory IFRS Adoption Improve Information Comparability? *Account. Rev.* **2012**, *87*, 1767–1789. [CrossRef]

17. DeFond, M.; Hu, X.; Hung, M.; Li, S. The Impact of Mandatory IFRS Adoption on Foreign Mutual Fund Ownership: The Role of Comparability. *J. Account. Econ.* **2011**, *51*, 240–258. [CrossRef]

18. Florou, A.; Pope, P.F. Mandatory IFRS Adoption and Institutional Investment Decisions. *Account. Rev.* **2012**, *87*, 1993–2025. [CrossRef]

19. Diamond, D.W.; Verrecchia, R.E. Disclosure, Liquidity, and the Cost of Capital. *J. Financ.* **1991**, *46*, 1325–1359. [CrossRef]

20. Easley, D.; O'Hara, M. Information and the Cost of Capital. *J. Financ.* **2004**, *59*, 1553–1583. [CrossRef]

21. Lambert, R.; Leuz, C.; Verrecchia, R.E. Accounting Information, Disclosure, and the Cost of Capital. *J. Account. Res.* **2007**, *45*, 385–420. [CrossRef]

22. Botosan, C.A. Disclosure Level and the Cost of Equity Capital. *Account. Rev.* **1997**, *72*, 323–349.

23. Botosan, C.A.; Plumlee, M.A. A Re-examination of Disclosure Level and the Expected Cost of Equity Capital. *J. Account. Res.* **2002**, *40*, 21–40. [CrossRef]

24. Barth, J.R.; Caprio, G., Jr.; Levine, R. Bank Regulation and Supervision: What Works Best? *J. Financ. Intermediat.* **2004**, *13*, 205–248. [CrossRef]

25. Bischof, J. The Effects of IFRS 7 Adoption on Bank Disclosure in Europe. *Account. Eur.* **2009**, *6*, 167–194. [CrossRef]

26. Flannery, M.J.; Houston, J.F. The Value of a Government Monitor for U. S. Banking Firms. *J. Money Credit Bank.* **1999**, *31*, 14–34. [CrossRef]

27. Flannery, M.J.; Kwan, S.H.; Nimalendran, M. Market Evidence on the Opaqueness of Banking Firms' Assets. *J. Financ. Econ.* **2004**, *71*, 419–460. [CrossRef]

28. Beltratti, A.; Stulz, R.M. The Credit Crisis around the Globe: Why Did Some Banks Perform Better? *J. Financ. Econ.* **2012**, *105*, 1–17. [CrossRef]

29. Ball, R.; Kothari, S.P.; Robin, A. The Effect of International Institutional Factors on Properties of Accounting Earnings. *J. Account. Econ.* **2000**, *29*, 1–51. [CrossRef]

30. Hail, L.; Leuz, C. International Differences in the Cost of Equity Capital: Do Legal Institutions and Securities Regulation Matter? *J. Account. Res.* **2006**, *44*, 485–531. [CrossRef]

31. Hail, L.; Leuz, C. Cost of Capital Effects and Changes in Growth Expectations around U.S. Cross-Listings. *J. Financ. Econ.* **2009**, *93*, 428–454. [CrossRef]

32. Bae, K.-H.; Tan, H.; Welker, M. International GAAP Differences: The Impact on Foreign Analysts. *Account. Rev.* **2008**, *83*, 593–628. [CrossRef]

33. Elton, E.J. Expected Return, Realized Return, and Asset Pricing Tests. *J. Financ.* **1999**, *54*, 1199–1220. [CrossRef]

34. Easton, P.D. PE Ratios, PEG Ratios, and Estimating the Implied Expected Rate of Return on Equity Capital. *Account. Rev.* **2004**, *79*, 73–95. [CrossRef]

35. Gode, D.; Mohanram, P. Inferring the Cost of Capital Using the Ohlson–Juettner Model. *Rev. Account. Stud.* **2003**, *8*, 399–431. [CrossRef]

36. Gebhardt, W.R.; Lee, C.M.C.; Swaminathan, B. Toward an Implied Cost of Capital. *J. Account. Res.* **2001**, *39*, 135–176. [CrossRef]

37. Claus, J.; Thomas, J. Equity Premia as Low as Three Percent? Evidence from Analysts' Earnings Forecasts for Domestic and International Stock Markets. *J. Financ.* **2001**, *56*, 1629–1666. [CrossRef]

38. Caprio, G.; Laeven, L.; Levine, R. Governance and Bank Valuation. *J. Financ. Intermediat.* **2007**, *16*, 584–617. [CrossRef]

39. West, S.G.; Aiken, L.S. *Multiple Regression: Testing and Interpreting Interactions*; Sage Publications: Thousand Oaks, CA, USA, 1991.

40. Easton, P.D.; Sommers, G.A. Effect of Analysts' Optimism on Estimates of the Expected Rate of Return Implied by Earnings Forecasts. *J. Account. Res.* **2007**, *45*, 983–1015. [CrossRef]

41. Petersen, M.A. Estimating Standard Errors in Finance Panel Data Sets: Comparing Approaches. *Rev. Financ. Stud.* **2009**, *22*, 435–480. [CrossRef]

42. Nobes, C.W. *GAAP 2001: A Survey of National Accounting Rules Benchmarked Against International Accounting Standards*; Andersen; BDO; Deloitte Touche Tohmatsu; Ernst & Young; Grant Thornton; KPMG; PriceWaterhouseCoopers: New York, NY, USA, 2001.

43. La Porta, R.; Lopez-de-Silanes, F.; Shleifer, A.; Vishny, R.W. Law and Finance. *J. Political Econ.* **1998**, *106*, 1113–1155. [CrossRef]

9

Evaluation and Classification of Mobile Financial Services Sustainability using Structural Equation Modeling and Multiple Criteria Decision-Making Methods

Komlan Gbongli [1,*], Yongan Xu [2,*], Komi Mawugbe Amedjonekou [3] and Levente Kovács [1]

[1] Institute of Finance and Accounting, Faculty of Economics, University of Miskolc, 3515 Miskolc-Egyetemvaros, Hungary; kovacs.levente@uni-miskolc.hu

[2] School of International Business, Southwestern University of Finance and Economics, 55 Guanghuacun Street, Qingyang District, Chengdu 610074, China

[3] Business School, York St John University, Lord Mayor's Walk, York Y031 7EX, UK; komi.amedjonekou@yorksj.ac.uk

[*] Correspondence: samxp12@yahoo.fr or pzkgbong@uni-miskolc.hu (K.G.); xyan88@swufe.edu.cn (Y.X.)

Abstract: Despite the fast emergent of smartphones in day-to-day activity, the sustainable development of mobile financial services (MFS) remains low partially due to online consumer's trust and perceived risk. This research broadens the trust and the perceived risk at the multi-dimensional for understanding and prioritizing alternatives of MFS decision. A combined methodology; structural equation modeling (SEM) with two multiple criteria decision-making (MCDM) methods such as a technique for order of preference by similarity to ideal solution (TOPSIS) and analytic hierarchy process (AHP) were applied for data analysis. The two steps SEM-TOPSIS techniques were adopted through a two-types survey on datasets consisting of 538 MFS users, and 74 both experienced MFS users and experts in Togo. The SEM is used for causal relationships and assigning weights for the TOPSIS input. TOPSIS was applied for providing MFS alternative classification, in which the results were compared with prior research using the SEM-AHP technique on the given population. The results via SEM revealed particularly strong support for the dispositional trust and perceived privacy risk. Trust has a negative relationship with perceived risk. Except for perceived time risk, all the antecedents of perceived risk and trust validated the proposed relationship. The findings of TOPSIS uncovered that mobile money transfer (MMT) remains the core application used, followed by mobile payment (MP) and mobile banking (MB) and, therefore, consistent with AHP. However, the TOPSIS technique is better suited to the problem of MFS selection for this study field. This research offers a novel and practical modeling and classification concept for researchers, companies' managers, and experts in the areas of information technology. The implications, limitations, and future research are provided.

Keywords: mobile financial services (MFS); trust; perceived risk; structural equation modeling (SEM); multiple-criteria decision-making (MCDM); technique for order preference by similarity to ideal solution (TOPSIS); analytic hierarchy process (AHP)

1. Introduction

As a part of the shift of technology in the financial business, mobile financial services have been exploring at an accelerate speed [1]. Innovations and technological expansion have emerged with significant advantages to the recent commercial market. Over the past few years, businesses have been redirecting their goals to making information system technology an essential part of their processes [2]. Therefore, more and more literature is diverted to the IS-related field [3]. The investigation of some existing studies which recommend integrating various theoretical models to understand the IT adoption has stressed that a comprehensive analysis in the context is required [2,4]. From these perspectives, an increasing number of researchers are focused on mobile financial services (MFS) considered as the development of the information system (IS) domain [5–8].

MFS refers to any financial transaction remotely conducted by the application of a mobile phone (e.g., smartphone or tablet) and mobile software (e.g., apps programs) either through banking service or network provider service [9,10]. MFS providers allow their consumers the flexibility to access their financial services (access information inquiry, bill payment, and money transfers) anywhere and anytime via a mobile phone, to support and improve service relationships by investing lots of resources using wireless Internet technology [11].

The studies of MFS that emphasized on electronic money transfer include three major mobile technologies-related fields of study, primarily mobile banking services (MB), mobile payment services (MP), and mobile money transfer (MMT) services [10]. MB remains part of the latest in a sequence of new mobile technological wonders [12]. Therefore, an expectation toward it should be for a significant impact on the market [13]. Payment today has now progressed to mobile devices (m-devices) identified as mobile financial services, particularly mobile payments [14]. Mobile money has appeared as a significant innovation with a potential expansion to financial inclusion in developing countries in various ways [15]. It is, therefore, growing access to financial services for a large number of people, who are entirely disregarded by banks because of longer travel distances or insufficient funds to fulfill the minimum deposit recommended for opening account in a bank [16,17], low-income population in developing countries [18], insofar, as it has several advantages [15,19,20]. In addition to the advantages granted to certain persons and companies, there are also advantages at the national economy level, primarily in emerging economies such as Hungary. The use of increasingly more accommodating tools may incentivize the suppressed use of cash, parallel to which, the countability of economic performance with statistical instruments continues to improve; meanwhile tax payment discipline also improves and the total social cost of payments decreases, etc., that is, overall the economy begins to whiten, leading to improved competitiveness [21].

While tremendous benefits are associated with adopting MFS as opposed to traditional payment methods, such as physical exchange notes, cheques, coins [18], the adoption rate is far from full utilization in many developing countries. This is characteristically the situation of West African Countries and particularly Togo. Given the statistical information on the Statista Portal (2016), the population using smartphones worldwide is predicted to be over five billion marks in 2019. Approximately 67% of the Togolese population subscribed to the mobile phone in 2015, while users of mobile Internet doubled between 2014 and 2015. However, the percentage rate of users of banking services is less than 15% [22] and, the rate of consumer acceptance of mobile banking remains trivial (around 1%) when considering the expectation [23]. It is, therefore, leading to deduct that mobile money services should fill this lacuna by providing significant input to increase the acceptance of MFS. This hope is far from being the case. The experiences of more developed countries also suggest the same, not technological limitations were the primary obstacle of the extension of the innovative payment solutions [24]. Therefore, the motives for the successful evolution or not together with the causes and motives for mobile money adoption, remain not understood sufficiently, which infers that the technology has not been extensively adopted. These trends reveal partial knowledge regarding the motivators and inhibitors that impact the acceptance of this mobile service [25].

Understanding why it is worth to select to use MFS can help in strategy development and allow businesses to effectively communicate benefits to their customers [26,27]. Mobile financial service operators might increase their attractiveness and competitiveness if they were able to enhance their strategies to satisfy the demand of their consumers. Therefore, there is a necessity of understanding the various requirements of MFS users and the comparative weight of each factor or criteria that could affect the demand of consumers. One possible motive for the existence of a gap between these could be the perception of risk that limits consumers' capability to make informed decisions to partake the benefit of MFS technology in Togo [28]. This is particularly true for emerging nations, mainly in an unstable country where the consideration of the loss of privacy in the security system and the associated risk played a crucial part in adopting IT [29]. Moreover, the studies in the past revealed that once there are risk issue concerns, the demand for trust becomes a necessity, since trust and risk are interrelated facets [28,30]. Not only the developing countries facing the issue of e-business but also the reflection of the online risk has called for a considerable attention among the developed countries like Hungary, particularly in 2014 when the case of fraud risk in electronic payment transactions ascended in Hungary (the case was discussed in the work of Kovács and David in detail [31]).

Driven by studies toward the multiple scopes for risk and trust and the central research on trust in contrast to risk in novel information technology perspective [32], we suppose that initiating research into novel IT artifacts such as this research could enlighten how trust and perceived risk could influence the ultimate adoption of novel technologies in developing countries.

The goal of this study is to disclose mechanisms related to behavior associated with MFS adoption and sustainable development when decision-making involves multiple criteria issues. One main research question is to understand how multi-dimensional trust and multi-faceted perceived risk perceptions affect a new emerging information technology such as MFS adoption at the individual level in an unstable country. Our approach differs from most prior studies that assess trust and risk perception of individual behavior. Indeed, most of the research that investigated the acceptance and application of communicative IT has been done within stable, capitalist, and highly-developed communities. Moreover, the majority of research undertakes that individuals have freedom of speech, and safety of their lives, basic protection and business offered by the government. However, little has been known regarding the adoption of IT in emerging and dynamic societies [33,34]. Therefore, we explore the fundamental trust and risk allied with MFS technology usage in high poverty.

The majority of prior research typically tests trust as a single construct [35–37] or investigates trust constructs and risk dimensions disjointedly [27,38]. In other words, how to effectively assess trust and risk concerns concurrently remains a black box. Drawing on research in information technology [39,40], we stress that multi-dimensional trust and perceived risk concepts may jointly play an integral part in individual behavior with regard to adopting a novel MFS, and it is of paramount importance for this to be investigated, particularly in developing countries such as Togo.

Furthermore, a plethora of research has been done in order to fully understand the factors that affect MFS adoption and its significance. However, most prior studies in this perspective have emphasized the general factors regarding the adoption of MFS, using explanatory statistical analysis as the research method [41,42]. The beta coefficients gained in multiple regression techniques can be considered as the relative weights of the constructs, however, their values are obtained indirectly via the testing result. Additionally, a negative value of beta can be found, making it quite complex for the justification of the importance of the resultant value [43]. Making decisions has continually been an essential activity in day to day life. Therefore, using services such as MFS necessitates a careful decision from an individual so that he/she would not regret his/her decision, ever since decision-making has emerged as a mathematical science today [44]. From there, multiple criteria decision-making (MCDM) techniques constitute a critical framework through which companies focus on which strategy to implement to meet the needs of consumers, to acquire the appropriate income, and to prosper in the competitive milieu [45].

In order to advance current IS researches, Esearch and Koppius [46] stressed that there is a necessity to integrate decision modeling methods in IS research to generate data estimates as well as methods for assessing the analytical power of the result. Therefore, applying a combined analytic method stressed how integrating two or multiple data analysis techniques in either methodology or investigation can patronize the confidence and validity in the resulting outcome [15,47]. Additionally, most managers make strategic decisions based on a single goal or dimension, but strategic planning is impacted by many different factors and regarded from several perspectives [48]. As the traditional notion of strategic planning lacks multidimensional prominence, this paper integrates the structural equation modeling and technique for order preference by similarity to ideal solution (SEM-TOPSIS) method to construct the relationships between decision factors for MFS adoption, while classifying the alternative of MFS. It is a unique decision support technique grounded in structural modeling.

The primary objectives of this research are: To explore the influential antecedent of trust and risk perception at the multidimensional level regarding MFS adoption in Togo; to propose and validate model MFS acceptance using an SEM technique by employing data collected through experts of MFS and MFS experienced users; to develop an SEM-TOPSIS-based model for multi-criteria decision-making by selecting the appropriate MFS type for MFS, grounded in experts' view, and by prioritizing the operative trust-risk factors while exposing the veiled relationship among the factors that influence customers in the MFS. The present study has the following contributions.

Primarily, a growing number of recent studies link the multiple criteria decision-making (MCDM) techniques to financial decision making [49]. In the majority of cases, the traditional model of MCDM considers the criteria (factors) are independently and hierarchically organized. Nevertheless, problems are often organized by interdependent criteria and dimensions and might even reveal feedback-like effects [50]. TOPSIS is one of the most extensively adopted decision methodologies in technology, engineering, management, science, and business. TOPSIS approaches, as part of MCDM, have an impact on improving the quality of decisions by generating the development more efficient, rational, and explicit. However, previous works have not sufficiently kept pace. Thus, we believe that there is a necessity for the methodical integration of SEM-TOPSIS to merge a recent study performed in this field of study. This study incorporates a complex multi-criteria decision-making problem by assessing types of multidimensional trust and risk in MFS that have rarely been investigated and touched in past studies. As such, a literature review is conducted, and then SEM analysis is used to construct a hierarchical structure for trust and risk factors, which includes a total of ten sub-factors. According to the identified criteria and sub-criteria and by considering relationships among them, TOPSIS is adopted for selecting the appropriate types of MFS, based on the critical factors that influence customers' trust and risk. Hence, the study contributes by proposing a solution that could effectively enhance trust and mitigation-perceived risk measures through a multi-level approach considered as a new added concept to planning strategy from the MFS perspective.

Second, one of the contributions of this research is based on the comparison of the results of both TOPSIS and analytical hierarchical process (AHP) technique, for a given model, to inspect if there are, indeed, noteworthy differences. The result of AHP is derived from the earlier work of Gbongli [10] in which the SEM-AHP technique has been applied for assessing the issues of risk and trust using the specified population. Similarly, the main work is derived from previous work in which SEM-TOPSIS has been extensively adopted on the equal given population [51]. As a result, this study shows that both approaches achieved comparable results and were well consistent and, in general, agreed with each other. In other words, both methods classify mobile money services as the most important MFS used, followed by mobile payment as the second and mobile banking as the last. However, the TOPSIS method is better suited to the problem of MFS selection for this study area since AHP requires a long process of pairwise comparison, and the requirement of the consistency ratio should also be considered in the process. The paper provides a detailed methodology application that could provide very useful insights for managers and researchers for their specific application.

The remainder of this paper is structured as follows. In Section 2, we offer a succinct overview of the literature and theory review. For Section 3, we present the theoretical framework. In Section 4, the description of the research methodology and the procedure of this research are presented. Section 5 provides findings based on the research objectives. We conclude the work with discussions of the findings, implications, limitations, and future study suggestions.

2. Literature and Theory Review

2.1. Understanding Mobile Financial Services (MFS)

The rapid adoption of mobile devices in developing countries [52], together with widespread mobile financial services, has recently drawn practitioners and academics' attention [53]. Since consumers are spending gradually more and more time in online and are "going mobile," financial digitalization is now driving banks and network companies' providers to undertake the most extensive transition in their history. Mobile financial services (MFS) denotes the financial services and financial transactions performed using the channel such as mobile devices [54].

MFS characterizes an area of innovation and strategic importance for global initiatives to counter poverty and mobile telecommunication providers [55]. It has been said to have carried about a positive shift in customers' perceptions in many countries. Mobile operators grasp MFS as an opportunity to engender revenue via an adjacent business (both basic payment and services) and recovery of cost and investments through enlarged data usage by consumers [56]. The goals of MFS are accompanied by various advantages for banks, such as the decreased use of cash, while cost-effectively serving the unbanked population, protecting current accounts and products. The major benefit of MFS regarding trade involves higher point-of-sale (PoS) throughput, real-time messaging to users, and fewer cost for cash handling. Accessing transaction information and ownership of the user interface are further viewed as an important perceived value of MFS. For the customer, MFS makes payments possible anytime, anywhere, and with the alleviated risk of theft (i.e., cash, particularly in underdeveloped communities) [55].

These advantages could be equally valid for Togo. Not much attention has been given to the empirical research on the adoption of MFS in Togo. Furthermore, in less affluent nations stricken with socio-political instability and vulnerability, MFS technologies may have different implications toward usage and are likely to impact the initial decisions to adopt [57,58]. The country of Togo sometimes encounters a kind of socio-political crisis. Given a negative socio-political and external influence such as the physical atmosphere of development and growth, policies, regulations, and social environment unsupportive of adoption are suggested to hinder innovation adoption [59]. MFS unavoidability might confront such challenges because of consumers' lack of trust in the novel wireless technology, and their risk perceptions. We thus stress that users' trust and risk perception may impact their adoption of MFS services.

2.2. Theory and Past Research

As an emergent service, mobile financial services (MFS) has not been widely adopted by users. Therefore, scholars have paid attention to assess the factors impacting their user adoption. Furthermore, technology adoption is one main area of focus for information systems (IS) researchers. A diversity of theoretical perspectives has been developed to study MFS adoption. More assertively toward another direction, the current literature on consumer behavior related to acceptance of IT, such as MFS, tends to elaborate on a theoretical model of technology adoption theories [60]. They often employ the traditional information system models to explain user adoption of IT like theory of reasoned action (TRA), motivational model, diffusion of innovation theory (DOI), technology acceptance model (TAM), innovation diffusion theory (IDT), theory of planned behavior (TPB), and unified theory of acceptance and use of technology (UTAUT). Numerous studies have employed these traditional frameworks to perform their researches, and the rest integrated either previous models or added new variables to construct models to carry out their study. They examine whether the models' theoretical constructs are likely to affect the consumer acceptance of an MFS [15,61–63] or assess whether consumers are ready to adopt m-payments grounded in the supposed factors [64].

The TRA model stipulates that a particular behavior is directed by the individual's intention to conduct that action, which itself hinges on the attitude to behavior and subjective norms [65]. For the TPB model, the perceived behavior was added to the attitude toward behavior and subjective norms that affect both the intentions of people's perceived behavior and actual behavior [66]. Past studies elucidated behavioral perception control as the degree to which one has control over launching a particular behavior as well as facing the circumstances, while the full volitional control over the behavior of interest is found limited [67]. Although their finding pinpointed the internal and external factors of perceived control, as an example, self-efficacy and facilitating condition, technology, and government sustenance, the utmost impact on the behavior is somehow associated with the type of innovation. The TAM model, as the extension to the TRA and TPB models, bears a significance of perceived usefulness and perceived ease of use factor to affect actual behavior geared toward innovation [68]. Based on the review of TAM literature, Marangunić and Granić [69] revealed seven past TAM-related studies. However, the goal of these works and the various analysis techniques adopted differ. For instance, Legris et al. [70] examine the question of whether the TAM explains actual use while Mortenson and Vidgen [71] conducted the review of TAM studies employing the computational literature review (CLR). Moreover, TAM [72] and its extended version has been used in various online milieu to assess the adoption of consumer's online-system [15,73–75].

The TRA model, however, has some drawbacks, comprising a major threat misleading between attitudes and norms because attitudes can commonly be viewed as norms and conversely. Similarly, further explanatory variables are required for TRA [76,77]. As such, TAM has then been successfully combined with TRA and TPB in parsimonious capability [78]. The theory of adoption, such as DOI theory [79], is a handy systemic background to define either adoption or non-adoption of new technology. The theory put forward is that people will be more likely to accept innovation grounded in the innovation facets and appearance of comparative benefit, compatibility, intricacy, trialability, and observability [80]. Regardless of the enlightened strength of this model, the weaknesses go a long way in decreasing its power. For instance, the relationship between attitude and espousal or rejection of innovation was restricted [81,82]; the innovation-decision process and the features of innovation remain unclear as well. The theory posits technology to pass via a linear stage; however, an intricate technology [83] has been perceived not on linear stages. Rendering to the critical review and meta-analysis of TAM [70], it was suggested as a useful model; although, it suffers from the trade-off of dropping information richness resulted from the investigation [84].

Despite the various advantages that might be incorporated into every theory or model, their competency in predicting and elucidating is due to the degree to which the predictor could get a sound proportion of variance explained in intention and usage behavior [85,86]. Even though the prevailing models are indicative of e-service or MFS acceptance behavior, many researchers believe that they are not sufficiently robust with regard to assessing all the aspects clients intend obviously throughout the various phases of their decision-making process and thus require further integration [87]. George's findings [88], after the review of previous information acceptance models, revealed that trust consideration could be a major laudatory and backup for an online vendor.

It is important to recall that trust and risk are interrelated facets [30], where the degree of importance of the situation depends on the impending outcome of risk. Given that the adoption of MFS becomes an important decision that consumers are required to make for a long-term impact, the function of risk is more likely to be vital. The extensive review of the literature revealed diverse antecedents to the adoption of mobile banking [27,89–92]. Studies were carried out in both developing and developed countries; however, a limited number have been conducted in Togo [7,93]. These outcomes are, therefore, insufficient to offer meaningful insights into predicting which multi-dimensional trust and risk influence customers' use of MFS in Togo while providing a strategy decision analysis framework for understanding the multiple factors that entail the decision of the acceptance. Moreover, many of these theories and models were used in developed countries, and their direct application in developing countries such as Togo might not be sufficiently robust for the economic situation of the country. Given that MFS belongs to information technology to which some adoption model might exist, it requires a distinctive conceptualization that might better pronounce the fact in emerging countries' situations.

Regarding these ends, this study uses components from both trust and risk dimensionality literature. It proposes conceptual research to envisage consumer appraisal of MFS (mobile banking, mobile payment, and mobile money transfer) adoption in Togo while ranking their perspective.

3. Theoretical Framework and Hypotheses

3.1. Antecedent of Trust

The concept of trust remains an intricate, multi-dimensional, and context-dependent paradigm [94]. Past researchers emphasize the diverse aspects of trust, a fact that frequently leads to discrepancies between numerous studies outcomes. After the appeal from Gefen et al. [32] for additional new IT-related research on trust, there is a need to collectively assess the most crucial trust's dimension, such as a disposition to trust, technology trust, and vendor trust that seems to impact MFS.

Some scholars have proposed trust dispositional, trust belief, structural assurance [95]. From others' point of view, the interpersonal trust, the dispositional trust, and institutional trust are also essential constituents of the trust dimension [96]. Others found the dimension of trust to be trusting behavior, dispositional to trust, and institution-based trust [97]. Disposition to trust denotes the general susceptibility for a person to trust others [98]. It is grounded in the personality, which explains the reason why some of us have a tendency to either trust or mistrust and doubt others [99,100]. Disposition to trust is, therefore, crucial for the establishment of initial trust and subsequently accommodating to less importance in the presence of pre-existed trust belief [101].

Technology trust is considered as an antecedent of trust. It connotes the readiness of an individual, or individual's technological dependency, to achieve a designated task by the positive feature incorporated in the technology [102] and the benefit arises from the particular technology [103]. With this view, technology trust refers to the role of technology in building a trusting relationship with the user [104]. From the above perspective, when an MFS user considers the technologies that are being applied to be reliable and consistent, then the probability to assess the aggregate service seems more promising, and trust will increase. Although admitting that the three-fold technology aspect affects the environment of MFS (i.e., website, network, and mobile technology), the present study intends to treat them as a whole without separating them. As such, the user or potential user is called upon the strong level of comprehensive understanding purposively for MFS optimum usage. Past research has revealed much importance and many benefits of technological trust in the behavioral field of application [102,105–107].

Vendor trust denotes the extent to which the consumer sees and believes that the vendor will accomplish the designated transactional requirements in risky or ambiguous conditions [108]. Many situations can raise consumer's trust toward the vendor. An online consumer who perceives the vendor in presenting an opportunistic behavior can create a kind of reluctance within that particular consumer. Earlier studies have revealed a negative relationship between the online vendor's opportunism and online consumer's trust [109]. Trust, and in specific the confidence in the mobile vendor, plays an exceptionally important role in the digital environment [110–113]. For Roger C. Mayer et al. [114], vendor ability, integrity, and benevolence are crucial vendor trust features, although ability can also be regarded as vendor competence [115]. By relating that logic to the MFS environment, vendors with a good reputation/integrity will be less expected to bear unscrupulous behaviors and threaten their status. As a result, we posit the succeeding three assumptions to inspect the causal effect relationships between trust's antecedents and trust in the MFS perspective.

Hypothesis 1. *The dispositional trust would significantly influence users' general trust in using MFS.*

Hypothesis 2. *The technological trust would significantly influence users' general trust in using MFS.*

Hypothesis 3. *The vendor trust would significantly influence users' general trust in using MFS.*

3.2. Antecedent of Perceived Risk

Perceived risk can denote a combination of uncertainty added to the severity of the consequence involved [116]. It is similarly taught as a kind of uncertainty and outcome [117]. In the psychological field, perceived risk is the emotional sensitivity and subjective thoughts of various objective risks. Although it is the derivative of the objectives risk, nevertheless, they are different from each other. From the perceptive of trust-risk relationship, prior researchers understood that the readiness to take risks is a general characteristic of all trust circumstances [28,118,119]. From this point, consumer trust could be noticed and subjected to the degree of the intricate risk presented in the situations [120]. Awkwardly perhaps, because of the complex nature of trust and risk variables, countless scholars have disregarded the function of risk perceptions [121]. E-commerce trust investigators have shown that, when trust increases, the trustee's perception of risk reduces and impacts their attitudes to the trustor, which successively, influences the readiness to procurement [122]. In the view of the risk management field, the risk is the construct associated with the cost of outcomes, empowering trust and risk as mirror images while both incorporate differing relationships [123]. The study focuses on the rapport among trust and risk [121], and the trust-related works and empirical confirmation predominantly emphasize on industrial relationships, nonetheless theoretical and empirical support encountered in MFS is limited. When people trust others, they believe that those they trust will act as anticipated, which diminishes the intricacy of the interaction. Understanding the high convolution of the relationship between trust and risk concept, and considering likewise the absence of scholarly unanimity that lack on how to account their relationship via model [124], this study takes the view of a mediating relationship [121] instead. On the mediating standpoint, if trust exists, then the risk perceived is reduced, which successively will impact the degree of decision-making to use MFS. Thus, higher trust in a technology would lower its perceived risk and consequently positively affect behavioral intention [125].

These ideas of risk and others will endure a detrimental dominance on the acceptance of MFS. For instance, Swaminathan et al. [126] revealed consumers' opposition to providing their credit card information through the Internet. With MFS, the consumers are required to entrust not only their credit card information but a whole account of information in most cases. Wide-ranging, trust ameliorates the consumer's conception toward online service and the related component, diminishing the level of the risk perception allied with the transaction process.

From the attribute of risk opinion, a plethora of researchers brought that studies on consumer's risk perception are a kind of a multi-facet concept [28,39,127], which becomes the root of the aggregate perceived risk. To date, perceived risk has been employed to elucidate both offline and online risk shopping behavior. The finding derived from the work of Featherman and Pavlou [127] on the consumer's adoption of e-services has been widely accepted, which classified perceived risk dimensions as an economic risk, social risk, time risk, functional risk, psychological risk, and privacy risk. Bellman et al. [128] informed regarding the prominence of time concerns and argued that it is a substantial predictor of online buying behavior. According to the finding, consumers in a hurry who have less time are more plausible to buy on the Internet. The perception of time risk can refer to the integration of time lost and determination expended in acquiring any item and service [129]. Grounded in this similar logic, the current study proposes that consumers are time-oriented, time-conscious, and therefore value the potential time they might spend in implementing, searching and learning the application process of the new MFS.

Security/privacy risk is categorized as an intrinsic loss undeviatingly to fraud, scam, or hacktivists haggling the security of the user of an e-service [130]. The security or privacy issues mostly arise when a customer is transferring money from his/her account or dealing with his/her secluded economic information, whereas others view this information without his/her consent. The perception of costs applied to the MFS application reveals fear among the consumers. Empirical evidence stressed that mobile banking acceptance is highly sustained by economic aspects such as beneficial fees regarding transaction service [131]. Alternatively, it is impeded by economic considerations (issues centered on basic fees for assessing mobile banking), like cost burden [132] or high payment incorporated in using mobile banking [133]. Therefore, the perception of cost risk tends to negate the adoption of mobile banking [134].

Centered on the work of Featherman and Pavlou [127] predominantly, and throughout the previous studies toward risk components so far; the present study deduces four important dimensions of risk perceived, which are expected to influence the consumer's overall risk concerning the MFS adoption. They are the perceived privacy risk, time, security, and financial risk in the form cost perceived. Hence, we can posit the following assumption based on the discussion being done under this section.

Hypothesis 4. *Consumer's general trust would negatively associate with the perceived risk in MFS.*

Hypothesis 5. *Perceived privacy risk would significantly influence users' perception of risk of using MFS.*

Hypothesis 6. *The Perception of time risk would significantly influence users' perceived risk of MFS.*

Hypothesis 7. *Perception of security risk would significantly influence users' perceived risk of MFS.*

Hypothesis 8. *Cost perceived would significantly influence users' aggregate perceived risk of using MFS.*

3.3. Antecedents of MFS Adoption

Under this section, three antecedents (dispositional trust, trust, perceived risk) of MFS adoption will be taken into consideration. Being part of a personality trait, a disposition to trust can denote an individual's predilection to show reliance on humanity and to support a trusting standpoint concerning others [135,136]. Many researchers hypothesize the disposition to trust as partaking a positive impact on trust toward online shopping websites [136]. This relationship was also supported in various IS research, particularly in e-commerce [94,137,138], and in mobile banking [139]. Accordingly, Gefen et al. [101] pointed out that disposition to trust is crucial, particularly for the development of early trust and befits less significant for established trust or pre-existing relationships trust beliefs. Once encountering people with trifling or no experience using the wireless Internet as a platform for financial transactions, a disposition to trust is predictable to affect their trusting perception on the Internet. People partaking high disposition to trust are more favorable to feel relaxed or secured when using wireless Internet for financial transactions [39]. Inferring from this lucidity to the MFS, we expect that consumers having a higher disposition to trust are more probable to espouse MFS than those with a lower disposition to trust.

The next antecedent of MFS adoption resides in risk perception. Since its application among consumer behavior literature [116], the conception of perceived risk has been reviewed from a multiplicity of viewpoints. The classical decision concept considers risk perception as a function of the distribution of probable outcomes of conduct, its likelihoods, and subjective values [140]. Accordingly, risk encompasses two dimensions: uncertainty and outcome, where there is the possibility of experiencing a loss as a consequence of a behavior and the significance accredited to the loss [141,142]. While various researchers have criticized this approach because of its strictness to apprehend a perceived risk variable equally to be ambiguous and indistinct [142], some others were heightened to this concept definition as expected utility theory [143,144]. Explicitly risk, therefore, carries on the subjectively driven expectancy of loss by the customer when denoting the perceived risk [145]. Internet banking and MFS, predominantly mobile banking, rely on a similar type of risk [146], only, the information media channels differ. Prior IS studies showed that the imperative attitudinal of perceived risks impact adoption behavior where much is based on the privacy risk and transaction security risk [6,147–150]. Preceding studies have equally supported the negative effect of the perceived risk of online usage and purchasing behavior [151–154]. Likewise, earlier researchers agreed that the more risk is perceived by someone in purchasing context, the less probable he/she will be resolved to buy [155]. Furthermore, the level of personal participation in the decision-making process exposes the degree of risk perceived combined with the significance attributed to the choice of the object while allowing for the desires, interest, and personal values of the individuals [156,157]. Based on the perception of risk assigned in past works as the main inhibitor elements of various IS arena; similarly, it is expected to affect the acceptance of MFS negatively.

Taking the antecedent of MFS from a different angle, the importance of trust has been revealed to be an extensive subject matter. Trust, combined with the previous definitions so far, denotes the readiness of one party to be exposed to the actions of another party deal with the hope that the other will accomplish the designated task needed to the trustor [30]. The empirical findings of Jarvenpaa and Tractinsky [158] revealed the trust element to influence the decision to purchase in various manifold cultures. The prominence of trust is so decisive that it may be extended to be viewed as the "wild wild west" of the 21st century [136]. The more MFS users or potential users believe and trust the services, the more they can develop an affirmative goal for its usage. User trust, which has been revealed to be an important adoption facilitator in many IS environments, lacks adequate inspection in the context of MFS as a whole. In line with the literature allied with the antecedent of adoption of MFS in this study, we can, therefore, posit as follows:

Hypothesis 9. *Disposition to trust would have a positive effect on an individual' espousal of MFS.*

Hypothesis 10. *User aggregate risk perceived would have a negative impact on the adoption of MFS.*

Hypothesis 11. *User general trust will positively influence an individual's acceptance to use MFS.*

3.4. Conceptual Framework

To assess how trust and risk perceptions at the multidimensional level affect the mobile financial services (MFS) acceptance in Togo, we propose a research model. Figure 1 summarizes the relationships described in the research hypotheses. The proposed model is used to identify several attributes as predictors of MFS. Based on the above discussion related to the suggested hypotheses, we considered three antecedents (dispositional trust, technology trust, and vendor trust) as a multi-dimensional trust for the general trust, four antecedents (privacy risk, time risk, security risk, and cost) regarded as multi-facet perceived risk for the aggregate perceived risk. The remaining three antecedents (dispositional trust, perceived aggregate, and general trust) are used for consumers' intention toward the adoption of mobile financial services. Demographic variables entailing age and education levels are included in the model as control variables.

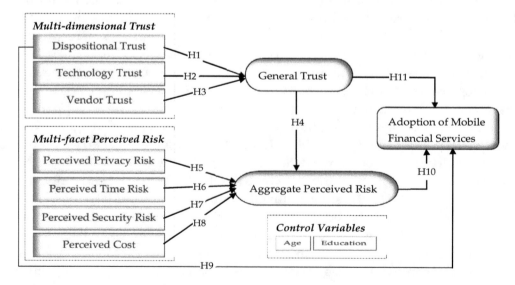

Figure 1. Proposed research model.

4. Research Methodology

4.1. Design and Data Collection

Various schools of thought questioned how data collected would be executed as well as the content of the studies. Among them, Cooper and Schindler [159] have suggested two approaches of scrutinizing issues: One technique called observational approach is to gather data on people, event, situations, and behavior; while the next one, the so-called communication approach, has considered the attitudes, expectations intentions, and motivator aspect.

This research, as a result, used data collection via the communication approach, taking a form of the survey since the motive of the study turns to capture the influential factor of MFS adoption once testing the research model. A survey instrument was then established for indicators and criteria development, which primarily got ratified after revising the suitability of the constructs by the chosen experts of MFS. The preliminary draft of the questionnaire was prepared in English then translated into French (the official language of Togo) for its assessment as well. Both questionnaires in English and French have been retained as to avoid any confusion related to the scope, purpose, and content; so far, allowing the comparison of the versions for discrepancies concerns, steadfastness to be easily acknowledged and established. Following the advice and the opinion from the experts, redundant and confusing items were either improved or removed. As a result, new items were included in the questionnaire lastly, permitting the validity of the survey instrument employed. The research model embodies ten factors; each factor remains evaluated with multiple items. Also, all items were accommodated from existent literature to increase content validity [160]. There were two types of questionnaires. The first type (SEM questionnaire) was divided into two parts. The first part was distributed with bio-data of the sample, and the second part answered the MFS questions using the five-point Likert scale bounded from strongly disagree (1) to strongly agree (5). The final measurement scales, items, and their sources are listed in "Appendix A".

For the second type of questionnaire (TOPSIS questionnaire), we arbitrarily contacted users and potential users and questioned them whether they had mobile MFS usage experience to ensure their familiarity to some extent as recommended [10,161]. Thus, those with two or more MFS experience years were further invited to fill the TOPSIS questionnaire format.

The empirical study took almost three months of the span for data collection because of the delay in obtaining some participants' responses and an awkward time-period indicated by some of them. Data were collected at some of the busiest and most crowded places of the capital town Lomé (i.e., Assivito, Dekon, Be, and Université de Lomé) where potential users and currents users of mobile financial services (MFS) can relatively be found and inspected better than in other sectors. Literate people filled in their survey questionnaires themselves, whereas for illiterates, help was given. The questionnaire took almost 10–15 min to complete by a given participant. The estimated accessible population of Lomé is 837,437 [162]. Therefore, the estimated adjusted sample size for this research should have a minimum of 399.8090 $\cong$ 400 [163]. In the situation which involves minor participants, informed consent has been given by legal representatives together with the minor participants "assent" before partaking in a study. An exception to this procedure was when teenagers are employed and living on their own.

Once the data collection procedure was completed, we examined all questionnaires and discarded cases with too many missing and or rushed responses.

As such, 538 questionnaires, which fulfilled the minimum requirement, were both ready and yielded usable samples. Among them, 294 (54.6%) were male and 244 (45.4%) female. Seventy-five (13.9%) respondents were aged below 18 years, 145 (27%) aged between 19–24 years, 199 (37%) aged between 25–30 years, and 119 (22.1%) aged above 31 years. Regarding educational qualifications, the majority of respondents (two hundred and sixty-seven) had a high school certificate or below, i.e., Baccalaureate (49.6%), 203 (37.7%) had a graduate degree, while 57 (10.6%) had a master's degree. The remaining 11 (2%) had a doctorate. Concerning MFS years of experiences, 187 (34.8%) of respondents claimed to have no experience with MFS, 194 (36.1%) used it for less than one year, 125 (23.2%) MFS usage ranged from the 1–2 years, 26 (4.8%) were found between 3–4 years of MFS experience. Only 6 (1.1%) had MFS experience for more than five years. Hence, very few respondents had MFS experience above three years from the deduction. Moreover, they are those respondents engaged in MFS application at the early stage of its implementation (Most MFS companies in Togo started launching their activities in the year 2013) and dwell on it.

4.2. Proposed Technique of Data Analysis: SEM-TOPSIS Methods

The SEM-TOPSIS technique was employed to construct the MFS evaluation decision support system. Therefore, SEM was utilized to generate critical criteria and weights, whereas TOPSIS was used to engender the rank and score of alternatives as well permitted the fullness of the data, improved the data accuracy via group decision making.

SEM is suitable to estimate and test casual relationships by employing a combination of statistical data and qualitative assumptions [15,164]. It remains a second-generation multivariate technique that tolerates the simultaneous assessment of multiple equations, embraces multiple regression analysis, factor analysis, and path model analysis [165]. SEM incorporates the whole analysis of construct concurrently rather than separately [166], with this application being emergent in the social sciences [167]. Accordingly, it is the handiest method adapted for checking causative relations between predictors and adoption behavior [168,169]. It offers greater flexibility in matching a theoretical model with a data sample when compared with techniques like PCA and factor analysis [170].

TOPSIS: Technique for Order Preference by Similarity to Ideal Solution. The various process of TOPSIS will be explained in the analysis section.

5. Data Analysis

5.1. Measurement and Hypotheses Testing with SEM Analysis

We performed exploratory factor analysis (EFA) employing maximum likelihood estimation with Promax because of the large sample of data set (n = 538) and its intricacy related to the outcome's elucidation, which is trivial in resolving the correlated. The EFA reveals the output of KMO as 0.809 and Bartlet's test of sphericity to be significant at $\alpha = 0.000$ with a Chi-square of 11,598.920, indicating the relevance for performing exploratory factor analysis [171]. Besides, the communalities for each variable were sufficiently high (lowest was 0.343, the majority were beyond 0.597, and the greatest was 0.975), showing the evidence that these variables were effectively correlated for factor analysis. The ten-factor model obtained a total variance explained with more than 60% along with all extracted factors partaking eigenvalue beyond 1.0.

To continue assessing our quantitative model, we settled the subsequent analysis in two phases [167]: first, via confirmatory factor analysis (CFA), we appraised both reliability and discriminant validity of the ten constructs [172]. The outcomes will achieve validity unless the researchers employ constructs that diverge from another construct in a similar model [172]. From the second step, we valued the structural model then SEM for hypotheses testing. These last two steps are adopted from previous studies [28,173]. Hence, we estimated the reliability of each construct based on three indices, such as composite reliability (CR), average variance extracted (AVE), and Cronbach's alpha (CA). The suggested values for good measures were at least 0.70, 0.50, and 0.70, respectively [174], (see Table 1). In patronage of convergent validity, the AVE found to be higher than 0.5 for all constructs, and all item factor loadings remain beyond the minimum threshold of 0.4 [175].

Table 1. Reliability and validity in confirmatory factor analysis (CFA).

	CR	AVE	MSV	MaxR (H)	(1)	(2)	(3)	(4)	(5)	(6)	(7)	(8)	(9)	(10)
(1)	0.846	0.647	0.227	0.848	**0.804**									
(2)	0.933	0.779	0.133	0.965	0.108	**0.883**								
(3)	0.904	0.704	0.087	0.975	0.216	0.067	**0.839**							
(4)	0.860	0.609	0.057	0.979	0.168	0.157	0.155	**0.780**						
(5)	0.855	0.664	0.227	0.981	0.476	0.020	0.230	0.144	**0.815**					
(6)	0.843	0.577	0.056	0.984	0.236	0.061	0.114	0.011	0.235	**0.760**				
(7)	0.856	0.600	0.133	0.985	0.041	0.365	0.044	0.238	−0.022	−0.072	**0.775**			
(8)	0.811	0.594	0.065	0.987	0.127	0.155	0.113	0.232	0.091	0.035	0.255	**0.771**		
(9)	0.798	0.571	0.013	0.987	0.102	0.098	0.065	−0.004	−0.035	0.086	0.075	0.115	**0.756**	
(10)	0.820	0.610	0.087	0.988	0.228	0.051	0.295	0.064	0.198	0.216	−0.042	0.019	0.104	**0.781**

Note: (1) DTrust: dispositional trust; (2) TTrust: technological trust; (3) Vtrust: vendor trust; (4) PPrivR: perceived privacy risk; (5) PTimeR: perceived time risk; (6) PSecurR: perceived security risk; (7) PCost: perceived cost; (8) PRisk: perceived risk; (9) AdMFS: adoption of MFS; (10) G-trust: general trust.

Moreover, all loadings of items arose in the corresponding construct, and no item loaded with the high value in another construct. This technique was espoused in past research [15,176,177]. As such, we established that our ten constructs displayed convergent validity (see Table 1 below).

We designed Table 2 to portray the goodness of fit of CFA and SEM. Apart from the goodness-of-fit index (GFI) for CFA slightly below the recommended, as this index is sensible to sample size, and in this study, we use large sample size (n = 538); for all indexes, our measurement model and structural model indicated sufficient goodness of fit.

Table 2. The goodness of fit (CFA and structural equation modeling (SEM)).

Indices	Abbreviation	CFA Value	SEM Value	Thresholds
Chi square	x^2	1068.904	30.445	p value > 0.05
Normed chi square	$x^2_{/DF}$	2.104	1.903	$1 < x^2/df < 3$
Root mean square residual	RMS or RMR	0.066	0.015	<0.08
Goodness-of-fit index	GFI	0.889	0.991	>0.90
Adjusted GFI	AGFI	0.862	0.955	>0.80
Normed fit index	NFI	0.900	0.941	>0.90
Comparative fit index	CFI	0.944	0.968	>0.93
Tucker-Lewis index	TLI	0.935	0.869	$0 < TLI < 1$
Root mean square error of approximation	RMSEA	0.045	0.041	<0.05 excellent fit <0.08 good fit

Before the structural model, we conducted a common method bias. Since the data for the variable were led through a single method (survey), we performed a test to check if a common factor might have been impacted our outcomes. Hence, the test adopted was an unmeasured latent factor suggested by Podsakoff et al. [178] and Siemsen et al. [178] toward studies that do not obviously measure a common factor, mentioned as a common latent factor (CLF) method. The most prevailing and best method in checking the CMB is the zero-constrained test where the CLF is involved along with Marker if accessible [178]. This approach checks whether the shared variance across all variables differs significantly from zero. In a case it is, then there are bias issues. To proceed, we computed the chi-square difference test among the unconstrained model and the model per all paths regarding the CLF constrained to be zero. Since the result is markedly different from zero, we can conclude that method bias does occur in our measures. Thus, moving to the causal model based on the result, CLF was retained for our structural model (by imputing composites in AMOS in the presence of CLF), which provided CMB-adjusted values.

We also check for invariance (configurable and metric) because of the presence of two groups, such as gender included in our data to see whether the factor and loading are adequately equivalent across groups. Davidov [179] has claimed that the assessment of path coefficients could only be useful if the invariance test has been done beforehand. The result signpost that the model fit of the unconstrained measurement models (per groups loaded distinctly) presented a sufficient fit ($\chi 2/DF = 1.623$, TLI = 0.928, CFI = 0.938, RMSEA = 0.034) when assessing a freely estimated model across genders. Grounded on the result, the model is configurally invariant. Once the model was constrained to be equal, the result of the chi-square difference test reveals the p-value (0.226) to be nonsignificant. So, the measurement model satisfies the benchmarks criteria for metric invariance across gender as well. Then and there, we move on making the composite from this measurement model to build SEM for verification of hypotheses testing. The results of the structured model, together with parameters, were obtained while controlling for age and education. The standardized path coefficients, path significances, and explained variance R^2 of the structural model (see Figure 2).

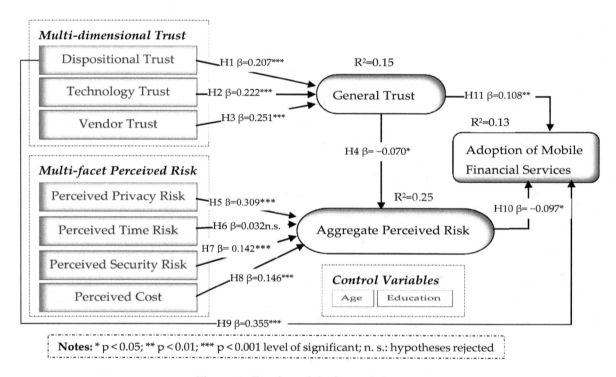

Figure 2. Final model after validation.

5.2. TOPSIS Analysis

The technique for order preference by similarity to ideal solution (TOPSIS) is a multiple criteria decision-making (MCDM) technique developed by Hwang and Yoon [180]. It is grounded in the criteria that the alternative should have the shortest distance from the positive ideal solution and the farthest from the negative ideal solution [181]. It has been extensively employed by researchers for the ranking of alternatives centered on different criteria [7,161,164,182,183]. When compared to other MCDM methods, TOPSIS necessitates limited subjective inputs from decision-makers [184] and remains a deterministic technique. It provides solution on both positive and negative way, which is beneficial for applications where there are considerations such as cost and benefits; and it is a rational method which works agreeably across various application areas [185]. Recall that the process of the SEM-TOPSIS can be characterized as follows. Primarily, SEM was applied to compute the hierarchical criteria and their relatives to ensure their significance. This is the reason why having the relative weightage obtained from SEM is reflected more valid than via any other method. The antecedent of trust and perceived risk given by the SEM model were deliberated for the relative weightage of the sub-criteria.

The computation of TOPSIS methods grounded on Hwang and Yoon [180], Lin and Tsai [186], and predominantly the one required for grouping decision Shih et al. [187] were adopted and presented as followed:

Step 1: construction of decision matrix D^k, $k = 1,\dots, K$ for each DM. The matrix structure can be viewed below:

$$D^k = \begin{array}{c} \\ A1 \\ A2 \\ \vdots \\ Ai \\ \vdots \\ Am \end{array} \overset{\begin{array}{c} n\ Criteria \\ X_1 \quad X_2 \ \dots\ X_J \ \dots\ X_n \end{array}}{\begin{bmatrix} x_{11}^k & x_{12}^k & \dots & x_{1j}^k & \dots & x_{1n}^k \\ x_{21}^k & x_{22}^k & \dots & x_{2j}^k & \dots & x_{2n}^k \\ \vdots & \vdots & \dots & \vdots & \dots & \vdots \\ x_{i1}^k & x_{i2}^k & \dots & x_{ij}^k & \dots & x_{in}^k \\ \vdots & \vdots & \dots & \vdots & \dots & \vdots \\ x_{m1}^k & x_{m2}^k & \dots & x_{mj}^k & \dots & x_{mn}^k \end{bmatrix}} \tag{1}$$

where A_i refers to the likely alternatives of the decision process i with $i = 1, \dots, m$; X_j denoting the attribute or criterion j, $j = 1,\dots, n$; with both quantitative and qualitative data. The value x_{ij}^k remains, therefore, the performance score of alternative A_i in relation to attribute X_j by decision-maker k, $k = 1,\dots, K$, while x_{ij}^k is the element of D^k. It is of importance to mention that there should be K decision-maker matrices designed for K participants of the group.

Step 2: the normalized decision matrix R^k, $k = 1, \dots, K$ is generated for each *DM*. Vis-à-vis to any *DM* k, the vector normalization technique is used for computing the element r_{ij}^k from the decision matrix R^k which can take any linear-scale transformation to preserve $0 \le r_{ij}^k \le 1$ inequality. Since we consider the vector normalization operation, then r_{ij}^k is given as:

$$r_{ij}^k = \frac{x_{ij}^k}{\sqrt{\sum_{j=1}^n \left(x_{ij}^k\right)^2}}, \tag{2}$$

where $i = 1,2,\dots,m$; $j = 1,2,\dots, n$; and $k = 1,2,\dots,K$. It is also necessary to clue that the vector normalization method makes provision as to which one represents a cost criterion for additional management. Moreover, there is no need to directly assess the weighted normalized as per the case of the original TOPSIS [188].

Step 3. The positive ideal solution V^{k+} (PIS), is made of all the best performance scores and the negative-ideal solution V^{k-} (NIS) is made of all the worst performance scores at the measures in the weighted normalized decision matrix for each DM $k = 1,\dots, K$. For any given *DM* k, his/her PIS and NIS can be characterized in the form of

$$PIS = V^{k+} = \left\{r_1^{k+}, \dots\dots, r_n^{k+}\right\} = \left\{\left(\max_i\ r_{ij}^k \ \middle|\ j \in J\right), \left(\min_i\ r_{ij}^k\ \middle|\ j \in J'\right)\right\} \tag{3}$$

$$NIS = V^{k-} = \left\{r_1^{k-}, \dots\dots, r_n^{k-}\right\} = \left\{\left(\min_i\ r_{ij}^k\ \middle|\ j \in J\right), \left(\max_i\ r_{ij}^k\ \middle|\ j \in J'\right)\right\} \tag{4}$$

where J is related to the benefit criteria and J' allied with the cost criteria, $i = 1,\dots,m$; $j = 1,\dots,n$; and $k = 1,\dots,K$.

Step 4. A weigh vector W is allocated to the attribute set for the group. Each DM will produce weights for attributes as w_j^k where $j = 1,\dots,n$ and $\sum_{j=1}^n w_j^k = 1$; and for each DM $k = 1,\dots,K$.

Each element of the weigh vector W will result from the operation of the corresponding components of the attributes' weights for every DM.

Step 5. Evaluate the separation measure through the positive ideal and the negative ideal solutions, $\overline{S_I^+}$ and $\overline{S_I^-}$, relatively to the group. Because of the group decision with respect to this research, this step requires two sub-steps, where the initial one considers the distance measure for individuals while the next one aggregates the measure for the group.

Step 5a. Assessment of the measure from PIS and NIS individually. The n-dimensional Euclidean distance can compute the distance of an alternative j to the ideal solution. Separation of each alternative from the positive ideal solution S_i^{k+} is then provided by the Equation (5) below:

$$S_i^{k+} = \sqrt{\sum_{j=1}^{n} w_j^k \left(v_{ij}^k - v_j^{k+} \right)^2}, \text{ for alternative } i, \, i = 1, \ldots, m \tag{5}$$

Similarly, separation from the negative ideal solution S_i^{k-} is then given by

$$S_i^{k-} = \sqrt{\sum_{j=1}^{n} w_j^k \left(v_{ij}^k - v_j^{k-} \right)^2}, \text{ for alternative } i, \, i = 1, \ldots, m. \tag{6}$$

Step 5b. Assessment of the measure from PIS and NIS for the group. In this part, the individual group measure of each alternative is to be integrated via an operation $\otimes$ for all DMs, $k = 1, \ldots, K$. As such, the two-fold measure of the PIS and NIS are presented below

$$\overline{S_i^+} = \overline{S_i^{1+}} \otimes \cdots \otimes \overline{S_i^{K+}}, \text{ for alternative } i, \tag{7}$$

$$\overline{S_i^-} = \overline{S_i^{1-}} \otimes \cdots \otimes \overline{S_i^{K-}}, \text{ for alternative } i. \tag{8}$$

Though this operation can provide various choices like geometric mean, arithmetic means with their related extended; this study pondered only on the geometric one for the group computation. Its calculation's formulae are below shown for PIS and NIS (Equations (9) and (10))

$$\overline{S_i^+} = \left(\prod_{k=1}^{K} S_i^{k+} \right)^{\frac{1}{K}}, \text{ for alternative } i, \tag{9}$$

$$\overline{S_i^-} = \left(\prod_{k=1}^{K} S_i^{k-} \right)^{\frac{1}{K}}, \text{ for alternative } i. \tag{10}$$

where $i = 1, \ldots, m; k = 1, \ldots, K$.

Step 6: The ranking score $\overline{C_i^*}$ is computed as

$$\overline{C_I^*} = \frac{\overline{S_i^-}}{\overline{S_i^+} + \overline{S_i^-}}, \, i = 1, \ldots, m \tag{11}$$

With $0 \leq \overline{C_I^*} \leq 1$. When C_I^* is close to 1, the alternative is considered as ideal; and when C_I^* is close to 0, the alternative is considered as non-ideal. The larger the index values, the higher the rank order, and so, the better the alternative' performance.

5.3. Case Study Using Combined SEM-TOPSIS Techniques

To establish the applicability of the suggested methodology (SEM-TOPSIS), a case study is carried out in this paper. The data examined were provided by respondents (74 MFS experienced users and experts) of mobile financial services, particularly for adopting the TOPSIS technique. The relative weightage is computed from the standardized total effect, normalized obtained from the SEM technique [10,189], and presented in Table 3. The weightings showed the importance of each sub-criteria for the MFS companies.

Table 3. Relative weightage of sub-criteria.

DTrust	TTrust	VTrust	PPrivR	PTimeR	PSecurR	PCost
0.265	0.128	0.177	0.200	0.021	0.109	0.101

Note: (1) DTrust: dispositional trust; (2) TTrust: technological trust; (3) Vtrust: vendor trust; (4) PPrivR: perceived privacy risk; (5) PTimeR: perceived time risk; (6) PSecurR: perceived security risk; (7) PCost: perceived cost.

To compute the relative weightage of MFS alternatives to each sub-criteria toward the criteria (trust and risk), the decision matrix of alternative performance evaluation (Equation (1) step 1) was created. Moreover, the output of the qualitative attribute from each alternative can also be set as discrete value or linguistic values (referring to Table 4) intentionally that the quantitative values could be set in the decision matrix above. Participants were asked to provide a set of values within the range of one to nine for the sub-criteria using Table 4 as measurement scale.

Table 4. Transformation of linguistic scale into quantitative values.

Linguistic Scale	Quantitative Values	
	Benefit-Max	Cost-Min
Very High	9	1
High	7	3
Average	5	5
Low	3	7
Very Low	1	9
Intermediate values between the two-adjacent judgment: (2,4,6,8)		

Following the procedure of the TOPSIS method, through a TOPSIS algorithm built-in MATLAB technical computing tool, the relative weightage of MFS allied with each sub-criterion is calculated and shown in Table 5. After aggregating the individual PIS and NIS via geometric mean from the Step 5b Equations (7) and (8), then the final score $\overline{C_i^*}$ is computed using Equation (11) of Step 6, followed by the ranking of the MFS alternatives as being portrayed in Figure 3 and Table 6.

Table 5. Summary of the relative weightage of mobile financial services (MFS) to each sub-criterion.

Relative Weightage of MFS to Each Sub–Criterion							
Sub–criteria weightage	0.265	0.128	0.177	0.200	0.021	0.109	0.101
Sub–criteria	DTrust	TTrust	VTrust	PPrivR	PTimeR	PSecurR	PCost
MB	5.40	4.78	6.23	−3.56	−7.53	−4.20	−6.50
MP	8.50	5.40	4.43	−2.34	−8.20	−5.00	−7.00
MMT	7.30	4.70	5.11	−1.42	−8.00	−4.48	−7.20

Note: MB: mobile banking; MP: mobile payment; MMT: mobile money transfer.

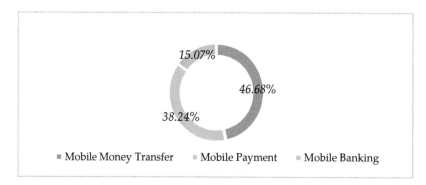

Figure 3. Classification of MFS alternatives using TOPSIS (% representation).

Table 6. Results of three alternatives of MFS ranking using TOPSIS.

MFS	$\overline{C_I^*}$	Rank	% Distribution of Coefficient
MMT	0.7454	1	46.68%
MP	0.6106	2	38.24%
MB	0.2407	3	15.07%

6. Discussion

New technology adoptions are impacted mainly by many factors, which may vary from technology concerns to the trust dimension, the perception of risk facets, and the behavior of users, to mention a few. The intricacy and significance related to the effort in elucidating the motives or reasons for users' adoption or rejection of new IT have led to the development of various concepts. Furthermore, there are a plethora of studies on the influence of trust and perceived risk with their determinant toward the adoption decision in an online environment.

Conversely to prior research works, this study scrutinizes the influence of critical variables such as multi-dimensional trust and perceived risk facets on the consumers' adoption behavior of MFS and incorporates each of them into the MFS alternative decision-making scenario. Some postulations were made toward the possible relationship among the factors. The findings are yet to be probed purposively to draw an important conclusion and implication. The result of the MFS structural model analysis regarded as a final model after validation is summarized and portrayed in Figure 2. To be specific, the discussion section is scheduled to be under two sections. The first section will be made with SEM methodology grounded on hypotheses results, which are comprised of three sets. First set: hypotheses associated with trust; second set: hypotheses associated with perceived risk; and third set: hypotheses associated with MFS adoption constructs. The last section of the discussion is booked for a succinct analysis of TOPSIS output obtained via the SEM-TOPSIS hybrid technique.

It should be mentioned that all hypotheses were tested when controlling for age and education. The reason for controlling variables is to support mitigating the unrelated effect. Moreover, its use contributes to improving the robustness and validity of the outcome. In terms of relationships, the study account for the p-value column allied with each variable where the related p-value of less than 0.05 indicates a significant relation associated. The results of the entire tested eleven hypotheses were statistically significant except for the relationship between perceived time risk (PTimeR) and perceived risk (PRisk, i.e., H6 as displayed from Figure 2).

The first set of hypotheses is related to trust, which was scrutinized by H1–H3. Empirical evidence is found to accept hypothesis H1 ($\beta = 0.207$, $p < 0.001$), which refers to the positive effect the disposition to trust has on general trust in MFS. Payne and Clark [190] showed that the general disposition to trust exerts substantial control on the trust among senior managers in an industrial context. Moreover, consumers' disposition to trust has been revealed to maintain a strong influence on their trust in an e-vendor. Although most of the previous studies did not plainly define the direction of the impact, the present study ratifies that disposition to trust and trust are positively related in MFS. Such information comes to back the knowledge that consumers who unveil a greater disposition to trust will more willingly trust the e-vendor [137] compared to those who will require more info [191]. However, our results are contradicted by earlier e-services [110], particularly in mobile banking. The reason might be that when consumers are to encounter a choice within MFS perspectives (mobile banking, mobile payment, mobile money), their trust disposition significantly affects the general trust more or less that of the single type of MFS. As a result, companies dealing with MFS should be aware of this critical effect and prepare for any competitive advantage strategies in the marketplace.

H2 (β = 0.222, p < 0.001) tested the effect of trust in technology on trust in general, and the findings stressed that technology trust has a strong positive impact on trust. Given technological trust as a sole antecedent of trust whereby the object upon which the trust remained imparted when referring to the inert technology [192], then, our empirical results are in line with previous findings in the context of mobile banking [110]. Furthermore, previous works [193] implicitly incorporated the concept of trust technology to trust with its importance being emphasized as a facilitator of e-commerce adoption.

Trust in the vendor was also found to have a positive influence on general trust, which supports H3 (β = 0.251, p < 0.001). The results of this research are reliable with the previous finding in which vendor trust has been defined as multi-dimensional and influential levers that the vendors could employ to build consumer trust [113]. Vendor trust remains so vital to promoting trust in changing a potential consumer from a curious viewer to one that will be ready to perform MFS. Thoughtful discerning of the essence and antecedents of consumer trust in MFS can support e-vendors with a set of controllable, strategic levers to develop such trust, which will encourage greater MFS acceptance and usage.

As a result, lack of consumer trust (trust disposition, technology trust, and vendor trust) in the overall online environment has been, and persists in being, a hamper to IS adoption [194] and thus to MFS. All these could serve as a clue to the concept that the consumers' espousal of MFS may be shaped accordingly.

The second set of hypotheses is associated with perceived risk. From this part, perceived risk has five antecedents, such as H4 and H5–H8. The investigation of the relationship between trust and perceived risk has been one of the main issues in the development of IS [195]. Our result shows that general trust has a negative influence on perceived risk, which supports H4 (β = −0.070, p < 0.05). The literature offers supportive studies on the import of this relationship [8,195]. Various researchers have also contributed to the belief that trust mitigates consumers' perceived risk [196–198] as well as affecting perceived benefit in e-commerce [199]. Lots of incentives that increase trust are similar incentives that reduce perceived risk. This result clarifies to some extent, the doubt related to the direction of the causality between trust and risk, which were found deficient from the past literature [121]. From H5–H8, the empirical study found to patronize all the hypotheses at a different level of p-value mention that each dimension of perceived risk has a positive influence on the overall perceived risk except H6 (see Figure 2). At that point, the moderate to weak positive relationships between the perceived risk (aggregate) and the risk component offers further reinforcement that risk can be researched as a multidimensional phenomenon [200]. These results are also consistent with the work of Featherman and Pavlou [127], which validated a majority of these antecedents as a risk dimension; therefore, being the influential element of the aggregated risk. Again, the outcomes reveal the multidimensional nature of perceived risk in information technology, mainly MFS. Boksberger et al. [201] are supporters of these findings in the area of air travel. Again, the results show that perceived privacy risk H5 (β = 0.309, p < 0.001) is indeed the predominant perceived risk dimension for the partakers of MFS, shadowed by the perceived cost H8 (β = 0.146, p < 0.001) and perceived security risk H7 (β = 0.142, p < 0.001). Moreover, this study confirms the positive effect of the perceived cost on the consumers' perceived risk, such as that the lower the cost, the more minor the perception of risk and the more the likelihood of MFS adoption. As such, the involvement aspect of the risk [202] is importantly observed when the price or cost is high, and the consumers risk losing money.

This research reveals no statistical evidence to support the hypothesis H6 ($\beta = 0.032$, $p < 0.342$) that perceived time risk has a positive influence on the aggregate perceived. Although H6 is rejected; the expected direction of the relationship is kept just so that the p-value is not statistically significant at 0.05. However, our findings are controverted by prior online payment research that has indicated a positive relationship between time risk and perceived risk [203]. It has stressed that consumers lack patience in waiting a long time because they are always delighted in pursuing new things [203]. Then, a longer waiting time for service delivery would deter the desire, impact their buying disposition or decision to adopt as well. In the view of this current study, the perceived risk dimension, such as perceived time risk, does not appear to impact the specific information technology acceptance, at least for the Togolese MFS investigated in this research. The reason may be related to the participants' (user and potential user) MFS experience. Since quite many of them lack experience in MFS, they might not be conscious regarding the real time needed for a service to be completed. This implies that the effect of time risk perceived is worthy of further development in future researches and MFS companies are encouraged to continue easing the transaction process of MFS in terms of time spent.

The third set of hypotheses is associated with the adoption of MFS. Among them, the hypothesis associated with the positive relationship that the dispositional trust has with MFS adoption was supported by the test result; hence, H9 ($\beta = 0.355$, $p < 0.001$) is accepted (Figure 2). This infers that when increasing the level of trust disposition, individuals tend to adopt MFS technologies without necessarily cogitating on the general trust. The finding is consistent with e-commerce adoption for SMEs [204]. Moreover, the scholars reported that indicators for the dispositional trust should be incorporated into empirical studies either as a moderating variable or as a precursor of trusting beliefs, intentions, and behaviors [205]. Being an antecedent of trust, a disposition to trust remains one of the most operative elements required during the launch phases of a relationship when parties are generally unacquainted with each other [206]. Given that MFS is still in the early stages of adoption in Togo, services providers are recommended to promote the variable that could increase the consumer's dispositional trust.

From Figure 3, perceived risk significantly negates the adoption and usage of MFS, rendering the support of H10 ($\beta = -0.097$, $p < 0.022$). It is so crucial to signpost the feasibility of this outcome to be enlightened by the theory of consumer behavior [116] allied with risk perception. The importance of perceived risk in the study also confirms previous studies that demonstrate that consumers' perceived risk is more efficacious at clarifying purchasing or adoption behavior inasmuch as consumers are more recurrently driven to avert mistakes than to capitalize on utility in purchasing [207]. This output is also coherent with a recent report on mobile payment adoption, which underlines rapid technology innovation while stressing the importance of perceived risk in the form of security [208,209].

Last but not least, the study entails and accepts the hypothesis H11 ($\beta = 0.108$, $p < 0.008$) in which general trust has a positive influence on MFS adoption. Generally, trust remains a vital factor in various economic and social relations involving uncertainty and reliance [210,211], particularly those regarding important decisions [212] and new technologies [198] as an MFS perspective. Accordingly, our findings are sustained via the idea that trust in business rests on the pertinent and crucial stimulus of behavior in general [213–215], and the facilitator factors for MFS adoption and usage in particular.

Under this set, it can then be deduced that both improving trust and decreasing risk continue to raise the likelihood level of consumers' engagement in MFS transaction. Companies are required to take the necessary precaution to balance the trade-off.

SEM-TOPSIS: It is noteworthy to recall that the second section of discussion concerns the output of MFS alternatives computation. The overall result from the TOPSIS technique shows the preference of each alternative regarding the various sub-criteria. The relative closeness $\overline{C_i^*}$ results obtained satisfies the sine qua non-condition, i.e., $0 \leq \overline{C_i^*} \leq 1$. Furthermore, TOPSIS technique is grounded on the principle that the higher the value of $\overline{C_i^*}$, the high the rank order, and consequently, the more the chosen alternatives are favored over others. The final result reveals that mobile money transfer (MMT) is the most preferable MFS to adopt and use with $\overline{C_i^*}$ tantamount to 0.7454 signifying 46.68% compared to the last two remainings. Mobile payment (MP) with 0.6106 (38.24%) was found to be the second MFS alternative used, whereas mobile banking (MB) adoption with 0.2407 (15.07%) is considered minor. This finding is relatively supported by the prior study on mobile banking and mobile payment, where 82% of participants under 35 years old have made mobile payments as compared to 79% who used mobile banking [216]. A similar past study has further shown that mobile payment usage among USA millennials was higher than that of mobile banking generally. The likely motive of the MFS preference acknowledged in this study can be explained based on the significant issues of concern toward perceived privacy risk. Using mobile money transfer or mobile payment service does not necessarily involve consumers' personal information or an account that needs to be connected to a bank account. By that, lots of end-users would rather opt for mobile money transfer and mobile payment than for mobile banking accordingly.

Table 7 below compares the outputs of TOPSIS and AHP and reveals the same results for the choice of the alternative ranking of mobile financial services (MFS). It was found that the outcomes were well consistent and, in general, agreed with each other. Based on the results of the ranking of the two techniques, mobile money transfer (MMT) was chosen as the most appropriate among the mobile financial services followed by mobile payment and mobile banking. However, there are slight differences found in the percentage of coefficient distribution among the classification of their alternatives. For instance, AHP reveals that MFS consumers have a high preference in using mobile money services (i.e., the difference in the percentage of coefficient: 13.32%) as compared to TOPSIS results. Contrarily, the TOPSIS result shows that consumers are more interested in using mobile payment when considering the difference in percentage sharing between the two techniques (i.e., the difference in the percentage of coefficient: 13.75%).

Table 7. Comparison between TOPSIS and analytic hierarchy process (AHP) outputs.

MFS Alternatives	TOPSIS % Distribution of Coefficient	TOPSIS Rank	AHP % Distribution of Coefficient	AHP Rank	The Difference in the % Distribution Coefficient
MMT	46.68%	1	60%	1	13.32%
MP	38.24%	2	24.49%	2	13.75
MB	15.07%	3	15.26%	3	0.19%

Note: The outputs of AHP are derived from the previous work of Gbongli [10].

However, the results regarding the difference in percentage distribution of coefficient between TOPSIS and AHP in terms of mobile banking selection remain trivial. These results stressed that MFS consumers would not prefer using mobile banking if they have a choice between the proposed mobile financial services (MFS).

The difference between the finding of TOPSIS and AHP in the choice of MFS depends on their strengths and weaknesses, which are thoroughly pronounced in the literature [161,217]. For instance, the core advantages of AHP over TOPSIS can be attributed to its intuitive appeal to decision-makers, and its ability to check inconsistencies. Furthermore, decision-makers find the pairwise comparison system of data input convenient and straightforward. However, the application of AHP leads to the decision problem being decomposed into numerous subsystems, which require a considerable number of pairwise comparisons to be completed. Therefore, it is a complex and time-consuming implementation. In the situation of TOPSIS, the non-linear relations between one-dimensional scores and distance ratios lead to the consideration of both negative and positive ideal solutions. Also, in the TOPSIS framework, we can use variables with different units of measurement. It is very simple and easy to implement so that it is adopted when the user prefers a simpler weighting approach. However, TOPSIS, in its standard and original form, is deterministic and does not embrace uncertainty in the calculations associated with final weightings.

7. Conclusions

The objective of this study was to examine the influence of both multidimensional trust and perceived risk facets at the individual level concurrently on the acceptance of mobile financial services (MFS) when prioritizing the MFS perspective. This paper's goal is to illuminate, to some extent, the MFS accessibility in Togo allied with the potential facilitators or inhibitor factors. Also, to evaluate them based on the consumer's experience and experts through a benchmark robust SEM-TOPSIS methodology. A qualitative study in the context of the Togolese was performed together with a literature review to derive the most probable factors that might influence end-users' perception of MFS since there was a scarcity of research investigating general trust and perceived risk antecedents. A quantitative study was then propelled to test the hypotheses formulated through the collected information obtained.

Our research model efficaciously integrates these dimensions, such as trust (dispositional trust, technological trust, and vendor trust), perceived risk (privacy, time, security, and cost) viewed as complex multidimensional factors. The data support the underlying assumption of the study except for H6 (see Figure 2). Mainly, our study is partially similar to the recent study done in Ghana (neighboring country of Togo) in which the perceived risk found to be related to the customer's trust in service providers regarding the adoption of mobile money [218]. In this line, our study provides more information to the various role-players of MFS about the necessity to emphasize on the trust and risk at the multidimensional level while making strategic and multicriteria decision-making.

Among the MFS alternative, the ranking result revealed mobile money to be the preferable MFS type used, followed by mobile payment and mobile banking with a minor percentage. When the ranking of TOPSIS was compared with those obtained by the AHP techniques in a similar given population, the findings were well consistent and, in general, approved with each other. However, a slight difference was found between both techniques and therefore placing TOPSIS better suited to the problem of MFS classification for the study area.

8. Implication

8.1. Implication for Practice

The outcomes of this study expose and validate the factors that impact consumers' adoption of MFS. First, the relative level of the path coefficients in our analysis model recommended that disposition to trust (an antecedent of trust) be the most salient factor that facilitates either directly or indirectly the adoption of MFS. The perceived privacy risk (an antecedent of perceived risk) as the next influential factor, however, hinders MFS adoption. Given this trusting disposition is developed throughout a lifetime [206] and reveals social impact over broad periods [198], it implies that there might be a presence of a cross-cultural difference in trust. If so, MFS companies' providers must expect various levels of trust, and thus, different proportions of MFS adoption as well. As a deduction, companies are recommended to be acquainted with building trust-based tools and for instance, increasing awareness and firms' reputations by keeping their promises while treating the customer as individuals, mainly in societies that acknowledge exhibiting a lower level of trust. MFS service providers could meritoriously upsurge adoption behavior by publicizing the advantages of MFS to potential consumers, seeing that the findings supported trust with all of its antecedents.

Moreover, by modeling perceived risk with various facets, this study's finding imparts numerous risk effect concerns. From this perspective, when companies propagandize their MFS services to ease the adoption issues, they should realistically underline a neutralizer or counter step for those risks' perceptions. The prominence of privacy risk and financial risk in the form of perceived cost as confirmed by this study and others prior research [219] signposts that customers still have doubts about the security of virtual transactions. For instance, these companies may stimulate a privacy risk protection strategy and grant technological support and anti-fraud to guarantee potential end-users minimal security risk. It is typical in the practice of emerging and developed countries (and it should be considered in developing countries as well) for payment service providers to try and promote trust in mobile financial services, in payments in general, as well as in other banking services by improving the general financial literacy of the population and small and medium enterprises. This is important, as those individuals who are familiar with financial processes and concepts demonstrate more trust toward financial services and can assess their risks better [220]. An increasingly popular practice is for certain governments to aid this process through an appropriate strategy and programs that serve the execution of that strategy. Because perceived time risk did not hold statistical significance in Togo, this phenomenon pinpoints that using MFS has little to do with the time spent. As such, service providers should preserve those features that ease the MFS application in the time-frame.

Lastly, the outcome of TOPSIS through an SEM-TOPSIS integrated study specifies that mobile money transfer (MMT) is indeed the predominant mobile financial service (MFS) alternative used in Togo followed by mobile payment (MP), while mobile banking (MB) is reflected as trifling. In general, MFS companies should concede that consumer trust and risk with their antecedent create a tremendous barrier to MFS transactions. This study still demonstrates that among the MFS companies, mobile money transfer companies are not powerless. It provides a practical guideline toward mobile financial service companies compared to the prevailing competitors within the related field such as online banking and ATM, for constructing more trust-based strategies to manipulate favorable consumer attitudes certainly, actions, and eventual transaction behavior whereas mitigating the perceived risk factors. Regarding MFS, companies offering mobile money transfer are suggested to sustain the adoption growth, while those performing mobile payment, mobile banking predominantly, are to bear their target consumers at the core of the business model by diversifying market strategy.

With regard to the above, we cannot ignore the network nature of the payments market, an essential characteristic of which is that the market's dynamics (all the services provided and their prices) depend on the cooperation between many actors. Therefore the optimizing and maximizing effect of the traditional, individual competition on efficiency does not necessarily prevail by itself [24]. This may account for why collaboration between actors plays a positive and decisive role in improvements in the fields of trust and encountered risks.

8.2. Implication for Methodology and Theory

This research remains the first to assess the multi-dimensional trust and perceived risk facet concurrently toward consumers' adoption decisions in mobile financial services while ranking their perspective.

The result obtained will open doors for scholars to explore further trust and perceived risk antecedents. It will support the theory of trust and risk literature in general and IT in particular, since many prior studies lacked conclusive outcomes about the directivity of the causative relationship between trust and perceived risk [30,121,211]. Our finding acknowledges the trust to be the potential predictor of risk in technology adoption. The scale items employed were greatly adopted from the prevailing studies in developed countries that are allied with technology acceptance adoption behavior, trust, and perceived risk. This section provides a crucial methodological implication for the marketing scholar, who might require a hint to cross-cultural appraisal concerning the application of scales, like those established in the United States and their relevance or relatedness in Togo. Our study outcomes not only enhance the clarification of mobile financial services adoption via the effect of trust and perceived risk but also hold some strategic implications for the global expansion of managerial implementation decision tools. This study provides a benchmark integrated methodology based on an SEM-MCDM application, which found lacking in the adoption decision in general. The theoreticians and practitioners should comprehend that the prominence of the integrated SEM-TOPSIS is rooted in its robustness to test multifarious postulations made, combined with the high level in ranking the countless alternatives when multiple criteria issues arise in decision making.

9. Limitation and Future Research

Notwithstanding some contributions to the literature, practical, theoretical, and methodological applications, all research unavoidably entails drawbacks that should be addressed. Our study outcomes are unique to Togo, although they are similar to IT in general and mobile financial transactions studies, predominantly. Preferably, a longitudinal study on our framework might need to gain a better understanding of how the variables relay over time. We expect future research will address these concerns. This research displays that time risk concerns are not significant antecedents of perceived risk. We hope that future research will further elucidate the relationship between time risk issues and adoption behavior in other populaces and circumstances. Emphasizing multi-dimensional trust and perceived risk influences; this research projected to offer a wide-ranging still parsimonious decision-making model for MFS acceptance. However, the present model expounds only 13.1% of the variance in behavior to adopt. Future studies can incorporate additional variables, such as usefulness, perceived ease of use, and familiarity, in an attempt to enhance the explanatory power. Based on the respondent's educational background, our distributed questionnaire appears to be limited to the more educated and technically competent elements of society, who would be more inclined to accept MFS applications. Therefore, researchers interested in MFS for adoption and sustainability should focus more on the underbanked population where illiterate people might be found in the majority. Comparison studies between statistical methods (regression or structural equation modeling (SEM)) and the MCDM method are welcome for future work.

Author Contributions: K.G. worked on the original idea, conducted the investigation and the conceptualization, coordinated the methodology, data analysis, and writing the research paper; Y.X. worked on the investigation and provided resources; K.M.A. provided support on the investigation; L.K. supervised the work. All authors have read and agreed to the published version of the manuscript.

Appendix A

Table A1. Measurement scales and items.

Measurement Scales
General Trust (G-trust) [221]
Mobile financial services are trustworthy (G-trust1)
Mobile financial services keep their promises(G-trust2)
Mobile financial services keep customers' interests first(G-trust3)
Dispositional Trust (DTrust) [222]
It is easy for me to trust a person/thing. (DTrust1)
My tendency to trust a person/thing is high. (DTrust2)
I tend to trust a person/thing even though I have little knowledge of it. (DTrust3)
Trusting someone or something is not difficult. (DTrust4)
Technology Trust (TTrust) [223]
I think the application of the mobile device for financial products or services will improve my decision on the financial transaction. (TTrust1)
I would like to try financial products such as money transfer using mobile devices application. (TTrust2)
I think there is no technical risk in using mobile phone technology to access financial products. (TTrust3)
Vendor Trust (Vtrust) [224]
The vendor can safeguard the interests of consumers. (Vtrust1)
The vendor hopes to maintain a good reputation. (Vtrust2)
Overall, the vendor is credible. (Vtrust3)
Perceived Risk (PRisk) [127]
Using MFS would expose me to any kind of risk perception. (PRisk1)

Table A1. *Cont.*

Measurement Scales
When MFS users' accounts suffer from fraud, they will have a possible loss of status in a social group. (PRisk2)
Overall, due to transaction errors, there might be a loss of money with high risk. (PRisk3)
I believe that the overall riskiness of mobile financial service systems is high. (PRisk4)
Perceived Privacy Risk (PPrivR) [158]
The chances of using MFS and losing control over the privacy of my payment information are high. (PPrivR1)
My Personal information could be exposed or access when using m-payment. (PPrivR2)
My Privacy information might be misused, sold or inappropriately shared. (PPrivR3)
Information about my MFS transactions would be known to others. (PPrivR4)
The potential loss of control over personal information is high with MFS. (PPrivR5)
Perceived Time Risk (PTimeR) [203]
Losing of Time could be caused by instability and low speed. (PTimeR1)
I might waste much time fixing payment errors if m-payment leads to a loss of convenience. (PTimeR2)
The possible time loss from having to set up and learn how to use MFS is high. (PTimeR3)
I may lose time when making a wrong procuring decision by wasting time seeking and making the purchase using MFS. (PTimeR4)
Perceived Security Risk (PSecurR) [225]
My personal information could be collected, tracked, and analyzed. (PSecurR1)
Losing my phone might allow criminal to gain access to my MFS PIN and other sensitive information. (PSecurR2)
I think my Identity can be stolen and used to do mobile payment transaction fraudulently. (PSecurR3)
MFS is one of the new useful IT applications, and I am aware of its security issues in the transactions. (PSecurR4)
If I lose the mobile phone as an MFS user, in the meantime, I could lose my e-money as well. (PSecurR5)
Perceived Cost (PCost) [134]
I have to pay higher costs when using MFS in comparison with other banking options. (PCost1)
Using mobile financial services is a cost burden to me. (PCost2)
It costs a lot to use mobile financial services. (PCost3)
MFS lacks promotion and other incentives according to the cost offers. (PCost4)
Adoption of Mobile Financial Services (AdMFS) [226]
I will opt for mobile financial services anytime I have the opportunity to use it. (AdMFS1)
I would embrace mobile financial services usage. (AdMFS2)
I think adopting a mobile device for fund transfer is attractive. (AdMFS3)
I will use Mobile Financial Services for all my financial transactions. (AdMFS4)
Mobile Financial services are the newest transaction tool that I opt to use. (AdMFS5)

References

1. Hsu, C.L.; Wang, C.F.; Lin, J.C.C. Investigating customer adoption behaviours in Mobile Financial Services. *Int. J. Mob. Commun.* **2011**, *9*, 477. [CrossRef]
2. Oliveira, T.; Faria, M.; Thomas, M.A.; Popovič, A. Extending the understanding of mobile banking adoption: When UTAUT meets TTF and ITM. *Int. J. Inf. Manag.* **2014**, *34*, 689–703. [CrossRef]
3. Agarwal, R.; Prasad, J. Are individual differences germane to the acceptance of new information technologies? *Decis. Sci.* **1999**, *30*, 361–391. [CrossRef]
4. Afshan, S.; Sharif, A.; Waseem, N.; Frooghi, R. Internet banking in Pakistan: An extended technology acceptance perspective. *Int. J. Bus. Inf. Syst.* **2018**, *27*, 383. [CrossRef]
5. Al-Jabri, I.M.; Sohail, M.S. Mobile banking adoption: Application of diffusion of innovation theory. *J. Electron. Commer. Res.* **2012**, *13*, 379–391.
6. Abrahão, R.; Moriguchi, S.N.; Andrade, D.-F. Intention of Adoption of Mobile Payment: An analysis in the light of the Unified Theory of Acceptance and Use of Technology (UTAUT). *Rev. Adm. Inov.* **2016**, *13*, 221–230. [CrossRef]
7. Gbongli, K.; Dumor, K.; Kissi Mireku, K. MCDM technique to evaluating mobile banking adoption in the Togolese banking industry based on the perceived value: Perceived benefit and perceived sacrifice factors. *Int. J. Data Min. Knowl. Manag. Process* **2016**, *6*, 37–56.
8. Muñoz-Leiva, F.; Climent-Climent, S.; Liébana-Cabanillas, F. Determinants of Intention to Use The Mobile Banking Apps: An Extension of The Classic TAM Model. *Span. J. Mark.* **2017**, *21*, 25–38. [CrossRef]

9.   Yen, Y.S.; Wu, F.S. Predicting the adoption of mobile financial services: The impacts of perceived mobility and personal habit. *Comput. Human Behav.* **2016**, *65*, 31–42. [CrossRef]

10.   Gbongli, K. A two-staged SEM-AHP technique for understanding and prioritizing mobile financial services perspectives adoption. *Eur. J. Bus. Manag.* **2017**, *9*, 107–120.

11.   Lin, H.F. An empirical investigation of mobile banking adoption: The effect of innovation attributes and knowledge-based trust. *Int. J. Inf. Manag.* **2011**, *31*, 252–260. [CrossRef]

12.   Mohammadi, H. A study of mobile banking loyalty in Iran. *Comput. Human Behav.* **2015**, *44*, 35–47. [CrossRef]

13.   Safeena, R.; Date, H.; Kammani, A.; Hundewale, N. Technology Adoption and Indian Consumers: Study on Mobile Banking. *Int. J. Comput. Theory Eng.* **2012**, *4*, 1020–1024. [CrossRef]

14.   Ooi, K.B.; Tan, G.W.H. Mobile technology acceptance model: An investigation using mobile users to explore smartphone credit card. *Expert Syst. Appl.* **2016**, *59*, 33–46. [CrossRef]

15.   Gbongli, K.; Xu, Y.; Amedjonekou, K.M. Extended Technology Acceptance Model to Predict Mobile-Based Money Acceptance and Sustainability: A Multi-Analytical Structural Equation Modeling and Neural Network Approach. *Sustainability* **2019**, *11*, 3639. [CrossRef]

16.   Jack, W.; Ray, A.; Suri, T. Transaction networks: Evidence from mobile money in Kenya. *Am. Econ. Rev.* **2013**, *103*, 356–361. [CrossRef]

17.   Kikulwe, E.M.; Fischer, E.; Qaim, M. Mobile money, smallholder farmers, and household welfare in Kenya. *PLoS ONE* **2014**, *9*, e109804. [CrossRef]

18.   Anderson, J. M-banking in developing markets: Competitive and regulatory implications. *Info* **2010**, *12*, 18–25. [CrossRef]

19.   Assadi, D.; Cudi, A. Le potentiel d'inclusion financiere du Mobile Banking. Une etude exploratoire. *Manag. Avenir* **2011**, *6*, 227–243. [CrossRef]

20.   Chaix, L.; Torre, D. Dominique Le double role du paiement mobile dans les pays en d'eveloppement. *Rev. Econ.* **2015**, *66*, 703–727.

21.   MNB. *National Bank of Hungary's Competitiveness Programme in 330 Points*; Magyar Nemzeti Bank: Budapest, Hungary, 2019; ISBN 978-615-5318-26-9.

22.   Couchoro, M.K. Challenges faced by MFIs in adopting Management information system during their growth phase: The case of Togo. *Enterp. Dev. Microfinanc.* **2016**, *17*, 115–131. [CrossRef]

23.   Financial Afrik Faible Taux Du Mobile Banking Au Togo. Available online: http://news.alome.com/cc/24339.html (accessed on 14 March 2019).

24.   Divéki, É.; Keszy-Harmath, Z.; Helmeczi, I. *Innovative Payment Solutions, MNB Surveys No. 85*; Magyar Nemzeti Bank: Budapest, Hungary, 2010; ISBN 1787-5293. (on-line).

25.   Hassan Hosseini, M.; Fatemifar, A.; Rahimzadeh, M. Effective factors of the adoption of mobile banking services by customers. *Kuwait Chapter Arab. J. Bus. Manag. Rev.* **2015**, *6*, 1–13. [CrossRef]

26.   Liébana-Cabanillas, F.; Sánchez-Fernández, J.; Muñoz-Leiva, F. Antecedents of the adoption of the new mobile payment systems: The moderating effect of age. *Comput. Human Behav.* **2014**, *35*, 464–478. [CrossRef]

27.   Johnson, V.L.; Kiser, A.; Washington, R.; Torres, R. Limitations to the rapid adoption of M-payment services: Understanding the impact of privacy risk on M-Payment services. *Comput. Human Behav.* **2018**, *79*, 111–122. [CrossRef]

28.   Gbongli, K.; Csordas, T.; Kissi Mireku, K. Impact of consumer multidimensional online trust-risk in adopting Togolese mobile money transfer services: Structural equation modelling approach. *J. Econ. Manag. Trade* **2017**, *19*, 1–17. [CrossRef]

29.   Gbongli, K.; Peng, Y.; Ackah, O. Selection and ranking of perceived risk associated with mobile banking in West Africa: An AHP Approach from customers' perspective. *Int. J. Sci. Eng. Res.* **2016**, *7*, 80–86.

30.   Mayer, R.C.; Davis, J.H.; Schoorman, F.D. An integrative model of organizational trust. *Acad. Manag. Rev.* **1995**, *20*, 709–734. [CrossRef]

31.   Kovács, L.; David, S. Fraud risk in electronic payment transactions. *J. Money Laund. Control.* **2016**, *19*, 148–157. [CrossRef]

32.   Gefen, D.; Benbasat, I.; Pavlou, P.A. A Research Agenda for Trust in Online Environments. *J. Manag. Inf. Syst.* **2008**, *24*, 275–286. [CrossRef]

33.   Wells, J.D.; Campbell, D.E.; Valacich, J.S.; Featherman, M. The Effect of Perceived Novelty on the Adoption of Information Technology Innovations: A Risk/Reward Perspective. *Decis. Sci.* **2010**, *41*, 813–843. [CrossRef]

34. Marett, K.; Pearson, A.W.; Pearson, R.A.; Bergiel, E. Using mobile devices in a high risk context: The role of risk and trust in an exploratory study in Afghanistan. *Technol. Soc.* **2015**, *41*, 54–64. [CrossRef]

35. Lee, K.C.; Chung, N. Understanding factors affecting trust in and satisfaction with mobile banking in Korea: A modified DeLone and McLean's model perspective. *Interact. Comput.* **2009**, *21*, 385–392. [CrossRef]

36. Gao, L.; Waechter, K.A. Examining the role of initial trust in user adoption of mobile payment services: An empirical investigation. *Inf. Syst. Front.* **2017**, *19*, 525–548. [CrossRef]

37. Alsaad, A.; Mohamad, R.; Ismail, N.A. The moderating role of trust in business to business electronic commerce (B2B EC) adoption. *Comput. Human Behav.* **2017**, *68*, 157–169. [CrossRef]

38. Lowry, P.B.; Vance, A.; Moody, G.; Beckman, B.; Read, A. Explaining and Predicting the Impact of Branding Alliances and Web Site Quality on Initial Consumer Trust of E-Commerce Web Sites. *J. Manag. Inf. Syst.* **2008**, *24*, 199–224. [CrossRef]

39. Luo, X.; Li, H.; Zhang, J.; Shim, J.P. Examining multi-dimensional trust and multi-faceted risk in initial acceptance of emerging technologies: An empirical study of mobile banking services. *Decis. Support Syst.* **2010**, *49*, 222–234. [CrossRef]

40. Park, S.; Tussyadiah, I.P. Multidimensional Facets of Perceived Risk in Mobile Travel Booking. *J. Travel Res.* **2017**, *56*, 854–867. [CrossRef]

41. Aktepe, A.; Ersöz, S.; Toklu, B. Customer satisfaction and loyalty analysis with classification algorithms and Structural Equation Modeling. *Comput. Ind. Eng.* **2015**, *86*, 95–106. [CrossRef]

42. Alzahrani, L.; Al-Karaghouli, W.; Weerakkody, V. Investigating the impact of citizens' trust toward the successful adoption of e-government: A multigroup analysis of gender, age, and internet experience. *Inf. Syst. Manag.* **2018**, *35*, 124–146. [CrossRef]

43. Shieh, L.F.; Chang, T.H.; Fu, H.P.; Lin, S.W.; Chen, Y.Y. Analyzing the factors that affect the adoption of mobile services in Taiwan. *Technol. Forecast. Soc. Chang.* **2014**, *87*, 80–88. [CrossRef]

44. Figueira, J.; Greco, S.; Ehrgott, M. Multiple criteria decision analysis: State of the art surveys. *Mult. Criteria Decis. Anal. State Art Surv.* **2005**, *78*, 859–890.

45. Valaskova, K.; Kramarova, K.; Bartosova, V. Multi Criteria Models Used in Slovak Consumer Market for Business Decision Making. *Procedia Econ. Financ.* **2015**, *26*, 174–182. [CrossRef]

46. Esearch, S.Y.R.; Koppius, O.R. Predictive Analytics in Information Systems Research. *MIS Q.* **2011**, *35*, 553–572.

47. Scott, J.E.; Walczak, S. Cognitive engagement with a multimedia ERP training tool: Assessing computer self-efficacy and technology acceptance. *Inf. Manag.* **2009**, *46*, 221–232. [CrossRef]

48. Hung, Y.H.; Chou, S.C.T.; Tzeng, G.H. Using MCDM methods to adopt and assess knowledge management. In *Communications in Computer and Information Science*; Springer: Berlin/Heidelberg, Germany, 2009; Volume 35, pp. 840–847.

49. Gupta, K.P.; Bhaskar, P.; Singh, S. Prioritization of factors influencing employee adoption of e-government using the analytic hierarchy process. *J. Syst. Inf. Technol.* **2017**, *19*, 116–137. [CrossRef]

50. Liou, J.J.H.; Tzeng, G.H. Comments on Multiple criteria decision making (MCDM) methods in economics: An overview. *Technol. Econ. Dev. Econ.* **2012**, *18*, 672–695. [CrossRef]

51. Gbongli, K.; Kovács, L. A Decision Analysis towards Mobile Financial Services Adoption and Sustainability in Togo: Structural Equation Modeling and TOPSIS Methodology. In Proceedings of the DSI 2019 Annual Meeting of Decision Sciences Institute, New Orleans, LA, USA, 23–25 November 2019; pp. 2080–2114.

52. Abu-Shanab, E.A.; Abu-Baker, A.N. Using and buying mobile phones in Jordan: Implications for future research and the Development of New Methodology. *Technol. Soc.* **2014**, *38*, 103–110. [CrossRef]

53. Laukkanen, T. Mobile banking. *Int. J. Bank Mark.* **2017**, *35*, 1042–1043. [CrossRef]

54. Hendricks, L.; Chidiac, S. Village Savings and Loans: A Pathway to Financial Inclusion for Africa's Poorest Households. *Enterp. Dev. Microfinance* **2011**, *22*, 134–146. [CrossRef]

55. Donovan, K. Mobile Money for Financial Inclusion. *Inf. Commun. Dev.* **2012**, *61*, 61–73. [CrossRef]

56. Dennehy, D.; Sammon, D. Trends in mobile payments research: A literature review. *J. Innov. Manag.* **2015**, *3*, 49–61. [CrossRef]

57. Lee, J.K.; Rao, H.R. Perceived risks, counter-beliefs, and intentions to use anti-/counter-terrorism websites: An exploratory study of government-citizens online interactions in a turbulent environment. *Decis. Support Syst.* **2007**, *43*, 1431–1449. [CrossRef]

58. Li, H.; Sarathy, R.; Xu, H. The role of affect and cognition on online consumers' decision to disclose personal information to unfamiliar online vendors. *Decis. Support Syst.* **2011**, *51*, 434–445. [CrossRef]

59. Wisdom, J.P.; Chor, K.H.B.; Hoagwood, K.E.; Horwitz, S.M. Innovation adoption: A review of theories and constructs. *Adm. Policy Ment. Health Ment. Health Serv. Res.* **2014**, *41*, 480–502. [CrossRef]

60. Safeena, R.; Date, H.; Hundewale, N.; Kammani, A. Combination of TAM and TPB in Internet Banking Adoption. *Int. J. Comput. Theory Eng.* **2013**, *5*, 146–150. [CrossRef]

61. Yan, H.; Yang, Z. Examining mobile payment user adoption from the perspective of trust. *Int. J. U E Serv. Sci. Technol.* **2015**, *8*, 117–130. [CrossRef]

62. Slade, E.L.; Williams, M.D.; Dwivedi, Y.K. Mobile payment adoption: Classification and review of the extant literature. *Mark. Rev.* **2013**, *13*, 167–190. [CrossRef]

63. Tam, C.; Oliveira, T. Understanding mobile banking individual performance. *Internet Res.* **2017**, *27*, 538–562. [CrossRef]

64. Slade, E.; Williams, M.; Dwivedi, Y.; Piercy, N. Exploring consumer adoption of proximity mobile payments. *J. Strateg. Mark.* **2015**, *23*, 209–223. [CrossRef]

65. Fishbein, M.; Ajzen, I. *Belief, Attitude, Intention and Behaviour: An Introduction to Theory and Research*; Addison-Wesley: Reading, MA, USA, 1975. [CrossRef]

66. Ajzen, I. From intentions to action: A theory of planned behavior. In *Action Control*; Springer: Berlin/Heidelberg, Germany, 1985; pp. 11–39. ISBN 978-3-642-69746-3.

67. Barua, P. The Moderating Role of Perceived Behavioral Control: The Literature Criticism and Methodological Considerations. *Int. J. Bus. Soc. Sci.* **2013**, *4*, 57–59.

68. Davis, F.D.; Bagozzi, R.P.; Warshaw, P.R. User acceptance of computer technology: A comparison of two theoretical models. *Manag. Sci.* **1989**, *35*, 982–1003. [CrossRef]

69. Marangunić, N.; Granić, A. Technology acceptance model: A literature review from 1986 to 2013. *Univers. Access Inf. Soc.* **2015**, *14*, 81–95. [CrossRef]

70. Legris, P.; Ingham, J.; Collerette, P. Why do people use information technology? a critical review of the technology acceptance model. *Inf. Manag.* **2003**, *40*, 191–204. [CrossRef]

71. Mortenson, M.J.; Vidgen, R. A computational literature review of the technology acceptance model. *Int. J. Inf. Manag.* **2016**, *36*, 1248–1259. [CrossRef]

72. Davis, F. Perceived usefulness, perceived ease of use, and user acceptance of information technology. *MIS Q.* **1989**, *13*, 319–340. [CrossRef]

73. Gefen, D.; Straub, D.; Mack, J.; Distinguished, R. The relative importance of perceived ease of use in IS adoption: A study of e-commerce adoption. *J. Assoc. Inf. Syst.* **2000**, *1*, 1–30. [CrossRef]

74. Pavlou, P.A. Integrating trust in electronic commerce with the technology acceptance model: Model development and validation. In Proceedings of the Seventh Americas Conference in Information Systems AMCIS, Boston, MA, USA, 3–5 August 2001; pp. 816–822.

75. Waite, K.; Harrison, T. Online banking adoption: We should know better 20 years on. *J. Financ. Serv. Mark.* **2015**, *20*, 258–272. [CrossRef]

76. Thompson, R.L.; Higgins, C.A.; Howell, J.M. Personal Computing—Toward a Conceptual-Model of Utilization. *MIS Q.* **1991**, *15*, 125–143. [CrossRef]

77. Webster, J.; Martocchio, J.J. Microcomputer Playfulness: Development of a Measure with Workplace Implications. *MIS Q.* **1992**, *16*, 201. [CrossRef]

78. Suh, B.; Han, I. The Impact of Customer Trust and Perception ofSecurity Control on the Acceptance ofElectronic Commerce. *Int. J. Electron. Commer.* **2003**, *7*, 135–161.

79. Rogers, E.M. *Diffusion of Innovations*; Free Press of Glencoe: New York, NY, USA, 1962.

80. Plouffe, C.R.; Vandenbosch, M.; Hulland, J. Intermediating technologies and multi-group adoption: A comparison of consumer and merchant adoption intentions toward a new electronic payment system. *J. Prod. Innov. Manag.* **2001**, *18*, 65–81. [CrossRef]

81. Karahanna, E.; Straub, D.W.; Chervany, N.L.; Karahanna, E. Information technology adoption across time: A cross-sectional comparison of pre-adoption and post-adoption beliefs. *MIS Q.* **1999**, *23*, 183–213. [CrossRef]

82. Chen, L.-D.; Gillenson, M.L.; Sherrell, D.L. Enticing online consumers: An extended technology acceptance perspective. *Inf. Manag.* **2002**, *39*, 705–719. [CrossRef]

83. Lyytinen, K.; Damsgaard, J. What's Wrong with the diffusion of innovation theory? The case of a complex and networked technology. *Reports Aalborg Univ. Dep. Comput. Sci.* **2001**, *187*, 1–20. [CrossRef]

84. Napaporn, K. Examining a Technology Acceptance Model of Internet Usage by Academics Within Thai Business Schools. Ph.D. Thesis, Victoria University, Melbourne, Australia, 2007.

85. Singleton, R.A.; Straits, B.C.; Straits, M.M. *Approaches to Social Research*, 2nd ed.; Oxford University Press: New York, NY, USA, 1993.

86. Taylor, S.; Todd, P.A. Understanding information technology usage: A test of competing models. *Inf. Syst. Res.* **1995**, *6*, 144–176. [CrossRef]

87. El-Kasheir, D.; Ashour, A.; Yacout, O. Factors affecting continued usage of internet banking among Egyptian customers. *Commun. IBIMA* **2009**, *9*, 252–263.

88. George, J.F. The theory of planned behavior and Internet purchasing. *Internet Res.* **2004**, *14*, 198–212. [CrossRef]

89. Aboelmaged, M.G.; Gebba, R.T. Mobile Banking Adoption: An Examination of Technology Acceptance Model and Theory of Planned Behavior. *Int. J. Bus. Res. Dev.* **2013**, *2*, 35–50. [CrossRef]

90. Shaikh, A.A.; Karjaluoto, H. Mobile banking adoption: A literature review. *Telemat. Inform.* **2014**, *32*, 129–142. [CrossRef]

91. Narteh, B.; Mahmoud, M.A.; Amoh, S. Customer behavioural intentions towards mobile money services adoption in Ghana. *Serv. Ind. J.* **2017**, *37*, 426–447. [CrossRef]

92. Alalwan, A.A.; Dwivedi, Y.K.; Rana, N.P. Factors influencing adoption of mobile banking by Jordanian bank customers: Extending UTAUT2 with trust. *Int. J. Inf. Manag.* **2017**, *37*, 99–110. [CrossRef]

93. Afawubo, K.; Agbagla, M.; Couchoro, K.M.; Gbandi, T. Socioeconomic determinants of the mobile money adoption process: The case of Togo. *Cah. Rech.* **2017**, *17*, 1–23.

94. Gefen, D.; Straub, D. Managing User Trust in B2C e-Services. *e-Serv.* **2003**, *2*, 7–24. [CrossRef]

95. Mcknight, D.H.; Chervany, N.L. What trust means in e-commerce customer relationships: An interdisciplinary conceptual typology. *Int. J. Electron. Commer.* **2001**, *6*, 35–59. [CrossRef]

96. Tan, F.B.; Sutherland, P. Online Consumer Trust: A Multi-Dimensional Model. *J. Electron. Commer. Organ.* **2004**, *2*, 40–58. [CrossRef]

97. Vidotto, G.; Massidda, D.; Noventa, S.; Vicentini, M. Trusting beliefs: A functional measurement study. *Psicologica* **2012**, *33*, 575–590.

98. Nor, K.M.; Pearson, J.M. An Exploratory Study Into The Adoption of Internet Banking in a Developing Country: Malaysia. *J. Internet Commer.* **2008**, *7*, 29–73. [CrossRef]

99. Schoorman, F.D.; Mayer, R.C.; Davis, J.H. An Integrative Model of Organizational Trust: Past, Present, and Future. *Acad. Manag. Rev.* **2007**, *32*, 344–354. [CrossRef]

100. Hallikainen, H.; Laukkanen, T. National culture and consumer trust in e-commerce. *Int. J. Inf. Manag.* **2018**, *38*, 97–106. [CrossRef]

101. Gefen, D.; Karahanna, E.; Straub, D.W. Trust and TAM in online shopping: An integrated mode. *MIS Q.* **2003**, *27*, 51–90. [CrossRef]

102. Mcknight, D.H.; Carter, M.; Thatcher, J.B. Trust in a Specific Technology: An Investigation of Its Components and Measures Trust in a specific technology: An investigation of its components and measures. *ACM Trans. Manag. Inform. Syst.* **2011**, *2*, 1–25. [CrossRef]

103. Muir, B.M.; Moray, N. Trust in automation. Part II. Experimental studies of trust and human intervention in a process control simulation. *Ergonomics* **1996**, *39*, 429–460. [CrossRef] [PubMed]

104. Misiolek, N.; Zakaria, N.; Zhang, P. Trust in organizational acceptance of information technology: A conceptual model and preliminary evidence. In Proceedings of the Decision Sciences Institute 33rd Annual Meeting, San Diego, CA, USA, 23–26 November 2002; pp. 1–7.

105. Meng, D.; Min, Q.; Li, Y. Study on trust in mobile commerce adoption—A conceptual model. In Proceedings of the International Symposium on Electronic Commerce and Security, Guangzhou, China, 3–5 August 2008; pp. 246–249.

106. Min, Q.; Meng, D.; Zhong, Q. An empirical study on trust in mobile commerce adoption. In Proceedings of the 2008 IEEE International Conference on Service Operations and Logistics, and Informatics, Beijing, China, 12–15 October 2008; Volume 1, pp. 659–664.

107. Lankton, N.K.; Harrison McKnight, D.; Wright, R.T.; Thatcher, J.B. Using expectation disconfirmation theory and polynomial modeling to understand trust in technology. *Inf. Syst. Res.* **2016**, *27*, 197–213. [CrossRef]

108. Bailey, B.P.; Gurak, L.J.; Konstan, J. Trust in Cyberspace. In *Human Factors and Web Development*, 2nd ed.; Ratner, J., Ed.; Lawrence Erlbaum Associates: Mahwah, NJ, USA, 2002.

109. Pavlou, P.A.; Liang, H.; Xue, Y. Understanding and Mitigating Uncertainty in Online Exchnge Relationships: A Principle—Agent Perspective. *MIS Q.* **2007**, *31*, 105–136. [CrossRef]

110. Liu, Z.; Min, Q.; Ji, S. An empirical study on mobile banking adoption: The role of trust. In Proceedings of the 2009 Second International Symposium on Electronic Commerce and Security, Nanchang, China, 22–24 May 2009; Volume 2, pp. 7–13.

111. Yang, S. Role of transfer-based and performance-based cues on initial trust in mobile shopping services: A cross-environment perspective. *Inf. Syst. E-Bus. Manag.* **2016**, *14*, 47–70. [CrossRef]

112. Yang, S.; Chen, Y.; Wei, J. Understanding consumers' web-mobile shopping extension behavior: A trust transfer perspective. *J. Comput. Inf. Syst.* **2015**, *55*, 78–87. [CrossRef]

113. Nilashi, M.; Ibrahim, O.; Reza Mirabi, V.; Ebrahimi, L.; Zare, M. The role of Security, Design and Content factors on customer trust in mobile commerce. *J. Retail. Consum. Serv.* **2015**, *26*, 57–69. [CrossRef]

114. Rogers, E.M. *Diffusion of Innovations*, 3rd ed.; Free Press: New York, NY, USA, 1983.

115. Bhattacherjee, A. Individual Trust in Online Firms: Scale Development and Initial test. *J. Manag. Inf. Syst.* **2002**, *19*, 211–242.

116. Bauer, R.A. Consumer behavior as risk taking. In *Risk Taking and Information Handling in Consumer Behavior*; Harvard University Press: Cambridge, MA, USA, 1960; pp. 389–398.

117. Cunningham, S.M. *The Major Dimensions of Perceived Risk, in Risk Taking and Information Handling in Consumer Behavior*; Harvard University: Cambridge, MA, USA, 1967; Volume 82–108.

118. Costigan, R.D.; Ilter, S.S.; Berman, J.J. A Multi-Dimensional Study of Trust in Organizations. *J. Manag.* **1998**, *10*, 303–316.

119. Johnson-George, C.; Swap, W.C. Measurement of specific interpersonal trust: Construction and validation of a scale to assess trust in a specific other. *J. Personal. Soc. Psychol.* **1982**, *43*, 1306–1317. [CrossRef]

120. Koller, M. Risk as a Determinant of Trust. *Basic Appl. Soc. Psych.* **1988**, *9*, 265–276. [CrossRef]

121. Gefen, D.; Srinivasan Rao, V.; Tractinsky, N. The conceptualization of trust, risk and their electronic commerce: The need for clarifications. In Proceedings of the 36th Annual Hawaii International Conference on System Sciences, HICSS 2003, Big Island, HI, USA, 6–9 January 2003.

122. Jarvenpaa, S.L.; Tractinsky, N.; Vitale, M. Consumer Trust in an Internet Store. *Inf. Technol. Manag.* **2000**, *1*, 45–71. [CrossRef]

123. Grandison, T.; Sloman, M. A survey of trust in internet applications. *IEEE Commun. Surv. Tutor.* **2000**, *3*, 2–16. [CrossRef]

124. Johnston, A.C.; Warkentin, M. The Online Consumer Trust Construct: A Web Merchant Practitioner Perspective. In Proceedings of the 7th Annual Conference of the Southern Association for Information Systems, Savannah, GA, USA, 27–28 February 2004; pp. 220–226.

125. Merhi, M.; Hone, K.; Tarhini, A. A cross-cultural study of the intention to use mobile banking between Lebanese and British consumers: Extending UTAUT2 with security, privacy and trust. *Technol. Soc.* **2019**, *59*, 101151. [CrossRef]

126. Swaminathan, V.; Lepkowska-White, E.; Rao, B.P. Browsers or Buyers in Cyberspace? An Investigation of Factors Influencing Electronic Exchange. *J. Comput. Commun.* **1999**, *5*. [CrossRef]

127. Featherman, M.S.; Pavlou, P.A. Predicting e-services adoption: A perceived risk facets perspective. *Int. J. Hum. Comput. Stud.* **2003**, *59*, 451–474. [CrossRef]

128. Bellman, S.; Lohse, G.L.; Johnson, E.J. Predictors of online buying behavior. *Commun. ACM* **1999**, *42*, 32–38. [CrossRef]

129. Murray, K.B.; Schlacter, J.L. The impact of services versus goods on consumers' assessment of perceived risk and variability. *J. Acad. Mark. Sci.* **1990**, *18*, 51–65. [CrossRef]

130. Lee, M.C. Predicting Behavioural Intention to Use Online Banking. In Proceedings of the 19th International Conference on Information Management, Taipei, Taiwan, 13–14 November 2008.

131. Yang, A.S. Exploring Adoption difficulties in mobile banking services. *Can. J. Adm. Sci.* **2009**, *26*, 136–149. [CrossRef]

132. Cruz, P.; Neto, L.B.F.; Muñoz-Gallego, P.; Laukkanen, T. Mobile banking rollout in emerging markets: Evidence from Brazil. *Int. J. Bank Mark.* **2010**, *28*, 342–371. [CrossRef]

133. Yao, H.; Zhong, C. The analysis of influencing factors and promotion strategy for the use of mobile banking/L'analyse d'influencer des facteurs et la stratégie de promotion pour l'usage des opérations bancaires mobiles. *Can. Soc. Sci.* **2011**, *7*, 60–63.

134. Luarn, P.; Lin, H.-H. Toward an understanding of the behavioral intention to use mobile banking. *Comput. Human Behav.* **2005**, *21*, 873–891. [CrossRef]

135. McKnight, D.H.; Cummings, L.L.; Chervany, N.L. Initial trust formation in new organizational relationships. *Acad. Manag. Rev.* **1998**, *23*, 473–490. [CrossRef]

136. McKnight, D.H.; Choudhury, V.; Kacmar, C. Developing and validating trust measures for e-commerce: An integrative typology. *Inf. Syst. Res.* **2002**, *13*, 334–359. [CrossRef]

137. Gefen, D. E-commerce: The role of familiarity and trust. *Omega* **2000**, *28*, 725–737. [CrossRef]

138. Kim, K.K.; Prabhakar, B. Initial Trust and the Adoption of B2C e-Commerce: The Case of Internet Banking. *ACM SIGMIS Database* **2004**, *35*, 50–64. [CrossRef]

139. Guangming, Y.; Yuzhong, M. A research on the model of factors influencing consumer trust in mobile business. In Proceedings of the 2011 International Conference on E-Business and E-Government, Shanghai, China, 6–8 May 2011; pp. 1–5.

140. Pratt, J.W. Risk Aversion in the Small and in the Large. *Econometrica* **1964**, *32*, 122–136. [CrossRef]

141. Kogan, N.; Wallach, M.A. *Risk-Taking: A Study in Cognition and Personality*; Rhinehart & Winston: New York, NY, USA, 1964.

142. Cox, D.F. *Risk Taking and Information Handling in Consumer Behavior*; Harvard University: Boston, MA, USA, 1967.

143. Bonoma, T.V.; Johnston, W.J. Decision making under uncertainty: A direct measurement approach. *J. Consum. Res.* **1979**, *6*, 177. [CrossRef]

144. Currim, I.S.; Sarin, R.K. A Procedure for Measuring and Estimating Consumer Preferences Under Uncertainty. *J. Mark. Res.* **1983**, *20*, 249–256. [CrossRef]

145. Cunningham, L.F.; Gerlach, J.H.; Harper, M.D.; Young, C.E. Perceived risk and the consumer buying process: Internet airline reservations. *Int. J. Serv. Ind. Manag.* **2005**, *16*, 357–372. [CrossRef]

146. Lee, M.S.Y.; McGoldrick, P.J.; Keeling, K.A.; Doherty, J. Using ZMET to explore barriers to the adoption of 3G mobile banking services. *Int. J. Retail Distrib. Manag.* **2003**, *31*, 340–348. [CrossRef]

147. Kim, K.K.; Prabhakar, B. Initial trust, perceived risk, and the adoption of internet banking. *ICIS 2000 Proc.* **2000**, *55*, 537–543.

148. Laforet, S.; Li, X. Consumers' attitudes towards online and mobile banking in China. *Int. J. Bank Mark.* **2005**, *23*, 362–380. [CrossRef]

149. Lee, E.; Kwon, K.; Schumann, D.W. Segmenting the non-adopter category in the diffusion of internet banking. *Int. J. Bank Mark.* **2005**, *23*, 414–437. [CrossRef]

150. Tan, M.; Teo, T.S.H. Factors Influencing the Adoption of Internet Banking. *J. AIS* **2000**, *1*, 1–42. [CrossRef]

151. Liang, T.-P.; Huang, J.-S. An empirical study on consumer acceptance of products in electronic markets: A transaction cost model. *Decis. Support Syst.* **1998**, *24*, 29–43. [CrossRef]

152. Liao, Z.; Cheung, M.T. Internet-based e-shopping and consumer attitudes: An empirical study. *Inf. Manag.* **2001**, *38*, 299–306. [CrossRef]

153. Kim, D.J.; Ferrin, D.L.; Rao, H.R. A trust-based consumer decision-making model in electronic commerce: The role of trust, perceived risk, and their antecedents. *Decis. Support Syst.* **2008**, *44*, 544–564. [CrossRef]

154. Pavlou, P.A. Consumer intentions to adopt electronic commerce—Incorporating trust and risk in the technology acceptance model. *Int. J. Electron. Commer.* **2003**, *7*, 101–134.

155. Dowling, G.R.; Staelin, R. A Model of Perceived Risk and Intended Risk-Handling Activity. *J. Consum. Res.* **1994**, *21*, 119. [CrossRef]

156. Assael, H. *Consumer Behavior and Marketing Action*, 6th ed.; South-Western College Publishing: Cincinnati, OH, USA, 1998.

157. Coulter, R.A.; Price, L.L.; Feick, L. Rethinking the Origins of invoivement and Brand Commitment: Insights from Postsociaiist Centrai Europe. *J. Consum. Res.* **2003**, *30*, 151–169. [CrossRef]

158. Jarvenpaa, S.L.; Tractinsky, N. Consumer trust in an Internet store: A cross cultural validation. *J. Comput. Mediat. Commun.* **1999**, *5*, 1–5. [CrossRef]

159. Cooper, D.R.; Schindler, P.S. *Business Research Methods*, 8th ed.; McGraw-Hill Irwin: Boston, MA, USA, 2003; ISBN 0199284989.

160. Straub, D.; Boudreau, M.; Gefen, D. Validation Guidelines for IS Positivist Validation Guidelines for IS Positivist. *Commun. Assoc. Inf. Syst.* **2004**, *13*, 380–427.

161. Gbongli, K. Integrating AHP-TOPSIS approach on prioritizing self-service technology (SST) decision making in financial institution (Togo). *Br. J. Math. Comput. Sci.* **2016**, *16*, 1–22.

162. N'Guissan, Y. Résultats définitifs du 4ème recensement général (RGPH4) au Togo. Available online: http://www.stat-togo.org/index.php/rgph (accessed on 25 March 2018).

163. Yamane, T. Statistics: An introductory analysis. *Harper Row* **1967**, *60*, 886.

164. Kumar Mittal, V.; Singh Sangwan, K. Development of a structural model of environmentally conscious manufacturing drivers. *J. Manuf. Technol. Manag.* **2014**, *25*, 1195–1208. [CrossRef]

165. Hair, J.F.; Black, W.C.; Babin, B.J.; Anderson, R.E.; Tatham, R.L. *Multivariate Data Analysis*, 7th ed.; Pearson: New York, NY, USA, 2010; ISBN 9788577804023.

166. Chin, W. The partial least squares approach to structural equation modeling. *Mod. Methods Bus. Res.* **1998**, *295*, 295–336.

167. Anderson, J.C.; Gerbing, D.W. Structural equation modeling in practice: A review and recommended two-step approach. *Psychol. Bull.* **1988**, *103*, 411–423. [CrossRef]

168. Schumacher, R.E.; Lomax, R.G. *A Beginner's Guide to Structural Equation Modeling*; Lawrence Erlbaum Associates: Mahwah, NJ, USA, 1996.

169. Hair, J.F.; Black, W.; Babin, B.; Anderson, R.; Tatham, R. *Multivariate Data Analysis*, 6th ed.; Pearson Prentice Hall, Pearson Education, Inc.: Upper Saddle River, NJ, USA, 2006; Volume 6, ISBN 909003868X.

170. Aloini, D.; Martini, A.; Pellegrini, L. A structural equation model for continuous improvement: A test for capabilities, tools and performance. *Prod. Plan. Control Manag. Oper.* **2011**, *22*, 628–648. [CrossRef]

171. Kaiser, H.F. An index of factorial simplicity. *Psychometrika* **1974**, *39*, 31–36. [CrossRef]

172. Campbell, D.T.; Fiske, D.W. Convergent and discriminant validity by the multitrait-multimethod matrix. *Psychol. Bull.* **1959**, *56*, 81–105. [CrossRef] [PubMed]

173. Zhou, T. Examining mobile banking user adoption from the perspectives of trust and flow experience. *Inf. Technol. Manag.* **2012**, *13*, 27–37. [CrossRef]

174. Fornell, C.; Larcker, D.F. Structural Equation Models with Unobservable Variables and Measurement Error: Algebra and Statistics. *J. Mark. Res.* **1981**, *18*, 382–388. [CrossRef]

175. Hair, J.F.; Anderson, R.E.; Tatham, R.L.; Black, W.C. *Multivariate Data Analysis*, 7th ed.; Prentice Hall: Upper Saddle River, NJ, USA, 2010. [CrossRef]

176. Zhou, T.; Lu, Y.; Wang, B. Integrating TTF and UTAUT to explain mobile banking user adoption. *Comput. Hum. Behav.* **2010**, *26*, 760–767. [CrossRef]

177. Hwang, Y. User experience and personal innovativeness: An empirical study on the Enterprise Resource Planning systems. *Comput. Human Behav.* **2014**, *34*, 227–234. [CrossRef]

178. Podsakoff, P.M.; MacKenzie, S.B.; Lee, J.; Podsakoff, N.P. Common method biases in behavioral research: A critical review of the literature and recommended remedies. *J. Appl. Psychol.* **2003**, *88*, 879–903. [CrossRef]

179. Davidov, E. A cross-country and cross-time comparison of the human values measurements with the second round of the European social survey. *Surv. Res. Methods* **2008**, *2*, 33–46.

180. Hwang, C.-L.; Yoon, K. *Multiple Attribute Decision Making: Methods and Applications: A State-of-the-Art Survey*; Springer: Berlin, Germany; New York, NY, USA, 1981; Volume 259.

181. Patil, S.K.; Kant, R. A fuzzy AHP-TOPSIS framework for ranking the solutions of Knowledge Management adoption in Supply Chain to overcome its barriers. *Expert Syst. Appl.* **2014**, *41*, 679–693. [CrossRef]

182. Mahdevari, S.; Shahriar, K.; Esfahanipour, A. Human health and safety risks management in underground coal mines using fuzzy TOPSIS. *Sci. Total Environ.* **2014**, *488*, 85–99. [CrossRef]

183. Dhull, S.; Narwal, M.S. Prioritizing the Drivers of Green Supply Chain Management in Indian Manufacturing Industries Using Fuzzy TOPSIS Method: Government, Industry, Environment, and Public Perspectives. *Process Integr. Optim. Sustain.* **2018**, *2*, 47–60. [CrossRef]

184. Vinodh, S.; Prasanna, M.; Hari Prakash, N. Integrated Fuzzy AHP-TOPSIS for selecting the best plastic recycling method: A case study. *Appl. Math. Model.* **2014**, *38*, 4662–4672. [CrossRef]

185. Behzadian, M.; Khanmohammadi Otaghsara, S.; Yazdani, M.; Ignatius, J. A state-of the-art survey of TOPSIS applications. *Expert Syst. Appl.* **2012**, *39*, 13051–13069. [CrossRef]

186. Lin, C.T.; Tsai, M.C. Location choice for direct foreign investment in new hospitals in China by using ANP and TOPSIS. *Qual. Quant.* **2010**, *44*, 375–390. [CrossRef]

187. Shih, H.S.; Shyur, H.J.; Lee, E.S. An extension of TOPSIS for group decision making. *Math. Comput. Model.* **2007**, *45*, 801–813. [CrossRef]

188. Shipley, M.F.; de Korvin, A.; Obid, R. A decision making model for multi-attribute problems incorporating uncertainty and bias measures. *Comput. Oper. Res.* **1991**, *18*, 335–342. [CrossRef]

189. Punniyamoorty, M.; Mathiyalagan, P.; Lakshmi, G. A combined application of structural equation modeling (SEM) and analytic hierarchy process (AHP) in supplier selection. *Benchmarking An Int. J.* **2012**, *19*, 70–92. [CrossRef]

190. Payne, R.; Clark, M. Dispositional and situational determinants of trust in two types of managers. *Int. J. Hum. Resour. Manag.* **2003**, *14*, 128–138. [CrossRef]

191. Salam, A.F.; Iyer, L.; Palvia, P.; Singh, R. Trust in e-commerce. *Commun. ACM* **2005**, *48*, 72–77. [CrossRef]

192. Lippert, S.K.; Forman, H. A supply chain study of technology trust and antecedents to technology internalization consequences. *Int. J. Phys. Distrib. Logist. Manag.* **2006**, *36*, 271–288. [CrossRef]

193. Pavlou, P.; Ratnasingam, P. Technology trust in B2B electronic commerce: Conceptual foundations. In *Business Strategies for Information Technology Management*; Kangas, K., Ed.; Idea Group Publishing: Hershey, PA, USA, 2001; pp. 200–215.

194. Aldridge, A.; White, M.; Forcht, K. Security considerations of doing business via the Internet: Cautions to be considered. *Internet Res.* **1997**, *7*, 9–15. [CrossRef]

195. Pavlou, A.P. Consumer acceptance of electronic commerce: Integrating trust and risk with the technology acceptance model. *Int. J. Electron. Commer.* **2003**, *7*, 69–103.

196. Cheung, C.; Lee, M.K.O. Trust in Internet Shopping: A Proposed Model and Measurement Instrument. In *Americas Conference on Information Systems*; AIS Electronic Library: Long Beach, CA, USA, 2000; pp. 680–689.

197. Kesharwani, A.; Bisht, S.S. The impact of trust and perceived risk on internet banking adoption in India: An extension of technology acceptance model. *Int. J. Bank Mark.* **2012**, *30*, 303–322. [CrossRef]

198. Fukuyama, F. Trust: The Social Virtues and the Creation of Prosperity. In *Trust the Social Virtues and the Creation of Prosperity*; Free Press: New York, NY, USA, 1995; p. 457. [CrossRef]

199. Ratnasingham, P.; Kumar, K. Trading partner trust in electronic commerce participation. *ICIS 2000 Proc.* **2000**, *56*, 544–552.

200. Zikmund, G.W.; Scott, E.J. A Multivariate Analysis of Perceived Risk Self-Confidence and Information Sources. *N. Am. Adv. Consum. Res.* **1974**, *1*, 406–416.

201. Boksberger, P.E.; Bieger, T.; Laesser, C. Multidimensional analysis of perceived risk in commercial air travel. *J. Air Transp. Manag.* **2007**, *13*, 90–96. [CrossRef]

202. Choffee, S.H.; McLeod, J.M. *Consumer Decisions and Information Use*; Ward, S., Robertson, T.S., Eds.; Consumer behavior: Theoretical sources; Prentice-Hall Inc.: Englewood Cliffs, NJ, USA, 1973.

203. Zhang, L.; Tan, W.; Xu, Y.; Tan, G. Dimensions of perceived risk and their influence on consumers' purchasing behavior in the overall process of B2C. In *Engineering Education and Management*; Zhang, L., Zhang, C., Eds.; Springer: Berlin/Heidelberg, Germany, 2012; Volume 111, pp. 1–11.

204. Chakuthip, A.; Brunetto, Y.; Rod, F.-W.; Sheryl, R. Trust, Social Network and Electronic Commerce Adoption. In *Handbook of Research on Electronic Collaboration and Organizational Synergy*; IGI Global: Hershey, NY, USA, 2007; pp. 452–471. [CrossRef]

205. Grabner-Kräuter, S.; Kaluscha, E.A. Empirical research in on-line trust: A review and critical assessment. *Int. J. Hum. Comput. Stud.* **2003**, *58*, 783–812. [CrossRef]

206. Rotter, J.B. Generalized expectancies for interpersonal trust. *Am. Psychol.* **1971**, *26*, 443–452. [CrossRef]

207. Mitchell, V. Consumer perceived risk: Conceptualisations and models. *Eur. J. Mark.* **1999**, *33*, 163–195. [CrossRef]

208. Manchiraju, S.; Vudayagiri, G.; Garg, G. Capgemini Top 10 trends in payment in 2016. Available online: https://www.capgemini.com/resource-file-access/resource/pdf/payments_trends_2016.pdf (accessed on 20 September 2019).

209. De Fouchier, R.; Larduinat, X. Connected living: How technology could impact daily lives by 2025—An International Study of Consumers Expectations for the Future of Mobile Technology. Available online: http://www.gemalto.com/brochures-site/download-site/Documents/documentgating/tel-wp-connected-living-2025.pdf (accessed on 25 September 2019).

210. Hosmer, L.T. Trust: The connecting link between organizational theory and philosophical ethics. *Acad. Manag. Rev.* **1995**, *20*, 379–403. [CrossRef]

211. Rousseau, D.M.; Sitkin, S.B.; Burt, R.S.; Camerer, C. Not so different after all: A cross-discipline view of trust. *Acad. Manag. Rev.* **1998**, *23*, 393–404. [CrossRef]

212. Luhmann, N. Trust and Power. *Coop. Trust* **1979**, *8*, 208. [CrossRef]
213. Konovsky, M.A.; Pugh, S.D. Citizenship behavior and social exchange. *Acad. Manag. J.* **1994**, *37*, 656–669.
214. Rossiter, C.M.; Barnett, P.W. *Communicating Personally: A Theory of Interpersonal Communication and Human Relationships*; The Bobbs-Merrill Company, Inc.: Indianapolis, IN, USA, 1975.
215. Schurr, P.H.; Ozanne, J.L. Influences on Exchange Processes: Buyers' Preconceptions of a Seller's Trustworthiness and Bargaining Toughness. *J. Consum. Res.* **1985**, *11*, 939. [CrossRef]
216. Fox, C.; Causey, E.; Cencula, D. *Study of Mobile Banking & Payments*, 3rd ed.; First Annapolis Consulting, Inc.: Annapolis, MD, USA, 2016.
217. Gavade, R.K. Multi-Criteria Decision Making: An overview of different selection problems and methods. *Int. J. Comput. Sci. Inf. Technol.* **2014**, *5*, 5643–5646.
218. Abdul-Hamid, I.K.; Shaikh, A.A.; Boateng, H.; Hinson, R.E. Customers' Perceived Risk and Trust in Using Mobile Money Services—an Empirical Study of Ghana. *Int. J. E-Bus. Res.* **2019**, *15*, 1–19. [CrossRef]
219. José Liébana-Cabanillas, F.; Sánchez-Fernández, J.; Muñoz-Leiva, F. Role of gender on acceptance of mobile payment. *Ind. Manag. Data Syst.* **2014**, *114*, 220–240. [CrossRef]
220. Kovács, L.; Terták, E. *Financial Literacy, Panacea or Placebo—A Central European Perspective*; Verlag Dashöfer: Bratislava, Slovakia, 2016.
221. Zhou, T. An empirical examination of continuance intention of mobile payment services. *Decis. Support Syst.* **2013**, *54*, 1085–1091. [CrossRef]
222. Lee, M.K.O.; Turban, E.; Matthew, K.O.; Lee, E.T. A trust model for consumer internet shopping. *Int. J. Electron. Commer.* **2001**, *6*, 75–91. [CrossRef]
223. Cheng, X.; Macaulay, L. Exploring Individual Trust Factors in Computer Mediated Group Collaboration: A Case Study Approach. *Gr. Decis. Negotiat.* **2014**, *23*, 533–560. [CrossRef]
224. Fang, Y.; Qureshi, I.; Sun, H.; McCole, P.; Ramsey, E.; Lim, K.H. Trust, Satisfaction, and Online Repurchase Intention: The Moderating Role of Perceived Effectiveness of E-Commerce Institutional Mechanisms. *MIS Q.* **2014**, *38*, 407–427. [CrossRef]
225. Tsiakis, T. Consumers' issues and concerns of perceived risk of information security in online framework. The marketing strategies. *Procedia Soc. Behav. Sci.* **2012**, *62*, 1265–1270. [CrossRef]
226. Sharma, S.K.; Govindaluri, S.M.; Al-Muharrami, S.; Tarhini, A. Predicting mobile banking adoption: A neural network approach. *J. Enterp. Inf. Manag.* **2016**, *29*, 222–237.

10

Macroeconomic Determinants of Nonperforming Loans of Romanian Banks

Teodor Hada [1], Nicoleta Bărbuță-Mișu [2,*], Iulia Cristina Iuga [3] and Dorin Wainberg [3,4]

[1] Department of Finance, "Bogdan Voda" University, 400525 Cluj-Napoca, Romania; teohada@yahoo.com
[2] Department of Business Administration, "Dunarea de Jos" University of Galati, 800008 Galati, Romania
[3] Department of Finance-Accounting, "1 Decembrie 1918" University of Alba Iulia, 510009 Alba Iulia, Romania; iuga_iulia@yahoo.com (I.C.I.); wainbergdorin@yahoo.com (D.W.)
[4] Department of Mathematics, "1 Decembrie 1918" University of Alba Iulia, 510009 Alba Iulia, Romania
* Correspondence: Nicoleta.Barbuta@ugal.ro.

Abstract: The banking sector plays an important role in the development of any economy. The performance of the loans in bank portfolios is a critical issue for the banking sector. The increased number of nonperforming loans (NPLs) after the financial crisis of 2008 has questioned the robustness of many banks and the stability of the entire sector. Our study aims to present the most important aspects related to NPLs and to investigate some macroeconomic determinant factors affecting the rate of NPLs in Romania. Based on a set of data for the period 2009–2019, the analysis of NPLs was made using linear regression. The results showed that all selected independent variables (exchange rates of the most used currencies (EUR, USD and CHF), unemployment rate, and inflation rate) have a significant impact on the dependent variable NPL. The study reveals strong correlations between NPLs and the macroeconomic factors studied and that the Romanian economy is clearly connected to the quality of the loan portfolios. Additionally, an econometric analysis of the empirical causes of NPLs shows that the RON–CHF exchange rate has been the main factor in increasing the NPL ratio in the last 5 years in Romania.

Keywords: nonperforming loans; macroeconomic factors; econometric model; exchange rate; unemployment rate; inflation rate

---

1. Introduction

The connection between nonperforming loans (NPLs) and bank losses has been analysed by authors from around the world and is considered a very important chapter in banking literature. Rising NPLs are often referred to as the failure of banks to manage credit policy.

In the last two decades, there has been a significant increase in the volume of loans granted by banks [1]. This increase was due to the process of deregulation of financial markets and the development of information technologies in the banking field. These processes have led to improved financial intermediation [2,3].

However, the financial crisis is also the result of the high NPL rate in the banking sector. The financial crisis of 2008 started in the USA and spread all over the world because all countries had trade relations with the USA. That crisis has been labelled as a cause of default on mortgages and loans. Increasing the NPL rate is the main reason for reducing bank revenues and, implicitly, for decreasing profits or recording losses. The reason for the NPL separation is the low repayment capacity of debtors, coupled with a high interest rate. Since 2008, the year of the onset of the global financial crisis, NPL levels have risen significantly.

As the existence of nonperforming loans, being a special category of loans, cannot be ignored, it is necessary to manage and separate this type of loan to a special portfolio of nonperforming loans.

The negative aspects and impact of these loans affect not only on the bank and its customers but also the economy on a macroeconomic level.

Bank practice has identified a multitude of causes generating nonperforming credits, grouped as follows, depending on the factors generating them:

- Macro level causes: political causes, economic causes, market causes, legislative causes, and competition causes.
- Causes generated by the loan beneficiaries: the weak management of the debtor companies.
- Causes independent of the customer's activity: fraud, takeovers, failure to comply with the provisions of the loan.
- Causes entirely due to the fault of the bank: a mistaken analysis of the customer's situation.

A flexible credit policy may also be the reason for a high volume of national credit, as happened in Romania. The bank sector serves the biggest part of the Romanian economy. The Romanian banks offer a large range of services to companies and individuals: conventional banking services, a variety of instruments for investments, and solutions for specialised financing. As the cornerstone of the national financial system and through its functions, the bank sector has special importance for the Romanian economy. The manner in which the bank sector develops its activity becomes an essential condition for the maintenance of financial stability and the insurance of sustainable economic development.

Therefore, it is clear why the NPL rate is crucial for banks. After the crisis in Romania in 2008, the unemployment rate increased significantly, the level of salaries of employees in state institutions decreased significantly—with a direct impact on NPLs (a large part of employees had contracted bank loans at that time)—and the inflation rate recorded significant changes. The exchange rates of RON–CHF, RON–EURO, and RON–USD almost doubled, affecting the repayment of loans (loans in progress and contracted before 2008) granted by banks in these currencies.

In this context, our study analyses the influence of certain macroeconomic factors from the category of the economic factors (the RON–CHF exchange rate, the RON–EUR exchange rate, the RON–USD exchange rate, the unemployment rate, the inflation rate) on the NPLs in the Romanian banking system. We mention that we chose the EUR, USD and CHF currencies due to their high proportion in Romanian foreign-currency credit granted to individuals and companies. Our paper compares the analysis before the initiation of the process of writing-off the unrecoverable NPLs (in 2014) and after 2014. Thus, the goal of this study is to present the most important aspects related to NPLs and to analyse the sensitivity of NPLs with respect to macroeconomic indicators in Romania. In particular, it uses regression analysis and a time series data set covering around 10 years (in the period 2009–2019) to examine the relationship between the nonperforming loan rate and some key macroeconomic variables that have changed significantly since 2008.

The paper is organised as follows. Section 2 offers a revision of the previous research on NPLs and influencing factors. Section 3 presents the data description and methodology used, including justification of the model used and tests developed. Section 4 shows the interpretation of the results based on the proposed model, compares the results of the models, and highlights similar results found in the literature. Section 5 presents the conclusions of our study, policy implications, and limitations.

2. Literature Review

There are many articles that have studied the links between the financial system and the economy. The most important examples are Bernanke and Gertler [4] and Bernanke, Gertler and Gilchrist [5] who developed the concept of the financial accelerator, arguing that credit markets are cyclical and that information asymmetry between creditors and debtors has an effect on amplifying and spreading shocks on the credit market. The Kiyotaki and Moore [6] model showed that if credit markets are imperfect, then relatively small shocks might be sufficient to explain business cycle fluctuations.

Competition has increased in the domestic and European banking markets, being strengthened by the deregulation process [7]. Banks have created permissive lending conditions to attract customers. Low interest rates, rising house prices and a stable economic environment characterised the precrisis period. This situation has led to the expansion of credit from both supply and demand. In our paper, we focus on the postcrisis period, characterised by high interest rates, falling house prices, and an unstable economic environment (rising unemployment, rising inflation, declining wages).

Several studies have examined the causes of NPLs and problem loans (e.g., Fernandez de Lis, Pagés and Saurina [8]; Boudriga, Taktak and Jellouli [9]; Espinoza and Prasad [10]).

An important number of studies in the literature on NPLs have focused exclusively on the role of macroeconomic or country-specific causes and have found that they have had the most significant effect. Espinoza and Prasad [10] tried to distinguish the determinants of NPLs for the Gulf Cooperative Council (GCC) banking system. The result of their study was that the NPL ratio increases when economic growth slows and risk aversion decreases, but also when interest rates rise. It is important to note that exchange rates and unemployment were not used as regressors due to the exchange rate regime and low and stable unemployment in the GCC countries.

Nkusu [11] used a methodology similar to that of Espinoza and Prasad [10]. He tested an econometric model that explains NPLs using only macrovariables and found that a worsening of the macroeconomic environment (i.e., a higher unemployment rate) is closely related to the problems of repayment/nonrepayment of loans and improving the macroeconomic environment implies a decrease in nonperforming loans. In recent years, interest in nonperforming loans and their determinants has increased significantly as we encounter more data published at the banking level by each country and at the level of the aggregate banking system. Many NPL studies have been published, whose results reveal important information about the quality of loan portfolios and, in general, the fragility of banks. Many researchers view NPLs as financial pollution with huge effects on both economic development and social life (e.g., Gonzales-Hermosillo [12], Barseghyan [13], Zeng [14]).

In the studies of Baboučak and Jančar [15] for the Czech Republic and Hoggarth, Logan and Zicchino [16] for the United Kingdom, the VAR methodology was used. They found that the important factors influencing financial stability and the quality of the loan portfolio were the dynamics of inflation and interest rates. Baboučak and Jančar [15] found evidence of a positive correlation between NPLs, unemployment rates and consumer price inflation, while GDP growth decreases the NPL rate. They also found that the actual appreciation of the effective exchange rate did not have an exaggerated influence on the NPL ratio. Regarding the Greek banking market, Louzis, Vouldis and Metaxas [17] examined the effect of various macroeconomic factors on NPLs, studying each type of loan in the nine largest Greek banks. The authors found that the real GDP growth rate, unemployment rate and lending rates have a strong negative effect on the NPL level, interpreting them as a sign of poor banking management.

Vogiazas and Nikolaidou [18] investigated the determinants of nonperforming creditors in the Romanian banking sector during the Greek crisis (December 2001–November 2010) and found that inflation and external GDP information are proportional and influence the credit risks of the banking system in the country. Our study is distinguished from the previous ones by investigating the impact of the exchange rate of the most used currencies (EUR, USD and CHF) on the granting of credit in Romania and the impact of unemployment and inflation rates on nonperforming loans after the crisis of 2008 (i.e., in the period 2009–2019, when the effects of the crisis were visible in all sectors of activity and especially on the banking system). We also present the most important determinants used in the literature for studying nonperforming loans, considering that the continuous analysis of the quality of the loans is a repetitive action, with several stages that are more important, namely, the stages before granting the credit, the granting of credit stage and the postgrant stage. Many studies have analysed various factors that can influence NPLs. In the next subsections, we present these factors grouped into the major factors of influence.

2.1. NPLs and NPL Data Analytics

Previous studies have examined the economic determinants of the NPL: "Greater capitalization, liquidity risks, poor credit quality, greater cost inefficiency and banking industry size significantly increase NPLs, while greater bank profitability lowers NPLs" [19]. The following variables significantly impact the NPL level: GDP real growth, share price, exchange rate and interest rate [20]. The assumption is that the macroeconomic variables and also the variables specific to the banks have an impact on the loan quality, depending on the loan category. For example, the NPLs from the Greek bank system can be mainly explained by macroeconomic variables (GDP, unemployment, interest rates, and public debts) and by the quality of the management [17].

Studies from various countries have identified the following factors that determine NPLs: inflation rate, unemployment rate, GDP level, ROA, ROE, liquidity, capital adequacy, size of the bank, volume of the deposits and interest rate [21]. For the saving banks, the GDP, the nonguaranteed loans and the net margins of interest affect NPLs, while for the commercial banks, the factors that affect NPLs are the size of the banks, their capital ratios and the expansion of their branches [7].

Knowledge-sharing processes and innovation processes of Islamic banks are integral parts of the survival and progress of business organisations. Another article conducted an empirical evaluation of the Czech public START program (funded by the European Regional Development Fund), a program that supported new entrepreneurs through zero-interest loans and credit guarantees. The obtained findings could not support the hypothesis of a positive impact of the programme on a firm's performance [22].

A model was created using latent variables of capital adequacy, operations, asset quality, size and profile of the countries in which they were based—this model can predict bank profitability. The study was conducted on the 100 largest banks between 2011 and 2015 [23].

2.2. NPLs and Macro Level Factors

Most studies considered macroeconomic factors as factors influencing NPLs.

The real GDP: Some authors have stated a negative relationship between GDP and NPLs [24,25]. Another study uses the data from the USA bank sector and takes into consideration real GDP per capita, inflation and total loans as independent variables, and the NPL ratio as a dependent variable. All the selected independent variables have a significant impact on the dependent variable, but, still, the values of the coefficients are not too high [26].

The economic growth: Another idea showed that NPLs affect the economy by slowing economic growth [27]. A study that analysed the situation in Hong Kong remarked that the NPL ratio grows together with the growth of the nominal interest rate but decreases once the inflation increases with economic growth [28].

The lending rate: Research on Italy found that the lending rate has a negative relationship with NPLs [24].

The unemployment rate: Some studies concluded that NPLs grow when the unemployment rate is high, while [29] showed that the unemployment rate has a negative impact on the quality of the bank loans [24]. NPLs increase when the unemployment rate grows and the debtors are confronted with difficulties related to the return of the loan [25].

The inflation: Inflation is positively connected to NPLs [29], while a lower inflation rate has a positive influence on the debtors' financial conditions and, eventually, on the recovery of the loans, meaning that it presents a positive relationship between the inflation rate and NPLs [30].

The market competition: The economic development of the country results in market growth. Market competition compels enterprises to increase their activity, i.e., to concentrate it [31]. Rahman et al. [32] sustained that taking effective measures to increase bank competition can create a level playing field for other banks and may reduce strict collateral requirements for companies.

The exchange rate: The high number of NPLs leads to a depreciation of the exchange rate [27] and hence NPLs have, as a result, a depreciation of the exchange rate [29]. At the same time, some authors affirmed that a depreciation of the national currency can lead to more NPLs [33].

The boom/recession/expansion period in the economy: The quality of bank loans of Italian banks is lower during recession periods and higher during expansion periods. The internal factors that influence NPLs are efficiency, the indicator of income from interest to total assets, and the slow growth of loans. The external factors affecting NPLs are the GDP and the interest rates [34].

The governance indicators: The governance indicators are significant factors influencing NPLs [35]. Using techniques for the estimation of data, a study examined the determinant factors of NPLs in the Turkish bank system. The results of the study showed that the determinant factors of NPLs changed after the crisis and that the macroeconomic and political determinant factors have a higher significance [36].

The bank concentration: Bank concentration may reduce NPLs by enhancing market power and boosting bank profits so that high profits can provide a "buffer" against adverse shocks [37]. Çifter [38] examined the effect of bank concentration on nonperforming loans (NPLs) for ten Central and Eastern European (CEE) countries and concluded that the relationship between the concentration of banks and NPLs, with regard to CEE countries, is ambiguous.

2.3. NPL and Nonspecific Factors

There is still a group of factors that we have included in the group of nonspecific factors because their influence differs from country to country. This group of factors would be the factors that influence trust in internet banking (such as provided information, e-banking system, a bank's website and bank characteristics). Another factor that falls into this group is perceived value. The results of the studies show that three components of perceived value (economic value, comfort value and emotional value) increase the intention to use banks that are only on the internet [39]. Another study contributed to the specialised literature on the correlation between ecological lending and credit risks and concluded that the institutional pressure of green credit policy has a positive effect on both the environmental performance and financial performance of banks [40]. Some authors combined the two large groups of factors in their studies. They found a positive relationship between GDP growth, inflation and bank performance, whereas a negative relationship between tax burden and performance [41]. The bad-management and moral-hazard hypotheses explain a significant part of NPLs [42].

3. Data and Methodology

3.1. The Dependent and Independent Variables

As defined in the literature, nonperforming loans are the loans that are delayed for a long period, according to the loan contract. According to Tesfaye [43], any loan that is not recovered in due time is known as nonperforming. The rate of nonperforming loans, according to the ABE definition, is calculated using the following formula: nonperforming exposures from loans and advances/exposures from loans and advances. According to the ABE definition, which was nationally implemented through Order 6/2014 of the National Bank of Romania, nonperforming exposures are the one of the following criteria: (1) there are significant exposures, with over 90 days' delay from the recovery date, and (2) it is considered that lacking a real guarantee, it is improbable for the debtor to integrally return his debts, disregarding the existence of a certain sum or a certain number of delays in payment.

In this study, we used the rate of nonperforming loans (NPLs) from the Romanian bank system as a dependent variable. With regard to the independent variables, we used the following macroeconomic factors: RON–CHF exchange rate (RON_CHF), RON–EUR exchange rate (RON_EUR), RON–USD exchange rate (RON_USD), the unemployment rate (UR) and the harmonised index of consumer prices (HICP) inflation rate.

The variables used in this article were selected from the total of possible variables based on the criterion of impact on nonperforming loans of the population, and, moreover, these variables changed significantly during the analysed period compared to the other variables listed above. Thus, following the documentation at a series of banks in Romania, we found that

- the variable unemployment rate influences the outstanding loans of the individuals because the credited persons have fewer possibilities to repay the loan taken due to a lack of income, the unemployment benefits being small in Romania (below 100 euro/month). We have considered this variable in the study because of the consequences of the crisis, which led to more bankruptcies, the reduction of activity in many sectors, followed by staff lay-offs or a reduction of monthly salaries, both from the private and public sectors. This situation increased the unemployment rate and implicitly reduced the income of individuals. In Romania, the majority of active persons used real estate loans, mortgage loans or personal loans for purchasing buildings or other durable goods that were granted in CHF, EUR and USD, and the individuals that were laid off or had their salaries cut found it impossible to reimburse credits and this generated the increase in NPLs;

- the inflation rate influenced the level of outstanding loans by the fact that a high inflation rate reduces the purchasing power of the population, generating the decrease of the population's real income because a great part of the income is used for consumption. Therefore, the reduction of the individuals' incomes leads to a reduction in the ability to repay loans. Thus, inflation can negatively affect the debtor's service capacity [44]. Inflation negatively affects the ability of debtors to repay creditors [11]. We expect a negative impact of inflation on NPLs as a rapid rise in prices exacerbates market frictions, forcing banks to exercise caution in lending [45].

- the RON–EUR, RON–USD and RON–CHF exchange rates significantly reduced the population's income and influenced a decrease in the credit repayment capacity by the fact that during the analysed period, the RON–CHF, RON–EUR, and RON–USD exchange rates increased permanently. The reduction of the population's income was generated by the fact that Romanian individuals received their salaries in RON and had to pay loans granted in EUR, USD and CHF. The increase in the exchange rate of these currencies generated an increase of monthly credit rate, and this situation made it impossible for individuals to pay their debts to banks.

3.2. Data

The study used an explanatory analysis and also an econometric analysis based on the data from 2009 until January 2019 in order to investigate the relationship between NPLs and the 5 macroeconomic factors selected and presented in Section 3.1. For each variable, 110 monthly values were considered. The data for our study were taken from the metadata database of the National Institute of Statistics of Romania (www.insse.ro), from the database of the National Bank of Romania (www.bnr.ro), and from the Eurostat database (https://ec.europa.eu/eurostat/data/database). For econometric analysis, we used the statistical package EViews.

A summary table of statistics for these variables is given below (Table 1).

Analysing data presented in Table 1, we found that the average rate of NPLs is 13.04%, the maximum value being 22.52%. Related to the evolution of the exchange rate, we can see that the RON–CHF exchange rate increased by 52.86% in the period analysed, the RON–EUR exchange rate increased by 14.91%, and the RON–USD exchange rate increased by 50.70%. The average unemployment rate was 6.29%, and the maximum value of the inflation rate was 5.98%.

A graphic representation of the NPL rate with 110 values (calculated monthly, starting at 1 December 2009 until 31 January 2019) is presented in Figure 1. We observe that the trend increases for the period 2009–2014 and decreases between 2015 and 2019. This makes us think that there may be a structural break in the NPL ratio.

Table 1. Descriptive statistics for the considered variables (Source: authors' estimations).

Variable	Mean	Std. Dev.	Min.	Max.
NPL	13.04	4.79	4.95	22.52
RON_CHF	3.75	0.38	2.80	4.28
RON_EUR	4.44	0.15	4.09	4.70
RON_USD	3.60	0.41	2.84	4.28
UR	6.29	1.09	3.70	7.90
HICP	97.62	4.90	84.03	105.98

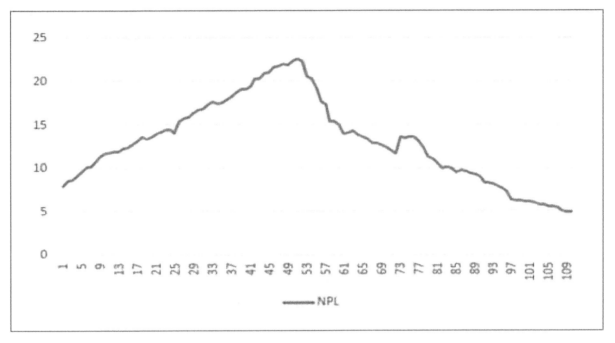

Source: database of the National Bank of Romania (www.bnr.ro)

Figure 1. The evolution of the NPL rate for the 2009–2019 period.

The novelty element in the general representation of banking activity from 2014 is the initiation of the process of writing-off the uncollectable nonperforming loans, following the recommendations of the National Bank of Romania, a process considered a necessary condition for the sustainable relaunch of credit. The year 2014 registered a significant decrease in nonperforming loans registered in the balance of the banks because of the operations of direct decrease in the value of unrecoverable loans, covered in a high percentage with adjustments for depreciation, that were made at the recommendation of the National Bank of Romania. Considering the limited efficiency of the techniques previously used by commercial banks in order to diminish the number of nonperforming loans—most often restructuration/rescheduling and foreclosure—the National Bank of Romania recommended the cleaning of portfolios in four stages:

- Writing-off the entirely provisioned nonperforming loan (the banks reserved their right to recover the loan).
- The integral forecasting and write-off of loans with a payment delay longer than 360 days.
- The integral forecasting and write-off of loans to companies in insolvency.
- An external audit of the provisions constituted according to IFRS and the guarantees.

The result of these activities was a decrease in the NPL rate from 20.4% in March to 13.9% in December 2014 (see Figure 1).

In our analysis, the dependent variable rate of NPLs is studied by considering as independent variables the exchange rates (RON–CHF, RON–EUR, RON–USD), the unemployment rate (UR) and the inflation rate (HICP), measured in the same statistic interval. As noted on the National Institute of Statistics of Romania website (www.insse.ro), we observe an upward trend of the inflation rate and a downward trend of the unemployment rate during the analysed period (starting on 1 December 2009 until 31 January 2019). From the National Bank of Romania website (www.bnr.ro), we observed an upward trend, with small oscillations for all three exchange rates (RON–CHF, RON–EUR, RON–USD).

The model chosen for studying the influence of the independent variables selected on the NPL rate is the multiple regression model, presented in the form of a linear relation:

$$y_i = \beta_1 x_{1i} + \beta_2 x_{2i} + \ldots + \beta_p x_{pi} + u_i, \tag{1}$$

where $i = 1, \ldots, n$, y_i represents the values of the explained variable Y, and $x_{1i}, x_{2i}, \ldots, x_{pi}$ are the values of the independent variables $X_1, \ldots, X_p$. The coefficients $\beta_1, \beta_2, \ldots, \beta_p$ are the parameters of the regression model, and u_i are the values of the residual variable.

3.3. The Estimation of the Parameters and the Validation of the Regression Model

In this section, we made a univariate analysis of the series analysing the presence of unit roots through the augmented Dickey–Fuller (ADF) test in order to determine the order of integration of each series.

The results of the augmented Dickey–Fuller test is presented in Table 2.

Table 2. Unit root test (source: authors' estimations).

Unit Root Test—ADF		
H0 = There is a Unit Root		
Variable	**Statistical Value of the Series in First Differences**	**Reject H0 at 95%**
NPL	−1.931625	Yes
RON_CHF	−1.695445	Yes
RON_EUR	−2.885321	Yes
RON_USD	−2.969274	Yes
UR	−4.433165	Yes
HICP	−1.359764	Yes

Notes: The number of lags was determined according to the Akaike criterion.

From the information provided in Table 2, we conclude that all the variables are first-order integrated, I(1).

4. Results and Discussion

4.1. Interpretation of the Obtained Results

In this section, we obtain the elements of the multiple regression model, as well as the values of certain indicators and tests for the appreciation of the validity and quality of the equation attached to the model. Therefore, after creating the group formed from the variables presented above, we defined the equation corresponding to the multiple regression model, with the rate of the nonperforming loans (NPLs) as the dependent variable and RON–CHF, RON–EUR, RON–USD, UR and HICP as independent variables, also defining the constant variable C, corresponding to the impact of other exogenous variables influencing NPLs, which are not considered in the present analysis. The estimation of the parameters in the equation of the regression model was made using the method of least squares.

The obtained values, representing, at the same time, the coefficients of the variables in the regression model and the results from the tests, are presented in Table 3.

Table 3. Estimations results (source: authors' estimations).

Dependent Variable: NPL				
Explanatory Variable	Coefficient	Std. Error	t-Statistic	Prob.
RON_CHF	1.695445	1.820228	0.931447	0.3538
RON_EUR	15.50740	3.957474	3.918510	0.0002
RON_USD	5.969274	1.460210	4.087956	0.0001
UR	4.433165	0.333343	13.29911	0.0000
HICP	0.339662	0.111708	3.040627	0.0030
C	−101.6536	13.38608	−7.593980	0.0000
R-squared	0.781285			
Adjusted R-squared	0.770770			
Prob(F-statistic)	0.000000			

One of the most important assumptions of any time series model is that the underlying process is the same across all observations in the sample. It is, therefore, necessary to analyse carefully the time series data that include periods of violent change (as we observed for the NPL ratio, in Figure 1). A tool that is particularly useful in this regard is the Chow test. The null hypothesis for the test is that there is no breakpoint (i.e., that the data set can be represented with a single regression line). We assumed that there is no structural break between the first five years and the last five years of the period.

As the content of Table 4 confirms, the null hypothesis is rejected, i.e., the regression is not stable over the considered data sets. Because of this structural break, we will estimate the model for the 2009–2014 period (Section 4.3) and 2015–2019 period (Section 4.4) separately.

Table 4. Regression stability test (Chow test; source: authors' estimations).

Score	C.V.	p-Value	Stable?	5.0%
21.813	2.461	0.00%	FALSE	

4.2. An Overview of the Period 2009–2019

From Table 3, we find a linear relationship between NPLs and their explanatory factors, statistically significant at a significance level of 1% (Prob(F-statistic) = 0.000). The sign of each coefficient is the expected one, being positive. If each of the considered macroeconomic components increases, nonperforming loans will also increase. All the variables studied place the level of NPLs at 78.12% (R-squared = 0.7812).

Therefore, based on the values above, we can affirm that the model of linear multiple regression can be accepted for the correlation and interdependence between the NPL rate and the macroeconomic indicators: the exchange rate, the unemployment rate, and inflation. However, as we mentioned before, this regression is not stable, according to the Chow test, and because of that, we have split the 2009–2019 period into two parts and will study each part separately.

In the Coefficient column from the results presented in Table 3, we have the coefficients of the equation of the regression model. The Variable column shows the names of the variables to which the coefficient corresponds. Each parameter estimated in this manner measures the contribution of the independent variable to the dependent variable. Hence, the regression equation is

$$NPL = 1.69 * RON/CHF + 15.50 * RON/EUR + 5.96 * RON/USD \\ + 4.43 * UR + 0.33 * INFL - 101.65 \tag{2}$$

Additionally, another method to verify the reliability of the regression parameters is represented by the method of confidence intervals. The confidence intervals are presented in Table 5. We have intervals with a confidence coefficient of 90% and 95%. Therefore, we can affirm with a confidence of

95% that the growth of one percent in the unemployment rate leads to the growth of NPLs between 3.77% and 5.09%.

Table 5. The confidence intervals (source: authors' estimations).

		Coefficient Confidence Intervals			
		90% CI		95% CI	
Variable	Coefficient	Low	High	Low	High
RON_CHF	1.695	−1.325	4.716	1.914	5.305
RON_EUR	15.50	8.939	22.075	7.659	23.355
RON_USD	5.969	3.545	8.392	3.073	8.864
UR	4.433	3.879	4.986	3.772	5.094
INFL	0.339	0.154	0.525	0.118	0.561
C	−101.653	−123.869	−79.437	−128.198	−75.108

An evaluation obtained for the considered values of this formula is given in Figure 2.

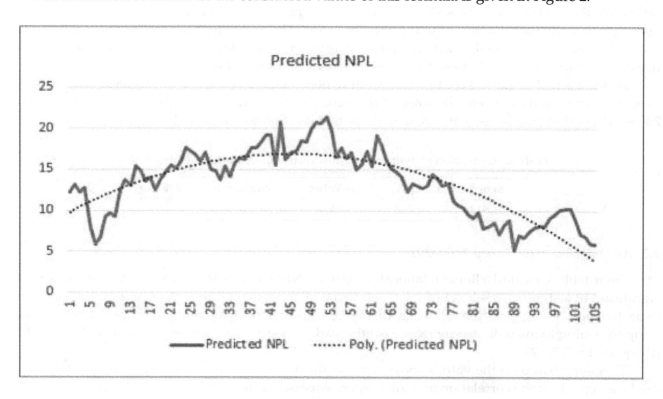

Figure 2. The graphic representation of the regression model for the 2009–2019 period.

As we can see, the trend line for the predicted NPL rate is described by a second-degree polynomial curve. This will sustain a separate study for each of the periods of 2009–2014 and 2015–2019.

4.3. A Model for the 2009–2014 Period

As we observed in Figure 1, NPL had an upward trend in the 2009–2014 period. The values of the regression model for this period are given in Table 6.

Here, we have the elements of the multiple regression model and also the values of certain indicators and tests for the appreciation of the reliability and quality of the equation attached to this model.

Thus, based on the values of these tests, we can affirm that the correlation and interdependence between the NPL and the considered independent variables are represented very well by a model of linear multiple regression.

Hence, the regression equation is

$$NPL = 1.76 * RON\_CHF + 9.50 * RON\_EUR + 2.40 * RON\_USD \\ + 2.55 * UR + 1.54 * INFL - 94.207 \tag{3}$$

From here, we can affirm that a growth of one unit in the RON–EUR exchange rate leads to a growth of the NPL rate by 9.5%. Our result is consistent with the study of Farhan et al. [46], who found that unemployment, inflation and exchange rates have a significant positive relationship with NPLs of the Pakistani banking sector. The findings obtained by Bock and Demyanets [27] imply that the exchange rate is one of the main determinants of NPLs.

Table 6. Estimation results for the 2009–2014 period (source: authors' estimations).

Dependent Variable: NPL				
Explanatory Variable	**Coefficient**	**Std. Error**	**t-Statistic**	**Prob.**
RON_CHF	1.716	1.686	1.018	0.113
RON_EUR	9.502	2.359	4.474	0.000
RON_USD	2.405	1.858	1.909	0.005
UR	2.550	1.602	0.913	0.265
INFL	1.547	1.087	6.270	0.000
Const.	−94.207	10.566	−7.950	0.000
R-squared	0.860568			
Adjusted R-squared	0.847893			
Prob(F-statistic)	0.000000			

Our results show that a growth of 1% in the unemployment rate will lead to a growth in the NPL rate by 2.55%. These are in line with the studies of Popa et al. [47], Ghosh [19], Makri et al. [48], Messai and Jouini [49] and Skarica [50]. This result is also reinforced by Louzis et al. [17], who found in their study that NPLs can be explained mainly by macroeconomic variables such as unemployment. The unemployment rate is one of the major determinants of NPLs, as stated by Nkusu [11]. According to Cifter's [38] study, the unemployment rate is the most important macroeconomic factor for NPLs, and a percentage increase in the unemployment rate increases NPLs by 3.61 percentage points for the group of countries analysed by him. Using GMM and quarterly data of Euro-area banks in the 1990–2015 period, Anastasiou et al. [51] found that macrovariables such as unemployment and growth exert a strong influence.

A growth of 1% in the inflation rate will determine a growth of the NPL rate by 1.54%. This result is similar to the study of Charalambakis et al. [52], who found that the key factors that can explain the movements in NPLs are the unemployment rate and the inflation rate. The results of the study by Donath et al. [53] showed that the variation of NPLs had a positive correlation with inflation as well as unemployment rates, which is the result found in our study.

In Table 7, we have the confidence coefficients intervals of 90% and 95% for our model. Hence, we can say, with a confidence of 95%, that an increase of 1% in the unemployment rate leads to an increase in the NPL rate of between 1.33% and 3.75%.

In Figure 3, we have the representation of the predicted NPL rate according to (3) for 61 values (calculated monthly, starting on 1 December 2009 until 31 December 2014). Here, the trend line for the predicted NPL rate is an upward linear one.

Table 7. The confidence intervals (source: authors' estimations).

		Coefficient Confidence Intervals			
		90% CI		95% CI	
Variable	Coefficient	Low	High	Low	High
RON_CHF	1.716	−1.105	4.537	−1.663	5.095
RON_EUR	9.502	2.209	16.796	0.766	18.239
RON_USD	2.405	−1.297	5.513	−2.682	6.127
UR	2.550	1.443	3.557	1.334	3.756
INFL	1.547	1.401	1.693	1.372	1.722
Const.	−94.207	−113.558	−74.857	−117.386	−71.028

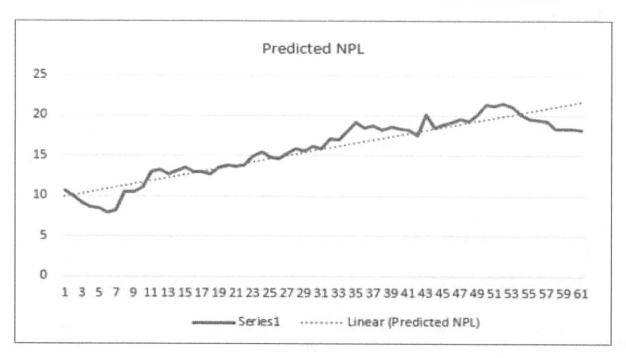

Figure 3. The graphic representation of the regression model for the 2009–2014 period.

4.4. A Model for the 2015–2019 Period

We observed in Figure 1 that NPL had an upward trend in the 2009–2014 period. The NPL level started to decrease in June 2014. The novelty element in the general view on the bank activity in 2014 was the initiation of the write-off process for uncollectible NPLs, following the recommendations of the National Bank of Romania to credit institutions. We formulated below the model of multiple regression based only on the data from the period 2015–2019 (the years when the NPL rate decreased) in order to observe if the same independent variables have a stronger impact on the NPL, similar to the previously formulated model.

We used the same techniques as above to study the mentioned period. Hence, in order to formulate the regression model, we defined the rate of nonperforming loans (NPLs) as a dependent variable.

The independent variables that are taken in consideration are the same: the exchange rates (RON–CHF, RON–EUR, RON–USD), the unemployment rate (UR) and the inflation rate (HICP), measured in the same statistic interval (from 1 December 2009 to 31 January 2019).

Using the same technique that we have described above, with the help of the software EViews, we obtained the elements of the multiple regression model and also the values of certain indicators and tests for the appreciation of the reliability and quality of the equation attached to this model. The obtained values, representing the coefficients of the variables in the model of linear multiple regression and, at the same time, the results of the tests on the model, are presented in Table 8.

Table 8. Estimations results (source: authors' estimations).

Dependent Variable: NPL				
Variable	Coefficient	Std. Error	t-Statistic	Prob.
RON_CHF	2.224377	1.824114	1.219429	0.2293
RON_EUR	−5.691265	3.409805	−1.669088	0.1024
RON_USD	−0.706060	1.189802	−0.593426	0.5560
UR	2.000545	0.218424	9.159005	0.0000
HICP	0.194019	0.075723	2.562230	0.0140
C	37.83326	15.77087	2.398933	0.0209
R-squared	0.954209			
Adjusted R-squared	0.948885			
Prob(F-statistic)	0.000000			

We will further present the manner in which we use these values in the study of linear regression with the five considered explanatory variables. The R-squared statistic: In the present case, we can appreciate that 95.4% of the NPL rate value is explained by the five considered independent variables. S.E. of regression (S): The fact that we have a value of S = 0.69 in the present case is another confirmation of the fact that the regression model is representative of the relationships between the considered variables. Another confirmation of the obtained model is given by the Fisher test, F-statistic, and its associated probability, Prob(F-statistic). The econometric model of multiple regression using the NPL rate as a dependent variable is a correct one and can be used in the analyses of macroeconomic forecasts. The statistic of the Durbin–Watson test (Durbin–Watson stat): In the present case, the value of the test is 0.85, corresponding to a positive linear dependence, meaning that a general growth of the values of the independent variables leads to a growth of the NPL rate.

Thus, based on the values of these tests, we can affirm that the correlation and interdependence between the NPL rate and macroeconomic indicators—the exchange rate, the unemployment rate and inflation—is represented very well in the model of linear multiple regression.

Hence, the regression equation is

$$NPL = 2.22 * RON/CHF - 5.69 * RON/EUR - 0.70 * RON/USD \\ + 2 * UR + 0.19 * INFL + 37.83 \tag{4}$$

We observe that the signs of the coefficients are different in this case. This will give us the right to say that the model has not given us consistent estimates and we expect endogeneity for this five-year period of 2015–2019.

An evaluation of this formula, obtained for the values of the independent variables considered for the calculation period, e.g., for 49 values (calculated monthly, starting on 1 January 2015 until 31 January 2019), is represented in Figure 4. We can affirm that for a growth of one unit in the RON-CHF exchange rate, the NPL rate will increase by 2.22%, while a growth of one percent in the unemployment rate will lead to a growth of 2% in the NPL rate. At the same time, we observe that the influence of the constant variable is important. Therefore, the factors taken into consideration in our analysis have an important impact on the dependent variables, determining its decrease by 37.83 units.

Here, the trend line for the predicted NPL rate is a downward linear one. In order to establish the significance level for each coefficient, we use the values of the Prob. column from Table 9. Another method for the confirmation of the validity of the regression parameters is the method of confidence intervals. We obtained the following intervals.

We obtained, as Table 9 shows, the intervals with a confidence coefficient of 90% and 95%. Therefore, in the example given, we can affirm with a confidence of 95% that an increase of 1% in the inflation rate leads to an increase of the NPL rate between 1.56% and 2.44%.

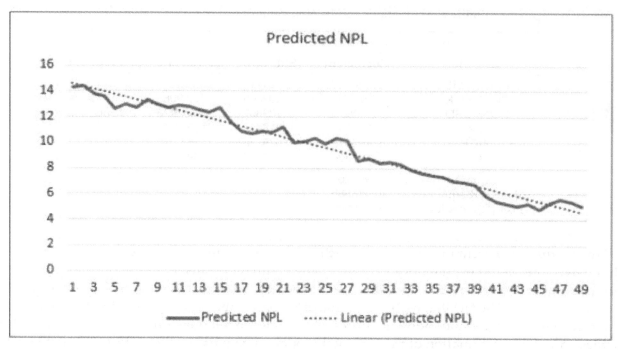

Figure 4. The graphic representation of the regression model for the 2015–2019 period.

Table 9. The confidence intervals (source: authors' estimations).

		Coefficient Confidence Intervals			
		90% CI		95% CI	
Variable	Coefficient	Low	High	Low	High
RON_CHF	2.224377	−0.842087	5.290842	−1.454299	5.903054
RON_EUR	−5.691265	−11.42339	0.040859	−12.56779	1.185263
RON_USD	−0.706060	−2.706201	1.294081	−3.105524	1.693405
UR	2.000545	1.633359	2.367731	1.560051	2.441039
HICP	0.194019	0.066724	0.321314	0.041310	0.346728
C	37.83326	11.32131	64.34521	6.028265	69.63825

4.5. Comparative Analysis for Periods Analysed

If we compare the influencing factors of the NFL rate analysed in this paper for both periods of 2009–2014 and 2015–2019, we may conclude that

- in the period 2009–2014, an increase in the RON–CHF exchange rate of 1% leads to an increase in the NPL rate of 1.70%, while, in the period 2015–2019, the same increase leads to an increase in the NPL rate of 2.22%, which shows that after the recommendations of the National Bank of Romania, the credits granted in CHF still remain a generating factor of NPLs in Romania. This is explained by the fact that due to the increase in the RON–CHF exchange rate, many debtors, after paying the monthly rate of the credit for 8–10 years, have a debt higher than the initial value of the credit.
- in the period 2009–2014, an increase in the RON–EUR exchange rate of 1% leads to an increase in the NPL rate of 9.50%, while in the period 2015–2019, the same increase leads to a decrease in the NPL rate of 5.69%, which shows that after the recommendations of the National Bank of Romania, the RON–EUR exchange rate is not a generating factor of NPLs in Romania.
- in the period 2009–2014, an increase in the RON–USD exchange rate of 1% leads to an increase in the NPL rate of 2.40%, while in the period 2015–2019, the same increase leads to a decrease of NPL rate with 0.71%, which shows that after the recommendations of the National Bank of Romania, the RON–USD exchange rate is not a generating factor of NPLs in Romania.

- in the period 2009–2014, an increase in the unemployment rate of 2.55% leads to an increase in the NPL rate of 2.40%, while in the period 2015–2019, the same increase leads to a decrease in the NPL rate of 2.00%, which shows that after 2014, the unemployment rate still remains a generating factor of NPLs in Romania.

- in the period 2009–2014, an increase in the inflation rate of 1% leads to an increase in the NPL rate of 1.55%, while in the period 2015–2019, the same increase leads to a decrease in the NPL rate of 0.19%, which shows that after 2014, the inflation rate is not a generating factor of NPLs in Romania, especially due to the Romanian government's efforts to maintain the inflation rate within the limits recommended by the European Union.

5. Conclusions

The present paper identifies several macroeconomic factors influencing the nonperforming loans rate in the Romanian banking system. The results are, in general, comparable to the results from other countries. The econometric analysis of the empirical determinants of the NPL rate presented in this paper shows that the exchange rate and the unemployment rate were the main causes for the growth of NPLs for both analysed periods of 2009–2014 and 2015–2019 (after 2014, what took place was the write-off of uncollectable NPLs at the recommendation of the National Bank of Romania). We applied in the present study an econometric model that helped us to identify the factors influencing the NPL rate in Romania, and we observed strong relations between the NPL rate and various macroeconomic factors. Our results are in general agreement with the literature because, from a macroeconomic perspective, the exchange rate, the unemployment rate and the inflation rate seem to be three supplementary factors affecting the NPL index, showing that the situation of the Romanian economy is clearly connected to the quality of loan portfolios. Related to the causes of nonperforming loans, after a literature review, we can conclude that nonperforming loans depend on several factors. We cannot make a list of all the causes because there are multiple causes, and these depend on macro-level factors and the specificity of each bank and its customers.

The writing-off process was individually transposed by a decrease of the number of banks registering NPL rates above the threshold for high risk, according to the ABE (up to 14% of the total number of Romanian credit institutions). The foreign currency loans continue to represent approximately 45% of total loans registered in Romania. An uncontrolled transaction of the exposure of RON to foreign currencies could have dramatic consequences on the situation of the foreign currency of the country and on the stability of the banking sector. The volatility of exchange rates, combined with the impact of the continued cutting of the workforce in Romania, along with the over-indebtedness of a significant part of the population, contribute to a growth of the causes for concern of the customers and the disturbance of the market, generating supplementary legislative and administrative pressure on the banks. In order to rectify the situation, during the last two years, Romanian banks have made new efforts in financial education and, supported by new regulations, mainly changed their position related to RON. The negative effects of COVID-19 on the Romanian economy are associated with expectations of increasing the probability of default in the real sector, as well as expectations of moderation of lending activity. In addition, the risk regarding uncertain and unpredictable legislative framework in the Romanian financial-banking field remains high, having the potential to put pressure on bank solvency and to limit access to the financing of potential borrowers.

The econometric analysis of the empirical causes of the NPL rate presented in this paper shows that the RON/CHF exchange rate has been the main factor in increasing the NPL ratio in the last 5 years in Romania. The coefficient of this explanatory variable is high from an economic point of view, proving that excessive credit in Swiss francs in the period 2006–2008 has significantly affected financial stability. High levels of NPLs are a legacy of the 2008 crisis.

The literature shows that the level of nonperforming loans must be at a low a level as possible because it affects the profitability of banks. For this aspect to become achievable, bank institutions must approach a prudent credit policy and create a connected environment between the present economic–financial context and the aspects related to the classification of risk.

Sustainable development needs to be applied in all the fields of activity, including the banking sector. Referring to the present context in the development of the credit system, we can easily observe the fact that credit operations are profitable and risky at the same time. In relation to international experience before the world crisis and to European experience in the recent past, we observed that a global strategy is more efficient in order to solve nonperforming loans. A multilateral strategy for solving nonpayment in the European bank system could combine more attentive supervision, institutional reforms for insolvency and the expansion of markets for the debts in difficulty. These measures need to be supported by an exchange of the fiscal regime and by reforms for the improvement of the access to information.

The problem of nonperforming loans is serious, and the recommended measures need to be applied as soon as possible. Some measures, such as stricter supervision, can be immediately implemented. Other measures, as the judicial reforms and the development of market infrastructure, will take more time to be implemented. As a result of our analysis performed on a period of ten years, 2009 to 2019, we can observe a series of transformations that have taken place in the evolution of nonperforming loans. The greatest challenge in fulfilling of the objectives of the sustainable development of banks is represented, on the one hand, by the understanding of the concept in relation to the business field, and, on the other hand, by the exclusive placement of sustainability within the exclusive responsibility of NGOs and governments. There is a need to understand that bank responsibility does not mean only philanthropic actions and sponsorships; there is more to it. The international bank community has proven, through the examples to be followed, that it understands the importance, necessity and reliability of sustainable development.

The limits of the present research refer to the focus on the influence of macroeconomic factors on the NPL rate without including nonspecific factors, such as the degree of implementation of e-banking (meaning internet banking and mobile banking), perceived value, and green credit policy.

The further directions of research may consist of studying the influence of some less quantifiable factors on the NPL rate, such as trust in banks, the e-banking system, ecological lending, and studying the competitive advantage of the Romanian banks entering into new business niches connected with sustainable development or integrating sustainable development into the banking sector.

Author Contributions: Conceptualization, T.H.; methodology, N.B.-M. and D.W.; validation, I.C.I. and D.W.; formal analysis, I.C.I. and N.B.-M.; investigation, I.C.I. and T.H.; resources, N.B.-M.; writing—original draft preparation, D.W., writing—review and editing, N.B.-M., D.W., and I.C.I. All authors have read and agreed to the published version of the manuscript.

Funding: This work was funded by the project "Excellence, Performance and Competitiveness in Research, Development and Innovation Activities at "Dunarea de Jos" University of Galati" ("EXPERT"), financed by the Romanian Ministry of Research and Innovation in the framework of Programme 1—Development of the National Research and Development System, subprogramme 1.2—Institutional Performance—Projects for Financing Excellence in Research, Development and Innovation, Contract no. 14PFE/17.10.2018.

Acknowledgments: This work was supported by the project "Excellence, Performance and Competitiveness in Research, Development and Innovation Activities at "Dunarea de Jos" University of Galati" ("EXPERT"), financed by the Romanian Ministry of Research and Innovation in the framework of Programme 1—Development of the National Research and Development System, subprogramme 1.2—Institutional Performance—Projects for Financing Excellence in Research, Development and Innovation, Contract no. 14PFE/17.10.2018. We also sincerely thank the anonymous reviewers and editors for their valuable comments and suggestions.

References

1. Cingolani, M. Finance Capitalism: A Look at the European Financial Accounts. *Panoeconomicus* **2013**, *60*, 249–290. [CrossRef]
2. Panopoulou, M. *Technological Change and Corporate Strategy in the Greek Banking Industry*; Center of Planning and Economic Research: Athens, Greece, 2005.

3. Rinaldi, L.; Sanchis-Arellano, A. *Household Debt Sustainability, What Explains Household Non-Performing Loans? An Empirical Analysis*; Working Paper Series 570; European Central Bank: Frankfurt, France, 2006.

4. Bernanke, B.; Gertler, M. Agency Costs, Net Worth, and Business Fluctuations. *Am. Econ. Rev.* **1989**, *79*, 14–31.

5. Bernanke, B.; Gertler, M.; Gilchrist, S. *The Financial Accelerator in a Quantitative Business Cycle Framework*; Working Paper No. 6455; NBER: Cambridge, MA, USA, 1998.

6. Kiyotaki, N.; Moore, J. Credit chains. *J. Political Econ.* **1997**, *105*, 211–248. [CrossRef]

7. Salas, V.; Saurina, J. Credit risk in two institutional regimes: Spanish commercial and savings banks. *J. Financ. Serv. Res.* **2002**, *22*, 203–224. Available online: https://link.springer.com/article/10.1023/A:1019781109676 (accessed on 17 May 2020). [CrossRef]

8. Fernandez de Lis, S.; Martinez Pagés, J.; Saurina, J. *Credit Growth, Problem Loans and Credit Risk Provisioning in Spain*; Banco de Espana Working Paper 18; Bank of Spain: Madrid, Spain, 2000.

9. Boudriga, A.; Taktak, N.; Jellouli, J. Bank Specific, Business and Institutional Environment Determinants of Nonperforming Loans: Evidence from MENA Countries. In Proceedings of the Economic Research Forum 16th Annual Conference, Cairo, Egypt, 9 January 2009.

10. Espinoza, R.A.; Prasad, A. *Nonperforming Loans in the GCC Banking System and Their Macroeconomic Effects*; Working Paper WP/10/224; International Monetary Fund: Washington, DC, USA, 2010.

11. Nkusu, M. *Non-Performing Loans and Macrofinancial Vulnerabilities in Advanced Economies*; WP/11/161, IMF Working Papers; IMF: Washington, DC, USA, 2011.

12. Gonzales-Hermosillo, B. Developing indicators to provide early warnings of banking crises. *Financ. Dev.* **1999**, *36*, 36–39.

13. Barseghyan, L. Non-performing loans, prospective bailouts, and Japan's slowdown. *J. Monet. Econ.* **2010**, *57*, 873–890. [CrossRef]

14. Zeng, S. Bank Non-Performing Loans (NPLS): A Dynamic Model and Analysis in China. *Mod. Econ.* **2012**, *3*, 100–110. [CrossRef]

15. Babouček, I.; Jančar, M. *Effects of Macroeconomic Shocks to the Quality of the Aggregate Loan Portfolio*; Working Paper Series, No. 1; Czech National Bank: Praha, Czech, 2005.

16. Hoggarth, G.; Logan, A.; Zicchino, L. *Macro Stress Tests of UK Banks*; BIS papers, No. 22; BIS: Basel, Switzerland, 2005.

17. Louzis, D.P.; Vouldis, A.T.; Metaxas, V.L. Macroeconomic and bank-specific determinants of non-performing loans in Greece: A comparative study of mortgage, business and consumer loan portfolios. *J. Bank. Financ.* **2012**, *36*, 1012–1027. [CrossRef]

18. Vogiazas, S.; Nikolaidou, E. Investigating the Determinants of Nonperforming Loans in the Romanian Banking System: An Empirical Study with Reference to the Greek Crisis. *Econ. Res. Int.* **2011**, *2011*, 1–13. [CrossRef]

19. Ghosh, A. Banking-industry specific and regional economic determinants of non-performing loans: Evidence from US states. *J. Financ. Stab.* **2015**, *20*, 93–104. [CrossRef]

20. Beck, R.; Jakubik, P.; Piloiu, A. Key Determinants of Non-performing Loans: New Evidence from a Global Sample. *Open Econ. Rev.* **2015**, *26*, 525–550. [CrossRef]

21. Salas, V.; Saurina, J. Deregulation, market power and risk behaviour in Spanish banks. *Eur. Econ. Rev.* **2003**, *47*, 1061–1075. [CrossRef]

22. Dvouletý, O. Effects of soft loans and credit guarantees on performance of supported firms: Evidence from the Czech Public Program START. *Sustainability* **2017**, *9*, 2293. [CrossRef]

23. Gemar, P.; Gemar, G.; Guzman-Parra, V. Modeling the sustainability of bank profitability using partial least squares. *Sustainability* **2019**, *11*, 4950. [CrossRef]

24. Bofondi, M.; Ropele, T. *Macroeconomic Determinants of Bad Loans: Evidence from Italian Banks*; Questioni di Economia e Finanza (Occasional Papers) No 89; Bank of Italy: Rome, Italy, 2011. Available online: https://www.bancaditalia.it/pubblicazioni/qef/2011_0089/index.html?com.dotmarketing.htmlpage.language=1 (accessed on 3 June 2020).

25. Jiménez, G.; Salas, V.; Saurina, J. Determinants of collateral. *J. Financ. Econ.* **2006**, *81*, 255–281. [CrossRef]

26. Saba, I.; Kouser, R.; Azeem, M. Determinants of Non-Performing Loans: Case of US Banking Sector. *Rom. Econ. J.* **2012**, *15*, 125–136.

27. Bock, R.; Demyanets, A. *Bank Asset Quality in Emerging Markets: Determinants and Spillovers*; Working Paper 12/71; IMF: Washington, DC, USA, 2012. Available online: https://www.imf.org/~{}/media/Websites/IMF/imported-full-text-pdf/external/pubs/ft/wp/2012/_wp1271.ashx (accessed on 3 June 2020).

28. Gerlach, S.; Peng, W.; Shu, C. *Macroeconomic Conditions and Banking Performance in Hong Kong SAR: A Panel Data Study*; BIS papers No. 22; Bank for International Settlements: Basel, Switzerland, 2005. Available online: https://www.bis.org/publ/bppdf/bispap22x.pdf (accessed on 3 June 2020).

29. Klein, N. *Non-Performing Loans in CESEE: Determinants and Impact on Macroeconomic Performance*; IMF Working Paper (P/13/72); IMF European Department: Pairs, France, 2013. Available online: https://www.imf.org/en/Publications/WP/Issues/2016/12/31/Non-Performing-Loans-in-CESEE-Determinants-and-Impact-on-Macroeconomic-Performance-40413 (accessed on 17 May 2020).

30. Abid, L.; Ouertani, M.N.; Zouari-Ghorbel, S. Macroeconomic and Bank-specific Determinants of Household's Non-performing Loans in Tunisia: A Dynamic Panel Data. *Procedia Econ. Financ.* **2014**, *13*, 58–68. [CrossRef]

31. Ginevičius, R. Determining market concentration. *J. Bus. Econ. Manag.* **2007**, *8*, 3–10. [CrossRef]

32. Rehman, R.U.; Zhang, J.; Ahmad, M.I. Political system of a country and its non-performing loans: A case of emerging markets. *Int. J. Bus. Perform. Manag.* **2016**, *17*, 241. [CrossRef]

33. Chaibi, H.; Ftiti, Z. Credit risk determinants: Evidence from a cross-country study. *Res. Int. Bus. Financ.* **2015**, *33*, 1–16. [CrossRef]

34. Quagliariello, M. Banks' riskiness over the business cycle: A panel analysis on Italian intermediaries. *Appl. Financ. Econ.* **2007**, *17*, 119–138. [CrossRef]

35. Anastasiou, D.; Bragoudakis, Z.; Malandrakis, I. Non-Performing Loans, Governance Indicators and Systemic Liquidity Risk: Evidence from Greece. *SSRN Electron. J.* **2019**. [CrossRef]

36. Vuslat, U. The Determinants of Nonperforming Loans before and After the Crisis: Challenges and Policy Implications for Turkish Banks. *Emerg. Mark. Financ. Trade* **2017**, *54*, 1–15. [CrossRef]

37. Beck, T.; Demirgüç-Kunt, A.; Levine, R. Bank concentration, competition, and crises: First results. *J. Bank. Financ.* **2006**, *30*, 1581–1603. [CrossRef]

38. Çifter, A. Bank concentration and non-performing loans in Central and Eastern European countries. *J. Bus. Econ. Manag.* **2015**, *16*, 117–137. [CrossRef]

39. Ahn, S.J.; Lee, S.H. The Effect of Consumers' Perceived Value on Acceptance of an Internet-Only Bank Service. *Sustainability* **2019**, *11*, 4599. [CrossRef]

40. Cui, Y.; Geobey, S.; Weber, O.; Lin, H. The impact of green lending on credit risk in China. *Sustainability* **2018**, *10*, 2008. [CrossRef]

41. Demirgüç-Kunt, A.; Huizinga, H. Determinants of commercial bank interest margins and profitability: Some international evidence. *World Bank Econ. Rev.* **1999**, *13*, 379–408. [CrossRef]

42. Berger, A.; DeYoung, R. Problem loans and cost efficiency in commercial banks. *J. Bank. Financ.* **1997**, *21*, 849–870. Available online: https://www.sciencedirect.com/science/article/pii/S0378426697000034 (accessed on 18 June 2020). [CrossRef]

43. Tesfaye, T. Determinants of Banks Liquidity and Their Impact on Financial Performance: Empirical Study on Commercial Banks in Ethiopia. Ph.D. Thesis, Addis Ababa University, Addis Ababa, Ethiopia, 2012.

44. Erdinc, D.; Abazi, E. The Determinants of NPLs in Emerging Europe, 2000–2011. *J. Econ. Political Econ.* **2014**, *1*, 112–125.

45. Boyd, J.; Levine, R.; Smith, B. The impact of inflation on financial market performance. *J. Monet. Econ.* **2001**, *47*, 221–248. [CrossRef]

46. Farhan, M.; Sattar, A.; Chaudhry, A.; Khalil, F. Economic Determinants of Non-Performing Loans: Perception of Pakistani Bankers. *Eur. J. Bus. Manag.* **2012**, *4*, 87–99.

47. Popa, I.D.; Cepoia, C.O.; Anghela, D.G. Liquidity-threshold effect in non-performing loans. *Financ. Res. Lett.* **2018**, *27*, 124–128. [CrossRef]

48. Makri, V.; Tsagkanos, A.; Bellas, A. Determinants of non-Performing loans: The case of eurozone. *Panoeconomicus* **2014**, *2*, 193–206. [CrossRef]

49. Messai, A.; Jouini, F. Micro and macro determinants of non-performing loans. *Int. J. Econ. Financ. Issues* **2013**, *3*, 852–860.

50. Skarica, B. Determinants of non-performing loans in Central and Eastern European countries. *Financ. Theory Pract.* **2014**, *38*, 37–59. [CrossRef]

51. Anastasiou, D.; Louri, H.; Tsionas, M. Determinants of non-performing loans: Evidence from Euro-area countries. *Financ. Res. Lett.* **2016**, *18*, 116–119.

52. Charalambakis, E.; Dendramis, Y.; Tzavalis, E. *On the Determinants of NPLs: Lessons from Greece*; Working Paper; Bank of Greece: Athens, Greece, 2017; ISSN 1109-6691.

53. Donath, L.; Cerna, V.; Oprea, I. Macroeconomic determinants of bad loans in Baltic countries and Romania. *SEA Pract. Appl. Sci.* **2014**, *4*, 71–80.

11

Micro-Operating Mechanism Approach for Regulatory Sandbox Policy Focused on Fintech

HaeOk Choi and KwangHo Lee ,*

Science and Technology Policy Institute, 508 Building B, Sejong National Research Complex 370, Sicheng-daero, Sejong 30147, Korea; hochoi@stepi.re.kr
* Correspondence: leekh@stepi.re.kr

Abstract: To determine the micro-operating mechanism(MoM) of enterprises participating in the regulatory sandbox policy in fintech, this study analyzes the structure of enterprise innovation competencies and derives relevant implications. The results reveal that large, middle-standing, and small and medium-sized enterprises focus on security, infrastructure, and user-related technology development, respectively, to enhance their innovation competencies. The security-related issues considered by large enterprises entail relatively high costs in initial technology development and are closely related to infrastructure building. Large enterprises are focused on developing overall security-related technologies, whereas middle-standing enterprises are striving to develop infrastructure-related technologies, with particular emphasis on elementary technologies. Small and medium-sized enterprises are also making efforts to develop user-centered technologies that can directly be used in fintech. As a method to implement regulatory sandboxes tailored to the needs of participating enterprises in South Korea, this study will help to determine the MoM of such participants and establish strategies to support them sustainably in terms of evidence-based policy.

Keywords: MoM(micro-operating mechanism); regulatory sandbox; fintech; type by enterprise; innovation competencies; patents data; evidence-based policy

1. Introduction

Many countries around the world are implementing regulatory reform through regulatory sandboxes, which were first attempted in the fintech field as a way to create new technologies and services that have been blocked by regulations [1–3]. However, due to the side effects of being transplanted overseas, we have begun to recognize the need for an institutional transplant process tailored to different financial environments and characteristics at individual companies by countries. Until now, research on the regulatory sandbox itself has been limited because it has been dominated by government-oriented studies [4,5]. This study focuses on the innovation capabilities of Korean companies participating in the regulatory sandbox within the fintech sector and aims to help establish a tailored policy based on a company's characteristics. To evaluate these ideas, this research utilized semantic analysis focusing on the contents and titles of patents, which are unstructured data, to overcome the limitations of earlier studies [6,7]. The former research mainly focused on the frequency and regional distribution of patents, so there was a limitation to utilize (unstructured data) the contents of patent creation. So, this research tries to utilize the characteristics of each company occurring in actual innovation creation activities. The micro-operation mechanism implies that it is necessary to design policies suitable for each characteristic by analyzing micro-structural characteristics appearing in the process of actual system implementation.

The regulatory sandbox policy in fintech began with concerns about the weakening of global competitiveness due to limitations imposed by the government's regulatory policy on the ability to rapidly develop technology [8]. In particular, data collection and utilization have important value through the transition to the data economy; as data-based services are launched, the fintech industry is being activated [9]. As new technologies and services are developed, efforts are being made to overcome difficulties caused by institutional voids in government policies [10]. In particular, the fintech field has high initial infrastructure costs which means that they should often be conducted as a government-led business. In this process, government-led system design should preemptively respond to regulations by selecting the impeding factors of new industries and services due to likely issues, such as overregulation, system vacancy, and system duplication. The regulatory sandbox promotes policies that value speed as a means of regulatory reform.

This study is significant since it helps to analyze the innovation competencies of the enterprises participating [11–13] in the regulatory sandbox policy. It is implemented as part of regulatory innovation and uses these competencies as a reference that establish related tailored policies in the future in terms of evidence-based policy.

2. Literature Review

The micro-operation mechanisms' theoretical evolution comes from the rational selection system, policy network model, and policy advocacy coalition model. These items explain the system and describe the mechanism of the policy process centered on the constituent variables within each theory. Nevertheless, there was a limitation in being unable to explain the specific mechanism of the policy process by linking macro and micro variables. Therefore, in order to overcome the limitations of existing studies, this study utilized ACI as a basic theoretical framework for research on micro-operation mechanisms.

Examining regulatory sandboxes using MoM (micro-operating mechanism), actor-centered institutionalism (ACI), which can analyze regulatory policy with a focus on interactions among actors within the system, was considered suitable for this study. Furthermore, the study utilized a scientific analytical technique to analyze innovation competencies [14–16], as well as unstructured data that were the contents or titles of patent data for each type of enterprise; accordingly, enterprises were categorized into different types to clarify their structures and characteristics.

ACI is suitable for examining the complex mechanisms of policies as a single theory, rather than an integration of multiple theories. Proposed by Scharpf [17,18], ACI postulates that policies are produced because of interactions among actors in institutional settings. It is similar to the rational choice model in that it focuses on actors' preferences and strategic choices. It also takes the same stance as historical institutionalism in that it acknowledges institutional influence over actors. However, institutional influence over actors merely restricts the scope of actors' appropriate actions; the specific action to be taken within that scope is determined by the actors' preferences and strategic choices. In other words, active actors are postulated, which distinguishes ACI from historical institutionalism, which focuses on the passive role of actors. Moreover, since it enables the formation of actors' preferences and strategic choices in the institutional context, ACI is different from the rational choice model, which limits the actors' preference for specific economic interests. In other words, ACI is a model that combines the rational choice model, which emphasizes the strategic choice of actors, and historical institutionalism, which stresses institution.

To date, research on ACI has focused on how the actors influenced by an institution behave, rather than how the institution influences the actors. Institutional settings that affect actors' choices are the remote causes of policy outcomes, whereas the results of actors' interactions are the proximate causes of policy outcomes [18] (p. 3). Therefore, ACI assumes policies to be linked to constellations and modes of interactions comprising institutional settings, actors with capabilities and orientations, combinations of strategies, and appropriate payoff [17].

First, the institutional setting is a factor that restricts the behaviors of participating actors since it serves as a venue for interactions among the actors and determines the overall framework of the game. However, since these constraints are not decisive, the final policy outcome is determined by the interactions among actors. Second, actors are composite constructs characterized by capabilities and orientations (preferences and perceptions) [18] (pp. 43–44). Capabilities are behavioral resources that enable or limit competencies, as well as the right to participate, refrain from participating, or make autonomous decisions in the policy process. In other words, they refer to not only financial and human resources but also the actors' competencies and roles defined by the law and sustained relationships. Orientations indicate perceptions of and preferences for the maintenance of status quo, causes of problems, efficacy in the behavioral process, and the process' outcomes [18] (pp. 62–63). Perception is a subjective cognitive orientation regarding phenomena, including facts and causal relations, and the criteria for judgment are established under a theory or an institutional structure that make autonomous decisions in the policy process. Furthermore, preference is a concept that is classified into interests, norms, identities, and interaction orientations [18] (p. 64). Third, constellations refer to the static picture that appears in interactions and combines actors' characteristics (perceptions, preferences, and capabilities) with a combination of strategies, represented by the game matrix [18] (pp. 44–72). Constellations comprise players who participate in the specific game, their strategy options, outcomes of a combination of strategies, and the preferences of these outcomes. These game constellations do not individually affect interactions but affect them in a configurational manner; hence, various elements must all be considered in the analysis. Game constellations in interactions appear at the level of potential conflicts in actual policy interactions. Moreover, they are related to the type of game, as that determines different aspects of how the conflicts will be resolved and how the players will maximize their interests by adjusting their strategies or making decisions with others. Therefore, constellations are the appropriate measure to determine the choices of players among actual policy options [17] (p. 72).

Finally, the variable of interactions is a dynamic aspect within which conflicts are developed; the types of interactions include unilateral action, negotiated agreement, majority vote, and hierarchical direction. These are standardized interaction types that appear in combination in real life and are influenced by the institutional structure [17] (p. 47). This aspect of interactions is a key variable that affects the determination of the direction of final policy outcomes along with the institutional setting.

Therefore, this study used ACI as a theoretical framework to determine the MoM of enterprises. The use of ACI helped to structuralize various entangled factors and determine their characteristics. This study's analysis of enterprise structural characteristics has implications for the establishment of tailored policies through regulatory sandboxes in fintech.

To date, studies on regulatory sandboxes have mostly focused on the introduction of regulatory institutions in certain countries [3,5–13] or on the current state of such institutions implemented in certain fields [1,14,15]. However, these studies have been limited by their inability to adequately determine the MoM innovation capacities. Therefore, this study is significant in that it analyzes innovation competencies as the MoM of enterprises participating in the regulatory sandbox policy in fintech and discusses its implications.

3. Methodology

By using patent contents, this study examined the MoM of enterprises participating in the regulatory sandbox policy in fintech. The structural characteristics and innovation competencies of participating enterprises were analyzed by using MoM of regulatory sandboxes and the presented methods to apply them back to tailored policies [19,20].

To do so, the study first adopted the regulatory sandbox policy as part of the regulatory innovation at the governmental level to create new industries and services that could overcome the difficulties caused by existing regulations. Accordingly, prior to analysis, this study conducted a literature review on the regulatory sandbox policy and examined various related trends.

Second, this study interviewed relevant experts (around 20 peoples between 1 April and 30 June 2020) to understand the innovation competencies of regulatory sandbox polices.

Third, this study searched for credit information data using a list of participants limited to participants in the fintech sector of the regulatory sandbox and classified them by type of enterprise into large, middle-standing, and small and medium-sized enterprises.

To search for patent data, the names of the participating enterprises were converted into applicant codes by utilizing the Korea Intellectual Property Rights Information Service of the Korean Intellectual Property Office. Using these applicant codes and categories, patent data spanning 10 years (from 1 July 2011 to 1 July 2020) were collected. Among the types of patent-related attribute data that were collected, unstructured data pertaining to titles and contents were used to examine the MoM of enterprises.

Further, a group network analysis using NetMiner, a network analytical tool, was performed on the collected data. The results were used to process the data and confirm the ratio by organization and group, then derive conclusions (see Figure 1).

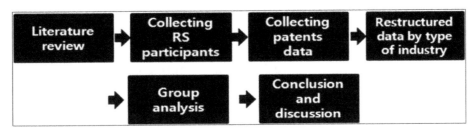

Figure 1. Research process.

4. Results

This study aimed to analyze the innovation competencies of enterprises participating in regulatory sandboxes in fintech. To clarify innovation competencies from a microscopic perspective, an analysis was conducted by classifying enterprises by type into large, middle-standing, and small and medium-sized enterprises based on patent data (see Figure 2).

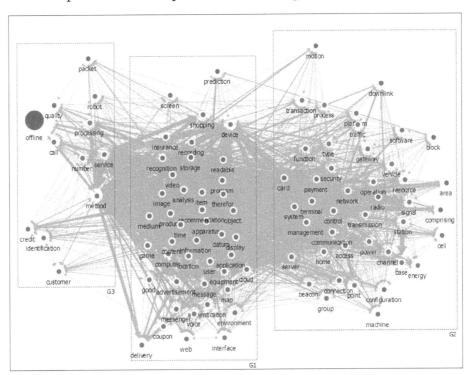

Figure 2. Results of group network analysis. Note: Nodes represent keywords, links show the relationship among nodes that appear as a result of analysis. The size of the nodes is related to their weight (the larger the node, the higher the frequency). Through semantic network analysis, the connection between nodes was visualized with the relationship frequencies.

The following shows the main keywords, frequency, and centrality of each group from the cluster group analysis result. As a result of patent analysis, companies in the fintech field that participate in the regulatory sandbox can be divided into three groups. These can be labeled as infrastructure-related issues (G1), complementary issues (G2), and G3 (user-related issues).

First, infrastructure-related issues (indicated as G1) represented major issues related to the infrastructure of fintech; relevant keywords were apparatus, device, information, and computer. These issues revealed that the infrastructure-related innovation competencies that can support security in enterprise are enhanced by the application of new technology in fintech. It is important to build infrastructure that can safely manage and distribute users' funds. Furthermore, it was indicated that the industry developed because of the advancement of infrastructure-related technology to supplement funds.

Second, security-related issues (G2) included keywords such as system, server, network, control, payment, and security. The establishment of security technology in fintech enterprises helps to protect users when a financial company needs to prove that users permitted its transactions. Currently, the issues in developing technology for security are concentrated in systems, servers, and networks. This shows that security-related issues are closely related to the overall system operations of fintech, which are closely related to G1 (infrastructure-related issues). In particular, security-related issues involve the overall system, unlike infrastructure-related issues, whereas infrastructure represents detailed physical technical factors.

Third, user-related issues (G3) showed high frequencies for keywords such as method, service, call, processing, and credit. This indicates that technology related to stability in fintech transactions has been developed through credit guarantee in transactions. This shows that technology has been developed in terms of methods and services for credit guarantee, since there is an urgent need to establish safeguards for users with the development of fintech (see Table 1).

Table 1. Results of group network analysis.

G1 (Infrastructure-Related Issues)				G2 (Security-Related Issues)				G3 (User-Related Issues)			
Keywords	Frequency	Degree Centrality	Node Betweenness Centrality	Keywords	Frequency	Degree Centrality	Node Betweenness Centrality	Keywords	Frequency	Degree Centrality	Node Betweenness Centrality
apparatus	3,538.00	0.990	0.052	system	3,352.00	0.990	0.052	method	7,541.00	0.990	0.052
device	1,185.00	0.867	0.033	server	904	0.847	0.032	service	1,950.00	0.939	0.045
information	826	0.878	0.039	network	690	0.735	0.020	call	129	0.378	0.003
computer	767	0.520	0.007	terminal	588	0.724	0.019	processing	107	0.367	0.003
medium	703	0.592	0.013	control	580	0.694	0.018	number	75	0.255	0.001
user	614	0.724	0.022	communication	412	0.612	0.011	credit	63	0.204	0.001
therefore	521	0.531	0.008	payment	345	0.469	0.008	customer	59	0.245	0.001
program	474	0.398	0.003	management	330	0.673	0.017	quality	57	0.245	0.001
datum	473	0.776	0.025	card	308	0.480	0.006	packet	55	0.224	0.001
content	447	0.582	0.010	signal	308	0.367	0.003	identification	51	0.235	0.001
advertisement	313	0.439	0.004	access	192	0.418	0.003	offline	50	0.112	0.000
video	311	0.367	0.003	transmission	168	0.408	0.004	robot	49	0.204	0.001
image	289	0.490	0.008	channel	156	0.327	0.002				
readable	282	0.224	0.001	station	151	0.367	0.002				
cloud	263	0.418	0.003	point	150	0.357	0.003				
application	239	0.571	0.010	resource	131	0.418	0.004				
equipment	210	0.459	0.005	radio	128	0.347	0.003				
message	209	0.449	0.004	security	126	0.378	0.002				
location	169	0.531	0.009	base	125	0.327	0.001				
authentication	150	0.398	0.004	power	95	0.347	0.003				
shopping	123	0.163	0.000	beacon	90	0.306	0.001				
recognition	112	0.327	0.002	area	89	0.173	0.000				

Table 1. *Cont.*

G1 (Infrastructure-Related Issues)				G2 (Security-Related Issues)				G3 (User-Related Issues)			
Keywords	Frequency	Degree Centrality	Node Betweenness Centrality	Keywords	Frequency	Degree Centrality	Node Betweenness Centrality	Keywords	Frequency	Degree Centrality	Node Betweenness Centrality
environment	104	0.306	0.001	transaction	86	0.296	0.002				
product	103	0.276	0.001	vehicle	86	0.276	0.001				
voice	102	0.327	0.001	energy	85	0.173	0.000				
delivery	93	0.184	0.000	connection	84	0.347	0.002				
web	90	0.265	0.001	traffic	83	0.296	0.002				
time	80	0.347	0.002	home	78	0.378	0.003				
recording	75	0.204	0.000	machine	77	0.214	0.001				
storage	74	0.327	0.003	cell	72	0.224	0.000				
coupon	71	0.224	0.001	function	72	0.367	0.002				
display	71	0.316	0.002	operation	68	0.327	0.002				
recommendation	67	0.184	0.000	motion	61	0.163	0.000				
analysis	62	0.337	0.002	downlink	58	0.143	0.000				
interface	58	0.235	0.000	software	58	0.235	0.001				
item	58	0.153	0.000	gateway	57	0.316	0.002				
messenger	57	0.173	0.000	platform	57	0.255	0.001				
object	56	0.245	0.001	type	56	0.337	0.003				
prediction	54	0.153	0.000	comprising	55	0.102	0.000				
screen	50	0.194	0.000	Configuration	55	0.286	0.002				
good	49	0.194	0.000	group	55	0.276	0.002				
map	49	0.184	0.000	process	53	0.235	0.001				
game	47	0.245	0.001	block	51	0.194	0.001				
insurance	47	0.163	0.000								

Note: As a result of the analysis, this table was able to obtain frequency, degree centrality, and node betweenness centrality results. The degree centrality represents the value of nodes on the graph, and the node betweenness centrality is a value expressed by quantifying the value between nodes, which is the result of analysis using a network analysis tool.

Subsequently, this study analyzed the structural characteristics of innovation competencies for each participant in a regulatory sandbox in finance. It was possible to understand the characteristics of each institution through the process of reclassifying the participants participating in the regulatory sandbox system in the fintech by institution.

First, large enterprises actively responded to security-related issues (G2) (35.3%). Furthermore, infrastructure-related (G1) and user-related (G3) issues showed the same ratio (32.4%).

Middle-standing enterprises showed the highest ratio of infrastructure-related issues (G1, 37.7%), which were followed by user-related issues (G3, 33.2%) and security-related issues (G2, 29.1%). Furthermore, it was found that middle-standing enterprises were focusing on the development of infrastructure-related and user-related technologies in fintech.

Finally, small and medium-sized enterprises showed the highest ratio of user-related issues (G3, 37.1%), which were followed by infrastructure-related issues (G1, 34.6%) and security-related issues (G2, 28.3%). In other words, small companies were developing technologies with a focus on users. (see Table 2).

Table 2. Results of group network analysis by industry categorization.

Division	Large-Sized Company		Enterprise of Middle-Standing		Small and Medium-Sized Enterprises		Total by Group
	Freq.	%	Freq.	%	Freq.	%	
G1 (infrastructure-related issues)	9290	32.4%	693	37.7%	275	34.6%	104.6%
G2 (security-related issues)	10121	35.3%	535	29.1%	225	28.3%	92.6%
G3 (user-related issues)	9297	32.4%	611	33.2%	295	37.1%	102.7%
Total	28708	100%	1839	100%	795	100%	-

Regarding the characteristics of each participating enterprise, the results show that large enterprises are focusing on the development of security-related technologies, whereas middle-standing enterprises are focusing on infrastructure-related technologies and small and medium-sized enterprises on user-related innovation competencies. Furthermore, large enterprises are developing security technologies that require relatively high initial costs, which play a key role in infrastructure building for fintech.

Security technology is switching the direction from ex-post exposure to ex-ante prevention for the development of digital technology, which indicates the need to establish a system for risk management and relevant risk prevention. Middle-standing enterprises are improving efficiency and safety in fintech by developing infrastructure-related technologies. Although infrastructure-related technologies are closely related to security-related technologies, they are different in that the former are more focused on detail. An examination of such microscopic mechanisms indicates that it is necessary to establish policies suited to the characteristics of each enterprise type to facilitate institutional development in fintech. (see Figure 3).

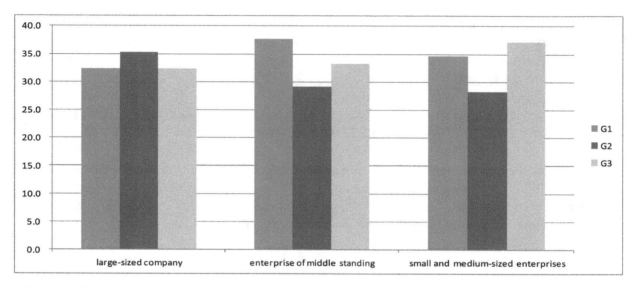

Figure 3. Group network analysis by industry categorization. Note: Data are classified by company and compared with the frequency of words belonging to each group.

5. Discussion

The current study analyzed the structural characteristics of the innovation competencies of participating enterprises after the implementation of the regulatory sandbox policy and helped use these characteristics to establish future policies in Korea. Furthermore, this study provides several implications for the development of a regulatory sandbox policy in terms of evidence-based policy.

To date, in the regulatory sandbox policy in Korea, a few policy makers have been effectively supplying policies that consider equity among participants. However, these policy makers have not made sufficient effort to determine the structure and characteristics of the innovation competencies of policy users in terms of the supply process [21–23] because policy makers do not have adequate time and funds to determine innovation competencies. Hence, the efficiency of user-centered policies can be improved by developing a scientific analysis method to analyze the competencies of policy users and including them in policies.

This study determined the MoM as a method to overcome policy failure by completely adopting the best practices implemented in other countries. The study results will help to implement regulatory sandbox policies tailored to the characteristics of South Korean participants to establish a differentiated system and establish strategies to support the participants' MoM.

To examine the MoM of regulatory sandboxes, this study used ACI, which analyzes policies focusing on interactions among actors. The application of ACI determines the institutional settings that affect the policies and examines how actors interact with different preferences and value systems under the constraints of institutional settings [19–24] to better explain the complicated aspects of the process of implementing regulatory sandboxes.

Future research projects can further explain the responses to regulations. For the successful execution of regulatory policies, it is necessary to obtain the compliance of subjects. Additional research using compliance theory must be conducted to explain the responses toward regulations [24–26].

This study has some limitations. It focuses on the innovation competencies of enterprises participating in the sandbox policy, rather than explaining the regulatory sandbox policy itself [27]. Therefore, in-depth discussions and considerations of the regulatory sandbox policy itself are necessary in the future.

6. Conclusions

This study focused on the structural characteristics of each type of enterprise participating in the regulatory sandbox policy and attempted to remove difficulties that new industries and services experiences during creation due to regulations. To examine the enterprises' MoM, this study collected and analyzed the patent data created by enterprises to analyze their characteristics and help design tailored policies in the future. The results of the analysis are as follows:

By analyzing the enterprise data by group, the innovation competencies of regulatory sandbox participants were classified into infrastructure-, security-, and user-related issues. Infrastructure- and security-related issues were closely related, and user-related issues occurred in the development of technologies related to stability in fintech transactions. Furthermore, it was found that fintech technology was developed with a focus on credit guarantee. Previously in Korea, the fintech sector was fostered by the private sector, but the intention is to have the government foster the section. Since the existing regulatory issues can be solved by the government's policy, the government's efforts can have a great impact on the technology development in the fintech field.

The results of the analysis for each type of enterprise reveal that large enterprises are focusing on security, middle-standing enterprises on infrastructure, and small and medium-sized enterprises on user-related issues to develop their innovation competencies. In particular, the security-related issues considered by large enterprises involve relatively high costs in terms of initial technology development and are closely related to the construction of infrastructures. Contrarily, small and medium-sized enterprises are developing technologies and services in fintech with a focus on users. Since the infrastructure sector in the fintech sector in Korea is a sector that requires a high initial cost, it is the role of the government to establish an institutional foundation for well-equipped infrastructure. Therefore, the government's institutional support for each of the infrastructure and technology development sectors should be strengthened in future institutional design of the fintech sector in Korea.

This study can be used to formulate regulatory sandbox policies in the future by determining the MoM of enterprises. In particular, it can be used as a reference to establish policies tailored to the characteristics of each organization type by analyzing the innovation competencies of each enterprise. The regulatory sandbox system in Korea is progressing at a rapid pace with the aim of creating new industries and services in all industries. However, in the process of solving the issues arising in the actual system process behind the creation of results through this sense of speed, a process of transplanting the system suitable for the characteristics of Korea is necessary. Therefore, this research suggests that there is a need for a policy alternative to feedback that can identify the characteristics of companies participating in the regulatory sandbox in the fintech sector and reflect this in the policy.

Author Contributions: Conceptualization, H.C.; methodology, H.C.; validation, H.C.; formal analysis, H.C.; investigation, H.C.; data curation, H.C.; writing—original draft preparation, H.C. and K.L.; writing—review and editing, H.C. and K.L. supervision, H.C. and K.L.; All authors have read and agreed to the published version of the manuscript.

Acknowledgments: This research is supported by STEPI (project number: T0200600, title: Agenda setting research project for technological regulation reform (4th year)). Also, this research is related to "Planning and research to establish basic plan for new industry regulation" (project number: I0202500).

References

1. Piri, M.M. The changing landscapes of fintech and regtech: Why the United States should create a federal regulatory sandbox. *Bus. Fin. L. Rev.* **2018**, *2*, 233.
2. Van der Waal, E.C.; Das, A.M.; van der Schoor, T. Participatory experimentation with energy law: Digging in a 'regulatory sandbox' for local energy initiatives in the Netherlands. *Energies* **2020**, *13*, 458. [CrossRef]
3. Hapsari, R.A.; Maroni, M.; Satria, I.; Ariyani, N.D. The existence of regulatory sandbox to encourage the growth of financial technology in Indonesia. *Fiat Justisia J. Ilmu Huk.* **2019**, *13*, 271–288. [CrossRef]
4. Edler, J. *Demand Oriented Innovation Policy. The Co-Evolution of Innovation Policy Encourage the Growth of Fina Systems and Governance*; Working Report No. 99; Office of Technology Assessment at the German Bundestag, TAB: Berlin, Germany, 2006; pp. 1–32.
5. Allen, H.J. Regulatory sandboxes. *Geo. Wash. L. Rev.* **2019**, *87*, 579.

6.   Sun, Y. Spatial distribution of patents in China. *Reg. Stud.* **2000**, *34*, 441–445. [CrossRef]
7.   Acs, Z.J.; Anselin, L.; Varga, A. Patents and innovation counts as measures of regional production of new knowledge. *Res. Policy* **2002**, *31*, 1069–1085. [CrossRef]
8.   Jenik, I.; Lauer, K. *Regulatory Sandboxes and Financial Inclusion*; CGAP: Washington, DC, USA, 2017.
9.   Zetzsche, D.A.; Buckley, R.P.; Barberis, J.N.; Arner, D.W. Regulating a revolution: From regulatory sandboxes to smart regulation. *Fordham J. Corp. Fin. L.* **2017**, *23*, 31. [CrossRef]
10.   Grant, A. Proposed Historical Policy Analysis of Project Catalyst's Regulatory Sandbox. Ph.D. Thesis, California State University, Northridge, CA, USA, 2020.
11.   Forsman, H. Innovation capacity and innovation development in small enterprises: A comparison between the manufacturing and service sectors. *Res. Policy* **2011**, *40*, 739–750. [CrossRef]
12.   Lewis, J.M.; Ricard, L.M.; Klijn, E.H. How innovation drivers, networking and leadership shape public sector innovation capacity. *Int. Rev. Adm. Sci.* **2018**, *84*, 288–307. [CrossRef]
13.   Mehrabani, S.E.; Shajari, M. Knowledge management and innovation capacity. *Manag. Res.* **2012**, *4*, 164. [CrossRef]
14.   Thomas, L.G. The case for a federal regulatory sandbox for Fintech companies. *NC Bank. Inst.* **2018**, *22*, 257.
15.   Buckley, R.P.; Arner, D.W.; Veidt, R.; Zetzsche, D.A. Building fintech ecosystems: Regulatory sandboxes, innovation hubs and beyond. *UNSW Law Res. Pap.* **2019**, 19–72. [CrossRef]
16.   Einav, L.; Levin, J. The data revolution and economic analysis. *Innov. Policy Econ.* **2014**, *14*, 1–24. [CrossRef]
17.   Scharpf, F.W. *Games Real Actors Play: Actor-Centered Institutionalism in Policy Research*; Westview Press: Boulder, CO, USA, 1997; p. 44.
18.   Scharpf, F. Institutions in comparative policy research. *Comp. Political Stud.* **2000**, *33*, 762–790. [CrossRef]
19.   Rudolph, M. User-friendly and tailored policy administration points. In Proceedings of the 1st International Conference on Information Systems Security and Privacy (ICISSP) Doctoral Symposium, Angers, France, 9–11 February 2015.
20.   Kim, S.S.; Rideout, C.; Han, H.W.; Lee, L.; Kwon, S.C. Implementing a targeted and culturally tailored policy, systems, and environmental nutrition strategy to reach Korean Americans. *Prog. Commun. Health Partnersh. Res. Educ. Action* **2018**, *12*. [CrossRef] [PubMed]
21.   Prajogo, D.I.; Ahmed, P.K. Relationships between innovation stimulus, innovation capacity, and innovation performance. *R&D Manag.* **2006**, *36*, 499–515. [CrossRef]
22.   Jørgensen, F.; Ulhøi, J.P. Enhancing innovation capacity in SMEs through early network relationships. *Creat. Innov. Manag.* **2010**, *19*, 397–404. [CrossRef]
23.   Etienne, J.; Schnyder, G. Improving the micro-foundations of actor-centered institutionalism. *SSRN* **2010**. [CrossRef]
24.   Etienne, J. Compliance theory: A goal framing approach. *Law Policy* **2011**, *33*, 305–333. [CrossRef]
25.   Crick, T.; Mateos-Garcia, J.; Bakhshi, H.; Westlake, S. Innovation Policy-Making in the Big Data Era. In *Proceedings of Data for Policy*; Cambridge University Press: Cambridge, UK, 2015; pp. 1–4.
26.   Kim, N.; Lee, H.; Kim, W.; Lee, H.; Suh, J.H. Dynamic patterns of industry convergence: Evidence from a large amount of unstructured data. *Res. Policy* **2015**, *44*, 1734–1748. [CrossRef]
27.   Authority Financial Conduct. Regulatory Sandbox. Available online: https://www.fca.org.uk/publication/research/regulatory-sandbox.pdf (accessed on 1 October 2016).

Permissions

List of Contributors

Mirjana Pejić Bach, Mislav Ante Omazić and Ana Aleksić
Faculty of Economics and Business, University of Zagreb, 10000 Zagreb, Croatia

Berislava Starešinić
Privredna banka Zagreb, 10000 Zagreb, Croatia

Sanja Seljan
Department of Information and Communication Sciences, Faculty of Humanities and Social Sciences, University of Zagreb, Ivana Lučića 3, 10000 Zagreb, Croatia

Witold Chmielarz and Marek Zborowski
Faculty of Management, University of Warsaw, Krakowskie Przedmiéscie 26/28, 00-927 Warsaw, Poland

Juan Camilo Mejia-Escobar
Departamento de Ingeniería de la Organización, Facultad de Minas, Universidad Nacional de Colombia, Avenida 80 No. 65-223 Medellín, Colombia
Facultad de Producción y Diseño, Institución Universitaria Pascual Bravo, Calle 73 No. 73A-226 Medellín, Colombia

Juan David González-Ruiz
Departamento de Economía, Facultad de Ciencias Humanas y Económicas, Universidad Nacional de Colombia, Cra. 65 #59a-110 Medellín, Colombia

Eduardo Duque-Grisales
Facultad de Ingeniería, Institución Universitaria Pascual Bravo, Calle 73 No. 73A-226 Medellín, Colombia

Esther Ortiz-Martínez and Salvador Marín-Hernández
Department of Accounting and Finance, University of Murcia, 3100 Murcia, Spain

Xiaofeng Hui
School of Economics and Management, Harbin Institute of Technology, Harbin 150001, China

Aoran Zhang
Antai College of Economics and Management, Shanghai Jiao Tong University, Shanghai 200030, China

Ana Alvarenga
Department of Information Science and Technology, Instituto Universitário de Lisboa (ISCTE-IUL), 1649-026 Lisboa, Portugal

Florinda Matos
Centre for Socioeconomic and Territorial Studies (DINÂMIA'CET-ISCTE), Instituto Universitário de Lisboa (ISCTE-IUL), 1649-026 Lisboa, Portugal

Radu Godina
UNIDEMI, Department of Mechanical and Industrial Engineering, NOVA School of Science and Technology, Universidade NOVA de Lisboa, 2829–516 Caparica, Portugal

João C. O. Matias
DEGEIT—Departamento de Economia, Gestão, Engenharia Industrial e Turismo, Universidade de Aveiro, Campus Universitário de Santiago, 3810–193 Aveiro, Portugal
GOVCOPP—Unidade de Investigação em Governança, Competitividade e Políticas Públicas, Universidade de Aveiro, Campus Universitário de Santiago, 3810–193 Aveiro, Portugal

Zia Ur Rehman, Muhammad Zahid and Muhammad Asif
Department of Management Sciences, City University of Science and IT, Peshawar 25000, Pakistan

Haseeb Ur Rahman
Institute of Management Sciences, University of Science and Technology, Bannu 28100, Pakistan

Majed Alharthi
Finance Department, College of Business, King Abdulaziz University, Rabigh 21911, Saudi Arabia

Muhammad Irfan
Electrical Engineering Department, College of Engineering, Najran University Saudi Arabia, Najran 61441, Saudi Arabia

Adam Glowacz
Department of Automatic, Control and Robotics, AGH University of Science and Technology, 30-059 Krakow, Poland

Sang-Giun Yim
School of Finance and Accounting, Kookmin University, Kookmin University, 77, Jeongneung-ro, Seongbuk-gu, Seoul 02707, Korea

Komlan Gbongli and Levente Kovács
Institute of Finance and Accounting, Faculty of Economics, University of Miskolc, 3515 Miskolc-Egyetemvaros, Hungary

Yongan Xu
School of International Business, Southwestern University of Finance and Economics, 55 Guanghuacun Street, Qingyang District, Chengdu 610074, China

Komi Mawugbe Amedjonekou
Business School, York St John University, Lord Mayor's Walk, York Y031 7EX, UK

Teodor Hada
Department of Finance, "Bogdan Voda" University, 400525 Cluj-Napoca, Romania

Nicoleta Bărbuță-Mișu
Department of Business Administration, "Dunarea de Jos" University of Galati, 800008 Galati, Romania

Iulia Cristina Iuga
Department of Finance-Accounting, "1 Decembrie 1918" University of Alba Iulia, 510009 Alba Iulia, Romania

Dorin Wainberg
Department of Finance-Accounting, "1 Decembrie 1918" University of Alba Iulia, 510009 Alba Iulia, Romania
Department of Mathematics, "1 Decembrie 1918" University of Alba Iulia, 510009 Alba Iulia, Romania

HaeOk Choi and KwangHo Lee
Science and Technology Policy Institute, 508 Building B, Sejong National Research Complex 370, Sichengdaero, Sejong 30147, Korea

Index

Printed in the USA
CPSIA information can be obtained
at www.ICGtesting.com
JSHW051407091023
49903JS00006B/312